THE MARK TWAIN PAPERS

1980

THE MYSTERIOUS STRANGER

by Mark Twain

THE MARK TWAIN PAPERS

*Of the projected fifteen volumes of this edition of
Mark Twain's previously unpublished works
the following have been issued to date:*

THE
MYSTERIOUS
STRANGER

by Mark Twain

Edited with an Introduction by
William M. Gibson

Mark Twain

UNIVERSITY OF CALIFORNIA PRESS
Berkeley and Los Angeles

CENTER FOR EDITIONS OF
AMERICAN AUTHORS
AN APPROVED TEXT
MODERN LANGUAGE
ASSOCIATION OF AMERICA

UNIVERSITY OF CALIFORNIA PRESS
Berkeley and Los Angeles, California
UNIVERSITY OF CALIFORNIA PRESS, LTD.
London, England

© 1969 The Mark Twain Company
Library of Congress Catalog Card Number: 70–105218
SBN 520-01661-0

Designed by Adrian Wilson
in collaboration with James Mennick

First paperbound edition
Manufactured in the United States of America

Acknowledgments

A T ONE TIME, the editors of the Iowa-California Edition of the writings of Mark Twain and the editors of The Mark Twain Papers, along with their respective publishers, intended to publish *Mark Twain's Mysterious Stranger Manuscripts* jointly, since the volume includes both published and unpublished writings. However, the published version is partly fraudulent, and the unpublished versions bulk larger than what had appeared in print. Moreover, the University of California Press has become the publisher for the Iowa edition (as it then was) as well as The Papers. Thus the book appears as a part of The Mark Twain Papers rather than under a double imprint.

This bit of editorial and publishing history will serve to explain my good fortune in having had two sets of editors to advise me and inspect my copy. My debt to the editorial board of The Papers— to Walter Blair and Henry Nash Smith—and to the Series Editor, Frederick Anderson, is large, and I am grateful to these scholars. I also owe particular thanks to John C. Gerber and Paul Baender, editors of the Iowa-California edition, who gave me professional counsel for several years prior to the decision to place this volume in The Papers, and to John S. Tuckey, who laid the foundation for this edition in his monograph, *Mark Twain and Little Satan, The Writing of* The Mysterious Stranger.

It is a pleasure to record a debt of a somewhat different kind, equally real, to three former students: John A. Costello, Priscilla H. Costello, and Miriam Kotzin. Mr. and Mrs. Costello, who typed the "No. 44" narrative from photocopy of the manuscript, deciphered and bracketed into their typescript many of Mark Twain's cancellations out of their own interest in the work. Miss Kotzin did me the service of retyping and checking against photocopy my own heavily corrected typescript of Twain's working notes for the three manuscripts. I owe these young scholars thanks. I am fortunate to have had the professional help of Bernard L. Stein for more than two years and of Victor Fischer for several months in establishing cancellations and completing the textual apparatus. And I appreciate assistance in proofreading from Mariam Kagan, Bruce T. Hamilton, Theodore Guberman, and Robert Hirst.

Barbara C. Gibson, my wife, at nearly every stage in the preparation of this edition invested hours and days in verifying copy against typescript and photocopy—only she knows how many—and in helping me "break" words or phrases heavily overscored.

Finally, I am grateful to the John Simon Guggenheim Foundation for the fellowship during which I began the editorial work; and to the Office of Education, Department of Health, Education and Welfare, and the National Endowment for the Humanities for providing me with indispensable travel and research assistance. The Office of Education has been the chief supporter of the Iowa edition; the National Endowment, the chief support of The Mark Twain Papers through the Center for Editions of American Authors, Modern Language Association of America.

Wɪʟʟɪᴀᴍ M. Gɪʙsᴏɴ

March 1968

Contents

Abbreviations

MTN   *Mark Twain's Notebook,* ed. Albert Bigelow Paine
                       (New York, 1935)

MTSatan   John S. Tuckey, *Mark Twain and Little Satan,
                       The Writing of* The Mysterious Stranger (West
                       Lafayette, Indiana, 1963)

MTTB   *Mark Twain's Travels with Mr. Brown,* ed. Frank-
                       lin Walker and G. Ezra Dane (New York, 1940)

MTW   Bernard DeVoto, *Mark Twain at Work* (Cam-
                       bridge, Massachusetts, 1942)

SCH   Dixon Wecter, *Sam Clemens of Hannibal* (Boston,
                       1952)

What Is Man?   *What Is Man? and Other Essays* (New York, 1917)

WWD   *Mark Twain's Which Was the Dream?,* ed. John S.
                       Tuckey (Berkeley and Los Angeles, 1967)

Introduction

M ARK TWAIN'S *The Mysterious Stranger, A Romance,* as published in 1916 and reprinted since that date, is an editorial fraud perpetrated by Twain's official biographer and literary executor, Albert Bigelow Paine, and Frederick A. Duneka of Harper & Brothers publishing company. When I first read the three manuscript versions of the narrative in the Mark Twain Papers, like other scholars who had seen them, I found this dismaying conclusion to be inescapable. John S. Tuckey first demonstrated the fact in 1963 in an admirable monograph in which he dated the composition of the manuscripts; [1] this publication of the texts themselves offers additional proof. Thus, half a century after a spurious version was delivered to an unsuspecting public in the form of a children's Christmas gift book, the manuscripts are presented here for the first time as they came from their author's hand.

Paine was able to publish the "final complete work"—he said in 1923—because he turned up its essential last chapter in a great batch of unfinished stories and fragments several years after Clemens died in 1910. [2] On the basis of incomplete evidence and wrong

---

[1] *MTSatan.*
[2] "Introduction," *DE,* XXVII, ix–x.

1

dating of manuscripts, Paine's successor as literary editor, Bernard DeVoto, argued that in completing *The Mysterious Stranger*, Mark Twain "came back from the edge of insanity, and found as much peace as any man may find in his last years, and brought his talent into fruition and made it whole again." [3] Two generations of readers have found the published tale as moving as DeVoto did. Although a very few readers and critics, notably Frederick A. G. Cowper and Edwin S. Fussell,[4] have been troubled by inconsistencies, especially in the final chapter, most have agreed that the melancholy fable, Twain's last important fiction, formed a kind of Nunc Dimittis.

The truth is that Mark Twain attempted at least four versions of the story, which survive in three manuscripts. *The Mysterious Stranger* represents, partially, the first manuscript in order of composition rather than the last, as DeVoto thought. None of the three is a finished work, although Twain did draft a "Conclusion of the book" for the third manuscript with the intent—never fulfilled—of completing this last version. Further, it is now clear that Paine, aided by Duneka, cut and bowdlerized the first manuscript heavily. He borrowed the character of the astrologer from the third manuscript and attributed to the new figure the grosser acts and speeches of a priest. Then he grafted the final chapter of the third manuscript to the broken-off first manuscript version by cutting half a

---

[3] *MTW*, p. 130.

[4] After suggesting that the generalized source for *The Mysterious Stranger* was chapter 20, "L'Hermite," of Voltaire's *Zadig*, and that Goethe's *Faust* might have contributed picturesque events, Cowper wrote in a footnote: "When he was over seventy, Mark Twain was going over with Paine a number of incomplete manuscripts. They found three forms of *The Mysterious Stranger* and agreed that one could easily be made ready for publication. Seemingly nothing was done to complete it. Twain died in 1910 and the story was not published until 1916. It is evidently not a finished work." His analysis appears in "The Hermit Story, as Used by Voltaire and Mark Twain," *In Honor of the Ninetieth Birthday of Charles Frederick Johnson*, ed. Odell Shepard and Arthur Adams (Hartford, 1928), p. 333. Fussell perceived a constant conflict in the published story between the author's "emotional reactions" and "his theoretical formulations,"—a conflict partially inherent in the manuscript on which the posthumous edition is based, it may be noted, and partially caused by Paine's editorial tampering ("The Structural Problem of *The Mysterious Stranger*," *Studies in Philology*, XLIX [January 1952], 103).

chapter, composing a paragraph of bridgework, and altering characters' names. Speaking of his great discovery among the confusion of papers, Paine said, "Happily, it was the ending of the story in its first form." [5] Although Paine's loyalty to Mark Twain was great and his rich accumulation of data about Mark Twain's life in *Mark Twain: A Biography* will always be valuable, two facts must be recorded here. He altered the manuscript of the book in a fashion that almost certainly would have enraged Clemens, and he concealed his tampering and his grafting-on of the last chapter, presumably to create the illusion that Twain had completed the story, but never published it. One bit of evidence proves this conclusively: in the all-important final chapter, on the manuscript the names "August" and "44," which Twain had given characters in the last version, are canceled, and "Theodor" and "Satan," characters in the first version, are substituted in Paine's hand.

A case can be made for Paine. When he and Duneka lifted the magician from the third manuscript, developed this figure into the astrologer, and used him as a kind of scapegoat, they thought they were acting to sustain and add to Mark Twain's reputation. They cut passages that they believed would offend Catholics, Presbyterians, and others for the same reason, and in cutting they did eliminate burlesque passages that clog the story. Moreover, as the experience of thousands of readers attests, the last chapter, although it was written for another version, does fit this version remarkably well. Certain "dream-marks" *do* suggest a dream-conclusion. But the major and inescapable charge in the indictment of Paine as editor of *The Mysterious Stranger* stands—he secretly tried to fill Mark Twain's shoes, and he tampered with the faith of Mark Twain's readers.

It follows that the serial text in *Harper's Monthly Magazine* (May through November 1916) and the text of the book (published in late October) possess no authority in the preparation of this edition. The text of the first edition remains chiefly an exhibition of the self-confident taste of the editor and his associate,

---

[5] "Introduction," *DE*, XXVII, x.

Duneka—and, it seems likely, of their desire to get out another book by "Mark Twain." One depressing aspect of their misrepresentational editorial work is that they commissioned N. C. Wyeth, a well-known illustrator of children's books, to illustrate their altered text, and they let the designer place a fine color engraving of that nonentity, the "borrowed" astrologer, on the front cover.

The Order of the Manuscripts

Three of Twain's holograph manuscripts in the Mark Twain Papers at the University of California in Berkeley provide the copy-text of this edition. Typescripts of the first and third manuscripts, with a few authorial corrections, possess subsidiary authority. Mark Twain's titles for each, in the order of composition, were "The Chronicle of Young Satan," "Schoolhouse Hill," and "No. 44, The Mysterious Stranger." His manuscript working-notes for the three versions, a long notebook entry about "little Satan, jr.," and a single discarded page of manuscript surviving from revision are included entire in appendixes. Explanatory notes follow.* The Textual Apparatus describes the texts, sets forth the editorial principles observed, lists the recovered cancellations, and gives all editorial choices or emendations. Here, as elsewhere in the University of California Press edition of The Mark Twain Papers, the intention is to set forth all the evidence for the making of the text.

The present dating of these works follows closely the conclusions of Tuckey, who in *Mark Twain and Little Satan* made a thorough examination not only of the manuscripts but of the whole body of documents in the Mark Twain Papers from 1897 through 1908, comparing papers, inks, and handwriting for dating clues and making skilled use of internal evidence as well.[6] Other literary evidence to be cited supports Tuckey's dating at every point.

Four versions of the narrative are to be distinguished in the three manuscripts:

Version A. The first may be called the "St. Petersburg Fragment" (Tuckey's "Pre-Eseldorf" pages). It consists of nineteen

---

[6] *MTSatan,* pp. 14–15.

* The reference here is to the original, clothbound edition (University of California Press, 1969).

manuscript pages preserved from a version of the story which was set in St. Petersburg. They were written after Mark Twain's arrival in Vienna in late September 1897 and were revised and worked into the early part of Version B. A number of canceled references to St. Petersburg identify the original setting. For black walnuts (which are Missouri trees) Twain later substituted chestnuts, for dollars he later substituted ducats, and for the village bank he wrote in the name of Solomon Isaacs, the moneylender. He substituted Nikolaus for Huck, Theodor for George (Tom in the notes), Father Peter for Mr. Black, Seppi for Pole, and Wilhelm Meidling for Tom Andrews "of good Kentucky stock." References that placed the story in the 1840's of the author's boyhood were deleted. The action includes Satan's lecture on the Moral Sense, Mr. Black's finding of the dollars, and the stir this discovery makes in the village.

Version B. "The Chronicle of Young Satan" ("Eseldorf," as DeVoto referred to it) is Mark Twain's own title for a story of some 423 manuscript pages which breaks off in mid-chapter in the court of an Indian rajah, where Satan is competing with the court magician. The main setting is Eseldorf, an Austrian village, in 1702; the action begins in May. The chief characters are the narrator Theodor Fischer and his youthful companions Seppi Wohlmeyer and Nikolaus Baumann; Father Peter and Father Adolf, the good and evil priests; Marget, the niece of Father Peter, and Ursula, their servant; Wilhelm Meidling, Marget's suitor; Lisa Brandt and her mother. Finally there is the stranger, known to the villagers as Philip Traum, although at home he is called Satan, after his uncle.

Mark Twain wrote "Chronicle" in three periods between November 1897 and September 1900, not long before he returned to the United States from Europe, free from his "long nightmare" of debt. In the first period from November 1897 through January 1898 in Vienna, Twain reworked the "St. Petersburg Fragment" into a plot sequence which develops the character of Father Adolf and then tells of the boys' first encounter with Satan, Father Peter's trial on the charge of stealing Father Adolf's gold, and Father

Peter's vindication.[7] Twain concluded in the following months, however, that he had resolved the conflict between the priests too rapidly, and apparently he decided that for Satan to drive Father Peter into a state of "happy insanity" at the very moment when the old man was proved innocent would provide the true ending he was seeking. So, returning to his manuscript between May and October 1899, Twain put aside the trial scene and developed further episodes, mixing into them Socratic dialogues on the workings of the Moral Sense.[8] Theodor recalls the story of the girls burned as witches because of fleabite "signs" and tells how Gottfried Narr's grandmother had suffered the same fate in their village.[9] The village is forced to choose between charging Father Adolf with witchcraft and suffering an Interdict. Fuchs and Meidling suffer pangs of jealousy because Lilly Fischer and Marget become infatuated with Satan and his knowledge and creative skills. This spurt of sustained composition ended approximately with Twain's summary passage early in chapter 6:

> What a lot of dismal haps had befallen the village, and certainly Satan seemed to be the father of the whole of them: Father Peter in prison . . . Marget's household shunned . . . Father Adolf acquiring a frightful and odious reputation . . . my parents worried . . . Joseph crushed . . . Wilhelm's heart broken . . . Marget gone silly, and our Lilly following after; the whole village prodded and pestered into a pathetic delirium about non-existent witches . . . the whole wide wreck and desolation . . . the work of Satan's enthusiastic diligence and morbid passion for business.

Twain wrote the remaining half of "Chronicle" from June through August 1900, in London and at nearby Dollis Hill. His hatred of cruelty (which would lead him to begin a book about

---

[7] In the present text, the sequence runs through chapters 1 and 2, the opening of chapter 3, and part of chapter 10. See _MTSatan_, pp. 38–39.

[8] These episodes, written in London and in Sanna, Sweden, constitute chapters 3 through 5 of the present text.

[9] The reference to Narr's grandmother, who "cured bad headaches by kneading the person's head and neck with her fingers," places the writing of this passage some time after July 1899. See Explanatory Notes.

lynchings in the United States) continued to manifest itself in passages that showed the burning of Frau Brandt at the stake for blasphemy, the punishment of the gamekeepers, Theodor's presence at the pressing to death of a gentlewoman in Scotland, and the Eseldorf mob's stoning and hanging of the "born lady."

Satan's freedom in time and space and his godlike powers also make possible two new strands of action: he changes the lives of Nick and Lisa to bring on their drowning, and he refers to future —that is, contemporary—events. In the spring and summer of 1900, Clemens was increasingly angered by the role of the European powers in the Boxer Rebellion; and, despite his admiration for the British and their institutions, he became increasingly committed to the cause of the Boer Republics. Satan refers sardonically to both situations in chapters 6 and 8.

Nearly all the episodes thus far lead to the deferred episode wherein Father Peter is exonerated and goes mad, the conclusion toward which Twain presumably had been working. But the pressure of world events and Twain's sense that he probably would not publish this book in his lifetime carried him on. King Humbert the Good of Italy was assassinated by an anarchist at Monza on 29 July 1900 and died excommunicated. Pope Leo XIII subsequently forbade priests to recite a "tender prayer" composed by Queen Margherita that already had been widely repeated in Italy and the Catholic world. Twain must almost at once have seized upon this as "proof" of the doctrine of papal infallibility.[10] His version of the event probably inspired the famous generalization on the power of laughter—and the failure of the human race to make use of its one great weapon. Then Twain added a parable on the price the British might have to pay for their tenure in India; and the Indian setting inspired him to begin another "adventure" of Satan and Theodor in the court of a rajah. At this point the manuscript ends.

Version C. "Schoolhouse Hill," or the Hannibal version, a fragment of 16,000 words, is first adumbrated in Mark Twain's notebook in November 1898. His entry begins:

---

[10] *MTSatan,* pp. 49–50.

Story of little Satan, jr, who came to ⟨Petersburg (Hannibal)⟩
went to school, was popular and greatly liked by ⟨Huck and Tom⟩
who knew his secret. The others were jealous, and the girls didn't
like him because he smelt of brimstone. *This* is the Admirable Crichton He was always doing miracles—his pals knew they were miracles,
the⟨y⟩ others thought them mysteries. He is a good little devil; but
swears, and breaks the Sabbath. By and by he is converted, and becomes a Methodist. and quits miracling. . . . As he does no more
miracles, even his pals⟨s⟩ fall away and disbelieve in him. When his
fortunes and his miseries are at the worst, his papa arrives in state in
a glory of hellfire and attended by a multitude of old-fashioned and
showy fiends—and *then* everybody is at the boy-devil's feet at once
and want to curry favor.

Little Satan, Jr., is also to perform tricks at jugglery shows, to try to
win Mississippi raftsmen to Christ, and to take Tom and Huck to
stay with him over Sunday in hell.[11] The complete entry, with
Mark Twain's working notes, shows that for the moment he had
put the trial sequence of "Chronicle" aside and was making a fresh
start in a mood of comedy. Whereas "Chronicle" is the first-person
narrative of young Fischer, the six chapters of November and
December 1898 are told by an omniscient narrator. Apparently, it
was to be both an essay in the correction of ideas and a comedy set
in the world of Tom Sawyer and Huckleberry Finn, whose boy-
hero would like to reform and save it.

The miraculous boy, now renamed 44, appears one winter morning in the St. Petersburg school and performs marvels by reading
books at a glance and learning languages in minutes. With Tom
and Huck on his side, he fights and puts down the school bully.
The Hotchkiss family take him into their home, where he feeds
and talks to the savage family cat. And, after saving Crazy Meadows and others from a blinding blizzard, he appears miraculously at
a séance. Here the manuscript ends.

In the rest of the story, Twain's notes suggest that he intended to

---

[11] Notebook 32, TS p. 50. MT's holograph manuscript of this and all other
notebooks cited are in MTP. The entry is printed with Mark Twain's working-
notes in Appendix B of this volume. Passages enclosed in angle brackets are
canceled in the original.

picture once more some of the life of his own Hannibal boyhood as a background for 44's tricks and miracles and reforms. But he also planned to introduce two serious actions. Forty-four was to fall in love with "Hellfire Hotchkiss" and to discover how tame, how "purely intellectual," was the happiness of hell compared to this mortal love. He was also to form an Anti-Moral-Sense Sunday-school and to print his own catechism with the aid of "slathers of little red . . . devils" specially brought up from hell. ("If Satan is around, and so much more intelligent and powerful than God, why doesn't He write a Bible?" Twain wrote in his notebook in June 1898).[12]

Why Mark Twain let this story lapse after a moderately promising beginning when he had dozens of ideas for continuing it is problematical. Perhaps certain inherent contradictions within the character of 44 and in his projected actions proved too great for Twain to resolve. Apparently he wanted to make his stranger both a boy and an angel, both a companion to Tom and Huck and a Prometheus-figure who was to enlighten the citizens of St. Petersburg concerning the damnable Moral Sense. The strain of this double purpose, only a little evident in "Chronicle," appears more clearly here.

Version D. "No. 44, The Mysterious Stranger," or "Print Shop" version, is a story of 530 manuscript pages, set like "Chronicle" in Austria, but in 1490, not long after the invention of printing. Late in 1902 Mark Twain altered the first chapter of his "Chronicle" manuscript to fit this new setting; but, intending to revise further, he left the linkages to his new version loose and imperfect. Father Adolf and Father Peter, for example, who are important in "Chronicle," play only minor roles in the new plot, and Marget and Wilhelm Meidling never reappear. Between November 1902 and October 1903, while in Florence for his wife's health, Twain wrote chapters 2 through 7 or 8, which represent the trials of No. 44 as a printer's devil in a "mouldering" castle. Most of the printers abuse him, but Katrina, the cook, and Heinrich Stein, the master, openly

---

[12] Notebook 32, TS p. 25.

support him, and August Feldner, the young narrator, secretly sympathizes with him. These chapters reach their climax when 44 masters the printing trade in a few hours, and, just as a major printing job is nearing completion, the compositors call a strike against the master.

Twain completed the next sequence, from chapters 8 or 9 through 25, in the first six months of 1904. In this stretch of narrative, 44 saves Stein from ruin with the help of the wandering jour printer Doangivadam and Katrina and August. He completes the Bible-printing contract by creating invisible Duplicates of the printing force (shades of Colonel Sellers as a scientist!), creates havoc in the castle by incarnating the Duplicates, and immolates himself before the entire group. In this fashion, the print-shop action comes to an end. Except for the parable of human suffering embodied in the plight of Johann Brinker and his family, Twain's new plot complications tend to be either fantastic or feeble. Forty-Four plays tricks on Balthasar Hoffman, the magician, and on Father Adolf, and he explains the difference in the human psyche between the Workaday-Self and the Dream-Self. By the time August Feldner/Martin von Giesbach falls in love with Marget Regen/Elisabeth von Arnim and grows jealous of Emil Schwarz, his Dream-Self's embodiment, Mark Twain has turned the idea of double personality into the triad of Waking-Self, Dream-Self, and Immortal Spirit and has even endowed Schwarz with some of the powers of 44. All these developments take place in something like a dramatic vacuum.

When Twain returned to the story in June and July 1905 in Dublin, New Hampshire, he evidently saw that his grip on the plot had weakened, for he destroyed some of the most recent pages and "Burned the rest (30,000 words) of the book this morning. Too diffusive"—that is, a block of the story following chapter 19. He managed to make his new matter (chapters 26 through 32) considerably livelier than his love story, although it is still "diffusive" and disjointed. Forty-Four transforms Marget's maid into a cat, plays Mister Bones in a Christy minstrel show, simultaneously attacks Mary Baker Eddy and Imperial Russia, undergoes a second apotheosis, and releases Emil Schwarz from the bonds of flesh. He satirizes a sentimental poem and turns time backward. Somehow, in the midst of this farrago of burlesque and satire, Twain created a minstrel-show vignette memorable for its humor and sentiment, and composed Schwarz's eloquent, serious, and startling plea for release from the bonds of "this odious flesh."

The plea of Schwarz to his alter ego for freedom also prefigures the "empty and soundless world" in which August is left after 44's historical pageant of skeletons has passed by. This episode, placed here as chapter 33, was written last, in 1908, and Twain may have intended it as an alternate ending to the whole. The "Conclusion of the book," however, is his own notation at the head of the dream-ending—the six manuscript pages written in the spring of 1904 and placed in this text as chapter 34. It seems more likely therefore that he wrote the pageant chapter as part of an effort—never fulfilled—to link the body of his story to the "Conclusion of the book."

Characters

Twice Mark Twain tried to place his fable of man's meanness and misery in "St. Petersburg" and the years of his boyhood, and twice he found it necessary to move it to Austria and a remoter era. Though he tended to regard time and place as unimportant and easily changeable, his effort to reuse the "Matter of Hannibal," as Henry Nash Smith has called it,[13] suggests that he may have been drawing characters from memory. The likelihood grows as one reads "Villagers of 1840–3," a manuscript of late 1897 which was written shortly before Twain composed the "St. Petersburg Fragment," the first sequence of "Chronicle," and "Schoolhouse Hill." For "Villagers" is an impressive set of thumbnail biographies of persons in Hannibal that suggests total recall, modified by black humor. Most of the names, as Dixon Wecter and Walter Blair have shown, were names of real persons, though a few, including the Clemenses', were disguised.[14]

In the "St. Petersburg Fragment," for example, Tom Sawyer and

---

[13] "Mark Twain's Images of Hannibal: From St. Petersburg to Eseldorf," *Texas Studies in English*, XXXVII (1958), 3–23.

[14] "Villagers of 1840–3" is included in *HH&T*. See also *SCH*, p. 128.

Huck Finn were the chums of "Pole" before the author made the names appropriately Austrian—Theodor, Nikolaus, and Seppi. Very likely the name "Pole" was derived from Napoleon Pavey, the son of a Hannibal hotel-keeper. In "Villagers" he "went to St. Louis. Gone six months—came back a striker, with wages, the envy of everybody." He "became second engineer. . . . Got drowned." Sam Clemens had lodged with a Pavey family as a young jour printer in St. Louis from 1852 to 1853.[15] Similarly, "Mr. Black" (Father Peter in "Chronicle" and "No. 44") is inspired by Orion Clemens, the good-hearted, dreamy, older brother who vacillated for a lifetime in his religions, jobs, and moods and who had no unkindness in him. Clemens for many years helped support Orion and his wife Molly; they aroused in him both sympathy and acute exasperation. In "Schoolhouse Hill" Oliver Hotchkiss, a more complex figure based on Orion, is still sympathetic but often comic. Twain identified him in a marginal note thus: "O had mental perception but no mental proportion." [16]

Contemporary events in Vienna as well as family and Hannibal history provided Mark Twain with ideas for characters in "Chronicle." Deputies Wohlmeyer and Fuchs in the Austrian parliament during the autumn of 1897 furnished only their names. Father Adolf, however, originally Father Lueger in the manuscript, derived distinct and unpleasant traits from Twain's repeated impressions of Dr. Karl Lueger, Burgomeister of Vienna and leader of the anti-Semitic Christian Socialists.[17] The priest's bull voice and gross physique come to mind in descriptions of Deputy Schönerer—"vast and muscular, and endowed with the most powerful voice in the Reichsrath." [18]

"Schoolhouse Hill" is closely related to "Villagers" and to Hannibal people other than Orion and Pamela Clemens. Tom and Sid Sawyer, Huck Finn, and Becky Thatcher reappear at a second remove from the humorist's boyhood friends. But the Scottish

---

[15] SLC to Frank E. Burrough, 15 December 1900 (TS in MTP).
[16] Orion Clemens had died on 11 December 1897.
[17] *MTSatan*, pp. 17–23.
[18] "Stirring Times in Austria," *Hadleyburg*, p. 323.

schoolmaster, Archibald Ferguson, is a semifictional representation of Sam Clemens's teacher, William O. Cross,[19] and the school bully, Henry Bascom, owes a substantial debt to the son of a Hannibal slave-trader, Henry Beebe, who "kept that envied slaughter-house" and to whom "Joe Craig sold . . . cats to kill in it." [20] Perhaps the most vital of all the characters is the elderly slave-woman Aunt Rachel, who reports so tellingly the offstage feats of 44. Though Twain may have been drawing on his memories of Aunt Hanner and Uncle Dan'l, his uncle John Quarles's slaves, who had served him more than once as models, he probably was thinking of Aunty Cord, a Negro servant in the Crane household at Elmira, whom he described to Howells in 1877 as "cook, aged 62, turbaned, very tall, very broad, very fine every way." [21] It was Aunty Cord, in the character of Aunt Rachel, whose "A True Story, Repeated Word for Word as I Heard It" Twain sent to the *Atlantic* in 1874. Of the "Villagers" characters in "Schoolhouse Hill," one more remains whose past life was to affect the plot. Crazy Meadows, whom 44 rescues from the blizzard, is identified in Twain's working notes as "Crazy Fields [who] lost wife, then child; because wife nursed sm. [small] pox patient who had no friend." Further notes linking "C. F." to Dr. James Radcliff of Hannibal, whose three sons went mad, indicate that Twain intended to present Fields's life history as a paradigm and a commentary on the Moral Sense.[22]

Mark Twain carried Father Peter and Father Adolf over from "Chronicle" to "No. 44, The Mysterious Stranger," but assigned them minor roles. Father Peter's niece, renamed Gretchen, quickly disappears. The magician, in contrast to his predecessor Merlin in *A Connecticut Yankee,* serves merely as a cog in the plot. And most of the compositors in Stein's print shop are present simply to

[19] Appendix B, *SCH,* pp. 131–133; *HH&T,* Appendix A.

[20] *Mark Twain's Letters to Will Bowen,* ed. Theodore Hornberger (Austin, 1941), p. 18. Even Dr. Wheelwright, "the stately old First-Family Virginian and imposing Thinker of the village," is probably a sketch from life of the "aged Virginian physician Dr. [Humphrey] Peake" as Wecter notes in *SCH,* p. 67; see also *HH&T,* Appendix A.

[21] *MTHL,* p. 195.

[22] Notebook 35, TS p. 12 (10 May 1902); MT's working-notes, in Appendix B; "Villagers," *HH&T.*

torment 44 and August Feldner. Four important characters, however, are new: Katrina, Doangivadam, the narrator August Feldner,
and Johann Brinker. Each possesses some vitality. All four are
related to Clemens's youth or to his early experience as a printer's
devil. Twain may have drawn Katrina (who is "swarthy") from his
memory of the Negro cook who fed him and two other apprentices
in the printing-shop kitchen of Joseph Ament, editor of the Hannibal *Missouri Courier*.[23] Unquestionably he modeled Doangivadam
upon Wales McCormick, a fellow apprentice in Ament's shop. As
Clemens remembered McCormick, he was a giant of seventeen or
eighteen, a "reckless, hilarious, admirable creature," high-spirited
and irreverent without limit—and therefore well suited to the
fictional role of defending his abused juniors.[24] For the most part,
August Feldner, the young narrator, is as fearful as his champion is
bold, and he comes to life most poignantly when he confesses that
the tough compositors fastened upon him a nickname so humiliating he could only hint at its meaning by an abbreviation: "B.-A."
he says in the text; "bottle-a'd" Twain writes in a marginal note;
"bottle-assed" is the word in printer's jargon. It is a fair guess that
August speaks for the youthful Clemens when he says that this
"small thing" shamed him "as few things have done since." Brinker's years as a blind and paralyzed deaf-mute—with the suffering
they bring for his mother and sisters—follow his performance of a
generous deed. His is the fate which Nikolaus Baumann in "Chronicle" escaped by his early death, and it is similar to that of Tom
Nash of Hannibal.

Satan, alias "No. 44," is the primary character in all three manuscripts and the most complex in his acts, his satirical bent, the "fatal
music of his voice," his Socratic way of speaking, and his origins.

---

[23] Probably in the summer of 1848 according to Wecter, *SCH*, p. 202. The
fictional Moses Haas, "never good for 600 on a fat take," sounds like the com-
positor-editor of Clemens's boyhood, "full of blessed egotism and placid self-
importance," who would "smouch all the poetry" on the day before publication
and "leave the rest to 'jeff' for the solid takes," described in "The Compositor,"
Hartford *Courant*, 20 January 1886.
[24] Autobiographical Dictation, 29 March 1906, TS in MTP; *MTA*, II, 276–
282; *SCH*, pp. 204–205, where Dixon Wecter notes the similarity.

To adapt Whitman's figure, he forms one side of a Square Deific.[25] In Mark Twain's theology, he is the truth-speaker momentarily banished from heaven, the preacher Koheleth, the new Prometheus who is "courteous to whores and niggers." [26] He thus usurps certain functions of Christ the consoler who, says the head clerk in "Captain Stormfield's Visit to Heaven," has saved as many worlds as there are gates into heaven—"none can count them." The Father of the Old Testament and Missouri Presbyterianism forms the second side of the square—severe, jealous, and vengeful. He is distinct from but sometimes shades into the eternal Creator, the third side, of whom Clemens thought in astronomical terms—a supernal Power not so much indifferent to men as wholly unaware of them. Forty-Four is speaking for this last, greatest deity when he tells Theodor that "Man is to me as the red spider is to the elephant."

Of the Quadernity, it is Satan the rebel, nonetheless, who figures most often in Twain's writings and who exhibits the richest development.[27] Young Clemens's first impression of the devil, recorded sixty years later, was so strong that, he says, he tried at age seven to write Satan's biography—only to be frustrated by the paucity of facts and his Sunday-school teacher's shocked resistance.[28] If this yarn seems something less than petrified fact, one must credit Clemens's claim that he had read the entire Bible by the time he entered his teens, and take seriously his remembered fear during a thunderstorm that the devil was coming to claim the soul of the original Injun Joe. Even more significant is his recollection of how he and others conspired to abuse the character of Satan in his mother's presence to see how she would react. As they had ex-

---

[25] I am expanding the trinity defined by Coleman O. Parsons in his "The Devil and Samuel Clemens," *Virginia Quarterly Review*, XXIII (Autumn 1947), 595–600. Much the fullest summary and discussion of influences in literature and life before Tuckey is Parsons's "The Background of *The Mysterious Stranger*," *American Literature*, XXXII (March 1960), 55–74. Behind Philip Traum, Parsons shows the figures of Pausanias in Adolf Wilbrandt's *The Master of Palmyra*, Goethe's Mephistopheles, the angel Jesrad in Voltaire's *Zadig*, and of course the boy Savior of the Apocryphal New Testament.

[26] See Appendix B.

[27] Satan's genealogy in Mark Twain's thought has been brilliantly outlined by Coleman Parsons; see note 25 above.

[28] "Is Shakespeare Dead?," *What Is Man?*, pp. 307–310.

pected, Jane Clemens was "beguiled into saying a soft word for the devil himself." She could not remain silent or passive when "hurt or shame [was] inflicted upon some defenseless person or creature"— not even the arch-sinner.[29] Years later, when as a cub pilot on the Mississippi he was reading Shakespeare and Milton, Clemens wrote in a letter to Orion, "What is the grandest thing in 'Paradise Lost' —the Arch-Fiend's terrible energy!" [30]

Then in 1867, shortly before he sailed for the Holy Land, the journalist Clemens encountered in a New York library another memorable figure in the apocryphal books of the New Testament. For his *Alta California* readers he quoted: "Jesus and other boys play together and make clay figures of animals. Jesus causes them to walk; also clay birds which he causes to fly, and eat and drink. The children's parents are alarmed and take Jesus for a sorcerer. . . ." The resemblance of the boy Jesus to Philip Traum is unmistakable.[31]

Satan in the Bible and *Paradise Lost* and the youthful Jesus of the Apocrypha are thus essential components of the matrix in which Mark Twain shaped his mysterious stranger. Thirty years later, the figure began to take form. The process began, it seems, with Clemens's bankruptcy, the death of Susy, and Jean's first epileptic seizures, and it continued during Olivia Clemens's decline into invalidism. In 1895 Twain recorded a dominant mood and a ruling idea in this notebook entry: "It is the strangest thing, that the world is not full of books that scoff at the pitiful world, and the useless universe and the vile and contemptible human race—books that laugh at the whole paltry scheme and deride it. . . . Why don't *I* write such a book? Because I have a family. There is no other reason." [32] That this question relates to the Mysterious

---

[29] *HH&T*, pp. 44–45.

[30] *MTB*, p. 146; Parsons, "The Devil and Samuel Clemens," p. 593.

[31] *MTTB*, pp. 252–253. This key source was first noted by Gladys Bellamy in *Mark Twain as a Literary Artist* (Norman, Oklahoma, 1950), pp. 352–353. See I. *Infancy*, Chapter XV, 1–7 and Chapter XIX, 3 and II. *Infancy*, Chapter I in *The Apocryphal New Testament*, 2d ed. (London: William Hone, 1820).

[32] Notebook 28, TS pp. 34–35 (10 November 1895). Clemens had long since learned the art of scoffing satire under the pseudonym Mark Twain, and also under the convention of a foreigner's writing letters home on his first visit to a

Stranger tales as well as to Twain's "gospel," *What Is Man?* (which he would begin in 1898), is hinted at in a cryptic entry made a month later, "What uncle Satan said." [33] By the summer of 1897 Twain was writing "Letters to Satan" inviting His Grace to "make a pleasure tour through the world," assuring Him, "You have many friends in the world; more than you think," particularly Cecil Rhodes and the European Concert.[34] Then comes the notation late in June, "Satan's boyhood—going around with other boys and surprising them with devilish miracles," and in these words the "St. Petersburg Fragment" and "The Chronicle of Young Satan" were born.[35]

During the next seven years while Mark Twain worked intermittently on the three related manuscripts,[36] he also composed a stream of notes and shorter pieces, finished and incomplete, published and unpublished, all concerning some diabolic or angelic stranger. Some time before the Clemens family left the Hotel Metropole in Vienna in the spring of 1898, Twain wrote "Conversations with Satan," a fragment in which the devil appears, dressed like an Anglican bishop, with the features of "Don Quixotte," Richelieu, or Sir Henry Irving playing Mephistopheles, to discuss cigars with Twain.[37] Later in 1898 Twain commented on or created three cognate characters. The first is the silent, august, black-clad figure of Death in Adolf Wilbrandt's "remarkable play," *The Master of Palmyra*, which Mark Twain saw at the Burg Theatre and praised warmly to American readers in the essay "About Play-Acting." [38]

---

new country—for example, Ah Song Hi's letters to Ching-Foo in Twain's early sketch, "Goldsmith's Friend Abroad Again" (*The Curious Republic of Gondour* [New York, 1919], pp. 75–109). Satan's "Letters from the Earth" is only one of several series that show Mark Twain an expert in the convention.

[33] Notebook 28, TS p. 51 (8 December 1895). One of the things that Satan said, "with discontent," was, "The trouble with you Chicago people is that you think you are the best people in hell—whereas you are merely the most numerous" (*MTN*, p. 324). The entry was made about 1 January 1897.

[34] *Europe*, pp. 211–220.

[35] Notebook 32a, TS p. 37; *MTSatan*, p. 31.

[36] Tuckey lists the dates of composition for all the manuscripts in a very useful table; *MTSatan*, p. 76.

[37] The manuscript, Paine 255 in MTP, has Mark Twain's room at the Metropole for its setting.

[38] *Hadleyburg*, pp. 235–251.

The second is the big, mysterious "passing stranger" of "The Man That Corrupted Hadleyburg," whom Richards in his delirium links to Satan and the "hell-brand." [39] The third is Twain's notebook hero-in-embryo, a descendant of Lilith, whose family escutcheon is a plain, clean slate, since he has no knowledge of good and evil, whereas the descendants of the Eve-branch bear the design of an apple core with the motto, "Alas!" [40]

Twain's opening allegation in "Concerning the Jews," published in September 1899, is that he has no prejudices of race, color, caste, or creed—not even a prejudice against Satan, "on account of his not having a fair show." A crucial passage follows in which he strongly defends Captain Dreyfus, announces that he will undertake Satan's rehabilitation himself—if he can get at the facts and find an unpolitic publisher—and concludes that "A person who has for untold centuries maintained the imposing position of spiritual head of four-fifths of the human race, and political head of the whole of it, must be granted the possession of executive abilities of the loftiest order." [41] This brilliant ironic passage, which may refer to "Chronicle" in the phrase about Satan's rehabilitation, ends most of Twain's peripheral attempts to sketch Satan or to use him for secondary argumentative ends. From the autumn of 1899 on, Twain concentrated his attention upon full, imaginative portraits of Satan and of 44 in the Mysterious Stranger stories. [42]

---

[39] *Hadleyburg*, pp. 2, 3, 67, 81. Twain offered the manuscript to a publisher on 2 November 1898 (Notebook 32, TS p. 48).

[40] Notebook 32, TS pp. 39–40 (September 1898). This descendant of Lilith may be the germ for Orrin Lloyd Godkin, one more disparager of the human race, in "Indiantown" (*WWD*, pp. 163–166).

[41] *Literary Essays*, "Definitive Edition" (New York, 1923), XXII, 264, 265.

[42] "The Stupendous Procession," a "fearful document" indeed as Paine called it, presents a pageant of warring nations, slaughter, and corpses presided over by a "Frivolous Stranger." The piece was intended for New Year's Day, 1902; *MTB*, pp. 1149–1150 prints a few paragraphs; MS is in MTP (DV345). "Sold to Satan" conjures up the devil, glowing with radium and clothed in a skin of polonium (*Europe*, pp. 326–338, written 1903–1904). "That Day in Eden (Passage from Satan's Diary)" sadly explicates man's acquisition of the Moral Sense as the saddest result of the Fall (*Europe*, pp. 339–346). The offensive stranger in "The Dervish and the Offensive Stranger" uneasily explains the downfall of the American Indians, the Filipinos, the Boers, and the Chinese (*Europe*, pp. 310–314). By 1905, the "aged stranger" of "The War Prayer" takes the place of a minister in a cathedral to pray for the total annihilation of the enemy

Mark Twain began many other fables and fictions in the last decade of his writing life and completed a few. But the Satanic stranger who visits the earth and pities and judges men, dominated his imagination and guided his pen in those years, trailing dozens of lesser characters in his angelic wake.

Acts and Concepts

Just as one may glimpse in Clemens's own experience the origins of many characters in "Chronicle," "Schoolhouse Hill," and "No. 44," one may also find in the records of his life adumbrations of acts and concepts in the three stories. Four of these may be termed, by a kind of bastard shorthand, protracted death by water, mob cowardice and cruelty, the Creation minimized, and quarrels and warfare. By developing such motifs, with varying degrees of success, Mark Twain was suggesting that men and women have no need of any hell "except the one we live in from the cradle to the grave." [43] The cause, he argued, was that the race was damned irrevocably, either by an indifferent-because-unconscious God or by the race's own defective nature—he never could decide which. Three other of Twain's concepts may be identified as the powers of laughter, music, and thought; the hierarchy of selves within the self; and the consoling view that life is a dream. These three qualify or explain the first four.

As I have suggested, Nikolaus Baumann's futile attempt in "Chronicle" to save Lisa Brandt from drowning anticipates Johann Brinker's rescue of Father Adolf from the icy river in "No. 44." Both events bring disease, paralysis, or crushing disaster to the rescuers and their families. Both stem from memories of the writer's boyhood. In 1906 Clemens recalled how he and Tom Nash had been skating on the Mississippi one frigid winter night when the

---

in the name of the "spirit of love" (*Europe*, pp. 394–398). As late as 1909 Mark Twain assumed the mask of Satan once again in the eleven "Letters from the Earth"—published in *Letters from the Earth*, ed. Bernard DeVoto (New York, 1962), pp. 3–55.

[43] Notebook 30, TS p. 53 (*post* 19 June 1896).

ice broke up; how he reached the shore safely, whereas the perspiring Nash boy had fallen into the icy water near shore; and how Tom had contracted scarlet fever as a result of the drenching, which left him stone-deaf and with impaired speech. He also remembered in 1898:

> I knew a man who when in his second year in college jumped into an ice-cold stream when he was overheated and rescued a priest of God from drowning; suffered partial paralysis, lay in his bed 38 years, unable to speak, unable to feed himself, unable to write; not even the small charity of quenching his mind was doled out to him—he lay and thought and brooded and mourned and begged for death 38 years.[44]

Similarly, in 1902, Twain made a note about Crazy Fields, whom he had presented briefly in "Schoolhouse Hill" as Crazy Meadows. Crazy Fields was associated by Clemens with old Dr. Radcliff in "Villagers" who declared on his deathbed: "Don't cry; rejoice—shout. This is the only valuable day I have known in my 65 years." Two sons of Dr. Radcliff of Hannibal had been born mad, and the third had gone mad after a career as a fine physician.[45] Late notes for "No. 44" add five more examples of blasted lives to these parables of good men's suffering.[46] Clemens's reaction to all these events, real and imaginary, was angry and rebellious. But the countermood of bitter resignation in Mark Twain is never very far away: as Theodor Fischer muses after the death of Lisa and Nikolaus, "Many a time, since then, I have heard people pray to God to spare the life of sick persons, but I have never done it."

Mob cowardice and mob cruelty, often abetted by the orthodox, figure again and again in the Mysterious Stranger manuscripts. Eleven girls of Eseldorf are burned together as witches because of "witch signs," or fleabites, on their bodies. The grandmother of Gottfried Narr is burned as a witch because she relieves pain by massage. Lisa Brandt's mother burns at the stake for blasphemy

---

after her daughter drowns. A Scottish mob will stone and crush a gentlewoman to death, Satan informs Theodor out of his fore-knowledge, because she is suspected of having Catholic sympathies.[47] Johann Brinker's mother, also suspected of witchcraft, is condemned to the stake by Father Adolf, whose life Brinker had saved at the cost of his own paralysis. Frau Brinker's decision to die in the fire rather than endure ostracism and starvation is moving and fitting in its context, no less so for the author's having found the germ of the episode in Cotton Mather's *The Wonders of the Invisible World*.[48] Other particular sources for some of these witchcraft episodes may yet be found in the histories Clemens read and reread; but no reader of "Goldsmith's Friend Abroad Again," which reports boys and policemen stoning and beating the Chinese in San Francisco, or of *The Prince and the Pauper* or *Huckleberry Finn* or *A Connecticut Yankee* or "The United States of Lyncherdom" would be surprised to find scenes of mob violence in these manuscripts.

Seeking to account for the special impact of these scenes, one remembers two scarifying events in Sam Clemens's early life. He once gave matches to a drunken tramp in the Hannibal jail so that he might smoke. During the night, before the jailer could unlock the door, he had to watch the man at the bars burning to death. He

[47] Several parallels exist in W. E. H. Lecky's account of how a Scottish mob stoned to death a certain Jane Corphar in 1704–1705. Accused of witchcraft, she had been released by the magistrates; but the minister of the town incited the mob to beat her in the presence of her two daughters. Eventually the mob had forced "a man with a sledge and horse to drive several times over her head" (*A History of England in the Eighteenth Century* [New York, 1892], II, 331–333). Mark Twain owned Lecky's *History*.

[48] Mather included in his book the report of a woman's confession at the stake, in Scotland in 1649:

As I must make answer to the God of Heaven, I declare I am as free from Witchcraft as any Child, but being accused by a Malicious Woman, and Imprisoned under the Name of a Witch, my Husband and Friends disowned me, and seeing no hope of ever being in Credit again, through the Temptation of the Devil, I made that Confession to destroy my own Life, being weary of it, and chusing rather to Die than to Live (Mr. Sinclare's *Invisible World* [London, 1862], p. 278; original edition, Boston, 1693).

Coleman Parsons in "The Background of *The Mysterious Stranger*" cites Sir Walter Scott's *Letters on Demonology and Witchcraft* (1830), letter IX.

also sat helplessly by in St. Louis while his beloved younger brother, Henry, slowly died of burns from a steamboat explosion.[49]

The most striking action in all three tales is Philip Traum's creating and destroying a race of Lilliputians, apparently for the sole purpose of amusing the three boys of the "Chronicle" story— the "Creation minimized," as I have called it. If, as John Hay once wrote Clemens, memory and imagination are the great gifts in a writer, they are nowhere more evident than in this demonstration by Satan. Here, in 1897 Mark Twain developed a donnée that he had noted only briefly thirty years earlier, when for his California newspaper readers he quoted from the Apocrypha: the youthful Savior in those books, like Philip Traum, often crippled or killed those who opposed his will.[50] So, from the apocryphal anecdote and his memory of *Gulliver's Travels* Twain developed his own version of the Creation, the Fall, and the Day of Doom, in which the unfallen angel and nephew of Satan acts the part of God. The Fall, it must be noted, is due in Twain's "Bible" to a quarrel between two workmen, who grapple like Cain and Abel in "a life and death struggle" until Satan crushes them with his fingers. As for the Judgment Day, it arrives by Satan's whim. Annoyed by the lamentation of the fingerling mourners around the two bodies, Satan mashes them into the ground, and then wipes out the whole race by fire and earthquake for the boys' entertainment. "As flies to wanton boys, are we to the gods;/They kill us for their sport," cries Gloucester in *King Lear*. The analogy is close.

As for the motif-in-action of quarreling and warfare, in all three versions of the story a sequence of personal fights and national battles substantiates Twain's contention that if the human race is not already damned, it ought to be. In 1897 Pudd'nhead Wilson observed that "The universal brotherhood of man is our most precious possession, what there is of it." [51] In 1899 Clemens said that he had proposed to the Emperor Franz Joseph "a plan to

[49] See also Parsons's citations in his "The Background of *The Mysterious Stranger*," pp. 65–68, particularly to chapter eight of Louisa May Alcott's *Little Men*.

[50] *MTTB*, pp. 252–253.

[51] *Following the Equator* (Hartford, 1897), p. 256, chapter 27.

exterminate the human race by withdrawing the oxygen from the air for a period of two minutes." [52] Behind these bits of mockery, one so sad and one so savage, is an old animus reawakened by contemporary wars. This same animus underlies many sardonic references in "Chronicle" and "No. 44" to Christian nations warring against other Christian nations and overwhelming pagan countries by conquest.

To illustrate: in "Chronicle," Theodor promises to tell, by and by, why Satan "chose China for this excursion." In 1897 Twain was defending the Emperor of China, and in 1899 he clearly sided with the "cautious Chinaman" as against "the Western missionary." [53] By 1900 he was writing his friend the Reverend Joseph H. Twichell, "It is all China, now, and my sympathies are with the Chinese. They have," he said, "been villainously dealt with by the sceptred thieves of Europe, and I hope they will drive all the foreigners out and keep them out for good." [54] Quite apparently Twain intended to make some exemplary use of the Chinese Boxers' struggle against the Powers, East and West. Satan develops the war-motif fully by showing the boys a theatrical or visionary "history of the progress of the human race" from Cain and Abel down through the sixty wars fought during the reign of Queen Victoria. Twain's last cinematic frames show England fighting what he called elsewhere a "sordid & criminal war" [55] against the Transvaal Republic and the Orange Free State in South Africa, and Europe "swallowing China"—proof, he explained, that "all the competent killers are Christian." Even Satan and Theodor's adventure with the "foreigner in white linen and sun-helmet," who cuffs the native juggler and thereby destroys the many-fruited tree and brings a fearful penalty upon himself, is a parable and prediction about British imperialism in India.[56] Finally, toward the end of the

---

[52] *MTB*, pp. 1079, 1235.
[53] *MTL*, p. 683.
[54] *MTL*, p. 699.
[55] *MTHL*, p. 715.
[56] Compare the tree-growing juggler in Ceylon and Dan Beard's picture, "The White Man's World," which shows the white man in the sun-helmet and illustrates Twain's assertion in the text, "The world was made for man—the white man" (*Following the Equator*, p. 339 and pp. 186–187).

"No. 44" manuscript, Mark Twain attempts simultaneously to sati-
rize Mary Baker Eddy and Czarist Russia. Mrs. Eddy had published
a telegram instructing her followers in the "Christian Silence dialect" to "cease from praying for peace and take hold of something
nearer our size," as Twain put it. He was bitterly disappointed
when the peace treaty between Russia and Japan was concluded at
Portsmouth in August 1905: as his recent article "The Czar's
Soliloquy" showed, he had hoped that Japan would win and the
Czar be overthrown.

The author's frame of mind, so often reflected in these war
scenes and "stupendous processions," may be summed up in a
statement that he made in the summer of 1900: "The time is grave.
The future is blacker than has been any future which any person
now living has tried to peer into." [57] Small wonder, then, that Philip
Traum should recount an up-to-date history of private and public
murder in "Chronicle" or that 44 should drag in by the heels Mary
Baker Eddy's proclamation about the Russo-Japanese War.[58]

Bitter and sad as the three "Mysterious Stranger" manuscripts
may be, they are not without affirmations: humor of all shades, the
love of music, and the power of imagination. Perhaps it was the

---

[57] "The Missionary in World-Politics," with letter to C. Moberly Bell, editor
of the London *Times;* unpublished MS in MTP.

[58] Why did Clemens fail to refer to the Spanish-American war in the Mysterious Stranger stories? Presumably the answer lies in the fact that the "Chronicle"
and "Schoolhouse Hill" were dropped before he returned to the United States in
October 1900, and that "No. 44" scarcely touches on war as a theme. In the fall
of 1900 Twain became convinced that the liberation of Cuba, which he applauded, was degenerating into imperialist war in the Philippines, and that even
British civilization could not justify the "single little shameful war" in South
Africa against the Boer Republics. He wrote four widely read and reprinted
attacks upon American missionaries and the European powers in China, upon
Chamberlain, McKinley and his administration, and upon the Czar of Russia.
They are "A Salutation-Speech from the Nineteenth Century to the Twentieth"
in the New York *Herald* of 30 December 1900; "To the Person Sitting in Darkness" in the *North American Review* of February 1901; "To My Missionary
Critics" in the same magazine for April 1901; and "The Czar's Soliloquy" in the
Review for March 1905. He joined the New England Anti-Imperialist League in
1900, and wrote much more, published and unpublished, on disarmament and
the possibility that new weapons might make war obsolete. For a discussion of
his anti-war writing from 1898 to 1902, see William M. Gibson, "Mark Twain
and Howells, Anti-Imperialists," *New England Quarterly,* XX (December 1947),
435–470.

contrast of bitter and affirmative strains that wrung from Livy Clemens, after she had heard her husband read the opening chapters of "Chronicle," the tribute, "It is perfectly horrible—and perfectly beautiful!" [59] The kind and quality of the humor vary greatly, as one might expect in Twain's unfinished work. When Philip Traum composes a narrative poem and a musical setting for it at the piano, he seems amateurish and boastful, whereas the antic dancing and singing presented by 44's Mister Bones mix humor and pathos effectively, perhaps because of Twain's lifelong delight in the Negro minstrel show. In the same way, 44's long talks with Mary Florence Fortescue Baker G. Nightingale (the chambermaid whom he has turned into a cat) represent burlesque spun out thin. But Aunt Rachel's amazed report of how 44 pacified and fed and talked to the fierce Hotchkiss cat, Sanctified Sal, is dramatic and finely humorous in the style of Uncle Remus or of Twain's own jumping-frog and blue-jay yarns. For all the slapstick Twain's avatars indulge in, they are the agents of a master humorist who is especially skilled in "black humor." I have already cited an instance in which Traum ridicules the doctrine of papal infallibility—a section Paine deleted from the published book. In a well known passage, Traum cries:

> Power, Money, Persuasion, Supplication, Persecution—these can lift at a colossal humbug,—push it a little—crowd it a little—weaken it a little, century by century: but only Laughter can blow it to rags and atoms at a blast. Against the assault of Laughter nothing can stand.

But Twain's illustrations never reached print. His account of how Robert Burns broke the back of the Presbyterian church and set Scotland free was to prove laughter's power. The general failure of readers to detect "the funniness of Papal Infallibility" would demonstrate how rarely mankind used that power.

Humor and music as catharsis and satire as correction are omnipresent in Mark Twain's theory and writings. The citizens of Hadleyburg, for example, restore their town's reputation for hon-

[59] *MTHL,* p. 699.

esty by laughing down their "incorruptible" leading citizens, whom another mysterious stranger has exposed. But in these stories and other late writings Twain could never quite decide·whether laughter was divine or only human. Pudd'nhead Wilson in 1897 insisted: "Everything human is pathetic. The secret source of Humor itself is not joy but sorrow. There is no humor in heaven." [60] Five years later Clemens observed, "We grant God the possession of all the qualities of mind except the one that keeps the others healthy; that watches over their dignity; that focuses their vision true— humor." [61] Of all the paradoxes in the three Mysterious Stranger stories, none is more paradoxical, or more sanative, than Twain's demonstrations of the power of laughter—was it *merely* human?— in the empty spaces of the universe.

Mark Twain put the concepts and actions thus far distinguished to real dramatic use in the plots of the Mysterious Stranger manuscripts. Only in "No. 44," the last, longest, and most diffuse version, did he develop a concept that resisted incorporation into the plot: that is, his speculative distinctions between Waking-Self, Dream-Self, and Immortal Soul and the resulting rather farcical incarnation of Emil Schwarz (Feldner's doppelgänger) and the printer's crew of Duplicates or Dream-Selves. How Twain arrived at this psychology is therefore as much a biographical question as it is a matter of literary genetics. Although Clemens in maturity was a champion of eighteenth-century rationalism, he grew up at a time when spiritualism and faith-cures roused widespread and lively interest, and he had long collected instances of "mental telegraphy," a power with which he endowed 44. In 1886 he and Howells collaborated in writing an absurd play, *Colonel Sellers as a Scientist,* in which one of Sellers's great schemes is to materialize the dead in order to build up a great supply of free labor (free, since the "materializees" neither slept nor ate). [62]

By the early 1890's Clemens was taking an increasing interest in

[60] *Following the Equator,* p. 119, chapter 10.
[61] Notebook 35 (1902), TS pp. 39–40.
[62] Walter J. Meserve, ed., *The Complete Plays of W. D. Howells* (New York, 1960).

mind-cures, which he associated with hypnotism, the work of J. H. Charcot's pupils, and the reports of the Society for Psychical Research.[63] Characteristically, his interest took two forms in alternation: a rational and satiric view and a speculative and psychological view. The first is exemplified earlier in the King's remark in *Huckleberry Finn*, "Layin' on o' hands is my best holt—for cancer and paralysis, and sich things"; Twain develops it amusingly at length in "Schoolhouse Hill" when Oliver Hotchkiss holds a séance. The second appears in Twain's sketch of 1876, "The Facts Concerning the Recent Carnival of Crime in Connecticut," a brilliant narration of the conflict between "Twain" and his conscience or superego, which ends by his murdering his conscience and enjoying the same exhilarating, amoral freedom that Schwarz enjoys in "No. 44."

The germ for Mark Twain's analysis of multiple selves in "No. 44," as Tuckey has observed, is a long notebook entry made in January 1897. In it Twain states that he has found "a new 'solution' of a haunting mystery." He had made a promising beginning himself in the "Carnival of Crime"; then Robert Louis Stevenson had come closer with Jekyll and Hyde; but, Twain continued, upon learning of a distinction which the French had been drawing between the waking person and the person under hypnosis, he had arrived at a new concept of duality. "My dream-self, is merely my ordinary body and mind freed from clogging flesh and become a spiritualized body and mind and with the ordinary powers of both enlarged in all particulars a little, and in some particulars prodigiously." The Dream-Self, he believes, is free in time and space, and "When my physical body dies my dream body will doubtless continue its excursion and activities without change, forever." [64]

No more than the image of the Dream-Self "as insubstantial as a dim blue smoke" finds its way into "Chronicle," in Philip Traum's lovely trick of thinning out like a soap bubble and vanishing. Many of the other distinctions and powers reappear directly and with embellishments, however, in the various incarnated Dream-Selves of "No. 44." Two of these distinctions are neither fantastic nor

[63] *MTSatan,* pp. 26–28; *MTHL,* p. 659.
[64] *MTN,* pp. 348–351.

farcical. Schwarz pleads eloquently with August and then with Number 44: "Oh, free me from . . . these bonds of flesh . . . this loathsome sack of corruption in which my spirit is imprisoned, her white wings bruised and soiled—oh, be merciful and set her free!" For the moment, Twain is able to take his idea of duality seriously and to lend Schwarz fictional life. The second distinction—that the dream body will continue on its excursion forever—foreshadows the "Conclusion of the book" and the prospect of August, as a "homeless Thought, wandering forlorn among the empty eternities!"

The "Conclusion of the book," which has so moved and challenged readers of *The Mysterious Stranger* since 1916, argues the extreme Platonic view that the final and only reality resides in the individual soul, all else being illusion—or that "life is a dream." (It is a view Emerson entertained only to reject it in *Nature*.) Although it is a key that fits nothing in the plot of the "Schoolhouse Hill" fragment, it does fit much of the action and imagery in "Chronicle" and nearly everything in the second half of "No. 44," the manuscript which it was written to conclude. The sources and analogues for it in Clemens's earlier writings, his reading, and his experience, enmeshed with his creation of Satan figures and his speculations about dreams, are extraordinarily various and complex. Here it may suffice to suggest only the chief sources of Twain's solipsistic idea.

Mark Twain began the "St. Petersburg Fragment" and "Chronicle" about a year after the death of his beloved daughter Susy, and he finished his "Conclusion of the book," "No. 44," in the summer of his wife Olivia Clemens's death. On the first anniversary of Susy's death he wrote one friend, "I suppose it is still with you as with us—the calamity not a reality, but a dream, which will pass, —*must* pass." [65] To another, he said six years later about Olivia's illness, "For a year and a half life, for this family, has been merely a bad dream." [66] Still later, after Olivia had died, he told Susan Crane of a lovely and blessed dream of Livy who leaned her head against

[65] SLC to Wayne MacVeagh, 22 August 1897, in MTP.
[66] SLC to T. B. Aldrich, 14 February 1904 (Harvard).

his while he repeated to her, "I was perfectly sure it was a dream, I never would have believed it wasn't." [67] This persistent sense of reality-in-dreams permeates Twain's long analysis of Waking- and Dream-Selves in a notebook entry of January 1897, and gave rise in the same month to an idea for a "farce or sketch" of people who seem to have "slept *backward* 60 years." [68] The dream motif began to carry over into his fiction, notably "My Platonic Sweetheart." This sketch of the summer of 1898 tells of a recurrent dream of idyllic meetings between the narrator and his charming girl, both timelessly young, in settings ranging from Missouri to India and ancient Athens—each dream like "Mohammed's seventy-year dream, which began when he knocked his glass over, and ended in time for him to catch it before the water was spilled." [69] In many respects this sketch anticipates the love passages and the ending of "No. 44." Twain kept on trying variations based upon his dream donnée. He began three stories of family disaster, the first of them called "Which Was the Dream?," also in the summer of 1898.[70] He conceived of "a drama in the form of a dream" [71] which he mentioned in a speech in 1900, and a year or two later he jotted down the idea, "divorce of the McWilliamses on account of his dream-wife and family." [72]

This welter of ideas in notes and fragments, this effort made over and over again to give form to the dream motif, began to come clear in the spring of 1904, not long before Twain either wrote or had firmly in mind his last chapter; it was in these months that he

---

[67] *MTL*, p. 777, 24 September 1905; *MTN*, p. 395, 24 September 1905.

[68] Notebook 31, TS pp. 41–43 (6 January 1897).

[69] *DE*, XXVII, 299.

[70] *MTHL*, pp. 675–678; *MTW*, pp. 118–120; and "Which Was the Dream?" in *WWD*.

[71] New York *Times*, "The Drama," 7 July 1900.

[72] Notebook 34 (1901), TS p. 21b. These notes and fragments are closely linked to Clemens's metaphor that the death of Susy had left the family helpless "derelicts" in an immense empty ocean. The metaphor recurs in letters to Francis H. Skrine, Twichell, and Howells. It becomes the setting of two manuscript fragments of the period, "The Enchanted Sea-Wilderness" (*WWD*, pp. 76–86) and "The Great Dark" (*WWD*, pp. 102–150). See SLC to Skrine, 19 January 1897, Roger Barrett Collection; to Twichell, 19 January 1897, *MTL*, p. 640; to Howells, 22 January 1898. *MTHL*, pp. 670–671.

probably wrote a note and he certainly wrote a letter couched in the language and imagery of the "Conclusion of the book." The note concerns "The intellectual & placid & sane-looking man whose foible is that life & God & the universe is a dream & he the only person in it—*not* a *person*, but a homeless & silly *thought* wandering forever in space." [73] The letter, dated 28 July, is in response to Twichell's question as to how life and the world had been looking to Clemens:

> (A *part* of each day—or night) as they have been looking to me the past 7 years: as being NON-EXISTENT. That is, that there is *nothing*. That there is no God and no universe; that there is only empty space, and in it a lost and homeless and wandering and companionless and indestructible *Thought*. And that I am that thought. And God, and the Universe, and Time, and Life, and Death, and Joy and Sorrow and Pain only a grotesque and brutal *dream*, evolved from the frantic imagination of that insane Thought.
>
> By this light, the absurdities that govern life and the universe lose their absurdity and become natural, and a thing to be expected. It reconciles everything, makes everything lucid and understandable: a God who has no morals, yet blandly sets Himself up as Head Sunday-school Superintendent of the Universe; Who has no idea of mercy, justice, or honesty, yet obtusely imagines Himself the inventor of those things; a human race that takes Him at His own valuation, without examining the statistics; thinks itself intelligent, yet hasn't any more evidence of it than had Jonathan Edwards in his wildest moments; a race which did not make itself nor its vicious nature, yet quaintly holds itself responsible for its acts.
>
> But—taken as unrealities; taken as the drunken dream of an idiot Thought, drifting solitary and forlorn through the horizonless eternities of empty Space, these monstrous sillinesses become proper and acceptable, and lose their offensiveness.

To this point in his letter, Clemens seems almost to merge himself into the character of the "sane-looking man" with the foible, or of 44 revealing the truth to August. But, Clemens explains to his old friend, the idea has become a part of him for seven years, for in that

---

[73] See MT's working notes, Appendix B.

time he has been working on an unfinished story. He continues: "And so, a part of each day Livy is a dream, and has never existed. The rest of it she is real, and is gone. Then comes the ache and continues." He concludes: "How well she loved you and Harmony, as did I, and do I, also." [74] Unquestionably Clemens endowed 44 with his own questionings and grievances and griefs.

It would be a mistake, however, to consider this letter unmixed autobiography. It is a moving document, written by Samuel Clemens, who suffers; it is equally a letter by Mark Twain, the long-committed artist who creates. Only a year before his death Clemens expressed elation at his discovery of a new literary form: writing untrammeled letters to his intimate friends like Howells or H. H. Rogers or Twichell and then not sending them. He told Howells, "When you are on fire with theology . . . you'll write it to Twichell, because"—in imagination—"it would make him writhe & squirm & break the furniture." [75] So, it appears, a literary impulse as well as private sorrow underlies the crucial letter to Twichell. It would also be a mistake to think that Twain had newly discovered the sense of cosmic loneliness which the "Conclusion" brilliantly imparts. More than thirty years earlier he had written, "I felt like the Last Man, neglected of the judgment, and left pinnacled in mid-heaven, a forgotten relic of a vanished world"; [76] this was his sensation as he stood above a sea of clouds on the crater edge at Haleakala, on Maui.

While Mark Twain wrestled with his final chapter—the only final chapter in the three manuscripts—he was attempting to cope with dream experiences and a haunting sense of isolation that had for long lain deep in his inner life. As Coleman Parsons first suggested, in completing the chapter Mark Twain evidently found powerful catalytic aid in *The Tempest*. [77] Schwarz's plea to the

---

[74] Dated Lee, Massachusetts, 28 July 1904 (MS at Yale University, TS in MTP).

[75] *MTHL*, p. 845.

[76] *Roughing It* (Hartford, 1872), p. 550, chapter 76.

[77] "The Background of *The Mysterious Stranger*," pp. 71–72. Clemens knew Shakespeare's plays well. On the Mississippi he heard George Ealer declaim Shakespeare, and read the plays in his spare time, and after he was a writer, he

"magician" for freedom from the bonds of "this odious flesh" recalls Ariel's eloquent pleas to Prospero for his release. Moreover, Traum and 44 share with Ariel the ability to enchant with music, the globe-girdling swiftness, the antic and mercurial moods (untroubled by any Moral Sense), and the power of melting "into air, into thin air," as none of their progenitors do—not Satan nor the child Jesus nor Pan nor the Admirable Crichton nor Twain's own Superintendent of Dreams. Prospero says:

> Our revels now are ended. These our actors,
> As I foretold you, were all spirits, and
> Are melted into air, into thin air;
> And, like the baseless fabric of this vision,
> The cloud-capp'd towers, the gorgeous palaces,
> The solemn temples, the great globe itself,
> Yea, all which it inherit, shall dissolve
> And, like this insubstantial pageant faded,
> Leave not a rack behind. We are such stuff
> As dreams are made on, and our little life
> Is rounded with a sleep.

Prospero's tone of great authority and reassurance as he speaks to the troubled young Ferdinand has its counterpart in the "gush of

---

burlesqued Shakespeare often. He cites Shakespeare as an example of supreme genius in "Chronicle," chapter 2. As early as 1873 Mark Twain quoted part of the dream-passage from *The Tempest* in "A Memorable Midnight Experience"; Howells located the passage for him in 1876; Mark Twain alluded to it again in 1889 in *A Connecticut Yankee;* and he quoted it at length in 1909 in the essay "Is Shakespeare Dead?" (*Europe*, p. 5; see *Yankee* [New York, 1889], p. 205, chapter XVII; *MTHL*, p. 127; *What Is Man?*, p. 362). Tuckey corroborates Twain's knowing *The Tempest*. After completing all but chapter 33 of "No. 44" (which was an afterthought), Clemens told his daughter Clara that he had broken his bow and burned his arrows—very probably his own version of Prospero's speech, "I'll break my staff, . . . / And deeper than did ever plummet sound / I'll drown my book" (*MTSatan*, p. 69). Finally, some part of the tone and imagery of 44's last speech to August may also derive from Belial's speech in Book II of *Paradise Lost:*

> To be no more; sad cure; for who would loose,
> Though full of pain, this intellectual being,
> Those thoughts that wander through Eternity. (146–148)

I am indebted to my former student Mrs. Barbara Fass for this brief but striking parallel.

thankfulness" which 44 releases in August and the "blessed and hopeful feeling" that his words will prove true. Satan's voice, like Prospero's, has "that fatal music" in it. Above all, what 44 reveals to August about the character of human life in the cosmos echoes and reechoes from Prospero's conclusion: life is as insubstantial as a dream.

If the similarities are strong, differences and difficulties (apart from *The Tempest*'s superiority) remain in Mark Twain's "Conclusion of the book." The almost unrelievedly dark tenor of his letter to Twichell is only half lightened in the "Conclusion" by blessed and hopeful feelings. Although 44's parting speech is credible insofar as one accepts his authority as a character and his premises in the argument, what is one to make of his urging August to "Dream other dreams, and better!"? Does the command to dream signify a command to create that "so potent art" of which Prospero and Shakespeare were masters? It is desirable here to repeat that Clemens valued the creative life above all other lives; it is a vulgar error to suppose he did not. The difficulty is that 44's injunction, whether in this or another meaning, cannot easily be assigned to a God hostile to men in an unmanageable or nonexistent universe. Of course, Clemens might have revised his manuscripts and this draft of a chapter, but as the chapter stands, the paradox remains: mold your life nearer to the heart's desire; life is at best a dream and at worst a nightmare from which you cannot escape.

The "Mysterious Strangers"

Almost universally, readers have accepted *The Mysterious Stranger, A Romance* as a finished, posthumously published work, and students of Twain have likewise credited Paine's story that his discovery of the last chapter enabled him to publish the complete tale. Only when John Tuckey published *Mark Twain and Little Satan* in 1963 were these readers and students disillusioned—although recently at least one critic, James M. Cox, has insisted that this posthumous edition of Mark Twain's last work "is not going to be superseded by any future text" and that it "is the closest thing to

Mark Twain's intention that we shall ever have." [78] But what Mark Twain actually wrote inevitably supersedes the Paine-Duneka patchwork text, and Mark Twain's "intention"—if by that we mean his effort to achieve a total effect in a completed work—was never fulfilled.

This is not to deny that the cut, cobbled-together, partially falsified text has the power to move and to satisfy esthetically despite its flaws. Perhaps it will last among some readers in preference to the unfinished fragmentary tales here published. But I think it possible that a writer or editor who is more sympathetic to Twain's divided mind and creative dilemma in his late life may, in the future, produce a better version than that pieced together by Paine and Duneka. Perhaps such a writer will imagine a new, wholly satisfying ending to "The Chronicle of Young Satan," or perhaps he will be able to condense, rework, and strengthen "No. 44, The Mysterious Stranger" and end it with Twain's last chapter in its proper place. To carry on, flesh out, and conclude "Schoolhouse Hill" would probably be even more difficult, and yet scarcely less rewarding. In any event, such a writer will begin with the texts that Mark Twain wrote in the form in which he left them, acknowledging openly when he selects or modifies or creates or concludes. Finally it must be said that these incomplete texts are Mark Twain's own fragments, large and small, with their own value and interest; and if he produced no finished narrative frieze, he did succeed in creating a multitude of various, memorable figures in the half-sculptured stones.

---

[78] *Mark Twain: The Fate of Humor* (Princeton, 1966), pp. 270, 272.

The Chronicle of Young Satan

Chapter 1

IT WAS 1702—May. Austria was far away from the world, and asleep; it was still the Middle Ages in Austria, and promised to remain so forever. Some even set it away back centuries upon centuries and said that by the mental and spiritual clock it was still the Age of Faith in Austria. But they meant it as a compliment, not a slur, and it was so taken, and we were all proud of it. I remember it well, although I was only a boy; and I remember, too, the pleasure it gave me.

Yes, Austria was far from the world, and asleep, and our village was in the middle of that sleep, being in the middle of Austria. It drowsed in peace in the deep privacy of a hilly and woodsy solitude where news from the world hardly ever came to disturb its dreams, and was infinitely content. At its front flowed the tranquil river, its surface painted with cloud-forms and the reflections of drifting arks and stone-boats; behind it rose the woody steeps to the base of the lofty precipice; from the top of the precipice frowned the vast castle, its long stretch of towers and bastions mailed in vines; beyond the river, to the left, was a tumbled expanse of forest-clothed hills cloven by winding gorges where the sun never penetrated; and to the right, lay a far-reaching plain dotted with little homesteads nested among orchards and shade-trees.

The whole region for leagues around was the hereditary property of a prince with a difficult name, whose servants kept the castle always in perfect condition for occupancy, but neither he nor his family came there oftener than once in five years. When they came it was as if the lord of the world had arrived, and had brought all the glories of its kingdoms along; and when they went they left a calm behind which was like the deep sleep which follows an orgy.

Eseldorf was a paradise for us boys. We were not overmuch pestered with schooling. Mainly we were trained to be good Catholics; to revere the Virgin, the Church and the saints above everything; to hold the Monarch in awful reverence, speak of him with bated breath, uncover before his picture, regard him as the gracious provider of our daily bread and of all our earthly blessings, and ourselves as being sent into the world with the one only mission, to labor for him, bleed for him, die for him, when necessary. Beyond these matters we were not required to know much; and in fact, not allowed to. The priests said that knowledge was not good for the common people, and could make them discontented with the lot which God had appointed for them, and God would not endure discontentment with His plans. This was true, for the priests got it of the Bishop.

It was discontentment that came so near to being the ruin of Gretel Marx the dairyman's widow, who had two horses and a cart, and carried milk to the market town. A Hussite woman named Adler came to Eseldorf and went slyly about, and began to persuade some of the ignorant and foolish to come privately by night to her house and hear "God's *real* message," as she called it. She was a cunning woman, and sought out only those few who could read— flattering them by saying it showed their intelligence, and that only the intelligent could understand her doctrine. She gradually got ten together, and these she poisoned nightly with her heresies in her house. And she gave them Bibles and hymn-books, to keep for their own, and persuaded them that it was no sin to read them.

One day Father Adolf came along and found the widow sitting

in the shade of the horse-chestnut that stood by her house, reading these books. He was a very loud and zealous and strenuous priest, and was always working to get more reputation, hoping to be a Bishop some day; and he was always spying around and keeping a sharp lookout on other people's flocks as well as his own; and he was dissolute and profane and malicious, but otherwise a good enough man, it was generally thought. And he certainly had talent; he was a most fluent and chirpy speaker, and could say the cuttingest things and the wittiest, though a little coarse, maybe—however it was only his enemies who said that, and it really wasn't any truer of him than of others; but he belonged to the village council, and lorded it there, and played smart dodges that carried his projects through, and of course that nettled the others; and in their resentment they gave him nicknames privately, and called him the "Town Bull," and "Hell's Delight," and all sorts of things; which was natural, for when you are in politics you are in the wasp's nest with a short shirt-tail, as the saying is.

He was rolling along down the road, pretty full and feeling good, and braying "We'll sing the wine-cup and the lass" in his thundering bass, when he caught sight of the widow reading her book. He came to a stop before her and stood swaying there, leering down at her with his fishy eyes, and his purple fat face working and grimacing, and said—

"What is it you've got there, Frau Marx? What are you reading?"

She let him see. He bent down and took one glance, then he knocked the book out of her hand and said angrily—

"Burn them, burn them, you fool! Don't you know it's a sin to read them? Do you want to damn your soul? Where did you get them?"

She told him, and he said—

"By God I expected it. I will attend to that woman; I will make this place sultry for her. You go to her meetings, do you? What does she teach you—to worship the Virgin?"

"No—only God."

"I thought it. You are on your road to hell. The Virgin will punish you for this—you mark my words." Frau Marx was getting frightened; and was going to try to excuse herself for her conduct, but Father Adolf shut her up and went on storming at her and telling her what the Virgin would do with her, until she was ready to swoon with fear. She went on her knees and begged him to tell her what to do to appease the Virgin. He put a heavy penance on her, scolded her some more, then took up his song where he had left off, and went rolling and zigzagging away.

But Frau Marx fell again, within the week, and went back to Frau Adler's meeting one night. Just four days afterward both of her horses died! She flew to Father Adolf, full of repentance and despair, and cried and sobbed, and said she was ruined and must starve; for how could she market her milk now? What *must* she do? tell her what to do. He said—

"I told you the Virgin would punish you—didn't I tell you that? Hell's bells! did you think I was lying? You'll pay attention next time, I reckon."

Then he told her what to do. She must have a picture of the horses painted, and walk on pilgrimage to the Church of Our Lady of the Dumb Creatures, and hang it up there, and make her offerings; then go home and sell the skins of her horses and buy a lottery ticket bearing the number of the date of their death, and then wait in patience for the Virgin's answer. In a week it came, when Frau Marx was almost perishing with despair—her ticket drew fifteen hundred ducats!

That is the way the Virgin rewards a real repentance. Frau Marx did not fall again. In her gratitude she went to those other women and told them her experience and showed them how sinful and foolish they were and how dangerously they were acting; and they all burned their books and returned repentant to the bosom of the Church, and Frau Adler had to carry her poisons to some other market. It was the best lesson and the wholesomest our village ever had. It never allowed another Hussite to come there; and for reward the Virgin watched over it and took care of it personally, and made it fortunate and prosperous always.

It was in conducting funerals that Father Adolf was at his best, if he hadn't too much of a load on, but only about enough to make him properly appreciate the sacredness of his office. It was fine to see him march his procession through the village, between the kneeling ranks, keeping one eye on the candles blinking yellow in the sun to see that the acolytes walked stiff and held them straight, and the other watching out for any dull oaf that might forget himself and stand staring and covered when the Host was carried past. He would snatch that oaf's broad hat from his head, hit him a staggering whack in the face with it and growl out in a low snarl—

"Where's your manners, you beast?—and the Lord God passing by!"

Whenever there was a suicide he was active. He was on hand to see that the government did its duty and turned the family out into the road, and confiscated its small belongings and didn't smouch any of the Church's share; and he was on hand again at midnight when the corpse was buried at the cross-roads—not to do any religious office, for of course that was not allowable—but to see, for himself, that the stake was driven through the body in a right and permanent and workmanlike way.

It was grand to see him make procession through the village in plague-time, with our saint's relics in their jeweled casket, and trade prayers and candles to the Virgin for her help in abolishing the pest.

And he was always on hand at the bridge-head on the 9th of December, at the Assuaging of the Devil. Ours was a beautiful and massive stone bridge of five arches, and was seven hundred years old. It was built by the Devil in a single night. The prior of the monastery hired him to do it, and had trouble to persuade him, for the Devil said he had built bridges for priests all over Europe, and had always got cheated out of his wages; and this was the last time he would trust a Christian if he got cheated now. Always before, when he built a bridge, he was to have for his pay the first passenger that crossed it—everybody knowing he meant a Christian, of course. But no matter, he didn't *say* it, so they always sent a jackass or a chicken or some other undamnable passenger across first, and so got the best of him. This time he *said* Christian, and wrote it in the bond himself, so there couldn't be any misunderstanding. And that isn't tradition, it is history, for I have seen that bond myself, many a time; it is always brought out on Assuaging Day, and goes to the bridge-head with the procession; and anybody who pays ten groschen can see it and get remission of thirty-three sins besides, times being easier for every one then than they are now, and sins much cheaper; so much cheaper that all except the very poorest could afford them. Those were good days, but they are gone and will not come any more, so every one says.

Yes, he put it in the bond, and the prior said he didn't want the bridge built yet, but would soon appoint a day—perhaps in about a week. There was an old monk wavering along between life and death, and the prior told the watchers to keep a sharp eye out and let him know as soon as they saw that the monk was actually dying. Towards midnight the 9th of December the watchers brought him word, and he summoned the Devil and the bridge was begun. All the rest of the night the prior and the Brotherhood sat up and prayed that the dying one might be given strength to rise up and walk across the bridge at dawn—strength enough, but not too much. The prayer was heard, and it made great excitement in heaven; insomuch that all the heavenly host got up before dawn and came down to see; and there they were, clouds and clouds of angels filling all the air above the bridge; and the dying monk tottered across, and just had strength to get over; then he fell dead just as the Devil was reaching for him, and as his soul escaped the angels swooped down and caught it and flew up to heaven with it, laughing and jeering, and Satan found he hadn't anything but a useless carcase.

He was very angry, and charged the prior with cheating him, and said *"this"* isn't a Christian," but the prior said "Yes it is, it's a *dead* one." Then the prior and all the monks went through with a great lot of mock ceremonies, pretending it was to assuage the Devil and reconcile him, but really it was only to make fun of him and stir up his bile more than ever. So at last he gave them all a solid good cursing, they laughing at him all the time. Then he raised a black storm of thunder and lightning and wind and flew away in it; and as he went the spike on the end of his tail caught on a capstone and tore it away; and there it always lay, throughout the centuries, as proof of what he had done. I have seen it myself, a thousand times. Such things speak louder than written records; for written records can lie, unless they are set down by a priest. The mock Assuaging is repeated every 9th of December, to this day, in memory of that holy thought of the prior's which rescued an imperiled Christian soul from the odious Enemy of mankind.

There have been better priests, in some ways, than Father Adolf, for he had his failings, but there was never one in our commune who was held in more solemn and awful respect. This was because he had absolutely no fear of the Devil. He was the only person I have ever known of whom that could be truly said. People stood in deep dread of him, on that account; for they thought there must be something supernatural about him, else he could not be so bold and so confident. All men speak in bitter disapproval of the Devil, but they do it reverently, not flippantly; but Father Adolf's way was very different; he called him by every vile and putrid name he could lay his tongue to, and it made every one shudder that heard him; and often he would even speak of him scornfully and scoffingly; then the people crossed themselves and went quickly out of his presence, fearing that something fearful might happen; and this was natural, for after all is said and done Satan is a sacred character, being mentioned in the Bible, and it cannot be proper to utter lightly the sacred names, lest heaven itself should resent it.

Father Adolf had actually met Satan face to face, more than once, and defied him. This was known to be so. Father Adolf said it himself. He never made any secret of it, but spoke it right out. And that he was speaking true, there was proof, in at least one instance; for on that occasion he quarreled with the Enemy, and intrepidly threw his inkstand at him, and there, upon the wall of his study was the black splotch where it struck and broke. The same was claimed for Luther, but no one believed it, for he was a heretic and liar. This was so, for the Pope himself said that Luther had lied about it.

The priest that we all loved best and were sorriest for, was Father

Peter. But the Bishop suspended him for talking around in conversation that God was all goodness and would find a way to save *all* his poor human children. It was a horrible thing to say, but there was never any absolute proof that Father Peter said it; and it was out of character for him to say it, too, for he was always good and gentle and truthful, and a good Catholic, and always teaching in the pulpit just what the Church required, and nothing else. But there it was, you see: he wasn't charged with saying it in the pulpit, where all the congregation could hear and testify, but only outside, in talk; and it is easy for enemies to manufacture *that*. Father Peter denied it; but no matter, Father Adolf wanted his place, and he told the Bishop, and swore to it, that he overheard Father Peter say it; heard Father Peter say it to his niece, when Father Adolf was behind the door listening—for he was suspicious of Father Peter's soundness, he said, and the interests of religion required that he be watched.

The niece, Marget, denied it, and implored the Bishop to believe her and spare her old uncle from poverty and disgrace; but Father Adolf had been poisoning the Bishop against the old man a long time privately, and he wouldn't listen; for he had a deep admiration of Father Adolf's bravery toward the Devil, and an awe of him on account of his having met the Devil face to face; and so he was a slave to Father Adolf's influence. He suspended Father Peter, indefinitely, though he wouldn't go so far as to excommunicate him on the evidence of only one witness; and now Father Peter had been out a couple of years, and Father Adolf had his flock.

Those had been hard years for the old priest and Marget. They had been favorites, but of course that changed when they came under the shadow of the Bishop's frown. Many of their friends fell away entirely, and the rest became cool and distant. Marget was a lovely girl of eighteen, when the trouble came, and she had the best head in the village, and the most in it. She taught the spinet, and earned all her clothes and pocket money by her own industry. But her scholars fell off one by one, now; she was forgotten when there were dances and parties among the youth of the village; the young fellows stopped coming to the house, all except Wilhelm Meidling

—and he could have been spared; she and her uncle were sad and forlorn in their neglect and disgrace, and the sunshine was gone out of their lives. Matters went worse and worse, all through the two years. Clothes were wearing out, bread was harder and harder to get. And now at last, the very end was come. Solomon Isaacs had lent all the money he was willing to put on the house, and gave notice that to-morrow he should foreclose.

Chapter 2

THREE OF us boys were always together, and had been so from the cradle, being fond of each other from the beginning, and this affection deepening as the years went on—Nikolaus Baumann, son of the principal judge of the local court; Seppi Wohlmeyer, son of the keeper of the principal inn, the "Golden Stag," which had a nice garden, with shade trees, reaching down to the river-side, and pleasure-boats for hire; and I was the third—Theodor Fischer, son of the church organist, who was also leader of the village band, teacher of the violin, composer, tax collector of the commune, sexton, and in other ways a useful citizen and respected by all. We knew the hills and the woods as well as the birds knew them; for we were always roaming them when we had leisure—at least when we were not swimming or boating or fishing, or playing on the ice or sliding down hill.

And we had the run of the castle park, and very few had that. It was because we were pets of the oldest serving-man in the castle—Felix Brandt; and often we went there, nights, to hear him talk about old times and strange things, and smoke with him (he taught us that), and drink coffee; for he had served in the wars, and was at the siege of Vienna; and there, when the Turks were defeated and driven away, among the captured things were bags of coffee, and the Turkish prisoners explained the character of it and how to make a pleasant drink out of it, and now he always kept coffee by him, to drink himself, and also to astonish the ignorant with. When it stormed he kept us all night; and while it thundered and lightened outside he told about ghosts and horrors of every kind, and of battles and murders and mutilations, and such things, and made it pleasant and cosy inside; and he told these things from his own experience largely. He had seen many ghosts in his time, and witches and enchanters, and once he was lost in a fierce storm at midnight in the mountains, and by the glare of the lightning had seen the Wild Huntsman rage by on the blast with his spectre dogs chasing after him through the driving cloud-rack. Also he had seen an incubus once, and several times he had seen the great bat that sucks the blood from the necks of people while they are asleep, fanning them softly with its wings and so keeping them drowsy till they die. He encouraged us not to fear supernatural things, such as ghosts, and said they did no harm, but only wandered about because they were lonely and distressed and wanted kindly notice and compassion; and in time we learned to not be afraid, and even went down with him in the night to the haunted chamber in the dungeons of the castle. The ghost appeared only once, and it went by very dim to the sight and floating noiseless through the air, and then disappeared; and we scarcely trembled, he had taught us so well. He said it came up sometimes in the night and woke him up by passing its clammy hand over his face, but it did him no hurt, it only wanted sympathy and notice. But the strangest thing was, that he had seen angels; actual angels out of heaven, and had talked with them. They had no wings, and wore clothes, and talked and looked and acted just like any natural person, and you would never know them for angels, except for the wonderful things they did which a mortal could not do, and the way they suddenly disappeared while you were talking with them, which was also a thing which no mortal could do. And he said they were pleasant and cheerful, not gloomy and melancholy, like ghosts.

It was after that kind of a talk, one May night, that we got up next morning and had a good breakfast with him and then went down and crossed the bridge and went away up into the hills on the left to a woody hill-top which was a favorite place of ours, and there we stretched out on the grass in the shade to rest and smoke and talk over those strange things, for they were in our minds yet, and impressing us. But we couldn't smoke, because we had been heedless and left our flint and steel behind.

Soon there came a youth strolling towards us through the trees, and he sat down and began to talk in a friendly way, just as if he knew us. But we did not answer him, for he was a stranger and we were not used to strangers and were shy of them. He had new and good clothes on, and was handsome and had a winning face and a pleasant voice, and was easy and graceful and unembarrassed, not slouchy and awkward and diffident like other boys. We wanted to be friendly with him, but didn't know how to begin. Then I thought of the pipe, and wondered if it would be taken as kindly meant if I offered it to him. But I remembered that we had no fire; so I was sorry and disappointed. But he looked up bright and pleased, and said—

"Fire? Oh, that is easy—I will furnish it."

I was so astonished I couldn't speak; for I had not said anything. He took the pipe and blew his breath on it, and the tobacco glowed red and spirals of blue smoke rose up. We jumped up and were going to run, for that was natural; and we did run a few steps, although he was yearningly pleading for us to stay, and giving us his word that he would not do us any harm, but only wanted to be friends with us and have company. So we stopped and stood, and wanted to go back, being full of curiosity and wonder, but afraid to venture. He went on coaxing, in his soft persuasive way; and when we saw that the pipe did not blow up and nothing happened, our confidence returned by little and little, and presently our curiosity got to be stronger than our fear, and we ventured back—but slowly, and ready to fly, at any alarm.

He was bent on putting us at ease, and he had the right art; one could not remain timorous and doubtful where a person was so earnest and simple and gentle and talked so alluringly as he did; no, he won us over, and it was not long before we were content and comfortable and chatty, and glad we had found this new friend. When the feeling of constraint was all gone, we asked him how he

had learned to do that strange thing, and he said he hadn't learned
it at all, it came natural to him—like other things—other curious
things.

"What ones?"

"Oh, a number; I don't know how many."

"Will you let us see you do them?"

"Do—please!" the others said.

"You won't run away again?"

"No—indeed we won't. Please do, won't you?"

"Yes, with pleasure; but you mustn't forget your promise, you
know."

We said we wouldn't, and he went to a puddle and came back
with water in a cup which he had made out of a leaf, and blew
upon it and threw it out, and it was a lump of ice, the shape of the
cup. We were astonished and charmed, but not afraid any more; we
were very glad to be there, and asked him to go on and do some
more things. And he did. He said he would give us any kind of
fruit we liked, whether it was in season or not. We all spoke at
once—

"Orange!"

"Apple!"

"Grapes!"

"They are in your pockets," he said, and it was true. And they
were of the best, too, and we ate them and wished we had more,
though none of us said so.

"You will find them where those came from," he said, "and
everything else your appetites call for; and you need not name the
thing you wish; as long as I am with you, you have only to wish and
find."

And he said true. There was never anything so wonderful and so
interesting. Bread, cakes, sweets, nuts—whatever one wanted, it
was there. He ate nothing himself, but sat and chatted, and did one
curious thing after another to amuse us. He made a toy squirrel out
of clay, and it ran up a tree and sat on a limb overhead and barked
down at us. Then he made a dog that was not much larger than a
mouse, and it treed the squirrel and danced about the tree, excited

and barking, and was as alive as any dog could be. It frightened the squirrel from tree to tree and followed it up until both were out of sight in the forest. He made birds out of clay and set them free and they flew away singing.

At last I made bold to ask him to tell us who he was.

"An angel," he said, quite simply, and set another clay bird free and clapped his hands and made it fly away.

A kind of awe fell upon us when we heard him say that, and we were afraid again; but he said we need not be troubled, there was no occasion for us to be afraid of an angel, and he liked us anyway. He went on chatting as simply and unaffectedly as ever; and while he talked he made a crowd of little men and women the size of your finger, and they went diligently to work and cleared and leveled off a space a couple of yards square in the grass and began to build a cunning little castle in it, the women mixing the mortar and carrying it up the scaffoldings in pails on their heads, just as our work-women have always done, and the men laying the courses of masonry—five hundred of those toy people swarming briskly about and working diligently and wiping the sweat off their faces as natural as life. In the absorbing interest of watching those five hundred little people make the castle grow step by step and course by course and take shape and symmetry, that feeling of awe soon passed away, and we were quite comfortable and at home again. We asked if we might make some people, and he said yes, and told Seppi to make some cannon for the walls, and told Nikolaus to make some halberdiers with breastplates and greaves and helmets, and I was to make some cavalry, with horses; and in allotting these tasks he called us by our names, but did not say how he knew them. Then Seppi asked him what his own name was, and he said tranquilly—

"*Satan*," and held out a chip and caught a little woman on it who was falling from the scaffolding and put her back where she belonged, and said "she is an idiot to step backward like that and not notice what she is about."

It caught us suddenly, that name did, and our work dropped out of our hands and broke to pieces—a cannon, a halberdier and a horse. Satan laughed, and asked what was the matter. It was a natural laugh, and pleasant and sociable, not boisterous, and had a reassuring influence upon us; so I said there was nothing much the matter, only it seemed a strange name for an angel. He asked why.

"Because it's—it's—well, it's *his* name, you know."

"Yes—he is my uncle."

He said it placidly, but it took our breath, for a moment, and made our hearts beat hard. He did not seem to notice that, but partly mended our halberdiers and things with a touch, handed them to us to finish, and said—

"Don't you remember?—he was an angel himself once."

"Yes—it's true," said Seppi, "I didn't think of that."

"Before the Fall he was blameless."

"Yes," said Nikolaus, "he was without sin."

"It is a good family—ours," said Satan; "there is not a better. He is the only member of it that has ever sinned."

I should not be able to make any one understand how exciting it all was. You know that kind of quiver that trembles around through you when you are seeing something that is so strange and enchanting and wonderful that it is just a fearful joy to be alive and look at it; and you know how you gaze, and your lips turn dry and your breath comes short, but you wouldn't be anywhere but there, not for the world. I was bursting to ask one question—I had it on my tongue's end and could hardly hold it back—but I was ashamed to ask it, it might be a rudeness. Satan set an ox down that he had been making, and smiled up at me and said—

"It wouldn't be a rudeness; and I should forgive it if it was. Have I *seen* him? Millions of times. From the time that I was a little child a thousand years old I was his second-best favorite among the nursery-angels of our blood and lineage—to use a human phrase—yes, from that time till the Fall; eight thousand years, measured as you count time."

"Eight—*thousand?*"

"Yes." He turned to Seppi, and went on as if answering something that was in Seppi's mind, "Why, naturally I look like a boy, for that is what I am. With us, what you call time is a spacious

thing; it takes a long stretch of it to grow an angel to full age."
There was a question in my mind, and he turned to me and
answered it: "I am sixteen thousand years old—counting as you
count." Then he turned to Nikolaus and said, "No, the Fall did not
affect me nor the rest of the relationship. It was only he that I was
named for who ate of the fruit of the tree and then beguiled the
man and the woman with it. We others are still ignorant of sin; we
are not able to commit it; we are without blemish, and shall abide
in that estate always. We—" Two of the little workmen were
quarreling, and in buzzing little bumble-bee voices they were cursing and swearing at each other; now came blows and blood, then
they locked themselves together in a life-and-death struggle. Satan
reached out his hand and crushed the life out of them with his
fingers, threw them away, wiped the red from his fingers on his
handkerchief and went on talking where he had left off: "We
cannot do wrong; neither have we any disposition to do it, for we do
not know what it is."

It seemed a strange speech, in the circumstances, but we barely
noticed that, we were so shocked and grieved at the wanton murder
he had committed—for murder it was, it was its true name, and it
was without palliation or excuse, for the men had not wronged him
in any way. It made us miserable; for we loved him, and had
thought him so noble and beautiful and gracious, and had honestly
believed he was an angel; and to have him do this cruel thing—ah,
it lowered him so, and we had had such pride in him. He went
right on talking, just as if nothing had happened: telling about his
travels, and the interesting things he had seen in the big worlds of
our solar system and of other solar systems far away in the remote-
nesses of space, and about the customs of the immortals that inhabit
them, somehow fascinating us, enchanting us, charming us in spite
of the pitiful scene that was now under our eyes: for the wives of
the little dead men had found the crushed and shapeless bodies and
were crying over them and sobbing and lamenting, and a priest was
kneeling there with his hands crossed upon his breast praying, and
crowds and crowds of pitying friends were massed about them,
reverently uncovered, with their bare heads bowed, and many with

the tears running down—a scene which Satan paid no attention to until the small noise of the weeping and praying began to annoy him, then he reached out and took the heavy board seat out of our swing and brought it down and mashed all those people into the earth just as if they had been flies, and went on talking just the same.

An angel, and kill a priest! an angel who did not know how to do wrong, and yet destroys in cold blood a hundred helpless poor men and women who had never done him any harm! It made us sick to see that awful deed, and to think that none of those poor creatures was prepared except the priest, for none of them had ever heard a mass or seen a church. And we were witnesses; we could not get away from that thought; we had seen these murders done and it was our duty to tell, and let the law take its course.

But he went talking right along, and worked his enchantments upon us again with that fatal music of his voice. He *made* us forget everything; we could only listen to him, and love him and be his slaves, to do with as he would. He made us drunk with the joy of being with him, and of looking into the heaven of his eyes, and of feeling the ecstasy that thrilled along our veins from the touch of his hand.

He had seen everything, he had been everywhere, he knew everything, and he forgot nothing. What another must study, he learned at a glance; there were no difficulties for him. And he made things live before you when he told about them. He saw the world made; he saw Adam created; he saw Samson surge against the pillars and bring the temple down in ruins about him; he saw Caesar's death; he told of the daily life in heaven, he had seen the damned writhing in the red waves of hell; and he made us see all these things, and it was as if we were on the spot and looking at them with our own eyes. And we *felt* them, too, but there was no sign that they were anything to him, beyond being mere entertainments. Those visions of hell, those poor babes and women and girls and lads and men shrieking and supplicating in anguish—why, we could hardly bear it, but he was as bland about it as if it had been so many imitation rats in an artificial fire.

And always when he was talking about men and women here in

the earth and their doings—even their grandest and sublimest—we were secretly ashamed, for his manner showed that to him they and their doings were of paltry poor consequence; often you would think he was talking about flies, if you didn't know. Once he even said, in so many words, that our people down here were quite interesting to him, notwithstanding they were so dull and ignorant and trivial and conceited, and so diseased and rickety, and such a shabby poor worthless lot all around. He said it in a quite matter-of-course way and without any bitterness, just as a person might talk about bricks or manure or any other thing that was of no consequence and hadn't feelings. I could see he meant no offence, but in my thoughts I set it down as not very good manners.

"Manners!" he said, "why it is merely the truth, and truth is good manners; manners are a fiction. The castle is done! Do you like it?"

Any one would have been obliged to like it. It was lovely to look at, it was so shapely and fine, and so cunningly perfect in all its particulars, even to the little flags waving from the turrets. Satan said we must put the artillery in place, now, and station the halberd-iers and deploy the cavalry. Our men and horses were a spectacle to see, they were so little like what they were intended for; for of course we had no art in making such things. Satan said they were the worst he had seen; and when he touched them and made them alive, it was just ridiculous the way they acted, on account of their legs not being of uniform lengths. They reeled and sprawled around as if they were drunk, and endangered everybody's lives around them, and finally fell over and lay helpless and kicking. It made us all laugh, though it was a shameful thing to see. The guns were charged with dirt, to fire a salute; but they were so crooked and so badly made that they all burst when they went off, and killed some of the gunners and crippled the others. Satan said we would have a storm, now, and an earthquake, if we liked, but we must stand off a piece, out of danger. We wanted to call the people away, too, but he said never mind them, they were of no consequence and we could make more, some time or other if we needed them.

A small storm-cloud began to settle down black over the castle, and the miniature lightning and thunder began to play and the ground to quiver and the wind to pipe and wheeze and the rain to fall, and all the people flocked into the castle for shelter. The cloud settled down blacker and blacker and one could see the castle only dimly through it; the lightnings blazed out flash upon flash and they pierced the castle and set it on fire and the flames shone out red and fierce through the cloud, and the people came flying out, shrieking, but Satan brushed them back, paying no attention to our begging and crying and imploring; and in the midst of the howling of the wind and volleying of the thunder the magazine blew up, the earthquake rent the ground wide and the castle's wreck and ruin tumbled into the chasm, which swallowed it from sight and closed upon it, with all that innocent life, not one of the five hundred poor creatures escaping.

Our hearts were broken, we could not keep from crying.

"Don't cry," Satan said, "they were of no value."

"But they are gone to hell!"

"Oh, it is no matter, we can make more."

It was of no use to try to move him; evidently he was wholly without feeling, and could not understand. He was full of bubbling spirits, and as gay as if this were a wedding instead of a fiendish massacre. And he was bent on making us feel as he did, and of course his magic accomplished his desire. It was no trouble to him, he did whatever he pleased with us. In a little while we were dancing on that grave, and he was playing to us on a strange sweet instrument which he took out of his pocket; and the music—there is no music like that, unless perhaps in heaven, and that was where he brought it from, he said. It made one mad, for pleasure; and we could not take our eyes from him, and the looks that went out of our eyes came from our hearts, and their dumb speech was worship. He brought the dance from heaven, too, and the bliss of paradise was in it.

Presently he said he must go away on an errand. But we could not bear the thought of it, and clung to him, and pleaded with him to stay; and that pleased him, and he said so; and said he would not go yet, but would wait a little while and we would sit down and talk a few minutes longer; and he told us Satan was only his *real* name and he was to be known by it to us alone, but he had chosen another one to be called by in presence of others; just a common one, such as people have—Philip Traum.

It sounded so odd and mean for such a being! But it was his decision, and we said nothing; his decision was sufficient.

We had seen wonders this day; and my thoughts began to run on the pleasure it would be to tell of them when I got home; but he noticed those thoughts, and said—

"No, all these matters are a secret between us four. I do not mind your *trying* to tell them, if you like, but I will protect your tongues, and nothing of the secret will escape from them."

It was a disappointment, but it couldn't be helped, and it cost us a sigh or two. We talked pleasantly along, and he was always reading our thoughts and responding to them, and it seemed to me that this was the most wonderful of all the things he did; but he interrupted my musings, and said—

"No, it would be wonderful for you, but it is not wonderful for me. I am not limited, like you. I am not subject to human conditions; I can measure and understand your human weaknesses, for I have studied them; but I have none of them. My flesh is not real, although it is firm to the touch, my clothes are not real, I am a spirit. Father Peter is coming." We looked around, but did not see any one. "He is not in sight yet, but you will see him presently."

"Do you know him, Satan?"

"No."

"Won't you talk with him when he comes? He is not ignorant and dull, like us, and he would so like to talk with you. Will you?"

"Another time, yes, but not now. I must go on my errand after a little. There he is; now you can see him. Sit still, and don't say anything."

We looked up and saw Father Peter approaching through the chestnuts. We three were sitting together in the grass, and Satan sat in front of us in the path. Father Peter came slowly along with his head down, thinking, and stopped within a couple of yards of us and took off his hat and got out his silk handkerchief and stood there mopping his face and looking as if he was going to speak to us, but he didn't. Presently he muttered, "I can't think what brought me here; it seems as if I was in my study a minute ago—but I suppose I have been dreaming along for an hour and have come all this stretch without noticing; for I am not myself in these troubled days." Then he went mumbling along to himself and walked *straight through* Satan, just as if nothing was there. It made us catch our breath to see it. We had the impulse to cry out, the way you nearly always do when a startling thing happens, but something mysteriously restrained us and we remained quiet, only breathing fast. Then the trees hid Father Peter after a little, and Satan said—

"It is as I told you—I am only a spirit."

"Yes, one perceives it now," said Nikolaus, "but *we* are not spirits. It is plain he did not see you, but were we invisible too? He looked at us, but he didn't seem to see us."

"No, none of us was visible to him, for I wished it so."

It seemed almost too good to be true, that we were actually seeing these romantic and wonderful things, and that it was not a dream. And there he sat, looking just like anybody—so natural, and simple, and charming, and chatting along again the same as ever, and—well, words cannot make you understand what we felt. It was an ecstasy; and an ecstasy is a thing that will not go into words; it feels like music, and one cannot tell about music so that another person can get the feeling of it. He was back in the old ages once more, now, and making them live before us. He had seen so much, so much! It was just a wonder to look at him and try to think how it must seem to have such experiences behind one.

But it made you seem sorrowfully trivial, and the creature of a day, and such a short and paltry day, too. And he didn't say anything to raise up your drooping pride any—no, not a word. He always spoke of men in the same old indifferent way—just as one speaks of bricks and manure-piles and such things; you could see that they were of no consequence to him, one way or the other. He didn't mean to hurt us, you could see that; just as we don't mean to insult a brick when we disparage it; a brick's emotions are nothing to us; it never occurs to us to think whether it has any or not.

Once when he was bunching the most illustrious kings and conquerors and poets and prophets and pirates and beggars together —just a brick-pile—I was shamed into putting in a word for man, and asked him why he made so much difference between men and himself. He had to struggle with that a moment; he didn't seem to understand how I could ask such a strange question. Then he said—

"The *difference* between man and *me?* The *difference* between a mortal and an immortal? between a clod and a spirit?" He picked up a wood-louse that was creeping along a piece of bark: "What is the difference between Homer and this? between Caesar and this?"

I said—

"One cannot compare things which by their nature and by the interval between them are not comparable."

"You have answered your own question," he said. "I will expand it. Man is made of dirt—I *saw* him made. I am not made of dirt. Man is a museum of disgusting diseases, a home of impurities; he comes to-day and is gone to-morrow, he begins as dirt and departs as a stench; I am of the aristocracy of the Imperishables. And man has the *Moral Sense*. You understand? he has the *Moral Sense*. That would seem to be difference enough between us, all by itself."

He stopped there, as if that settled the matter. I was sorry, for at that time I had put a dim idea of what the moral sense was. I merely knew that we were proud of having it, and when he talked like that about it it wounded me and I felt as a girl feels who thinks her dearest finery is being admired, and then overhears strangers making fun of it. For a while we were all silent, and I, for one, was depressed. Then Satan began to chat again, and soon he was sparkling along in such a cheerful and vivacious vein that my spirits rose once more. He told some very cunning things that put us in a gale of laughter; and when he was telling about the time that Samson tied the torches to the foxes' tails and set them loose in the Philistines' corn and was sitting on the fence slapping his thighs and laughing, with the tears running down his cheeks, and lost his

balance and fell off the fence, the memory of that picture got *him*
to laughing, too, and we did have a most lovely and jolly time. By
and by he said—

"I am going on my errand, now."

"Don't!" we all said, "don't go; stay with us. You won't come
back."

"Yes, I will, I give you my word."

"When? To-night? To-morrow? Say when?"

"It won't be long. You will see."

"We like you."

"And I you. And as a proof of it I will show you something fine
to see. Usually when I go, I merely vanish; but now I will dissolve
myself and let you see me do it."

He stood up, and it was quickly finished. He thinned away and
thinned away until he was a soap-bubble, except that he kept his
shape. You could see the bushes through him as clearly as you see
things through a soap-bubble, and all over him played and flashed
the delicate iridescent colors of the bubble, and along with them
was that thing shaped like a window-sash which you always see on
the globe of the bubble. You have seen a bubble strike the carpet
and lightly bound along two or three times before it bursts. He did
that. He sprang—touched the grass—bounded—floated along—
touched again—and so on, and presently exploded,—*puff!* and in
his place was vacancy.

It was a strange and beautiful thing to see. We did not say
anything, but sat wondering, and dreaming, and blinking; and
finally Seppi roused up and said, mournfully and sighing—

"I reckon none of it has happened."

Nikolaus sighed and said about the same.

I was miserable to hear them say it, for it was the same cold fear
that was in my own mind. Then we saw poor old Father Peter
wandering along back, with his head bent down, searching the
ground. When he was pretty close to us he looked up and saw us,
and said—

"How long have you been here, boys?"

"A little while, Father."

"Then it is since I came by, and maybe you can help me. Did you come up by the path?"

"Yes, Father."

"That is good. I came the same way. I have lost my wallet. There wasn't much in it, but a very little is much to me, for it was all I had. I suppose you haven't seen anything of it?"

"No, Father, but we will help you hunt."

"It is what I was going to ask of you. Why, here it is!"

We hadn't noticed it; yet there it lay, right where Satan stood when he began to melt—if he did melt, and it wasn't a delusion. Father Peter picked it up, and looked very much surprised.

"It is mine," he said, "but not the contents. This is fat; mine was flat; mine was light, this is heavy."

He opened it; it was stuffed as full as it could hold, with gold coins. He let us gaze our fill; and of course we did gaze, for we had never seen so much money at one time before. All our mouths came open to say "Satan did it!" but nothing came out. There it was, you see—we couldn't tell what Satan didn't want told; he had said so himself.

"Boys, did you do this?"

It made us laugh. And it made him laugh, too, as soon as he thought what a foolish question it was.

"Who has been here?"

Our mouths came open to answer, but stood so for a moment, because we couldn't say "nobody," for it wouldn't be so, and the right word didn't seem to come; then I thought of the right one, and said it—

"Not a human being."

"That is so," said the others, and let their mouths go shut.

"It is *not* so," said Father Peter, and looked at us very severely. "I came by here a while ago, and there was no one here, but that is nothing; some one has been here since. I don't mean to say that the person didn't pass here before you came, and I don't mean to say you saw him, but some one *did* pass, that I know. On your honor— you saw no one?"

"Not a human being."

"That is sufficient; I know you are telling me the truth."

He began to count the money on the path, we on our knees eagerly helping to stack it in little piles.

"It's eleven hundred ducats-odd!" he said, "oh, dear, if it were only mine—and I *need* it so!" and his voice broke and his lips quivered.

"It *is* yours, sir!" we all cried out at once, "every heller!"

"No—it isn't mine. Only four ducats are mine; the rest . . . . ."

He fell to dreaming, poor old soul, and caressing some of the coins in his hands, and forgot where he was, sitting there on his heels with his old gray head bare, and it was pitiful to see.

"No," he said, waking up, "it isn't mine. I can't account for it. I think some enemy . . . . . it must be a trap."

Nikolaus said—

"Father Peter, with the exception of Father Adolf you haven't a *real* enemy in the village—nor Marget, either. And not even a *half* enemy that's rich enough to chance eleven hundred ducats at one dash to do you a mean turn. I'll ask you if that's so, or not?"

He couldn't get around that argument, and it cheered him up.

"But it isn't mine, you see—it isn't mine, in any case."

He said it in a wistful way, like a person that wouldn't be sorry, but glad, if somebody would contradict him.

"It *is* yours, Father Peter, and we are witness to it—aren't we, boys?"

"Yes, we are—and we'll stand by it, too."

"Bless your hearts, you do almost persuade me, you do, indeed. If I had only a hundred and eighty ducats of it! The house is mortgaged for it, and we've no home for our heads if we don't pay to-morrow. And that four ducats is all we've got in the—"

"It's yours, every bit of it, and you've got to take it—we are bail that it's all right, aren't we Theodor? aren't we Seppi?"

We two said yes; and Nikolaus stuffed the money back into the shabby old wallet and made the owner take it. So he said he would use two hundred of it, for his house was good enough security for that, and would put the rest at interest till the rightful owner came for it; and on our side we must sign a paper showing how he got the money—a paper to show to the villagers as proof that he had not got out of his troubles dishonestly.

Chapter 3

It MADE immense talk next day, when Father Peter paid Solomon Isaacs in gold and left the rest of the money with him at interest. Also, there was a pleasant change: many people called at the house to congratulate, and a number of cool old friends became kind and friendly again; and to top all, Marget was invited to a party.

And there was no mystery; Father Peter told the whole circumstance just as it happened, and said he could not account for it, only it was the plain hand of Providence, so far as he could see. One or two shook their heads and said privately it looked more like the hand of Satan; and really that seemed a surprisingly good guess for ignorant people like that. Some came slyly buzzing around and tried to coax us boys to come out and "tell the *truth;*" and promised they wouldn't ever tell, but only wanted to know for their own satisfaction, because the whole thing was so curious. They even wanted to buy the secret, and pay money for it; and if we could have invented something that would answer—but we couldn't; we hadn't the ingenuity, so we had to let the chance go by, and it was a pity.

We carried that secret around without any trouble, but the other one, the big one, the splendid one, burnt the very vitals of us, it was so hot to get out and we so hot to *let* it out and astonish people with it. But we had to keep it in; in fact it kept *itself* in: Satan said it would, and it did. We went off every day and got to ourselves in the woods, so that we could talk about Satan, and really that was the only subject we thought of or cared anything about, and day and night we watched for him and hoped he would come, and we got more and more impatient all the time. We hadn't any interest in the other boys any more and wouldn't take part in their games and enterprises. That kind of boys seemed so tame, after Satan; and their doings so trifling and commonplace after his adventures in antiquity and the constellations, and his miracles and meltings and explosions and all that.

During the first day we were in a state of anxiety, on account of one thing, and we kept going to Father Peter's house on one pretext or another, to keep track of it. That was the gold coin; we were afraid it would crumble and turn to dirt, like fairy money. If it did . . . . but it didn't. At the end of the day no complaint had been made about it; so after that we were satisfied that it was real gold, and dropped the anxiety out of our minds.

There was a question which we wanted to ask Father Peter, and finally we went there the second evening, a little diffidently, after drawing straws, and I asked it, as casually as I could, though it did not sound as casual as I wanted, because I did not know how—

"What is the moral sense, sir?"

He looked down surprised, over his great spectacles, and said—

"Why, it is the faculty which enables us to distinguish good from evil."

It threw some light, but not a glare, and I was a little disappointed, also in some degree embarrassed. He was waiting for me to go on; so, in default of anything else to say, I asked—

"Is it valuable?"

"*Valuable!* Heavens, lad, it is the one thing that lifts man above the beasts that perish and makes him heir to immortality!"

This did not remind me of anything further to say, so I got out, with the other boys, and we went away with that kind of indefinite sense you have often had of being filled but not fatted. They wanted me to explain, but I was tired.

We passed out through the parlor, and there was Marget at the spinet teaching Marie Lueger. So one of the deserting pupils was back; and an influential one, too: the others would follow. Marget jumped up and ran and thanked us again, with the tears in her eyes —this was the third time—for saving her and her uncle from being turned into the street, and we told her *again* we hadn't done it; but that was her way, she never could be grateful enough for anything a person did for her: so we let her have her say. And as we passed through the garden, there was Wilhelm Meidling sitting there waiting, for it was getting toward the edge of the evening, and he would be asking Marget to take a walk along the river with him when she was done with the lesson. He was a young lawyer, and succeeding fairly well and working his way along, little by little. He was very fond of Marget, and she of him. He had not deserted along with the others, but had stood his ground all through, although it had injured him in people's esteem and made his business fall off more or less. His faithfulness was not lost on Marget and her uncle. He hadn't so very much talent, but he was handsome and good, and these are a kind of talents themselves and help along. He asked us how the lesson was getting along, and we told him it was about done. And maybe it was so; we didn't know anything about it, but we judged it would please him, and it did; and didn't cost us anything.

On the fourth day comes Father Adolf home from the ancient priory up the valley, where he had heard the news, I reckon. He had a private talk with us, and was very much interested, and we told him all about it. He sat there studying and studying a while to himself, then he asked—

"How many ducats did you say?"

"Eleven hundred and seven, sir."

Then he said, as if he was talking to himself—

"It is ve-ry singular. Yes . . . . . very strange. A cu-rious coincidence."

Then he began to ask questions, and went over the whole ground, from the beginning, we answering. By and by he said—

"Eleven hundred and six ducats. It is a large sum."

"*Seven,*" said Seppi, correcting him.

"Oh, seven, was it? Of course a ducat more or less isn't of consequence, but you said eleven hundred and six, before."

It would not have become us to say he was mistaken, but we knew he was. Nikolaus said—

"Since your reverence says we said it, we did; but we meant to say seven."

"Oh, it is no matter, lad, it was merely that I noticed the discrepancy. It is several days, and you cannot be expected to remember precisely. One is apt to be inexact when there is no particular circumstance to impress the count upon the memory."

"But there *was* one, Father," said Seppi, eagerly.

"What was it, my son," asked Father Adolf, indifferently.

"First, we all counted the piles of coin, each in turn, and all made it the same—eleven hundred and six. But I had slipped one out, for fun, when the count began, and now I slipped it back and said, 'I think there is a mistake—there are eleven hundred and seven; let us count again.' We did, and of course I was right. They were astonished; then I told how it came about."

Father Adolf asked us if this was so, and we said it was.

"That settles it," he said. "I know the thief, now. Lads, the money was stolen."

Then he went away, leaving us very much troubled, and wondering what he could mean. In about an hour we found out; for by that time it was all over the village that Father Peter had been arrested for stealing a great sum of money from Father Adolf. Everybody's tongue was loose and going. Many said it was not in Father Peter's character and must be a mistake; but the others shook their heads and said misery and want could drive a suffering man to almost anything. About one detail there were no differences: all agreed that Father Peter's account of how the money came into his hands was just about unbelievable, it had such an impossible look. *Our* characters began to suffer, now. We were Father Peter's only witnesses; how much did he probably pay us to back up his fantastic tale? People talked that kind of talk to us pretty freely and frankly, and were full of scoffings when we begged them to believe we had really told only the truth. Our parents were harder on us than any one else. Our fathers said we were disgracing our families, and they commanded us to purge ourselves of our lie, and there was no limit to their anger when we continued to say we had spoken true. Our mothers cried over us and begged us to give back our bribe and get back our honest names and save our families from shame, and come out and honorably confess. And at last we were so worried and harassed that we *tried* to tell the whole thing, Satan and all—but no, it wouldn't come out. We were hoping and longing, all the time, that Satan would come and help us out of our trouble, but there was no sign of him.

Within an hour after Father Adolf's talk with us Father Peter was in prison and the money sealed up and in the hands of the officers of the law. The money was in a bag, and Solomon Isaacs said he had not touched it since he had counted it; his oath was taken that it was the same money, and that the amount was eleven hundred and seven ducats. Father Peter claimed trial by the ecclesiastical court, but Father Adolf didn't want that, and said an ecclesiastical court hadn't jurisdiction over a suspended priest. The Bishop upheld him. That settled it; the case would go to trial in the civil court. The court would not sit for some time to come. Wilhelm Meidling would be Father Peter's lawyer and do the best he could, of course, but he told us privately that a weak case on his side and all the power and prejudice on the other made the outlook bad.

So Marget's new happiness died a quick death. No friends came to condole with her, and none were expected; an unsigned note withdrew her invitation to the party. There would be no scholars to take lessons. How could she support herself? She could remain in the house, for the mortgage was paid off, though the government and not poor Solomon Isaacs had the mortgage-money in its grip for the present. Old Ursula, who was cook, chambermaid, housekeeper, laundress and everything else for Father Peter, and had been Marget's nurse in earlier years, said God would provide. But she said that from habit, for she was a good Catholic and such speeches were a slang of the trade; but she meant to help in the providing, to make sure, if she could find a way.

We boys wanted to go and see Marget and show friendliness for her, but our parents were afraid of offending Father Adolf, and wouldn't let us. He was going around inflaming everybody against Father Peter and saying he was an abandoned thief and had stolen eleven hundred and seven gold ducats from him. He said he knew he was the thief from that fact, for it was exactly the sum which he had lost and which Father Peter pretended he had "found."

In the afternoon of the fourth day after the catastrophe old Ursula appeared at our house and asked for some washing to do, and begged my mother to keep this a secret, to save Marget's pride, who would stop this project if she found it out, yet Marget had not enough to eat and was growing weak. Ursula was growing weak herself, and showed it; and she ate of the food that was offered her like a starving person, but could not be persuaded to carry any home, for Marget would not eat charity food. She took some clothes down to the stream to wash them, but we saw from the window that handling the bat was too much for her strength; so she was called back and a trifle of money offered her, which she was afraid to take, lest Marget should suspect; then took it, saying she would explain that she found it in the road. To keep it from being a lie and damning her soul, she got me to go and drop it, while she watched; then she went along by there and found it, and exclaimed with surprise and joy, and picked it up and went her way. Like the rest of the village she could tell every-day lies fast enough, and without taking out any precautions against fire and brimstone on their account; but this was a new kind of lie and it had a dangerous look because she hadn't had any practice in it. After a week's practice it wouldn't have given her any trouble. It is the way we are made.

I was in trouble, for how would Marget live? Ursula could not find a coin in the road every day—perhaps not even a second one. And I was ashamed, too, for not having been near Marget, and she so in need of friends; but that was my parents' fault, not mine, and I couldn't help it.

I was walking along the path, feeling very down-hearted, when a most cheery and tingling freshening-up sensation went rippling through me, and I was too glad for any words; for I knew by that sign that Satan was by. I had noticed it before. Next moment he was alongside of me and I was telling him all my trouble and what had been happening to Marget and her uncle. While we were talking we turned a curve and saw old Ursula resting in the shade of a tree, and she had a lean stray kitten in her lap and was petting it. I asked her where she got it, and she said it came out of the woods and followed her; and she said it probably hadn't any mother or any friends and she was going to take it home and take care of it. Satan said—

"I understand you are very poor; why do you want to add another mouth to feed? Why don't you give it to some rich person?"

Ursula bridled at this, and said—

"Perhaps *you* would like to have it. You must be rich, with your fine clothes and quality airs." Then she sniffed, and said, "Give it to the rich—the idea! The rich don't care for anybody but themselves; it's only the poor that have feeling for the poor, and help them. The poor and God. God will provide for this kitten."

"What makes you think so?"

Ursula's eyes snapped with anger.

"Because I know it!" she said. "Not a sparrow falls to the ground without His seeing it."

"But it falls, just the same. What good is *seeing* it fall?"

Old Ursula's jaws worked, but she could not get any words out for the moment, she was so horrified. When she got her tongue she stormed out—

"Go about your business, you puppy, or I will take a stick to you!"

I could not speak, I was so scared. I knew that with his notions about the human race Satan would consider it a matter of no consequence to strike her dead, there being "plenty more;" but my tongue stood still, I could give her no warning. But nothing happened; Satan remained tranquil; tranquil and indifferent. I reckon he couldn't be insulted by Ursula, any more than the King could be insulted by a tumble-bug. The old woman jumped to her feet when she made her remark; and did it as briskly as a young girl. It had been many years since she had done the like of that. That was Satan's influence; he was a fresh breeze to the weak and the sick, wherever he came. His presence affected even the lean kitten, and it skipped to the ground and began to chase a leaf. This surprised Ursula, and she stood looking at the creature and nodding her head wonderingly, her anger quite forgotten.

"What's come over it?" she said. "A while ago it could hardly walk."

"You have not seen a kitten of that breed before," said Satan.

Ursula was not proposing to be friendly with the mocking stranger, and she gave him an ungentle look and retorted—

"Who asked you to come here and pester me, I'd like to know? And what do you know about what I've seen and what I haven't seen?"

"You haven't seen a kitten with the hair-spines on its tongue pointing to the front, have you?"

"No—nor you either."

"Well, examine this one and see."

Ursula was become pretty spry, but the kitten was spryer, and she could not catch it, and had to give it up. Then Satan said—

"Give it a name, and maybe it will come."

Ursula tried several names, but the kitten was not interested.

"Call it Agnes. Try that."

The creature answered to the name and came. Ursula examined its tongue.

"Upon my word it's true," she said. "I have not seen this kind of a cat before. Is it yours?"

"No."

"Then how did you know its name so pat?"

"Because all cats of that breed are named Agnes; they will not answer to any other."

Ursula was impressed.

"It is the most wonderful thing!" Then a shadow of trouble came into her face, for her superstitions were aroused, and she reluctantly put the creature down, saying, "I suppose I must let it go; I am not afraid—no, not exactly that, though the priest—well, I've heard people—indeed many people . . . . And besides, it is quite well, now, and can take care of itself." She sighed, and turned to go, murmuring, "It is such a pretty one, too, and would be such company—and the house is so sad and lonesome these troubled days . . . . . Miss Marget so mournful and just a shadow, and the old master shut up in the jail."

"It seems a pity not to keep it," said Satan.

Ursula turned quickly—just as if she was hoping some one would encourage her.

"Why?" she asked, wistfully.

"Because this breed brings luck."

"Does it? Is it true? Young man, do you know it to be true? How does it bring luck?"

"Well, it brings money, anyway."

Ursula looked disappointed.

"Money? A cat bring money—the idea! You could never sell it here; people do not buy cats here; one can't even give them away." She turned to go.

"I don't mean sell it. I mean have an income from it. This kind is called the Lucky Cat. Its owner finds four silver groschen in his pocket every morning."

I saw the indignation rising in the old woman's face. She was insulted. This boy was making fun of her. That was her thought. She thrust her hands into her pockets and straightened up to give him a piece of her mind. Her temper was all up, and hot. Her mouth came open and let out three words of a bitter sentence . . . . . . then it fell silent, and the anger in her face turned to surprise, or wonder, or fear, or something, and she slowly brought out her hands from her pockets and opened them and held them so. In one was my piece of money, in the other lay four silver groschen. She gazed a little while, perhaps to see if the groschen would vanish away, then she said, fervently—

"It's true—it's true—and I am ashamed and beg forgiveness, oh dear master and benefactor!" and she ran to Satan and kissed his hand, over and over again, according to the Austrian custom.

In her heart she probably believed it was a witch-cat and an agent of the devil; but no matter, it was all the more certain to be able to keep its contract and furnish a daily good living for the family, for in matters of finance even the piousest of our peasants would have more confidence in an arrangement with the devil than with an archangel. Ursula started homeward, with Agnes in her arms, and I said I wished I had her privilege of seeing Marget.

Then I caught my breath, for we were there! There in the parlor, and Marget standing looking at us, astonished. She was feeble and pale, but I knew that those conditions would not last in Satan's atmosphere, and it turned out so. I introduced Satan—that is, Philip Traum,—and we sat down and talked. There was no constraint. We were simple folk, in our village, and when a stranger was a pleasant person we were soon friends. Marget wondered how we got in without her hearing us. Traum said the door was open, and we walked in and waited until she should turn around and greet us. This was not true; no door was open; we entered through the walls, or the roof, or down the chimney, or somehow; but no matter, what Satan wished a person to believe, the person was sure to believe, and so Marget was quite satisfied with that explanation. And then the main part of her mind was on Traum, anyway; she couldn't keep her eyes off him, he was so beautiful. That gratified me, and made me proud. I hoped he would show off, some, but he didn't. He seemed only interested in being friendly and telling lies. He said he was an orphan. That made Marget pity him. The water came into her eyes. He said he had never known his mamma; she passed away while he was a young thing; and said his papa was in shattered health, and had no property to speak of—in fact none of any earthly value—but he had an uncle in business down in the tropics, and he was very well off and had a monopoly, and it was from this uncle that he drew his support. The very mention of a kind uncle was enough to remind Marget of her own, and her eyes filled again. She said she hoped their two uncles would meet, some day. It made me shudder. Philip said he hoped so, too, and that made me shudder again.

"Maybe they will," said Marget; "does your uncle travel much?"

"Oh, yes, he goes all about; he has business everywhere."

"Then he may come here—I hope he will. I should be so glad to see him. What is his business?"

"Souls."

"Shoe-souls?"

"Yes. He trades in them. Buys them."

She asked where he lived; but Philip generalised on that, and merely said it was a foreign country.

"Is he a foreigner himself? Was he born there?"

"Well, no. No, he was an emigrant."

"Is it a trying climate?"

"For some—yes; but he doesn't mind it."

"Acclimated, I suppose."

"Yes."

"Is it a colony?"

"Yes."

"What nationality?"

"Mixed. But mainly French."

"And so that is the language in use?"

"It is the official language."

And so they went on chatting, and poor Marget forgot her sorrows for one little while, anyway. It was probably the only really bright and cheery hour she had known lately. I saw she liked Philip, and I knew she would; anybody would. And when he told her he was studying for the ministry I could see that she liked him better than ever. And then, when he promised to get her admitted to the jail so that she could see her uncle, that was the capstone. He said he would give the guards a little present, and she must always go in the evening after dark, and say nothing, "but just show this paper and pass in, and show it again when you come out"—and he scribbled some queer marks on the paper and gave it her, and she was ever so thankful, and right away was in a fever for the sun to go down; for in that old cruel time prisoners were not allowed to see their friends, and sometimes they spent years in the jails without ever seeing a friendly face. I judged that the marks on the paper were an enchantment, and that the guards would not know what they were doing, nor have any memory of it afterward; and that was indeed the way of it. Ursula put her head in at the door, now, and said—

"Supper's ready, Miss." Then she saw us and looked frightened, and motioned me to come to her, which I did, and she asked if we had told about the cat. I said no, and she was relieved, and said please don't; for if Miss Marget knew, she would think it was an unholy cat and would send for a priest and have its gifts all purified out of it, and then there wouldn't be any more dividends. So I said we wouldn't tell, and she was satisfied. Then I was beginning to say

good-bye to Marget, but Satan interrupted and said, ever so politely
—well, I don't remember just the words, but anyway he as good as
invited himself to supper, and me, too. Of course Marget was
miserably embarrassed, for she had no reason to suppose there
would be half enough food for a sick bird. Ursula heard him, and
she came straight into the room, not a bit pleased. At first she was
astonished to see Marget looking so fresh and rosy, and said so; then
she spoke up in her native tongue, which was Bohemian and
said—as I learned afterward—

"The impudent thing! inviting himself when nobody's asked
him. It's just like him—I've never seen the beat of him for making
himself easy on a short acquaintance. Send him packing, Miss
Marget—there's not victuals enough."

Before Marget could speak, Satan had the word, and was talking
back at Ursula in her own language—which was a surprise for her,
and for her mistress, too. He asked—

"Didn't I see you down the road a while ago?"

"Yes, sir."

"Ah, that pleases me; I see you remember me."

"Why, of course, sir. Nobody that sees you once can forget you, I
reckon. And besides, you are so good, and so—so—so aggravating."

"Can you keep a secret?"

"I can try, sir. For your goodness, though; not for your aggravat-
ingness."

He stepped to her and whispered, "I told you it is a Lucky Cat.
Don't be troubled—it will provide."

That sponged the slate of Ursula's feelings clean of its anxieties,
and a deep financial joy shone in her eyes. The cat's value was
augmenting. It was getting full time for Marget to take some sort of
notice of Satan's invitation, and she did it in the best way, the
honest way that was natural to her. She said she had little to offer,
but that we were welcome if we would share it with her.

We had supper in the kitchen, and Ursula waited at table. A
small fish was in the frying-pan, crisp and brown and tempting, and
one could see that Marget was not expecting such respectable food
as this. Ursula brought it, and Marget divided it between Satan and

me, declining to take any of it herself; and was beginning to say she did not care for fish to-day, but she did not finish the remark. It was because she noticed that another fish had appeared in the pan. She looked surprised, but did not say anything. She probably meant to inquire of Ursula about this, later. There were other surprises: flesh, and game, and wines and fruits—things which had been strangers in that house lately; but Marget made no exclamations, and did what she could to look unsurprised, which was human and natural. Satan talked right along, and was entertaining, and made the time pass pleasantly and cheerfully; and although he told a good many lies it was no harm in him, for he was only an angel and did not know any better. They do not know right from wrong; I knew this, because I remembered what he had said about it. He accomplished one thing which I was glad of—he got on the good side of Ursula. He praised her to Marget, confidentially, but speaking just loud enough for Ursula to hear. He said she was a fine woman, and he hoped some day to bring her and his uncle together. Very soon Ursula was mincing and simpering around in a ridiculous girly way, and smoothing out her gown and prinking at herself like a foolish old hen, and all the time pretending she was not hearing what Satan was saying. I was ashamed, for it showed us to be what Satan considered us, a silly race and trivial. Satan said it was time his uncle was married, for he entertained a great deal, and always had company staying with him, and to have a clever woman presiding over the festivities would double the attractions of the place.

"But your uncle is a gentleman, isn't he?" asked Marget.

"Yes," said Satan, indifferently; "some even call him a Prince, out of compliment, but he is not bigoted; to him personal merit is everything, rank nothing."

Marget thought he must be a most lovable gentleman and much sought after. Satan said he was; and a great help to the clergy—but for him they would have to go out of business.

My hand was hanging down by my chair; Agnes came along and licked it; by this act a secret was revealed. I started to say "It is all a mistake; this is just a common ordinary cat; the hair-needles on her tongue point inward, not outward." But the words did not come, because they couldn't. Satan smiled upon me, and I understood. It was as if he had said, "I know your thought, but you will keep it to yourself."

When it was dark Marget took food and wine and fruit, in a basket, and hurried away to the jail, and Satan and I walked toward my home. I was thinking to myself that I should like to see what the inside of a jail was like; Satan overheard the thought, and the next moment we were in the jail. We were in the torture-chamber, Satan said. The rack was there, and the other instruments, and there was a smoky lantern or two hanging on the walls and helping to make the place look dim and dreadful. There were people there, —a priest and executioners,—but as they took no notice of us, it meant that we were invisible. A young man lay bound, and Satan said he was suspected of being an unsound Catholic, and the priest and the executioners were about to inquire into it. They asked the man to confess to the charge, and he said he could not, for it was not true. Then they drove splinter after splinter under his nails, and he shrieked with the pain. Satan was not disturbed, for it was only a human being, but I could not endure it, and had to be whisked out of there. I was faint and sick, but the fresh air revived me, and we walked toward my home. I said it was a brutal thing.

"No, it was a *human* thing. You should not insult the brutes by such a misuse of that word—they have not deserved it;" and he went on talking like that. "It is like your paltry race—always lying, always claiming virtues which it hasn't got, always denying them to the Higher Animals, which alone possess them. No brute ever does a cruel thing—that is the monopoly of the snob with the Moral Sense. When a brute inflicts pain he does it innocently; it is not wrong; for him there is no such thing as wrong. And he does not inflict pain for the pleasure of inflicting it—only man does that. Inspired by that mongrel Moral Sense of his! A Sense whose function is to distinguish between right and wrong, with liberty to choose which of them he will do. Now what advantage can he get out of that? He is always choosing, and in nine cases out of ten he prefers the wrong. There shouldn't *be* any wrong; and without the Moral Sense there *couldn't* be any. And yet he is such an unreasoning creature that he is not able to perceive that the Moral Sense degrades him to the bottom layer of animated beings and is a shameful possession. Are you feeling better? Let me show you something."

In a moment we were in a French village. We walked through a great factory of some sort, where men and women and little children were toiling in heat and dirt and a fog of dust; and they were clothed in rags, and drooped at their work, for they were worn, and half-starved, and weak and drowsy. Satan said—

"It is some more Moral Sense. The proprietors are rich, and very holy; but the wage they pay to these poor brothers and sisters of theirs is only enough to keep them from dropping dead with hunger. The work-hours are fifteen per day, winter and summer—from 5 in the morning till 8 at night—little children and all. And they walk to and from the pig-sties which they inhabit—four miles each way, through mud and slush, rain, snow, sleet and storm, daily, year in and year out. They get four hours of sleep. They kennel together, three families in a room, in unimaginable filth and stench; and disease comes, and they die off like flies. Have they committed a crime, these poor mangy things? No. Have they offended the priest? No; they are his pets—they fatten him with their farthings, or he would have to work for his living. What have they done, that they are punished so? Nothing at all, except getting themselves born into your foolish race. You have seen how they treat a misdoer there in the jail, now you see how they treat the innocent and the worthy. Is your race logical? Are these ill-smelling innocents better off than that heretic? Indeed, no, his punishment is trivial compared with theirs. They broke him on the wheel and mashed him to rags and pulp after we left, and he is dead, now, and free of your precious race; but these poor slaves here—why, they have been dying for years, and some of them will not escape from life for years to come. It is the Moral Sense which teaches the factory-proprietors the difference between right and wrong—you perceive the result. They think themselves better than dogs. Ah, you are such an illogical, unreasoning race! And paltry—oh, unspeakably!"

Then he dropped all seriousness and just overstrained himself making fun of us, and deriding our pride in our warlike deeds, our great heroes, our imperishable fames, our mighty Kings, our ancient aristocracies, our venerable history—and laughed and laughed till it was enough to make a person sick to hear him; and finally he sobered a little and said "but after all, it is not all ridiculous, there is a sort of pathos about it when one remembers how few are your days, how childish your pomps, and what shadows you are!"

Presently all things vanished suddenly from my sight, and I knew what it meant. The next moment we were walking along in our village; and down toward the river I saw the twinkling lights of the Golden Stag. Then in the dark I heard a joyful cry—

"He's come again!"

It was Seppi Wohlmeyer. He had felt his blood leap and his spirits rise in a way that could mean only one thing, and he knew Satan was near although it was too dark to see him. He came to us and we walked along together, and Seppi poured out his gladness like water. It was as if he was a lover and had found his sweetheart which had been lost. Seppi was a smart and animated boy, and had enthusiasm and expression, and was a contrast to Nikolaus and me. He was full of the last new mystery, now—the disappearance of Hans Oppert, the village loafer. People were beginning to be curious about it, he said. He did not say anxious—curious was the right word, and strong enough. No one had seen Hans for a couple of days.

"Not since he did that brutal thing, you know," he said.

"What brutal thing?" It was Satan that asked.

"Well, he is always clubbing his dog, which is a good dog, and is his only friend, and is faithful, and loves him, and does no one any harm; and two days ago he was at it again, just for nothing—just for pleasure—and the dog was howling and begging, and Theodor and I begged, too, but he threatened us, and struck the dog again with all his might and knocked one of its eyes out, so that it hung down; and he said to us, 'There, I hope you are satisfied, now— that's what you have got for him by your damned meddling'—and he laughed, the heartless brute." Seppi's voice trembled with pity and anger. I guessed what Satan would say, and he said it.

"There is that misused word again—that shabby slander. Brutes do not act like that, but only men."

"Well, it was inhuman, anyway."

"No it wasn't, Seppi, it was human—quite distinctly human. It is not pleasant to hear you libel the Higher Animals by attributing to them dispositions which they are free from, and which are found nowhere but in the human heart. None of the Higher Animals is tainted with the disease called the Moral Sense. Purify your language, Seppi; drop those lying phrases out of it."

He spoke pretty sternly—for him—and I was sorry I hadn't warned Seppi to be more particular about the words he used. I knew how he was feeling. He would not want to offend Satan; he would rather offend all his kin. There was an uncomfortable silence, but relief soon came, for that poor dog came along, now, with that eye hanging down, and went straight to Satan, and began to moan or mutter brokenly, and Satan began to answer in the same way, and it was plain that they were talking together in the dog language. We all sat down in the grass, in the moonlight, for the clouds were breaking away, now, and Satan took the dog's head in his lap and put the eye back in its place, and the dog was comfortable, and wagged his tail and licked Satan's hand, and looked thankful and said the same—I knew he was saying it, though I did not understand the words. Then the two talked together a bit, and Satan said—

"He says his master was drunk."

"Yes, he was," said we.

"And an hour later he fell over the precipice there beyond the Cliff Pasture."

"We know the place, it is three miles from here."

"And the dog has been often to the village, begging people to go there, but he was only driven away and not listened to."

We remembered it, but hadn't understood what he wanted.

"He only wanted help for the man who had misused him, and he thought only of that, and has had no food nor sought any. He has watched by his master two nights. What do you think of your race? Is heaven reserved for *it*, and this dog ruled out, as your teachers tell you? Can your race add anything to this dog's stock of morals and magnanimities?" He spoke to the creature, who jumped up, eager and happy, and apparently ready for orders, and impatient to execute them. "Get some men; go with the dog—he will show you that carrion; and take a priest along to arrange about insurance, for death is near."

With the last word he vanished, to our sorrow and disappointment. We got the men and the priest, and we saw the man die. Nobody cared but the dog, but he mourned and grieved, and licked the dead face, and could not be comforted. The man had died without the last sacraments, for he was unconscious and the priest refused them. We buried him where he was, and without a coffin, for he had no money, and no friend but the dog, and he could not be buried in holy ground, for he had died in sin. We buried him without any funeral services, for in the circumstances the priest would not perform them, of course, nor countenance the unholy burial with his presence. If we had been an hour earlier the priest would have been in time to send that poor creature to heaven, but now he was gone down into the awful fires, to burn forever. It seemed such a pity that in a world where so many people have difficulty to put in their time, one little hour could not have been spared for this poor creature who needed it so much, and to whom it would have made the difference between eternal joy and eternal pain. It gave me an appalling idea of the value of an hour, and I thought I could never waste one again without remorse and terror. Seppi was depressed and grieved, and said it must be so much better to be a dog and not run such awful risks. We took this one home with us and kept him for our own. Seppi had a very good thought as we were walking along, and it cheered us up and made us feel much better. He said the *dog* had forgiven the man that had wronged him so, and maybe God would accept that absolution in place of the priest's, though it was furnished gratis and therefore was not really official and regular.

Chapter 4

THERE WAS a very dull week, now, for Satan did not come, nothing much was going on, and we boys could not venture to go and see Marget, because the nights were moonlit and our parents might find us out if we tried. But we came across Ursula a couple of times taking a walk in the meadows beyond the river to air the cat, and we learned from her that things were going well. She had natty new clothes on and bore a prosperous look. The four groschen a day were arriving without a break but were not being spent for food and wine and such things—the cat attended to all that. Marget was enduring her forsakenness and isolation fairly well, all things considered, and was cheerful, by help of Wilhelm Meidling. She spent an hour or two every night in the jail with her uncle, and had fattened him up with the cat's contributions. But she was curious to know more about Philip Traum, and hoped I would bring him again. Ursula was curious about him herself, and asked a good many questions about his uncle. It made the boys laugh, for I had told them the nonsense Satan had been stuffing her with. She got no satisfaction out of us, our tongues being tied. Ursula gave us a small item of information: money being plenty now, she had taken on a servant to help about the house and run errands. She tried to tell it in a commonplace matter-of-course way, but she was so set up by it and so vain of it that her pride in it leaked out pretty plainly. It was beautiful to see her veiled delight in this grandeur, poor old thing, but when we heard the name of the servant we wondered if she had been altogether wise; for although we were young, and often thoughtless, we had fairly good perception in some matters. This boy was Gottfried Narr, a dull good creature with no harm in him and nothing against him, personally; still, he was under a cloud, and properly so, for it had not been six months

since a social blight had mildewed the family—his grandmother
had been burnt as a witch. When that kind of a malady is in the
blood it does not always come out with just one burning. Father
Adolf had often said so, and had warned the people to keep a
lookout on those Narrs. Just now was not a good time for Ursula
and Marget to be having dealings with a member of such a family,
for the witch-terror had risen higher during the past year than it
had ever reached in the memory of the oldest villagers. The mere
mention of a witch was almost enough to frighten us out of our
wits. This was natural enough, because of late years there were
more kinds of witches than there used to be; in old times it had
been only old women, but of late years they were of all ages—even
children of eight and nine; so it was getting so that *anybody* might
turn out to be a familiar of the devil—age and sex hadn't anything
to do with it. In our little region we had tried to extirpate the
witches, but the more of them we burned the more of the breed
rose up in their places.

Once, in a school for girls only ten miles away, the nuns found
that the back of one of the girls was all red and inflamed, and they
were greatly frightened, believing it to be the devil's marks. The
girl was scared, and begged them not to denounce her, and said it
was only fleas; and indeed that is what it looked like; but of course
it would not do to let the matter rest there. All the girls were
examined, and eleven out of the fifty were badly marked, the rest
less so. A commission was appointed, but the eleven only cried for
their mothers and would not confess. Then they were shut up, each
by herself, in the dark, and put on black bread and water, for ten
days and nights; and by that time they were haggard and wild, and
their eyes were dry and they did not cry any more, but only sat and
mumbled, and would not take the food. Then one of them confessed, and said they had often ridden through the air on broom-
sticks to the witches' sabbath, and in a bleak place high up in the
mountains had danced and drunk and caroused with several
hundred other witches and with Satan, and all had conducted
themselves in a scandalous way and had reviled the priests and blas-
phemed God. That is what she said—not in narrative form, for she

was not able to remember any of the details without having them called to her mind one after the other; but the commission did that, for they knew just what questions to ask, they being all written down by the Pope for the use of witch-commissions two centuries before. They asked "Did you do so and so?" and she always said yes, and looked weary and tired and took no interest in it. And so when the other ten heard that this one had confessed, they confessed too, and answered yes to the questions. Then they were burnt at the stake all together, which was just and right; and everybody went from all the countryside to see it. I went, too; but when I saw that one of them was a bonny sweet girl I used to play with, and looked so pitiful there chained to the stake and her mother crying over her and devouring her with kisses and clinging around her neck and saying "Oh, my God! oh, my God!" it was too dreadful and I went away.

It was bitter cold weather when Gottfried's grandmother was burnt. It was charged that she had cured bad headaches by kneading the person's head and neck with her fingers—as *she* said—but really by the devil's help, as everybody knew. They were going to examine her, but she stopped them, and confessed straight off that her power was from the devil. So they appointed to burn her next morning early, in our market square. The officer who was to prepare the fire was there first, and prepared it. She was there next,—brought by the constables, who left her and went to fetch another witch. Her family did not come with her. They might be reviled, maybe stoned, if the people were excited. I came, and gave her an apple. She was squatting at the fire, warming herself, and waiting; and her old lips and hands were blue with the cold. A stranger came next. He was a traveler, passing through; and he spoke to her gently, and seeing nobody but me there to hear, said he was sorry for her. And he asked her if what she had confessed was true, and she said no. He looked surprised, and still more sorry, then, and asked her—

"Then why did you confess?"

"I am old and very poor," she said, "and I work for my living. There was no way but to confess. If I hadn't, they might have set

me free. That would ruin me; for no one would forget that I had
been suspected of being a witch, and so I would get no more work,
and wherever I went they would set the dogs on me. In a little
while I should starve. The fire is best, it is soon over. You have been
good to me, you two, and I thank you."

She snuggled closer to the fire, and put out her hands to warm
them, the snow-flakes descending soft and still on her old gray head
and making it white and whiter. The crowd was gathering, now,
and an egg came flying, and struck her in the eye, and broke and
ran down her face. There was a laugh, at that.

I told Satan all about the eleven girls and the old woman, once,
but it did not affect him. He only said it was the human race, and
what the human race did was of no consequence. And he said he
had seen it made; and it was not made of clay, it was made of mud
—part of it was, anyway. I knew what he meant by that—the
Moral Sense. He saw the thought in my head, and it tickled him
and made him laugh. Then he called a bullock out of a pasture and
petted it and talked with it, and said—

"There—*he* wouldn't drive children mad with hunger and fright
and loneliness, and then burn them for confessing to things invented for them which had never happened. And neither would he
break the hearts of innocent poor old women and make them afraid
to trust themselves among their own race; and he would not insult
them in their death-agony. For he is not besmirched with the Moral
Sense, but is as pure from it as the angels are, and knows no wrong
and never does it."

Lovely as he was, Satan could be cruelly offensive when he
chose; and he always chose, when the human race was brought to
his attention. He always turned up his nose at it, and never had a
kind word for it. I do not see how a person can act so.

Well, as I was saying, we boys doubted if it was a good time for
Ursula to be hiring a member of the Narr family. We were right.
When the people found it out they were naturally indignant. And
moreover, since Marget and Ursula hadn't enough to eat, them-
selves, where was the money to come from to feed another mouth?
That is what they wanted to know; and in order to find out, they

stopped avoiding Gottfried and began to seek his society and have sociable conversations with him. He was pleased—not thinking any harm, and not seeing the trap—and so he talked innocently along, and was no discreeter than a cow.

"Money!" he said, "they've got plenty of it. They pay me two groschen a week, besides my keep. And they live on the fat of the land, I can tell you; the Prince himself can't beat their table."

This astonishing statement was conveyed to Father Adolf on a Sunday morning when he was returning from mass. He was deeply moved, and said—

"Hell and flinders! this must be looked into."

He said there was witchcraft at the bottom of this outrage, and told the villagers to resume relations with Marget and Ursula in a private and unostentatious way and keep both eyes open. They were to keep their own counsel, and not rouse the suspicions of the household. The villagers were at first a bit reluctant to enter such a dreadful place, but the priest said they would be under his protection while there, and no harm would come to them, particularly if they carried a trifle of holy water along and kept their beads and crosses handy. This satisfied them and made them willing to go; envy and malice made the baser sort even eager to go.

And so poor Marget began to have company again, and was as pleased as a cat. She was like 'most anybody else—just human, and happy in her prosperities and not averse from showing them off a little; and she was humanly grateful to have the warm shoulder turned to her and be smiled upon by her friends and the village again; for of all the hard things to bear, to be cut by your neighbors and left in contemptuous solitude is maybe the hardest.

The bars were down, and we could all go there now, and we did —our parents and all. Day after day. The cat began to strain herself. She provided the top of everything for those companies, and in abundance—among them many a dish and many a wine which they had not tasted before and which they had not even heard of except at second hand from the Prince's servants. And the table-ware was much above ordinary, too.

Marget was troubled at first, and pursued Ursula with questions to an uncomfortable degree; but Ursula stood her ground and stuck to it that it was Providence, and said no word about the cat. Marget knew that nothing was impossible to Providence, but she could not help having doubts that this effort was from thence, though she was afraid to say so, lest disaster come of it. Witchcraft occurred to her, but she put the thought aside, for this was before Gottfried joined the household, and she knew Ursula was pious and a bitter hater of witches. By the time Gottfried arrived Providence was established, unshakably intrenched, and getting all the gratitude. The cat made no murmur, but went on composedly working the commissariat and improving in style and prodigality by experience.

In any community, big or little, there is always a fair proportion of people who are not malicious or unkind by nature, and who never do unkind things except when they are overmastered by fear, or when their self-interest is greatly in danger, or some such matter as that. Eseldorf had its proportion of such people, and ordinarily their good and gentle influence was felt, but these were not ordinary times—on account of the witch-dread—and so we did not seem to have any gentle and compassionate hearts left, to speak of. Every person was frightened at the unaccountable state of things at Marget's house, not doubting that witchcraft was at the bottom of it, and fright frenzied their reason. Naturally there were some who pitied Marget and Ursula for the danger that was gathering about them, but naturally they did not say so—it would not have been safe. So the others had it all their own way, and there was none to advise the ignorant girl and the foolish old woman and warn them to modify their doings. We boys wanted to warn them, but we backed down when it came to the pinch, being afraid Father Adolf would find it out. We found that we were not manly enough nor brave enough to do a generous action when there was a chance that it could get us into trouble. Neither of us confessed this poor spirit to the others, but did as other people would have done—dropped the subject and talked about something else. And I know we all felt mean, eating and drinking Marget's fine things along with those companies of spies, and petting her and complimenting her with the rest, and seeing with self-reproach how foolishly happy she was, and never saying a word to put her on her guard. And indeed she was happy, and as proud as a princess, and so grateful to have friends again. And all the time those people were watching with all their eyes and reporting all they saw to Father Adolf.

But he couldn't make head nor tail of the situation. There must be an enchanter somewhere on the premises, but who was it? Marget was not seen to do any jugglery, nor was Ursula, nor yet Gottfried; and still the wines and dainties never ran short, and a guest could not call for a thing and not get it. To produce these effects was usual enough with witches and enchanters—that part of it was not new; but to do it without any incantations, or even any rumblings or earthquakes or lightnings or apparitions—*that* was new, novel, wholly irregular. There was nothing in the books like this. Enchanted things were always unreal: gold turned to dirt in an unenchanted atmosphere, food withered away and vanished. But this test failed, in the present case. The spies brought samples: Father Adolf prayed over them, exorcised them, swore at them, but it did no good; they remained sound and real, they yielded to natural decay only, and took the usual time to it.

Father Adolf was not merely puzzled, he was also exasperated; for these evidences very nearly convinced him—privately—that there was no witchcraft in the matter. It did not wholly convince him, for this could be a new kind of witchcraft. There was a way to find out, as to this: if this prodigal abundance of provender was not brought in from the outside but produced on the premises, there was witchcraft, sure.

Marget announced a party, and invited forty people; the date for it was seven days away. This was Father Adolf's opportunity. Marget's house stood by itself, and could be easily watched. All the week it was watched night and day. Marget's household went out and in as usual, but they carried nothing in their hands, and neither they nor others brought anything to the house. This was ascertained. Evidently rations for forty people were not being fetched. If they were furnished any sustenance it would have to be made on the premises. It was true that Marget went out with a basket every evening, but the spies ascertained that she always brought it back empty.

The guests arrived at noon, and filled the place. Father Adolf followed, after a little, without an invitation. His spies informed him that neither at the back nor the front had any parcels been brought in. He entered, and found the eating and drinking going on finely, and everything going on in a lively and festive way. He glanced around and perceived that many of the cooked delicacies and all of the native and foreign fruits were of a perishable character, and he also recognised that these were fresh and perfect. No apparitions, no incantations, no thunder. That settled it. This was witchcraft. And not only that, but of a new kind—a kind never dreamed of before. It was a prodigious find, an illustrious find—and he the discoverer of it! The announcement of it would resound throughout the world, penetrate to the remotest lands, paralyse all the nations with amazement—and carry his name with it, and make him renowned forever. It was a wonderful piece of luck, a splendid piece of luck; the glory of it made him dizzy.

All the house made reverence to him, Marget seated him, Ursula ordered Gottfried to bring a special table for him, then she decked it and furnished it, and asked for his orders.

"Bring me what you will," he said.

The two servants brought supplies from the pantry, together with white wine and red—a bottle of each. The priest took some water, blessed it, then sprinkled it over everything, bottles and all; then bowed his head and said grace. He poured out a beaker of red wine, drank it off, poured another, then began to eat, with a grand appetite.

I was not expecting Satan, for it was more than a week since I had seen him or heard of him, but now he came in—I knew it by the feel, though people were in the way and I could not see him. I heard him apologising for intruding; and he was going away, but Marget urged him to stay, and he thanked her and stayed. She brought him along, introducing him to the girls, and to Meidling and to some of the elders; and there was quite a rustle of whispers:

"It's the young stranger we hear so much about and can't get a sight of, he is away so much." "Dear, dear, but he is beautiful—what is his name?" "Philip Traum." "Ah, it fits him!" (You see, Traum is German for Dream.) "What does he do?" "Studying for the minis-try, they say." "His face is his fortune—he'll be a cardinal some day." "Where is his home?" "Away down somewhere in the tropics, they say—has a rich uncle down there." And so on. He made his way at once; everybody was anxious to know him and talk with him. Everybody noticed how cool and fresh it was, all of a sudden, and wondered at it, for they could see that the sun was beating down the same as before, outside, and the sky clear of clouds, but no one guessed the reason, of course.

Father Adolf had drunk his second beaker; he poured a third. He set the bottle down, and by accident overturned it. He seized it before much was spilt, and held it up to the light, saying "What a pity—it is royal wine." Then his face lighted with joy or triumph or something, and he said—

"Quick—bring a bowl."

It was brought—a four-quart one. He took up that two-pint bottle and began to pour; went on pouring, and still pouring, the red liquor gurgling and gushing into the white bowl and rising higher and higher up its sides, everybody staring and holding their breath—and presently the bowl was full to the brim.

"Look at the bottle," he said, holding it up; "it is full yet!" I glanced at Satan, and in that moment he vanished. The priest rose up, flushed and excited, crossed himself, and began to thunder in his bull voice: "This house is bewitched and accursed!" People began to cry and shriek and crowd toward the door. "I summon this detected household to . . . ." I saw Satan, a transparent film, melt into the priest's body; then the priest put up his hand, and appar-ently in his own big voice said, "Wait—remain where you are." All stopped where they stood. "Bring a funnel." Ursula brought it, trembling and scared, and he stuck it in the bottle and took up the great bowl and began to pour the wine back, the people gazing and dazed with astonishment, for they knew that the bottle was already full before he began. He emptied the whole of the bowl into the bottle, then smiled out over the room, chuckled, and said, indifferently, "It is nothing—anybody can do it!"

A frightened cry burst out everywhere, "Oh, my God, *he* is possessed!" and there was a tumultuous rush for the door which swiftly emptied the house of all who did not belong in it except us boys and Meidling. We boys knew the secret, and would have told it if we could, but we couldn't. We were very thankful to Satan for furnishing that good help at the needful time.

Marget was pale, and crying, Meidling looked kind of petrified; Ursula the same; but Gottfried was the worst—he couldn't stand, he was so weak and scared. For he was of a witch family, you know, and it would be bad for him to be suspected of witching a priest. Agnes came loafing in, looking pious and unaware, and wanted to rub up against Ursula and be petted, but Ursula was afraid of her and shrank away from her, but pretending she was not meaning any incivility, for she knew very well it wouldn't answer to have strained relations with that kind of a cat. But we boys took Agnes and petted her, for Satan would not have befriended her if he had not had a good opinion of her, and that was endorsement enough for us. He seemed to trust anything that hadn't the Moral Sense.

Outside the guests scattered in every direction and fled in a pitiable state of terror, gasping out to all they met, that Father Adolf was possessed of a devil; and such a tumult they made with their running and sobbing and shrieking and shouting that soon all the village came flocking from their houses to see what had happened, and they thronged the street and shouldered and jostled each other in their excitement and fright; and then Father Adolf appeared and they fell apart in two walls like the cloven Red Sea, and down this lane Father Adolf came striding and mumbling, and where he passed the lanes surged back in packed masses, and fell silent with awe, and their eyes stared and their breasts heaved, and several women fainted; and when he was gone by, the crowd swarmed together and followed him at a distance, talking excitedly and asking questions and finding out the facts. Finding out the facts and passing them on to others, with improvements; improvements which soon enlarged the bowl of wine to a barrel and made the one bottle hold it all and yet remain empty to the last.

When Father Adolf reached the market square he went straight to a juggler fantastically dressed, who was keeping three brass balls in the air and took them from him and faced around upon the approaching crowd and said—

"This poor clown is ignorant of his art. Come forward and see an expert perform."

So saying he tossed the balls up one after the other and set them whirling in a slender bright oval in the air, and added another, then another and another and so on—no one seeing whence he got them —adding, adding, adding, the oval lengthening and lengthening all the time, his hands moving so swiftly that they were just a web or a blur and not distinguishable as hands; and such as counted said there were now a hundred balls in the air. The spinning great oval reached up twenty feet in the air and was a shining and glinting and wonderful sight. Then he folded his arms and told the balls to go on spinning without his help—and they did it. After a couple of minutes he said, "There, that will do," and the oval broke and came crashing down and the balls scattered abroad and rolled every whither. And wherever one of them came, the people fell back in dread, and no one would touch it. It made him laugh, and he scoffed at the people and called them cowards and old women. Then he turned and saw the tight-rope, and said foolish people were daily wasting their money to see a clumsy and ignorant varlet degrade *that* beautiful art—now they should see the work of a master. With that he made a spring into the air and lit firm on his feet on the rope. Then he hopped the whole length of it back and forth on one foot, with his hands clasped over his eyes; and next he began to throw summersaults, both backward and forward, and threw twenty-seven.

The people murmured, and were deeply scandalised to see a priest do such worldly things; but he was not disturbed, and went on with his antics just the same. Finally he sprang lightly down and walked away, and passed up the road and around a corner and disappeared. Then that great pale, silent, solid crowd drew a deep breath, and looked into each others' faces as if they said, "Was it real? Did you see it, or was it only I—and was I dreaming?" Then they broke into a low murmur of talking, and fell apart in couples and moved toward their homes, still talking in that awed way with their faces close together and laying a hand on an arm and making other such gestures as people make when they have been deeply impressed by something.

We boys followed behind our fathers, and listened, catching all we could of what they said; and when they sat down in our house and continued their talk they still had us for company. They were in a sad mood, for it was certain, they said, that disaster for the village must follow this awful visitation of witches and devils.

"They have not ventured to lay their hands upon an anointed servant of God before," said my father; "and how they could have dared it this time I cannot make out; for he wore his crucifix—isn't it so?"

"Yes," said the others, "we saw it."

"It is serious, friends, it is very serious. Always before, we had a protection. It has failed."

The others shook, as with a sort of chill, and muttered those words over—

"It has failed."

"God has forsaken us."

"It is true," said Seppi Wohlmeyer's father, "there is nowhere to look for help."

"The people will realise this," said Nikolaus's father the judge, "and despair will take away their courage and their energies. We have indeed fallen upon evil times."

He sighed, and Wohlmeyer said in a troubled voice—

"The report of it will go about the country and our village will be shunned, as being under the displeasure of God. The Golden Stag will know hard times."

"True, neighbor," said my father, "all of us will suffer—all in repute, many in estate. And good God!"

"What is it!"

"*That* can come—to finish us!"

"Name it—*um Gottes Willen!*"

"The Interdict!"

It smote like a thunderclap, and they were like to swoon with the terror of it. Then the dread of this calamity roused their energies, and they stopped brooding and began to consider ways to avert it. They discussed this, that and the other way, knowing all the time that there was but one *best* way, yet all being afraid to mention it. But it had to come out at last: the witch-commission must summon the priest and put him on his trial, and *somebody* must go and call the commission's attention to its duty, for otherwise it would shirk its duty, naturally fearing to proceed against a priest, and they, like all the community, being hardly less afraid of this particular priest than of the strangely intrepid devil that was in him. Whoever pushed the commission to its work would be in trouble, for Father Adolf would know of it promptly through betrayal of the informer by the commission, and would mark that man.

They were in a trying position, now: if they moved in this matter and the priest escaped the stake, he would ruin them; if they kept silence, there was the possible interdict, a calamity of which they would get their share. They talked and talked till the afternoon was far spent, then confessed that at present they could arrive at no decision. So they parted sorrowfully, with oppressed hearts which were filled with bodings.

While they were saying their parting words I slipped out and set my course for Marget's house to see what was happening there. I met many people, but none of them greeted me. It ought to have been surprising, but it was not, for they were so distraught with fear and dread that they were not in their right minds, I think; they were white and haggard, and walked like persons in a dream, their eyes open but seeing nothing, their lips moving but uttering nothing, and worriedly clasping and unclasping their hands without knowing it.

At Marget's it was like a funeral. She and Wilhelm sat together on the sofa, but saying nothing, and not even holding hands. Both were steeped in gloom, and Marget's eyes were red from the crying she had been doing. She said—

"I have been begging him to go, and come no more, and so save himself alive. I cannot bear to be his murderer. This house is bewitched, and no inmate of it will escape the fire. But he will not go; and he will be lost with the rest."

Wilhelm said he would not go; if there was danger for her, his place was by her and there he would remain. She said dear sweet things to him for that, and he said they made him very happy, but he could not change his mind. Then she began to cry again, and it was all so mournful that I wished I had stayed away. There was a knock, now, and Satan came in, fresh and cheery and beautiful, and brought that winy atmosphere of his and changed the whole thing. He never said a word about what had been happening, nor about the awful fears which were freezing the blood in the hearts of the community, but began to talk and rattle on about all manner of gay and pleasant things; and next about music—an artful stroke which cleared away the remnant of Marget's depression and brought her spirits and her interest broad awake. She had not heard any one talk so well and so knowingly on that subject before; and she was so uplifted by it and so charmed that what she was feeling lit up her face and came out in her words, and Wilhelm noticed it and did not look as pleased as he ought to have done. And next Satan branched off into poetry, and recited some, and did it well, and Marget was charmed again; and again Wilhelm was not as pleased as he ought to have been, and this time Marget noticed it and was remorseful, and said—

"Wilhelm writes poetry, and I think it is beautiful."

Then she went on to tell about a poem he had written the day before, and she and Satan persuaded him to read it. He was greatly pleased and mollified, and not hard to persuade. It was a very stirring tale about a girl who was carried off by bandits, and was followed through a thunderous and stormy night by her lover, who rescued her and drove off the captors, killing several of them in a brave fight, but in his turn receiving wounds of which he died just as the morning sun was brightening the world with hope and happiness. It was moving and fine, and he read it well, and was entitled to praise, and got it in full measure from both Marget and Satan.

Next, Marget proposed that Wilhelm and Philip vary the entertainment with a game of chess, and she would look on. I knew what her idea was. She was proud of Wilhelm's poetical success and of the praise it had won from Philip, and she wanted to show off Wilhelm still further and raise him still higher in the stranger's esteem; for Wilhelm was champion at chess in all that region and accustomed to giving the odds of a castle to the next best man. But it was my opinion that she was making a mistake this time; she would better try to show off Wilhelm in some other way, it seemed to me.

Satan said he was ready to play, and glad. Then he added, in his frank and confident way, that he was a good player, and so, to be fair, he would play against both of them if they were willing. It amused Wilhelm, who said—

"I see you don't know my reputation; but let it be as you say."

At the associated pair's ninth move, Satan said—

"There, the game is mine: checkmate in nineteen moves. Let us play another."

He was going to re-set the pieces; but Wilhelm stopped him, and said—

"Ah, wait. We will see about that. You will probably change your opinion before many minutes. I'm not in the habit of surrendering to remote possibilities."

"But this isn't a remote possibility, it is a certainty."

"I don't see how you can know that. And I don't begin to believe it. Let us continue."

"Very well. It is your privilege—but it wastes time."

He moved. The couple made an answering move, and Satan said—

"You are worse off, now: checkmate in fourteen moves."

Wilhelm was annoyed, but he said nothing; only bit his lip. Satan moved; the couple studied a painful while; considered and discussed various moves, then made one. Satan said—

"Checkmate in eleven moves"—and moved queen's castle.

Wilhelm flushed, but held his peace. After cautious deliberation the couple decided upon a move and made it.

"Checkmate in seven moves," said Satan, advancing his queen.

Wilhelm was sorely tried, but he kept his temper. Kept it, but continued the game, and was finally checkmated, of course.

"It is a defeat," he said, "and I confess it. I believe you are stronger than I am." Then he added, "particularly in guessing."

Guessing those checkmates so far ahead was what he meant; but Satan made no comment. Wilhelm asked the odds of a knight, and they played again. Wilhelm lost. Then he took the odds of both knights and was again defeated. His temper almost got the better of him, now. He said, ironically, that perhaps Philip could even give his queen away and beat him. But Satan said—

"Yes. Let us begin."

Of course he beat him. I think he could have beaten him with a pawn. Wilhelm was so vexed, by this time, that Marget cast about for a change of subject, to save the situation. She chose music, and it was a good selection. The talk flowed pleasantly along, and things were soon in a satisfactory condition again. By and by Marget said—

"Surely, with your knowledge of music, you must be able to play. You do play, don't you?"

"Oh, certainly," said Satan, "I am a good player."

It was strange, the way he could say such things as that, and not exasperate people. It didn't seem conceited, in him, any more than it would seem conceited in a fish to say "Yes, I am a good swimmer."

"Then do play something. The spinet is old and jingly-jangly and a little out of tune, but you won't mind that, will you."

"Oh, no, I can make it musical. Let me see—what shall I play? I will play the poem—we will chase the bandits and rescue the captive girl."

"Oh, that will be lovely! But can you make it up as you go along?"

"Yes, that is easy."

I was in raptures to see him show off so. It was a great long poem, and just the thing. He sat down, and his fingers began to glide up and down the keys. It was a wonder to look at those two people sitting there, their lips parted and their breath hardly coming, the picture of astonishment. For this was no music such as they had ever heard before. It was not one instrument talking, it was a whole vague, dreamy, far-off orchestra—flutes, and violins, and silver horns, and drums, and cymbals, and all manner of other instruments, blending their soft tones in one rich stream of harmony. And it was mournful and touching; for this was the lover realising his loss. Then Satan began to chant the words of that poor fellow's lament—gentle and low; and the water rose in those two people's eyes, for they had heard no voice like that before, nor had any one heard the like of it except in heaven, where it came from. Little by little the music and the singing rose louder out of the distance—the lover was coming, he was on his way. And ever the singing and the music grew; and the storm began to gather and move toward us, with the wind sighing, the thunder muttering and the lightning playing; and on it came, just as if you could see it, and see the lover's horse racing and straining down in the pursuing front of it; and so, with a boom and a roar and a crash it burst upon us in one final grand explosion of noble sounds, and then the battle began, the victory was won, the storm passed, the morning came, and the lover lay dying in the maiden's arms, with her tears falling upon his face and the precious music of her endearments fading upon his ear.

It was finished, and we sat drowned in that ecstasy, and numb and dumb and only half conscious. When we came out of it Satan was gone. All sat thinking—going over the details of that marvelous picture painted in music, and trying to fix them in the memory for a perpetual possession. Finally Marget rose up, half dazed, and went to the spinet and stood looking at it. She struck a chord. Of course

she got only the old effeminate tinkle-tankle the thing was born
with. She turned away with a sigh.

"Ah, how did he do it?" she said.

"And how did he remember that long poem and never miss a
word?" said Wilhelm. "I think he is the Devil."

"Or an angel," said Marget. "Tell me about him, Theodor; tell
me all you know."

But I got away; saying I should be punished if I was not home to
supper.

Chapter 5

NEXT DAY everybody was talking—but under their breath.
They were talking sharply critical talk about the witch-commission.
"Why haven't the commission summoned Father Adolf for examination? if it were some friendless old woman who had done those
Satanic miracles with the bowl, the bottle and the brazen balls,
would they be so lax?" That is what the public said—in a whisper.
Always confidentially; adding, "Please don't quote *me*—don't say *I*
said anything." You see they were prompt to blame the committee
for being afraid of Father Adolf, yet at the same time they forgot to
despise their own cowardice in not holding up the committee's
hands and encouraging them to their duty. And they forgot that in
despising the committee for being so brave when friendless old
women were concerned, they were only despising themselves, for
that was their own daring attitude toward friendless old women.
Satan would have had a laugh at all this if he had been about. He
would have said "It is like the human race; they have a fine large
opinion of themselves, with nothing to found it on."

I had five days' holiday, now, on my uncle's farm in the country,
and when I got back another question was puzzling the people:
"What has become of Father Adolf?" No one knew. He had not
been seen since his performance on the tight rope.

Meantime Satan had been going about quite freely, getting

acquainted with everybody, chatting with everybody, and charming the whole village and winning its gratitude by beguiling its mind from its troubles by diverting its interest to cheerfuler matters. Among his new acquaintances were the families of us boys, and their admiring talk of him was a great satisfaction to us, but we were not able to reveal our relations with him and boast about it, which we should have been so glad to do. My mother said to my father, with a shade of suspicion in her tone—

"There is something strange about him—I can't quite make him out. He is a gentleman—his clothes and his breeding show it; and yet he seems to associate with any kind of characters that come along, Rupert."

"Yes, that comes out in his talk, Marie," said my father.

"It is plain that he makes no sort of distinction between Fuchs the rich brewer and Hansel the loafing tinker—just as soon put in his time with the one as with the other."

"Yes, and not only that, but he speaks of them as if the *value* of the two was the same—their value to the world and the village."

"Well," said my mother with a slight sniff, "maybe that is the right word, though I couldn't see that he attached anything that a body might really describe as *value* to either of them."

My father had to grant that that was the correcter way of putting it.

"But he is young," he added; "in years he is but a youth, and that is the prig-time of life. He will get over it when he is older and has found out something about life and the world. Experience will teach him a lot of things which he doesn't know now."

My mother reflected a little, then said—

"But *is* he such a boy, Rupert? He looks it, and all that, but there's times when he doesn't talk like a boy. You said, yourself, that he was curiously well up in the law for such a lad, and that he talked about legal procedure like a person who had played the game."

Mother had cornered him again. But she was not vain of it, being more or less accustomed to it, and always expecting him to be pretty random and to need watching when he wasn't on the Bench.

"He may be a good deal of a boy, and no doubt he is," continued my mother, "but I can see that he is a superior one and smart beyond his years. In my opinion he is going to make his way in this world. Particularly if he goes into a profession."

"He is studying for the ministry," said my father.

My mother glanced up with interest.

"Orthodox, I suppose?" said she.

"As I understand it—yes."

"Then he can't marry, and I hope he will not come here too much."

"Why?"

"Because if I know the signs, our Lilly was interested in him the minute she saw him."

"Is that so, Marie?"

"Love at first sight if I know the indications."

"Marie, if your eyes and your instincts have not put you in error, this may be a serious matter."

"Well, we shall see. Theodor, bring your sister."

I fetched her, and on the way I told her what the occasion was, for we were loyal comrades and always posted each other when we could and when it might be useful. Mother stated her charge, and Lilly met it frankly and without embarrassment. She said she was interested in Philip Traum.

"Is he interested in you?"

"Ah, as to that, I do not know."

"What do you think?"

"I think—well, I think he is not."

"I am very, very glad to hear it, my child, and you will be glad, too, when you learn that he can never marry."

I thought poor Lilly's cheek lost a little of its color.

"Can . . . . . never marry?" she said with a sort of gasp. "Why, mother?" and her eyes lost somewhat of their sparkle.

"Because he is studying for the ministry. He is going to be a priest."

"That is a mistake, Mütterchen!" and the color came back and the eyes brightened; "he told me so himself."

"He did, did he? Upon my word the confidences have begun to flow early! So he is not to be a priest. I do not know whether to be glad or sorry." She looked bothered, and went on talking, with the look in her eyes of one who is thinking aloud without being conscious of it: "So beautiful,—such a gentleman—doubtless rich. . . ." Then she broke out with "I do wish we could know something *about* him before this thing goes any further. Did he tell you anything about himself? . . . . . but *that* would be worth nothing; it might be all lies, of course."

"Ah, no—no, mother, you wrong him, indeed you do. He is not capable of telling a lie."

It took me so unprepared that the laugh was half out before I could stop it; but I turned it into a strangle, and no one knew it was anything but that.

"Oh, of course you would think he couldn't tell a lie, but that is no proof. What did he say about himself? Anything? Where does he live when he is at home?"

"His country seat—"

"He has a country seat . . . . . um . . . . . well, that is something, anyway. And I must say that his clothes and his style are a sort of—of—"

"Corroborative evidence," suggested my father, helping her out.

"Yes. Where is his country seat?"

"In Austria or Germany, I think, but he didn't say."

"What is the name of it?"

"Himmelreich."

"The Kingdom of Heaven! What a modest name."

"Blasphemous, you would better say," said my father, with censure in his voice.

Mother went on questioning, and getting answers, and growing gradually reconciled to the perplexing situation and fortifying herself to entertain the idea of taking Satan into the family in the quality of son-in-law if the worst should come to the worst, so to speak; and finally she said—

"Well, there's one comfort: he is but a child, yet, and so are you;

and we shall know all about him long before either of you is old enough to marry. I hope his character is good, and his morals; he seems to have a fair enough nature."

"Oh, a beautiful nature, mother."

"Of course *you* think so, but that is nothing to the point."

"He is ever so kind-hearted, mother, and admires rattlesnakes."

Mother came near fainting.

"Ad—mires rattlesnakes! Is he insane?"

"No. But he has read all about them, and admires their noble character."

"Their noble character—the most infamous beast that crawls! What rubbish is this you are talking?"

"But mother, it is not so unreasonable when he explains it. He says this, to the credit of the rattlesnake: that he never takes advantage of any one, and has none of the instincts of an assassin; that he never strikes without first giving warning, and then does not strike if the enemy will keep his distance and not attack him. Isn't that true of the rattlesnake, papa?"

"Well—yes, it is. I had not thought of it before. The truth is, it is better morals than some men have."

"I am so glad you think so, papa; it is what *he* says."

"Oh, if *he* says it, that settles it," said my mother, not well pleased to be caught in the minority. Then I could see she wanted a change of subject, and had her eye out for a pretext. She seemed to find it, and said, "There, you'd better run along and get at your embroidery; if you haven't finished it in thirty days—"

"It happens that it's already finished!" cried Lilly, without trying to conceal how vain she was about it.

"Finished? When?"

"Day before yesterday."

"The idea! Very well, you can pull it all out and do it over again. And next time, do it right."

"It is done right—I'll bring it and you can see for yourself," and she ran and brought it.

It was a little picture, wrought in threads of silk and gold and silver. My mother was astonished, and said—

"Dear me, it is finer than the original—much finer. It is easily forty days' work. How is it that it took you ten days to merely start it, and only one day to complete it? And certainly the workmanship is beyond praise for grace and beauty and perfection. Dear, dear, the exquisite delicacy of it! It's just a dream!"

"It didn't take a day, it took only twenty minutes. *He* did it."

My mother was astonished again, and asked dozens of questions, and got all the particulars, and grew more and more astonished all the time. Then she examined the work in this and that and the other light, hanging it on the wall, on a chair, spreading it on the table, her eyes speaking her wondering and worshiping delight in it, and her lips muttering all the time, "Marvelous creature, amazing creature," and Lilly stood drinking it all in, happy and proud as a person could be.

"Well," said mother at last, "it strikes a body dumb, I must say. He is a most singular creature, take him how you will. Embroiders like an angel, and admires rattlesnakes; a most unaccountable mixture in the matter of tastes. With his gifts he will get along. He doesn't need any better profession than this, and I hope he will stick to it, and make a name for himself. That is his intention, isn't it?"

"No," said my sister, "he looks higher."

"Higher? What is he going to be?"

"An author."

"Author of what?"

"When he has finished his education at Heidelberg, he is going to write the history of the Roman jurisprudence and codify the Roman laws."

"That kitten?"

"He is not a kitten, mamma, and it isn't right for you to call him such names."

"Child, then—I'm not particular. But the bare idea of it—eight weeks old, so to speak, and already planning a flight like that; it does seem to me to smack of self-conceit. But no matter, it's no affair of mine, but I know one thing: if he were my child I would see to it that he stuck to his embroidery, that I would. There's the makings of a man in him if he had the right kind of a mother. Poor thing, it is a shame that he has been allowed to grow up in this helter-skelter fashion. His mother was a Pole, probably; I never did think much of those Poles."

She had probably never had an opinion about the Poles before, but she was in the humor to hit somebody a thump and the Poles happened to turn up in her head just in time to be useful.

There was one very noticeable thing: in all this conversation the name of young Joseph Fuchs the brewer's son and heir was not mentioned once. It was another instance of the fact that wherever Satan came people dropped other interests out of their minds for the time and they could not seem to think of anything but him. It was the same now. Apparently no one had thought of Joseph Fuchs, not even my father; yet my father was a steady-going practical man, and a judge. This was strange, for Joseph was the best catch in the region, and was courting my sister, apparently with her approval, and certainly with the approval of papa and mamma. And yet all of a sudden comes this revolution, and my mother is dazzled, and turned topsy-turvy, and sets herself to contemplating Satan as a possible son-in-law, just as if there was no impropriety about it and nothing in the way; and if papa was surprised at it or dissatisfied, he gave no sign of it. It was Satan's influence; it had put the family under an enchantment. Not purposely, of course; for these people belonged to the human race and it would not have occurred to him to interest himself in their small affairs—unasked—one way or the other; either to help them or to hurt them. The villagers, high and low, were all bugs to him, and by his nature he seemed unable to take a bug seriously.

Joseph Fuchs was twenty-one and a good enough young fellow. He wouldn't ever be likely to set the river on fire, but that was nothing—there was plenty of company of this calibre, he was with the majority. He took an innocent pleasure in his clothes and in his father's riches, but that was natural enough in one whose people had been poor no long time back; and he was likely to take a seat which commanded a mirror if it came handy, but nobody minded it, since it did him good and harmed no one. These were the outside tinselings of his character, but there was gold back of them; he was honest and clean and true, and had warm affections and deep feelings.

Just as mamma had finished her slat at the Poles, Joseph came in. The effect was curious; the family looked a trifle startled; much as if he was a half-remembered disappearance come back out of the long ago. It took them half a moment or two to wake up and pull themselves together; then they set him a chair where he could face the mirror, and gave him welcome and asked after his people, and so worked off the restraint that was in the atmosphere and got things going in a more or less natural and comfortable fashion. Joseph had not noticed anything; it was not to be expected that he would. He did not even seem to notice that Lilly's welcome did not come from her eyes, according to custom, but only from her mouth; but I noticed it. I was sorry, too; for this was a man, and could meet her on her own human level, and make her brief breath of life happy, and share with her the peace and oblivion of the grave afterward; whereas in her innocence and ignorance she was fixing her heart of flesh upon a spirit, a wanderer of the skies, an object as unattainable as a comet and not more competent to meet the requirements of a this-world fellowship.

Being asked for the news, Joseph said—

"Oh, there isn't any, of course, except the new stranger. It's all Philip Traum here, Philip Traum there, Philip Traum yonder— nothing but Philip Traum; but I suppose that that is no news to you—of course it isn't. Father is infatuated with him; so is everybody—in fact I don't mind saying I include myself. Well, you know, he *is* a wonderful creature; now there's no getting around that." His voice took on a grave tone, and he added, "That youth is doing things which can get him into trouble—*can*, I say, though I hope they won't."

Lilly paled a little, and asked—

"What kind of things?"

"Well, things which the people can't understand; strange things which set them to shaking their heads and talking under their breath. This morning he jumped off the bridge and saved old Haas from drowning; did it without an effort, they say, fat and monstrous as old Haas is."

"It was a brave fine act," said Lilly; "surely there was nothing about that for people to criticise and shake their heads over."

"Well, you see, that wasn't the worst of it—I mean, that wasn't all of it. They might have overlooked the miracle of strength displayed, but they say the water didn't wet his clothes. They couldn't account for that."

"Do you believe the water didn't wet his clothes, Joseph?"

"Well, you know, they *say* it didn't. They believed it, I am quite sure of it; and the police must have believed it, too, for when they heard of it they arrested him."

"What a shame! and he had been doing such a brave thing. Papa, you will order them to set him free—you can't refuse."

"Don't you worry," said Joseph, "he's already free."

"How is that?"

"He wouldn't go with them."

"Did they try to make him?" my father asked.

"Yes, but he only made fun of them. They tried to carry him off by force, but they hadn't the strength; they couldn't budge him from where he stood. Then they were afraid; for he said that if they tried it again he would throw them in the river. Now you know that for some reason or other they *were* afraid, for if they hadn't been they would have summoned more help, that being the usual course; but this they did not do. They only crossed themselves and looked foolish. Then they asked him to come to headquarters and fill up the usual form which requires a stranger to give his address, name, age, religion, occupation, whence he is from, how long he proposes to stay, and all that; and he wouldn't do it, and laughed at them again, and walked off about his business, no one interfering. He doesn't seem to be afraid of anybody or any thing. Oh, yes, everybody is talking! Among other things, about his chess and his music—have you heard of that?"

"No."

"Well, then, it's because it only came out yesterday evening, I suppose; but it is started, now, and you'll hear plenty about it soon.

It happened four or five days ago, and yesterday evening Wilhelm Meidling lost his temper and told about it. The way of it was this."

Then Joseph told all about the four chess games and that wonderful music.

"Do you see?" he continued, "it's all as astounding as Father Adolf's bowl and bottle, and his jugglery and gymnastics in the market square. Very well. Put this and that together, and what do you arrive at? This: we all know Father Adolf is possessed of a devil; that being the case, what is the matter with Philip Traum?"

It was a hard hit and sudden. It made them all jump. But Joseph didn't see it; he went tinkling right along:

"Well, now, that's my news; what's yours? You know Philip the Magician, as I call him; have you been favored yet? has he been exhibiting here?"

It was another hit. It made them look unwell. Mother glanced at Lilly, and she slid the embroidery out of sight. Joseph was having a very successful time with his random gun, but he didn't know it.

Mother replied, a little stiffly, that Mr. Traum had not been exhibiting here. The others said nothing, and Joseph laughed pleasantly and remarked—

"A pity, too, for I suppose they'll burn him, soon, and then you'll naturally be sorry you haven't a sample to remember him by."

"*Don't* talk so!" said Lilly. "Such things are not matter for jesting."

"Well, then, I won't. But seriously, you know, people *are* talking, and he ought to be careful. That is what I tell him, and it's what father tells him; but he is so young and volatile and carefree that it hasn't any effect; he only laughs at it. Another thing: he has gone and made an enemy of the very man who could be most useful to him some day if he should get into trouble, and that man is Wilhelm Meidling, a good lawyer and a rising one."

"How has that happened?"

"I don't know; but anyway it's so. Meidling let it out yesterday evening. Meidling is drinking again—I suppose you know that?"

Mother said she had heard something of the sort.

"Well, it's true. He drops in at the Golden Stag pretty often just here lately."

"Ah, poor Marget!" said Lilly; "she has troubles enough, she might have been spared this one. She takes it hard—of course?"

"I suppose so, but one can't know—no one goes there."

That hit Lilly, right in the heart—I could see it. She got up, saying—

"I am ashamed of myself; I must go to her; you must let me, mother. It is ungrateful in the happy to forsake the unhappy, whatever others may do."

"No, no!" spoke up Joseph, alarmed; "none of that! Keep clear away from there—it is not safe!"

Poor fellow, he naturally supposed that *he* was the cause of her happiness, and in his pride and joy he put what should have been an appeal into the form of a kind of bridegroom-elect command, without thinking. Lilly straightened up, gave him a freezing look, and said—

"I beg your pardon. Who are you to dictate to me what I shall do?"

It was pitiful to see how he was crushed. He couldn't say a word, but only fumbled with his hands and looked stunned and vacant. Neither my father nor my mother seemed to know anything to do to relieve the situation; and so, when Wilhelm Meidling came walking in, now, he seemed like a kind of angel of deliverance, specially commissioned by Providence, and I think he hadn't any doubts that my parents were glad to see him. Lilly's welcome was not so pronounced, by a good deal; he had interrupted her project, and she had to put it by and sit down—which she did, but she couldn't have looked sociable and amiable if she had tried.

Five days had made a great and sorrowful change in Meidling. The old pleasant and friendly light had gone out of his eyes, his complexion was unwholesome, his skin puffy, his hands tremulous, his spirit moody and sour. He was a little under the influence of liquor, but not seriously so.

By way of a beginning, mother asked after Marget.

"I don't know how she is," answered Wilhelm drearily, and with a sigh.

"You don't?" said mother, surprised at his manner and troubled by his statement. "Why, how does that come?"

"I don't suppose it would interest you," he said, in that same dreary way, and looked around upon our faces wistfully, just as a person does who is carrying a burden upon his heart and finds it too heavy to bear, and is longing to talk about his trouble if he could find encouragement and a friendly ear. My mother saw and understood, for in her nature there was her sex's native sympathy for creatures in distress; she soon smoothed Wilhelm's path for him and made his traveling of it easy for him. Once more we heard about the chess games and the music; then this followed:

"Next day Traum was there again. More than half an hour; and did another amazing musical miracle. Marget read a tale to him out of a book—a prose one; then he sat down and played it and sang it, turning it into rhymed verse as he went along—a marvelous achievement, one is obliged to confess. In the parts where the tale was military and stirring, he filled the place with the crash of military bands; and through the music you could hear the hoof-beats of charging cavalry, the boom and thunder of artillery, the clash of steel, along with another sound that was heartbreaking—the perfectly counterfeited shrieks and cries and supplications of wounded and dying men. Such human voices! and they seemed to be in the room. Of course in the room, though really the room was a battlefield, and we saw the fight, as in a vision. When the scene of the tale changed and was soft and tender and romantic, with moonlight, and shimmering lakes, and the breath of flowers in the air, you heard only the distant strains of violins and oboes and aeolian harps. You understand, he finds all this variety of instruments in that old crazy spinet.

"When he was taking his departure Marget forgot all decorum and begged him, supplicated him, implored him to stay. And that was not all: she told him she could not live with him out of her sight!"

It made the family jump; and Lilly turned a ghastly white, then

flushed red and her eyes blazed. Her lips worked, but she held in.
Joseph saw this, and there was a painful wonder in his eyes.

My mother showed distress. She was doing aimless things and
fumbling with her hands like a person who has been knocked out
of his bearings. She started to ask, in a hesitating way, if Philip was
in love with Marget, but Wilhelm was not conscious of anything
but his own affair; so he never heard her, but went right on:

"Traum wouldn't stay; but going out at the door, Marget still
pleading, he said as indifferently as if he were asking the time of
day, 'I can't stop now, but I'll come every day, if you like.' "

"He doesn't love her!"

It was Lilly. It was out before she could stop it; her feelings had
got the best of her. Joseph's head was bowed; if he had been
looking at his face in the glass, he would have seen a spasm.
Wilhelm looked at Lilly in a vague half-conscious way as if he sort
of wondered why she should show so much interest, then he
touched his dry lips with his tongue and went on:

"Marget's eyes were humid and brilliant, her face was flushed,
she was in a state of exaltation, she was like a person intoxicated
with adorable emotions. I said, 'You are in love with him.' She
answered, 'I am, and I glory in it; I worship him!' "

Lilly patted the floor with her foot, and the indignant breath
came short through her parted lips, but she kept control of her
tongue this time.

"I argued with her, reasoned with her, but it did no good. I said
he was a stranger, an adventurer whom nobody knew. She said it
was nothing to her; she loved him, and did not care who he was nor
what he was. Still I reasoned and persuaded. I said he was possessed
of a devil. She only said 'I would God I were possessed of the mate
to it.' It was awful to hear her say that. I told her he was indifferent
to her, and that he had not shown by a single word or sign that he
cared for her in anything more than a friendly way. She said, 'I
cannot help it, I love him; he does not love me now, but he is
coming every day, and I have a right to hope and I *will* hope.' It
was a bitter hour for me. We parted, without a caress; she did not

even put out her hand; then her conscience smote her and she put it out, saying 'Forgive me—good-night—and let us be friends.'

"It is a madness, you see; it is enchantment—she is not to blame. I have not been back. He goes every day; I have it from Gottfried. Marget's love was my whole fortune; and it is lost."

A silence fell. Every one sat as still as a statue. And the pride and the hopes and the happiness of each had received a stroke and been brought low. It was dismal, and like a funeral. Presently Wilhelm cast an appealing glance at my father, who started to get up, but Wilhelm motioned him back, as if to say, "Never mind—I know the way." So he passed into the back room. The liquor was there.

Soon we heard a brisk step, and the next moment Satan came tripping in as cheerful as a bird, and his coming was like the sea-breeze invading a sick-room. Everybody's spirits rose, and the welcome that shone in Lilly's face was another pang for Joseph. Satan greeted every one heartily by name and handshake; and in the midst of it Wilhelm came reeling in with our butcher-knife in his hand. He flourished it, and shouted "Stand back!" which they naturally did, being taken by surprise, and the women screamed; and as Satan faced about, Wilhelm sprang at him and brought down the knife with a deadly lunge. But it only touched Satan's breast, and fell to the floor.

For just an instant Satan's eyes glowed with a dangerous light but it was gone as swiftly as it had come, and he was saying to the company—

"Don't be disturbed, he was only playing."

Wilhelm looked perplexed and ashamed, and said haltingly— punctuating with a hiccup here and there—

"No, it is not entitled to so charitable a construction as that, and I make the humblest apologies to the company for my conduct. It was not myself that was acting, it is foreign to my nature; my sleep has been broken, I have been drinking more than is good for me, and for a moment my reason was affected, I think. I have done wrong, and am sorry. I had no right to proceed against his life."

Satan could do what he pleased with any one. It pleased him to smooth away Wilhelm's feeling of humiliation, and soften his resentment, and banish the liquor-fogs from his brain and the dulness from his eye and the depression from his spirit, and restore to him his normal self and make him cheerful and comfortable; and by the crafts and witcheries of his tongue he did it. In no long time Wilhelm was discussing chess with him, the company were assisting in the debate, and things were going along as smoothly as ever. And at last when Wilhelm said he wished a record had been kept of those four remarkable games, so that he could lighten his dull hours by studying them, Satan said he would make the record.

"From memory?" my father asked, "after five days?" I think he meant it for irony; but irony was not his best hold.

Satan did not reply; but took some sheets of paper and filled them with the record of the games, in—well, in the time it takes to count ten, I should say, or perhaps fifteen. You could not see his hand move over the paper, it was just a whiz and a blur. Wilhelm examined the record in detail. Then,

"It is correct," he said.

"Marvelous!" said the others.

"You've got your sample," murmured Joseph. Lilly gave him a look which excused him from further comment.

Chapter 6

WHEN I looked in on Lilly that night after she was abed, her eyes were red and she had been crying; but I found that the source of it was not Satan's indiscriminate ways, but only resentment against Marget for her attitude toward him. She thought it was scandalous in Marget to act so, considering that she already had a lover. I was surprised at this remark; it seemed illogical, and I said so.

"You are in love with Philip Traum yourself, and *you* had another lover."

She flew out at me and said—

"The cases are not the same—they are far different."

I suppose it was a mistake to ask her to point out the difference, but I did it, not knowing much about women then—nor now, probably. Her temper warmed up, and she said—

"If you can't see the difference, it would be useless for me to try to make you. Oh, you *are* so stupid!"

I could not see that that was an answer, and I said so. I said—

"Look at the cases—coolly and dispassionately—just as if it were other people, and you not concerned. There's Marget and Wilhelm, engaged; on the other side you and Joseph, as good as engaged. A stranger comes along, and you and Marget brush your lovers aside and fall in love with him. If it is scandalous in Marget, why then it seems to me—"

"Now that's enough—I don't want to hear any more about it. I never saw such a wandering mind."

"Wandering mind, indeed! Where is my mind wandering, I'd like to know?"

"Yes, I should think you would. But don't try—nobody can find out. You'll only fatigue yourself."

It was a shame to put me down like that and walk over me, so to speak, when I was certainly in the right. I ought to have known that when a woman gets her head set, particularly in a love matter, she hasn't any sense and isn't any more movable by argument than a stump is; but I was but a lad, and didn't know the crazy make of them.

I dropped the matter, since I had to, and then I went at the matter which I had mainly come to talk about. For Lilly's own happiness I wanted to save her while there was yet time, from irrevocably engaging her heart in this hopeless chase. So I led up to it in a grave and impressive introduction of some length, and when I believed I had sufficiently prepared her for the blow, I said—

"My dear, dear sister, be warned: he does not love you, and he never can."

Storm-fires began to gather in her eyes, and she rose and sat up in the bed and looked me over, much as a comet looks a little dog over that has been trying to help it conduct its excursion in the safest way.

"*You* think so!" she said. "I wish to ask you a question or two—you who are so fond of reasoning and arguing and inferring, and think yourself so competent in such matters. What do you know about Philip Traum? Nothing. Are you intimate with him? Certainly not. Is your mind capable of intimacy with a mind like his? Hardly. Have you ever encountered such a mind before? Answer me."

"Well—no."

"Is there any one else in the world who can bring out of a simpering old spinet the music of the spheres?"

"No."

"Is there any one else who can carry four games of chess in his memory a week? Or transmute prose into poetry without reflection or preparation? Or turn a would-be assassin into a fireside comrade in ten minutes by the clock? Or do this?" and she drew that embroidery from under her pillow and displayed it. "Come—infer me an inference. What do you infer from these things?"

"Well, that he—that he is not like anybody else."

She snatched at that as triumphantly as if I had given my whole case away:

"You've said it! Very well, then, since he is not like anybody else, it is argument that he is governed by laws that are not the laws which govern other people's actions. Do we know what the laws are which govern him?"

Of course I knew, but it was not my privilege to let out that fact, so I blinked the truth and said no.

"Very well, then, you see where you have landed. *You* don't know, and can't know, that he will never love me; so you need not bother yourself any more about the matter. Through my sympathies, my perceptions and my love *I* know him; know him as no one else knows him; know him as no one else can ever know him. And you shall not take my golden hope from me—no one shall! He will love me yet, and only me."

There was a glory in her eyes that made her beautiful. I had not the heart to spoil it; so I kept back the words that were upon my lips: "Marget is probably saying these same things herself."

I went to my bed with heavy thoughts. What a lot of dismal haps had befallen the village, and certainly Satan seemed to be the father of the whole of them: Father Peter in prison, on account of the money laid in his way by Satan, which furnished Father Adolf the handy pretext he needed; Marget's household shunned and under perilous suspicion on account of that cat's work—cat furnished by Satan; Father Adolf acquiring a frightful and odious reputation, and likely to be burnt at the stake presently—Satan responsible for it; my parents worried, perplexed, distressed about their daughter's new love-freak and the doubtfulness of its outlook; Joseph crushed and shamed; Wilhelm's heart broken and dissipation laying its blight upon his character, his ambition and his fair repute; Marget gone silly, and our Lilly following after; the whole village prodded and pestered into a pathetic delirium about non-existent witches and quaking in its shoes: the whole wide wreck and desolation of hearts and hopes and industries the work of Satan's enthusiastic diligence and morbid passion for business. And he, the author of all the trouble, was the only person concerned that got any rapture out of it. By his spirits one would think he was grateful to be alive and improving things.

I fell asleep to pleasant music presently—the patter of rain upon the panes and the dull growling of distant thunder. Away in the night Satan came and roused me and said—

"Come with me. Where shall we go?"

"Anywhere—so it is with you."

Then there was a fierce glare of sunlight, and he said—

"This is China."

That was a grand surprise, and made me sort of drunk with vanity and gladness to think I had come so far—and so much, much further than anybody else in our village, including Bartel Sperling, who had such a great opinion of his travels. We buzzed around over that Empire for more than half an hour and saw the whole of it. It was wonderful, the spectacles we saw; and some were beautiful, others too horrible to think. For instance—however, I will go into that by and by, and also why Satan chose China for this excursion instead of another place—it would interrupt my tale to do it now. Finally we stopped flitting, and lit.

We sat upon a mountain commanding a vast landscape of mountain-range and gorge and valley and plain and river, with cities and villages slumbering in the sunlight, and a glimpse of blue sea on the further verge. It was a tranquil and dreamy picture, beautiful to the eye and restful to the spirit. If we could only make a change like that whenever we wanted to, the world would be easier to live in than it is, for change of scene shifts the mind's burdens to the other shoulder and banishes old shop-worn wearinesses from mind and body both.

We talked together, and I had the idea of trying to reform Satan and persuade him to lead a better life. I told him about all those things he had been doing, and begged him to be more considerate and stop making people unhappy. I said I knew he did not mean any harm, but that he ought to stop and consider the possible consequences of an act before launching it in that impulsive and random way of his; then he would not make so much trouble. He was not hurt by this plain speech, he only looked amused and surprised, and said—

"What, *I* do random things? Indeed I never do. *I* stop and consider possible consequences? Where is the need? I *know* what the consequences are going to be—always."

"Oh, Satan, then how could you do those things?"

"Well, I will tell you, and you must understand it if you can. You belong to a singular race. Every man is a suffering-machine and a happiness-machine combined. The two functions work together harmoniously, with a fine and delicate precision, on the give-and-take principle. For every happiness turned out in the one department the other one stands ready to modify it with a sorrow or a pain—maybe a dozen. In most cases the man's life is about equally divided between happiness and unhappiness. When this is not the case the unhappiness predominates—always; never the other. Sometimes a man's make and disposition are such that his misery-machinery is able to do nearly all the business. Such a man goes through life almost ignorant of what happiness is. Everything he touches, everything he does, brings a misfortune upon him. You have seen such people? To that kind of a person life is not an advantage, is it? it is only a disaster. Sometimes, for an hour's happiness a man's machinery makes him pay years of misery. Don't you know that? It happens every now and then. I will give you a case or two, presently. Now the people of your village are nothing to me—you know that, don't you?"

I did not like to speak out too flatly, so I only said I had suspected it.

"Well, it is true that they are nothing to me. It is not possible that they should be. The difference between them and me is abysmal, immeasurable. They have no intellect."

"No intellect?"

"Nothing that resembles it. At a future time I will examine what man calls his mind and give you the details of that chaos, then you will see and understand. Men have nothing in common with me— there is no point of contact. They have foolish little feelings, and foolish little vanities and impertinences and ambitions, their foolish little life is but a laugh, a sigh, and extinction; and they have no sense. Only the Moral Sense. I will show you what I mean. Here is a red spider, not so big as a pin's head; can you imagine an elephant being interested in him; caring whether he is happy or isn't; or whether he is wealthy or poor; or whether his sweetheart returns his love or not; or whether his mother is sick or well; or whether he is looked up to in society or not; or whether his enemies will smite him or his friends desert him; or whether his hopes will suffer blight or his political ambitions fail; or whether he shall die in the bosom of his family or neglected and despised in a foreign land? These things can never be important to the elephant, they are nothing to him, he cannot shrink his sympathies to the microscopic size of them. Man is to me as the red spider is to the elephant. The elephant has nothing against the spider, he cannot get down to that remote level—I have nothing against man. The elephant is indifferent, I am indifferent. The elephant would not take the trouble to do the spider an ill turn; if he took the notion he might do him a good turn, if it came in his way and cost nothing. I have done men good service, but no ill turns.

"The elephant lives a century, the red spider a day; in power, intellect and dignity, the one creature is separated from the other by a distance which is simply astronomical. Yet in these and in all qualities man is immeasurably further below me than is the wee spider below the elephant.

"Man's mind clumsily and tediously and laboriously patches little trivialities together, and gets a result—such as it is. My mind *creates!* Do you get the force of that? Creates anything it desires—and in a moment. Creates without materials; creates fluids, solids, colors—anything, everything—out of the airy nothing which is called Thought. A man imagines a silk thread, imagines a machine to make it, imagines a picture, then by weeks of labor embroiders it on a canvas with the thread. I *think* the whole thing, and in a moment it is before you—created.

"I *think* a poem—music—the record of a game of chess—any-thing—and it is there. This is the immortal mind—nothing is beyond its reach. Nothing can obstruct my vision—the rocks are transparent to me, and darkness is daylight. I do not need to open a book; I take the whole of its contents into my mind at a single glance, through its cover; and in a million years I could not forget a single word of it, or its place in the volume. Nothing goes on in the skull of any man, bird, fish, insect or other creature which can be hidden from me. I pierce the learned man's brain with a single glance, and the treasures which cost him three-score years to accu-mulate are mine; he can forget, and he does forget, but I retain.

"Now then, I perceive by your thoughts that you are understand-ing me fairly well. Let us proceed. Circumstances might so fall out that the elephant could like the spider—supposing he can see it—but he could not *love* it. His love is for his own kind—for his equals. An angel's love is sublime, adorable, divine, beyond the imagination of man—infinitely beyond it! But it is limited to his own august order. If it fell upon one of your race for only an instant it would consume its object to ashes."

I thought of poor Marget and poor Lilly.

"Give yourself no uneasiness," he said, "they are safe. No, we cannot love men, but we can be harmlessly indifferent to them; we can also like them, sometimes. I like you and the boys, I like Father Peter, and for your sakes I am doing all these things for the villagers."

He saw that I was thinking a sarcasm, and he explained his position.

"I *have* wrought well for the villagers, though it does not look like it on the surface. Your race never know good fortune from ill. They are always mistaking the one for the other. It is because they cannot see into the future. What I am doing for the villagers will bear good fruit some day; in some cases to themselves, in others to unborn generations of men. No one will ever know that I was the cause, but it will be none the less true for all that. Among you boys you have a game: you stand a row of bricks on end a few inches apart; you push a brick, it knocks its neighbor over, the neighbor knocks over the next brick—and so on till all the row is prostrate. That is human life. A child's first act knocks over the initial brick, and the rest will follow inexorably. If you could see into the future, as I can, you would see everything that was ever going to happen to that creature; for nothing can change the order of its life after the first event has determined it. That is, nothing *will* change it, because each act unfailingly begets *an* act, that act begets another, and so on to the end, and the seer can look forward down the line and see just when each act is to have birth, from cradle to grave."

"Does God order the career?"

"Foreordain it? No. The man's circumstances and environment order it. His first act determines the second and all that follow after. But suppose, for argument's sake, that the man should skip one of these acts; an apparently trifling one, for instance: suppose it had been appointed that on a certain day, at a certain hour and minute and second and fraction of a second he should snatch at a fly, and he *didn't* snatch at the fly. That man's career would change utterly, from that moment; thence to the grave it would be wholly different from the career which his first act as a child had arranged for him.

Indeed it might be that if he had snatched at the fly he would have ended his career on a throne; and that omitting to do it would set him upon a career that would lead to beggary and a pauper's grave. For instance: if at any time—say in boyhood—Columbus had skipped the triflingest little link in the chain of acts projected and made inevitable by his first childish act, it would have changed his whole subsequent life and he would have become a priest and died obscure in an Italian village, and America would not have been discovered for two centuries afterward. I know this. To skip any one of the billion acts in Columbus's chain would have wholly changed his life. I have examined his billion of possible careers, and in only one of them occurs the discovery of America. You people do not suspect that all of your acts are of one size and importance, but it is true: to snatch at an appointed fly is as big with fate for you as is any other appointed act—"

"As the conquering of a continent, for instance?"

"Yes.

"Now then, no man ever *does* drop a link—the thing has never happened; even when he is trying to make up his mind as to whether he will do a thing or not, that *itself* is a link, an act, and has its proper place in his chain; and when he finally decides and acts, that also was the thing which he was absolutely certain to do. You see, now, that a man will never drop a link in his chain. He cannot. If he made up his mind to try, *that* project would itself be an unavoidable link—a thought bound to occur to him at that precise moment, and made certain by the first act of his babyhood."

It seemed so dismal!

"He is a prisoner for life," I said, sorrowfully, "and cannot get free."

"No, of himself he cannot get away from the consequences of his first childish act. But I can free him."

I looked up wistfully.

"I have changed the careers of a number of your villagers."

I tried to thank him, but found it difficult, and let it drop.

"I shall make some other changes. You know that little Lisa Brandt."

"Oh, yes, everybody does. My mother says she is so sweet and so lovely that she is not like any other child. She says she will be the pride of the village when she grows up; and its idol, too, just as she is now."

"I will change her future."

"Make it better?" I asked, with some misgivings.

"Yes. And I will change the future of Nikolaus."

I was glad, this time, and said—

"I don't need to ask about *his* case; you will be sure to do generously by him."

"It is my intention."

Straight off I was building that great future of Nicky's in my imagination, and had already made a renowned General of him and Hofmeister at the Court, when I noticed that Satan was waiting for me to get ready to listen again. I was ashamed of having exposed my cheap imaginings to him, and was expecting some sarcasms, but it did not happen. He proceeded with his subject:

"Nicky's appointed life is 62 years."

"That's grand!" I said.

"Lisa's, 36. But as I told you, I shall *change* their lives. Two minutes and a quarter from now Nikolaus will wake out of his sleep and find the rain blowing in. It was appointed that he should turn over and go to sleep again. But *I* have appointed that he shall get up and close the window first. That trifle will change his career entirely. He will rise in the morning two minutes later than the chain of his life had appointed him to rise. By consequence, thence-forth nothing will ever happen to him in accordance with the details of the old chain."

He took out his watch and sat looking at it a few moments, then said—

"Nikolaus has risen to close the window. His life is changed, his new career has begun. There will be consequences."

It made me feel creepy, it was so uncanny.

"But for this change certain things would happen twelve days from now. For instance, Nikolaus would save Lisa from drowning. He would arrive on the scene at exactly the right moment—four minutes past 10—the long-ago appointed instant of time—and the water would be shoal, the achievement easy and certain. But he will arrive some seconds too late, now; Lisa will have struggled into deeper water. He will do his best, but both will drown."

"Oh, Satan, oh, dear Satan," I cried, with the tears rising in my eyes, "save them! don't let it happen, I can't bear to lose Nikolaus, he is my loving playmate and friend; and think of Lisa's poor mother!"

I clung to him and begged and pleaded, but he was not moved. He made me sit down again, and told me I must hear him out.

"I have changed Nikolaus's life, and this has changed Lisa's. If I had not done this, Nikolaus would save Lisa; then he would catch cold from his drenching; one of your race's fantastic and desolating scarlet fevers would follow, with pathetic after-effects: for forty-six years he would lie in his bed a paralytic log, deaf, dumb, blind, and praying night and day for the blessed relief of death. Shall I change his life back?"

"Oh, no! Oh, not for the world, not for the world! In charity and pity, leave it as it is."

"It is best so. I could not have changed any other link in his life and done him so good service. He had a billion possible careers, but not one of them was worth living; they were charged full with miseries and disasters. But for my intervention he would do his brave deed twelve days from now,—a deed begun and ended in six minutes—and get for all reward those forty-six years of sorrow and suffering I told you of. It is one of the cases I was thinking of a while ago when I said that sometimes an act which brings the actor an hour's happiness and self-satisfaction is paid for—or punished? —by years of suffering."

I wondered what poor little Lisa's early death would save her from. He answered the thought:

"From ten years of pain and slow recovery from an accident, and then from nineteen years of pollution, shame, depravity, crime, ending with death at the hands of the executioner. Twelve days hence she will die; her mother would save her life if she could. Am I not kinder than her mother?"

"Yes—oh, indeed yes; and wiser."

"Father Peter's case is coming on, presently. He will be acquitted, through unassailable proofs of his innocence."

"Why Satan, how can that be? Do you really think it?"

"Indeed I know it. His good name will be restored, and the rest of his life will be happy."

"I can believe it. To restore his good name will have that effect."

"His happiness will not proceed from that cause. I shall change his life that day, for his good. *He* will never know his good name has been restored."

In my mind—and modestly—I asked for particulars, but Satan paid no attention to my thought. Next, my mind wandered to Father Adolf, and I wondered where he might be.

"In the moon," said Satan, with a fleeting sound which I believed was a chuckle. "I've got him on the cold side of it, too. He doesn't know where he is, and is not having a pleasant time; still, it is good enough for him. I shall need him presently; then I shall bring him back and possess him again. He has a long and cruel and odious life before him, but I will change that, for I have no feeling against him and am quite willing to do him a kindness. I think I will get him burnt."

He had such strange notions of kindness. But angels are made so, and do not know any better. Their ways are not like our ways; and besides, human beings are nothing to them; they think they are only freaks.

It seemed to me odd that he should put the priest so far away; he could have dumped him in Germany just as well, where he would be handy.

"Far away?" said Satan. "To me no place is far away; distance does not exist, for me. The sun is less than a hundred million miles from here, and the light that is falling upon us has taken eight minutes to come; but I can make that flight, or any other, in a

fraction of time so minute that it cannot be measured by a watch. I
have but to *think* the journey, and it is accomplished."

I held out my hand and said—

"The light lies upon it; think it into a glass of wine, Satan."

He did it. I drank the wine.

"Break the glass," he said.

I broke it.

"There—you see it is real. The villagers thought the brass balls
were magic-stuff and as perishable as smoke. They were afraid to
touch them. You are a curious lot—your race. But come along, I
have business. I will put you to bed." Said and done. Then he was
gone; but his voice came back to me through the rain and darkness,
saying, "Yes, tell Seppi, but no other."

It was the answer to my thought.

Sleep would not come. It was not because I was proud of my
travels and excited about having been around the big world to
China, and feeling contemptuous of Bartel Sperling, "the traveler,"
as he called himself, and looked down upon us others because he
had been to Vienna once and was the only Eseldorf boy who had
made such a journey and seen the world's wonders. At another time
that would have kept me awake, but it did not affect me now. No,
my mind was filled with Nikolaus, my thoughts ran upon him only,
and the good days we had seen together at romps and frolics in the
woods and the fields and the river in the long summer days, and
skating and sliding in the winter when our parents thought we
were at school. And now he was going out of this young life, and
the summers and winters would come and go, and we others would
rove and play as before, but his place would be vacant, we should
see him no more. To-morrow he would not suspect, but would be as
he had always been, and it would shock me to hear him laugh, and
see him do lightsome and frivolous things, for to me he would be a
corpse, with waxen hands and dull eyes, and I should see the
shroud around his face; and next day he would not suspect, nor the
next, and all the time his handful of days would be wasting swiftly
away and that awful thing coming nearer and nearer, his fate

closing steadily around him and no one knowing it but Seppi and me. Twelve days—only twelve days. It was awful to think of. I noticed that in my thoughts I was not calling him by his familiar names, Nick and Nicky, but was speaking of him by his full name, and reverently, as one speaks of the dead. Also, as incident after incident of our comradeship came thronging into my mind out of the past, I noticed that they were mainly cases where I had wronged him or hurt him, and they rebuked me and reproached me, and my heart was wrung with remorse, just as it is when we remember our unkindnesses to friends who have passed behind the veil, and we wish we could have them back again, if for only a moment, so that we could go on our knees to them and say "Have pity, and forgive."

Once when we were nine years old he went a long errand of nearly two miles for the fruiterer, who gave him a splendid big apple for reward, and he was flying home with it almost beside himself with astonishment and delight, and I met him, and he let me look at the apple, not thinking of treachery, and I ran off with it, eating it as I ran, he following me and begging; and when he overtook me I offered him the core, which was all that was left; and I laughed. Then he turned away, crying, and said he had meant to give it to his little sister. That smote me, for she was slowly getting well of a sickness, and it would have been a proud moment for him, to see her joy and surprise and have her caresses. But I was ashamed to say I was ashamed, and only said something rude and mean, to pretend I did not care, and he made no reply in words, but there was a wounded look in his face as he turned away toward his home which rose before me many times in after years, in the night, and reproached me and made me ashamed again. It had grown dim in my mind, by and by, then it disappeared; but it was back, now, and not dim.

Once at school, when we were eleven, I upset my ink and spoiled four copy-books, and was in danger of severe punishment; but I put it upon him, and he got the whipping.

And only last year I had cheated him in a trade, giving him a large fish-hook which was partly broken through, for three small sound ones. The first fish he caught broke the hook, but he did not know I was blameable, and he refused to take back one of the small hooks which my conscience forced me to offer him, but said "a trade is a trade; the hook was bad, but that was not your fault."

No, I could not sleep. These little shabby wrongs upbraided me and tortured me; and with a pain much sharper than one feels when the wrongs have been done to the living. Nikolaus *was* living, but no matter: he was to me as one already dead. The wind was still moaning about the eaves, the rain still pattering upon the panes.

In the morning I sought out Seppi and told him. It was down by the river. His lips moved, but he did not say anything, he only looked dazed and stunned, and his face turned very white. He stood like that, a few moments, the tears welling into his eyes, then he turned away and I locked my arm in his and we walked along thinking, but not speaking. We crossed the bridge and wandered through the meadows and up among the hills and the woods, and at last the talk came, and flowed freely; and it was all about Nikolaus and was a recalling of the life we had lived with him. And every now and then Seppi said, as if to himself:

"Twelve days!—less than twelve."

We said we must be with him all the time; we must have all of him we could, the days were precious, now. Yet we did not go to seek him. It would be like meeting the dead, and we were afraid. We did not say it, but that was what we were feeling. And so it gave us a shock when we turned a curve and came upon Nikolaus face to face. He shouted gaily—

"Hi-hi! what is the matter? Have you seen a ghost?"

We couldn't speak, but there was no occasion; he was willing to talk for us all, for he had just seen Satan and was in high spirits about it. Satan had told him about our trip to China, and he had begged Satan to take him a journey, and Satan had promised. It was to be a far journey, and wonderful and beautiful; and Nikolaus had begged him to take us, too, but he said no, he would take us some day, maybe, but not now. Satan would come for him on the

13th, and Nikolaus was already counting the hours, he was so impatient.

That was the fatal day. We were already counting the hours, too.

We wandered many a mile, always following paths which had been our favorites from the days when we were little, and always we talked about the old times. All the blitheness was with Nikolaus; we others could not shake off our depression. Our tone toward Nikolaus was so strangely gentle and tender and yearning that he noticed it, and was pleased; and we were constantly doing him deferential little offices of courtesy, and saying, "Wait, let me do that for you," and that pleased him, too. I gave him seven fish-hooks —all I had—and made him take them; and Seppi gave him his new knife and a humming-top painted red and yellow—atonements for swindles practised upon him formerly, as I learned later, and probably no longer remembered by Nikolaus now. These things touched him, and he said he could not have believed that we loved him so; and his pride in it and gratefulness for it cut us to the heart we were so undeserving of them. When we parted at last, he was radiant and said he had never had such a happy day.

As we walked along homewards, Seppi said—

"We always prized him, but never so much as now, when we are going to lose him."

Chapter 7

Next day and every day we spent all of our spare time with Nikolaus; and also added to it time which we (and he) stole from work and other duties, and this cost the three of us some sharp scoldings and some threats of punishment. Every morning two of us woke with a start and a shudder, saying, as the days flew along, "Only ten days left;" "only nine days left;" "only eight;" "only seven." Always it was narrowing. Always Nikolaus was gay and happy, and always puzzled because we were not. He wore his invention to the bone, trying to invent ways to cheer us up, but it was only a hollow success; he could see that our jollity had no heart in it, and that the laughs we broke into came up against some obstruction or other and suffered damage and decayed into a sigh. He tried to find out what the matter was, so that he could help us out of our trouble or make it lighter by sharing it with us; so we had to tell many lies to deceive him and appease him.

But the most distressing thing of all was, that he was always making plans, and often they went beyond the 13th! Whenever that happened, it made us groan in spirit. All his mind was fixed upon finding some way to conquer our depression and cheer us up; and at last, when he had but three days to live, he fell upon the right idea and was jubilant over it: a boys' and girls' frolic and dance in the woods, up there where we first met Satan, and this was to occur on the 14th. It was ghastly; for that was his funeral-day. We couldn't venture a protest; it would only have brought a "Why?" which we could not answer. He wanted us to help him invite his guests, and we did it; one can refuse nothing to a dying friend. But it was dreadful; for really we were inviting them to his funeral.

It was an awful eleven days; and yet, with a lifetime stretching back between to-day and then, they are still a grateful memory to me, and beautiful. In effect they were days of companionship with one's sacred dead, and I have known no comradeship that was so close or so precious. We clung to the hours and the minutes, counting them as they wasted away, and parting with them with that pain and bereavement which a miser feels who sees his hoard filched from him coin by coin by robbers and is helpless to prevent it.

When the evening of the last day came we stayed out too long; Seppi and I were in fault for that, we could not bear to part with Nikolaus; so it was very late when we left him at his door. We lingered near, a while, listening; and that happened which we were fearing. His father gave him the promised punishment, and we heard his shrieks. But we listened only a moment, then hurried away, remorseful for this thing which we had caused. And sorry for the father, too; our thought being, "If he only knew—if he only knew!"

In the morning Nikolaus did not meet us at the appointed place, so we went to his home to see what the matter was. His mother said—

"His father is out of all patience with these goings on, and will not have any more of it. Half the time when Nick is needed he is not to be found; then it turns out that he has been gadding around with you two. His father gave him a flogging last night. It always grieved me before, and many's the time I have begged him off and saved him, but this time he appealed to me in vain, for I was out of patience myself."

"I wish you had saved him just this one time," I said, my voice trembling a little, "it would ease a pain in your heart to remember it some day."

She was ironing, at the time, and her back was partly toward me. She turned about with a startled or wondering look in her face and said—

"What do you mean by that?"

I was not prepared, and didn't know anything to say, so it was awkward, for she kept looking at me; but Seppi was alert and spoke up:

"Why of course it would be pleasant to remember; for, the very reason we were out so late was that Nikolaus got to telling us how good you are to him, and how he never got whipped when you were by to save him; and he was so full of it, and we so full of the interest of it that none of us noticed how late it was getting."

"Did he say that? did he?" and she put her apron to her eyes.

"You can ask Theodor—he will tell you the same."

"It is a dear good lad, my Nick," she said. "I am sorry I let him get whipped; I will never do it again. To think—all the time I was sitting here last night fretting and angry at him he was loving me and praising me! Dear, dear, if we could only know! then we shouldn't ever go wrong; but we are only poor dumb beasts groping around and making mistakes. I shan't ever think of last night without a pang."

She was like all the rest; it seemed as if nobody could open a mouth, in these wretched days, without saying something that made us shiver. They were "groping around," and did not know what sorrowfully true things they were saying by accident.

Seppi asked if Nikolaus might go out with us.

"I am sorry," she answered, "but he can't. To punish him further, his father doesn't allow him to go out of the house to-day."

We had a great hope! I saw it in Seppi's eyes. We thought, "if he cannot leave the house, he cannot be drowned." Seppi asked—to make sure—

"Must he stay in all day, or only the morning?"

"All day. It's such a pity, too; it's a beautiful day, and he is so unused to being shut up. But he is busy planning his party, and maybe that is company for him. I do hope he isn't too lonesome."

Seppi saw that in her eye which emboldened him to ask if we might go up and help him pass his time.

"And welcome!" she said, right heartily. "Now I call that *real* friendship, when you might be abroad in the fields and the woods, having a happy time. You *are* good boys, I'll allow that, though you don't always find satisfactory ways of proving it. Take these cakes —for yourselves—and give him this one, from his mother."

The first thing we noticed when we entered Nikolaus's room was the clock. A quarter to 10. Could that be correct? Only such a few minutes left to live! I felt a contraction at my heart. Nikolaus jumped up and gave us a glad welcome. He was in good spirits over his plannings for his party, and had not been lonesome.

"Sit down," he said, "and look at what I've been doing. And I've finished a kite that you will say is a daisy. It's drying, in the kitchen; I'll fetch it."

He had been spending his penny-savings in fanciful trifles of various kinds, to go as prizes in the games, and they were marshaled with fine and showy effect upon the table. He said—

"Examine them at your leisure while I get mother to touch up the kite with her iron if it isn't dry enough yet."

Then he tripped out and went clattering down stairs, whistling "Die Trommeln sagen pom-pom-pom."

We did not look at the things; we couldn't take any interest in anything but the clock. We sat staring at it in silence, listening to the ticking, and every time the minute-hand jumped, we nodded recognition—one minute fewer to cover in the race for life or for death. Finally Seppi drew a deep breath and said—

"Two minutes to ten. Seven minutes more and he will pass the death-point. Theodor, he is going to be saved! he's going to—"

"Hush, I'm on needles!—watch the clock, and keep still."

Five minutes more. We were panting, with the strain and the excitement.

Another three minutes, and there was a footstep on the stair.

"Saved!" and we jumped up and faced the door.

The old mother entered, bringing the kite.

"Isn't it a beauty?" she said. "And dear me, how he has slaved over it; ever since daylight, I think, and only finished it a while before you came." She stood it against the wall, and stepped back to take a view of it. "He drew the pictures his own self, and I think they are very good. The church isn't so very good, I'll have to admit, but look at the bridge—any one can recognise the bridge in a minute. He asked me to bring it up. . . . . . Dear me, it's seven minutes past ten, and I—"

"But where is *he?*"

"He? Oh, he'll be here soon—he's gone out a minute."

"Gone *out?*"

"Yes. Just as he came down stairs little Lisa's mother came in and said the child had wandered off somewhere, and as she was a little uneasy I told Nikolaus to never mind about his father's orders—go and look her up . . . . . Why, how white you two do look; I do believe you are sick. Sit down; I'll fetch you something. That cake has disagreed with you. It *is* a little heavy, but I thought—"

She disappeared without finishing her sentence, and we hurried at once to the back window and looked toward the river. There was a great crowd at the other end of the bridge, and people were flying toward that point from every direction.

"Oh, it is all over—poor Nikolaus! Why did she let him get out of the house!"

"Come away," said Seppi, half sobbing, "come quick—we can't bear to meet her—in five minutes she will know."

But we were not to escape. She came upon us at the foot of the stairs, with her cordials in her hand, and made us come in and sit down and take the medicine. Then she watched the effect, and it did not satisfy her; so she made us wait longer, and kept upbraiding herself for giving us the unwholesome cake.

Presently the thing happened which we were dreading. There was a sound of tramping and scraping outside, and a crowd came solemnly in, with heads uncovered, and laid the two drowned bodies on the bed.

"Oh, my God!" that poor mother cried out, and fell on her knees, and put her arms about her dead boy and began to cover the wet face with kisses. "Oh, it was I that sent him, and I have been his death. If I had obeyed, and kept him in the house, this would not have happened. And I am rightly punished—I was cruel to him last night, and him begging me, his own mother, to be his friend."

And so she went on and on, and all the women cried, and pitied her, and tried to comfort her, but she could not forgive herself and could not be comforted, and kept on saying if she had not sent him out he would be alive and well now, and she was the cause of his death.

It shows how foolish people are when they blame themselves for anything they have done. Satan knows, and he said nothing happens that your first act hasn't *arranged* to happen and made inevitable; and so, of your own motion you can't ever alter the scheme or do a thing that will break a link. Next we heard screams, and Frau Brandt came wildly plowing and plunging through the crowd with her dress in disorder and her hair flying loose, and flung herself upon her dead child with moans and kisses and pleadings and endearments; and by and by rose up almost exhausted with her outpourings of passionate emotion, and clenched her fist and lifted it toward the sky, and her tear-drenched face grew hard and resentful, and she said—

"For nearly two weeks I have had dreams and presentiments and warnings that death was going to strike what was most precious to me, and day and night and night and day I have groveled in the dirt before Him praying Him to have pity on my innocent child and save it from harm—and *here* is His answer!"

Why, He *had* saved it from harm—but she did not know.

She wiped the tears from her eyes and cheeks, and stood awhile gazing down at the child and caressing its face and its hair with her hand, then she spoke again in that bitter tone—

"But in His hard heart is no compassion. I will never pray again."

She gathered her dead child to her bosom and strode away, the crowd falling back to let her pass, and smitten dumb by the awful words they had heard. Ah, that poor woman! It is as Satan said, we do not know good fortune from bad, and are always mistaking the one for the other. Many a time, since then, I have heard people pray to God to spare the life of sick persons, but I have never done it.

Both funerals took place at the same time in our little church next day. Everybody was there, including the party-guests. Satan was there, too; which was proper, for it was on account of his efforts that the funerals had happened. Nikolaus had departed this life without absolution, and a collection was taken up for masses, to get him out of purgatory. Only two-thirds of the required money was gathered, and the parents were going to try to borrow the rest, but Satan furnished it. He told us privately that there was no purgatory, now, it having been discarded because it did not pay, there being none but Catholic custom for it; but he had contributed in order that Nikolaus's parents and their friends might be saved from worry and distress. We thought it very good of him, but he said money did not cost him anything.

At the graveyard the body of little Lisa was seized for debt by a carpenter to whom the mother owed fifty groschen for work done the year before. She had never been able to pay this, and was not able now. The carpenter took the corpse home and kept it four days in his cellar, the mother weeping and imploring about his house all the time; then he buried it in his brother's cattle-yard, without religious ceremonies. It drove the mother wild with grief and shame, and she forsook her work and went daily about the town cursing the carpenter and blaspheming the laws and the Emperor and the church, and it was pitiful to see. Seppi asked Satan to interfere, but he said that the carpenter and the rest were members of the human race and were acting quite neatly, for that species of animal. He would interfere if he found a horse acting in such a way, and we must inform him when we came across that kind of a horse doing that kind of a human thing, so that he could stop it. We believed this was sarcasm, for of course there wasn't any such horse.

But after a few days we found that we could not abide that poor woman's distress; so we begged Satan to examine her several possible careers, and see if he could not change her, to her profit, to a new one. He said the longest of her careers as they now stood gave her forty-two years to live, and her shortest one twenty-nine, and that both were charged with grief and hunger and cold and pain. The only improvement he could make would be to enable her to skip a certain link three minutes from now; and he asked us if he should do it. This was such a short time to decide in, that we went to pieces with nervous excitement, and before we could pull ourselves together and ask for particulars he said the time would be up in a few more seconds; so then we gasped out—

"Do it!"

"It is done," he said; "she was going around a corner, I have turned her back; it has changed her career."

"Then what will happen, Satan?"

"It is happening now. She is having words with Fischer, the weaver. In his anger Fischer will straightway do what he would not have done but for this accident. He was present when she stood over her child's body and uttered those blasphemies."

"What will he do?"

"He is doing it now—betraying her to a priest. In three days she will go to the stake."

We could not speak; we were frozen with horror, for if we had not meddled with her career she would have been spared this awful fate. Satan noticed these thoughts, and said—

"What you are thinking is strictly human-like; that is to say, foolish. The woman is advantaged. Die when she might, she would go to heaven. By this prompt death she gets twenty-nine years' more of heaven than she is entitled to, and escapes twenty-nine years of misery here."

A moment before we were bitterly making up our minds that we would ask no more favors of Satan for friends of ours, for he did not seem to know any way to do a person a kindness but by killing him; but the whole aspect of the case was changed now, and we were glad of what we had done and full of happiness in the thought of it.

After a little I began to feel troubled about Fischer, and asked timidly—

"Does this episode change Fischer's life-scheme, Satan?"

"Change it? Why, certainly. And radically. If he had not met Frau Brandt a while ago he would die next year, thirty-four years of age. Now he will live to be ninety, and have a pretty prosperous and comfortable life of it, as human lives go."

We felt a great joy and pride in what we had done for Fischer, and were expecting Satan to sympathise with this feeling; but he showed no sign, and this made us uneasy. We waited for him to speak, but he didn't; so, to assuage our solicitude we had to ask him if there was any defect in Fischer's good luck. Satan considered the question a moment, then said, with some hesitation—

"Well, the fact is, it is a delicate point. Under his several former possible life-careers he was going to *heaven*."

We were aghast.

"Oh, Satan! and under this one—"

"There, don't be so distressed. You were sincerely trying to do him a kindness; let that comfort you."

"Oh, dear, dear, *that* cannot comfort us. You ought to have *told* us what we were doing, then we wouldn't have acted so."

But it made no impression on him. He had never felt a pain or a sorrow, and did not know what they were, in any really informing way. He had no knowledge of them except theoretically—that is to say, intellectually. And of course that is no good. One can never get any but a loose and ignorant notion of such things except by experience. We tried our best to make him comprehend the awful thing that had been done and how we were compromised by it, but he couldn't seem to get hold of it. He said he did not think it important where Fischer went to, in heaven he would not be missed, there were "plenty there." We tried to make him see that he was missing the point entirely; that Fischer, and not other people, was the proper one to decide about the importance of it; but it all went for nothing, he said he did not care for Fischer, there were plenty more Fischers.

The next minute Fischer went by, on the other side of the way, and it made us sick and faint to see him, remembering the doom that was upon him, and we the cause of it. And how unconscious he was that anything had happened to him! You could see by his elastic step and his alert manner that he was well satisfied with himself for doing that hard turn for poor Frau Brandt. He kept glancing back over his shoulder expectantly. And sure enough, pretty soon Frau Brandt followed after, in charge of the officers and wearing jingling chains. A mob was in her wake, jeering and shouting "Blasphemer and heretic!" and some among them were neighbors and friends of her happier days. Some were trying to strike her, and the officers were not taking as much trouble as they might to keep them from it.

"Oh, stop them, Satan!" It was out before we remembered that he could not interrupt them for a moment without changing their whole after-lives. He puffed a little puff toward them with his lips and they began to reel and stagger and grab at the empty air; then they broke apart and fled in every direction, shrieking, as if in intolerable pain. He had crushed a rib of each of them with that little puff. We could not help asking if their life-chart was changed.

"Yes, entirely. Some have gained years, some have lost them. Some few will profit in various ways by the change, but only that few."

We did not ask if we had brought poor Fischer's luck to any of them. We did not wish to know. We fully believed in Satan's desire to do us kindnesses, but we were losing confidence in his judgment. It was at this time that our growing anxiety to have him look over our life-charts and suggest improvements began to fade out and give place to other interests.

For a day or two the whole village was in a chattering turmoil over Frau Brandt's case and over the mysterious calamity that had overtaken the mob, and at her trial the place was crowded. She was easily convicted of her blasphemies, for she uttered those terrible words again and said she would not take them back. When warned that she was imperiling her life she said they could take it and welcome, she did not want it, she would rather live with the professional devils in perdition than with these amateurs in the village. They accused her of breaking all those ribs by witchcraft, and asked her if she was not a witch? She answered scornfully—

"No. If I had that power would any of you holy hypocrites be alive five minutes? No, I would strike you all dead. Pronounce your sentence and let me go; I am tired of your society."

So they found her guilty, and she was excommunicated and cut off from the joys of heaven and doomed to the fires of hell; then she was clothed in a coarse robe and delivered to the secular arm, and conducted to the market place, the bell solemnly tolling the while. We saw her chained to the stake, and saw the first thin film of blue smoke rise on the still air. Then her hard face softened, and she looked upon the packed crowd in front of her and said with gentleness—

"We played together once, in long-gone days when we were innocent little creatures. For the sake of that, I forgive you."

We went away then, and did not see the fires consume her, but we heard the shrieks, although we put our fingers in our ears. When they ceased we knew she was in heaven notwithstanding the excommunication; and we were glad of her death and not sorry that we had brought it about.

Chapter 8

ONE DAY, a little while after this, Satan appeared again. We were always watching out for him—Seppi and I—and longing for him; for life was never very stagnant when he was by. He came upon us at that place in the woods where we had first met him.

Being boys, we wanted to be entertained, and we asked him to do a show for us.

"Very well," he said, "would you like to see a history of the progress of the human race?—its development of that product which it calls Civilization?"

We said we should.

So, with a thought, he turned the place into the Garden of Eden, and we saw Abel praying by his altar; then Cain came walking toward him with his club, and did not seem to see us, and would have stepped on my foot if I had not drawn it in. He spoke to his brother in a language which we did not understand; then he grew violent and threatening, and we knew what was going to happen, and turned away our heads for the moment; but we heard the crash of the blows and heard the shrieks and the groans; then there was silence, and we saw Abel lying in his blood and gasping out his life, and Cain standing over him and looking down at him, vengeful and unrepentant.

Then the vision vanished, and was followed by a long series of unknown wars, murders and massacres. Next, we had the Flood, and the Ark tossing around in the stormy waters, with lofty mountains in the distance showing veiled and dim through the rain. Satan said—

"The progress of your race was not satisfactory. It is to have another chance, now."

The scene changed, and we saw Noah lying drunk on Ararat.

Next, we had Sodom and Gomorrah, and "the attempt to discover two or three respectable persons there," as Satan described it. Next, Lot and his daughters in the cave.

Next came the Hebraic wars, and we saw the victors massacre the survivors and their cattle, and save the young girls alive and distribute them around.

Next, we had Jael; and saw her slip into the tent and drive the nail into the temples of her sleeping guest; and we were so close that when the blood gushed out it trickled in a little red stream to our feet and we could have stained our hands in it if we had wanted to.

Next we had Egyptian wars, Greek wars, Roman wars, hideous drenchings of the earth with blood; and we saw the treacheries of the Romans toward the Carthaginians, and the sickening spectacle of the massacre of those brave people. Also we saw Caesar invade Britain—"not that those barbarians had done him any harm, but because he wanted their land, and desired to confer the blessings of civilization upon their widows and orphans," as Satan explained.

Next Christianity was born. Then, ages of Europe passed in review before us, and we saw Christianity and Civilization march hand in hand through those ages, "leaving famine and death and desolation in their wake, and other signs of the progress of the human race," as Satan observed.

Then the Holy Inquisition was born; "another step in your progress," Satan said. He showed us thousands of torn and muti-lated heretics shrieking under the torture, and other thousands and thousands of heretics and witches burning at the stake, "always in the pleasant shade flung by the peaceful banner of the cross," as Satan remarked. And in the midst of these fearful spectacles, as an incidental matter, we had a marvelous night-show, by the light of flitting and flying torches—the butchery of Christian by Christian in France on Bartholomew's Day.

And always we had wars, and more wars, and still other wars—all over Europe, all over the world. "Sometimes in the private interest of royal families," Satan said, "sometimes to get more land, sometimes to crush a weak nation; but never a war started by the aggressor for any clean purpose—there is no such war in the history of your race."

"Now," said Satan, "you have seen your progress down to the present, and you must confess that it is wonderful—in its way. We must now exhibit the future. In a year or two we shall have Blenheim and Ramillies. Look!"

He showed us those awful slaughters.

"You perceive," he said, "that you have made continual progress. Cain did his murder with a club; the Hebrews did their murders with javelins and swords; the Greeks and Romans added protective armor and the fine arts of military organisation and generalship; the

Christian has added guns and gunpowder; two centuries from now
he will have so greatly improved the deadly effectiveness of his
weapons of slaughter that all men will confess that without the
Christian Civilization war must have remained a poor and trifling
thing to the end of time. In that day the lands and peoples of the
whole pagan world will be at the mercy of the sceptred bandits of
Europe, and they will take them. Furnishing in return, the blessings of civilization.

"Nine years from now a Prussian prince will be born who will
steal Silesia; plunge several nations into bloody and desolating wars;
lead a life of treachery and general and particular villainy, and be
admiringly called 'the Great.' Sixty-six years from now a Corsican
will be born who will deluge Europe with blood and spread the
Christian civilization far and wide. He also will be called 'the
Great.' A trifle before his day, England will begin to swallow India.
In his early manhood there will be a Revolution in France whose
bloody exhibitions will be a more terrible thing to see than even
France will have known since the Bartholomew Day. All through
the next century there will be wars—wars everywhere in the earth.
Wars for gain—each one a crime on the part of the provoker of it.
An English queen will reign more than sixty years, and fight more
than sixty wars during her reign—spreading civilization generously; also with profit. England, desiring a weak State's diamond
mines, will take them—by robbery, but courteously. Desiring another weak State's gold mines, her statesmen will try to seize them
by piracy; failing, they will manufacture a war and take them in
that way; and with them the small State's independence.

The Christian missionary will exasperate the Chinese; they will
kill him in a riot. They will have to pay for him, in territory, cash,
and churches, sixty-two million times his value. This will exasperate the Chinese still more, and they will injudiciously rise in revolt
against the insults and oppressions of the intruder. This will be
Europe's chance to interfere and swallow China, and her band of
royal Christian pirates will not waste it. Now then, I will show you
this long array of crimson spectacles, so that you can note the

progress of civilization from the time that Cain began it down to a period a couple of centuries hence."

Then he began to laugh in the most unfeeling way, and make fun of the human race, although he knew that what he had been saying shamed us and wounded us. No one but an angel could have acted so; but suffering is nothing to them, they do not know what it is, except by hearsay.

More than once Seppi and I had tried in a humble and diffident way to convert him; and as he had remained silent we had taken his silence as a sort of encouragement; necessarily, then, this talk of his was a disappointment to us, for it showed that we had made no deep impression upon him. The thought made us sad, and we knew, then, how the missionary must feel when he has been cherishing a glad hope and has seen it blighted. We kept our grief to ourselves, knowing that this was not the time to continue our work.

Satan laughed his unkind laugh to a finish, then he said—

"It is a remarkable progress. In five or six thousand years five or six high civilizations have risen, flourished, commanded the wonder of the world, then faded out and disappeared; and not one of them except the latest, ever invented any sweeping and adequate way to kill people. They all did their best, to kill being the chiefest ambition of the human race and the earliest incident in its history, but only the Christian Civilization has scored a triumph to be proud of. Two centuries from now it will be recognised that all the competent killers are Christian; then the pagan world will go to school to the Christian: not to acquire his religion, but his guns. The Turk and the Chinaman will buy those, to kill missionaries and converts with."

By this time his theatre was at work again: and before our eyes nation after nation drifted by, during two centuries, a mighty procession, an endless procession, raging, struggling, wallowing through seas of blood, smothered in battle-smoke through which the flags glinted and the red jets from the cannon darted; and always we heard the thunder of the guns and the cries of the dying.

"And what does it amount to?" said Satan, with his evil chuckle. "Nothing at all. You gain nothing; you always come out where you went in. For a million years the race has gone on monotonously propagating itself and monotonously re-performing this dull nonsense—to what end? No wisdom can guess! Who gets a profit out of it? Nobody but a parcel of usurping little monarchs and nobilities who despise you; would feel defiled if you touched them; would shut the door in your face if you proposed to call; whom you slave for, fight for, die for, and are not ashamed of it, but proud; whose existence is a perpetual insult to you and you are afraid to resent it; who are mendicants supported by your alms, yet assume toward you the airs of benefactor toward beggar; who address you in the language of master to slave and are answered in the language of slave to master; who are worshiped by you with your mouth, while in your hearts—if you have one—you despise yourselves for it. The first man was a hypocrite and a coward, qualities which have not yet failed in his line: it is the foundation upon which all civilizations have been built. Drink to their perpetuation! drink to their augmentation! drink to—"

Then he saw by our faces how much we were hurt, and he cut his sentence short and stopped chuckling, and his manner changed. He said gently—

"No, we will drink each other's health, and let civilization go. The wine which has flown to our hands out of space by my desire, is earthly, and good enough for that other toast, but throw away the glasses—we will drink this one in wine which has not visited this world before."

We obeyed, and reached up and received the new cups as they descended. They were shapely and beautiful goblets, but they were not made of any material that we were acquainted with. They seemed to be in motion, they seemed to be alive; and certainly the colors in them were in motion. They were very brilliant and sparkling, and of every tint, and they were never still, but flowed to and fro in rich tides which met and broke and flashed out dainty explosions of enchanting color. I think it was most like opals washing about in waves and flashing out their splendid fires. But there is nothing to compare the wine with, just as there was never anything to compare Satan's music with. We drank it, and felt a strange and witching ecstasy go stealing through us, and Seppi's eyes filled and he said worshipingly—

"We shall be there some day, and then—"

He glanced furtively at Satan, and I think he hoped Satan would say "Yes, you will be there some day," but Satan seemed to be thinking about something else, and said nothing. This made me feel ghastly, for I knew he had heard; nothing, spoken or unspoken, ever escaped him. Poor Seppi looked distressed, and did not finish his remark. The goblets rose, and clove their way into the sky, a triplet of radiant sundogs, and disappeared. Why didn't they stay? It seemed a bad sign, and depressed me. Should I ever see mine again? would Seppi ever see his?

Until this day I do not know. I never asked, and Seppi never asked. It is best not to inquire too far, in some matters, if you want to be comfortable. I had doubts about Seppi's ever seeing his goblet again, and I know he had doubts in my case, for some reason or other. These doubts restrained us and we did not pry into each other's fate further than concerned the present life.

You must never picture Satan as a solitary, but always with a lot of vagrant animals tagging around after him. Animals could not let him alone, they were so fascinated with him; and this was mutual, for he felt the same way toward them. He often said he would not give a penny for human company when he could get better. You see they were fond of each other because in a manner they were kin, through their mutual property in the absence of the Moral Sense. And kin in another particular, too—to him, as to them, there were no unpleasant smells. He said that unpleasant smells were an invention of Civilization—like modesty, and indecency. He said that to the pure all smells were sweet, to the decent all things were decent. He said that the natural man, the savage, had no prejudices about smells, and no shame for his God-made nakedness. Through intimacy with him we came to enjoy the society of many animals which had previously been repulsive to us, but we drew the line at the polecat. He did not; and so when he wanted to play with that creature we kept our distance. Indeed we were obliged to do this, it was not an affectation; for, while a polecat is undoubtedly a comely and graceful animal to look at, none but an angel can get any real joy out of its company. As for me, I would rather live in solitude. Seppi felt the same way.

Of course out there in the woods we had a perfect managerie on hand. The wild creatures trooped in from everywhere, and climbed all over Satan, and sat on his shoulder and his head, and rummaged his pockets, and made themselves at home—squirrels, rabbits, snakes, birds, butterflies, every creature you could name; and the rest would sit around in a crowd and look at him and admire him and worship him, and chatter and squawk and talk and laugh, and he would answer back in their own languages.

And they often beguiled him to do unlawful things. They would tell him of friends of theirs caught in traps by poachers in the prince's preserves, and would lead the way and show him, and he would release the creatures and destroy the traps. There was a reward out for the transgressor, and the keepers were on the watch, but he did not care. This time it was as usual. A rabbit came with a pitiful tale and he started, we following and protesting as far as the fence, and he changing himself into a rough and ragged poacher as he went. He got a broken-legged rabbit out of a trap, healed it with a touch and let it go—and there were the keepers in ambush, and swarmed out and surrounded him, catching him in the act. Four of them. The chief keeper, Conrad Bart, spoke his mind freely, calling Satan hard names, and said—

"We have you at last, lousy vagabond, and now you shall pay with usury for the trouble and worry you have given us, and the nights of watching, and the scouting and the fatigue. And also for the deridings and revilings his Highness has discharged upon us for being less cunning than you and letting you outwit us so long. Oh, yes, you shall pay!"

Satan said—

"It is a mistake; you think me a poacher, but I am not. I give you my honor I am innocent."

All the keepers laughed at that, and said "He gives us his honor —*he!*" and Bart said he ought not to tell lies, he had no art in it.

"I am not lying," said Satan. "I am a stranger; you do not know me; you have not seen me before; then how can you know whether it is I whom you have been seeking, or another?"

Bart said, with an airy toss of his head—

"It is plain that whether I know you or not, you do not know *me;* or you would know that I do not waste my time and my master's in bartering arguments with your kind of vermin. Now then, drop it. And answer: what is your name, and where are you from?"

"I do not choose to tell my name, nor where I am from. And you are mistaken in thinking I do not know you. I know the four of you; and I know things about each of you which you would not like the magistrates to find out."

It made them very angry, and three of them were for lashing him to a tree and flogging the insolence out of him; but Bart said—

"Wait—let him speak, we shall lose nothing. For each separate lie that he tells he shall have a separate flogging. Begin. What do you know about Caspar, there?"

"That at midnight, ten nights ago, in a lonely place he hid something which the owner would much like to recover."

"It is a lie!" shouted Caspar, and the others slapped their thighs in malicious joy to see Caspar snapped up in that startling and ungracious fashion.

"Then let us go and fetch it," said Satan.

"Agreed!" said all but Caspar, and were for starting; but Caspar begged, and took back the "lie," and said he had spoken hastily.

"Then confess," said Satan.

"I do," said Caspar, but with an ill grace, and with a nod of his head as much as to say "you will pay for this," whereat the others made merry again.

"It was a good guess, tramp," said Bart, "and saves you one thrashing. But you are not out of the woods yet. Try again. What do you know about Johan?"

"That he also possesses something which does not belong to him. It is a piece of gold, and has a secret mark upon it. I know the owner and the mark. Also, I know where the gold-piece is."

Johan burst into a wordy fury and called Satan the most shameful names, and threw off his jacket and challenged him to fight, but Satan was not moved. Then Johan's temper got so much the better of him that he made a mistake; for he swore he hadn't a gold-piece and dared Satan to prove the contrary.

"He has sewed it up in the lining of his jacket, there," said Satan.

Johan jumped for the jacket, but the others were too quick for him; and in the lining they found the coin.

Things were beginning to look serious. The men lost their levity, and looked nonplussed and ill at ease. There was a moment's silence, then Bart said, with the manner of one who has been relaxing himself with a childish game, but is tired of it and would return to matters of dignity and importance—

"Well, enough of this nonsense. Bind the loafer and fetch him along."

"Ah," said Conrad, with a sneer, "it is that way that the cat jumps, is it?"

"What do you mean?" said Bart.

"I mean that you've got *us* exposed, and now you would sneak out yourself."

"Take back the words!"

"I won't take them back. You know you don't dare to let this devil's imp tell what he knows about you. Do you hear?—you don't dare."

"It's a lie!" Then, his temper being up and hot, *he* made a mistake. "If he knows anything about me that I am hiding, let him out with it. Come—speak up, poacher and spy; and mind, if you utter so much as half a lie about me, I will not leave a whole bone in your body."

"I shall say only the truth," said Satan. "First, then, from to-day you will not be a keeper, but will be kept. You will be a public show and a curiosity, and will earn your family's living in that way."

This made the others laugh, but not Bart.

"Damn your prophecies!" he cried. "Confine yourself to what you *know* about me."

"Very well. Eighteen years ago a man was murdered near this village, for money. I know where the body lies; and with the body are the proofs that you did the murder, and not Jacob Hein whom you sent to the gallows for it."

Before you could think, Bart's gun was at Satan's breast and his finger on the trigger. But he never pulled it; Satan turned him to stone—clothes, gun and all.

And while those others were staring at this strange statue he turned himself into Father Adolf. They took only one glance at him, then fled away, crossing themselves, and soon they had spread the news, and set the persecuted village wild once more. The way Satan was acting, he was sure to greatly injure Father Adolf's character, which was bad enough already, but I did not say anything. It would have been of no use; Satan would have said, "He is only a human being—it is of no consequence."

Seppi was sorry for Bart's family, but Satan said he had done them a favor; that Bart was a fortune to them, now; they could exhibit him and get rich.

We met the crowds coming up, but he had already told us to keep away from him, and we were obeying. He said he should not be favorably received, and he was right. They fell apart and gave him a wide passage and were cruelly afraid of him, and showed his ecclesiastical authority a servile deference by uncovering to him and making humble obeisance; but the minute his back was to them they stoned him. They fairly rained missiles upon him, which struck and bounded off in sprays, but he didn't mind it, but strode contentedly along, acting like a person who was refreshing himself with a shower-bath, and much obliged.

Then we turned back. It was pitiful to see the family, their grief was so bitter. They flung their arms around the statue, and kissed it and cried over it, and could not be comforted. All the crowd admired the statue, and were full of wonder at its minute fidelities to fact, even the least little frayed and torn places in the clothes being exactly preserved, while as a portrait the work was perfection, and the murderous expression in countenance and attitude splendidly lifelike and animated and true; so true and so real that when women found themselves suddenly in front of the malignant face and the marble gun they gave a little screech and jumped aside. The birds in the game-bag were perfectly rendered, and so was a fly that was on the left cheek; it was like the frozen flies you find on the panes, winter mornings, white-shrouded in glinting frost. Siebold the drunken artist was there, and he said there was not another work of art in Europe that could match this one for modeling and tone.

The coroner's jury took their seats and reverently uncovered their heads, and the keepers were sworn and gave testimony. They said they caught the priest red-handed, and that by the power of his devil he had for the moment taken upon himself the semblance of a poacher, which deceived them and they did not suspect it was the priest. A quarrel followed, and the poacher tried to kill deceased, whereupon deceased, in self-defence, pulled his gun upon the poacher, but before he could fire, deceased, by black magic and devil's arts, turned deceased into the present rock, as here exhibited; then assumed his own proper shape and said with many ribald oaths that if any durst lay a hand upon him, by God he would perpetuate *his* substance likewise.

Then the jury rendered a verdict that deceased had come to his death by the visitation of God. Also the fly.

The coroner was not willing to accept the verdict, because it included the fly.

The jury insisted that they could not exclude the fly without irreverence, since God in His inscrutable wisdom had seen fit to honor the humble animal with an equal share in His visitation.

The coroner said it was manifest to any thoughtful mind that the overtaking of the fly by the visitation was an accident, and not intentional.

The foreman retorted, "if there has been an accident, then a verdict cannot be reached at all, since we have no way of determining which of the parties fell by accident and which by intention."

The coroner advanced the theory that the foreman was an ass; which made a great stir, Siebold the drunken artist and some others approving, and were called to order, and silence enjoined upon them. The coroner continued, "To the reflecting mind there is no difficulty here. The intention would necessarily be directed against the party in chief, which would be deceased, by right of his superior dignity as man, office-bearer and Christian, and not against the party of the second part, who, being without estate, position or legal recognition, cannot in reason claim precedence over the party of the first part in a so grave matter as the present, wherein the divine grace has manifestly purposed a rebuke to but one party and not both."

The foreman responded with some heat: "How do *you* know there was an accident? Is it in the character of the Deity to deal in accidents? (*Siebold*—Good!) Is He so poor a marksman as to fire at one and bring down two? (*Siebold*—Good again!) How do you know what the fly had been doing? Are you in the secret of the privacies of God? Is it your high privilege to sit in judgment upon His acts and determine for Him which of them are intentional and which of them are due to heedlessness and inattention—at *your* salary? It is self-conceit gone mad, it is blasphemous impertinence."

Several excited Jurymen. Stand by the verdict! stand by it!

The Foreman. Trust me to do my whole duty. Sir, this jury cannot concede, without the most awful irreverence, that an all-compassionate Providence would lift its hand against even so humble a creature as a fly without just and righteous cause. We cannot and will not concede that this fly fell by accident. This fly was guilty of an offence which is hidden from us and which we are not privileged to pry into. What it did is a secret between itself and its Creator (and perhaps the coroner!) but it *was* guilty, and that guilt is witnessed and forever established by its fate. Let it be a lesson to us all.

The Coroner. Then you stand to your verdict.

The Foreman, impressively. God helping us, we do; and to the issue we do solemnly commit our lives, our fortunes and our sacred honor. (*Voices.* Amen!) "Not even a sparrow falls," and so forth and so forth; and neither does a fly. This Christian—such as he was

—this alleged Christian fell by the dispensation of God; this fly likewise. Such is the verdict, and by it we stand or fall. *Wir können nicht anders.*

All the assemblage burst into a bravo of applause.

The Coroner, with dignity. Remove the fly from the image, and exclude it from the verdict. On no other terms will I accept a finding of the court.

The Foreman, sternly. It shall not be done.

The Coroner. The inquest is closed. There is no verdict. The absence of a verdict determining the cause of the man's death debars me from issuing the necessary burial-permit; deceased must therefore remain unburied—that is, in consecrated ground. He may be a suicide.

The family began to wail and plead, but the coroner was firm, saying, with a wave of his hand toward the image—

"The law must be respected. Remove the petrifaction."

It was loaded into a six-ox van by twenty-two men and followed to the Bart homestead by the weeping family and by the public, who walked uncovered, and there it was housed from view and crape hung upon the door. There was a wake that night, and next day the customary funeral-feast; and in every way the due and usual decencies were observed, even to the sending out of invitations (with the date blank), to the funeral. After some months, when the season of first-mourning had expired, the public exhibition began, and was inordinately successful, children and servants half price, and crowds coming from all over the Empire, and even from foreign countries, and many Italian image-dealers paying a commission for the privilege of making and selling small casts of it. The family quickly grew rich, and in the next generation obtained nobility in Germany at the usual rates. After many, many years it was sold, and passed from hand to hand and country to country, and now for a long time it has been in the Pitti palace in Florence, earning its living as a Roman antique.

Chapter 9

I wanted to know my whole history in advance, but I never asked Satan for it. I was afraid, for it might be an unhappy history. I could change it if I had the plan of it, but any change might happen to be for the worse. I knew this because Satan had shown me other people's lives and I saw that in nearly all cases there would be little or no advantage in altering them. He made maps of these lives, as cross-lined and intricate as spider-webs, and pointed out to me that while each change in a billion would introduce a new career, I could not trace any one of them very far without perceiving that as a rule it only skipped one kind of unhappiness to land in one of a different breed, and not any easier to bear. And there was another deterrent: I believed that to know my whole life beforehand would take the interest out of it. It would be destitute of surprises. No glad event could stir me, I should have discounted all its possible effects long before it arrived. I should fix my attention on coming griefs and calamities mainly, and be mourning and suffering on their account all the dragging years till their appointed dates came round and the disasters fell.

So I conquered my curiosity and left the secret of my future sealed, and I am sure it was best so. I did ask for Seppi's future, and got it instantly, beautifully printed in many large volumes, which I hid away and still possess. But I read only a page or two in the beginning. They spoiled a couple of days for me, for during that time Seppi was merely a weariness to me, because every smart remark he made had a stale sound—I had read it in the book; and there was no surprise in anything he did—I had read it in the book. After that, he was interesting again; for I allowed him to do his day and say his say, and then at night reviewed the performance in the book to see that he had been honest and had not skipped anything.

I found afterward that he had my life, and was following the same system. When we grew to manhood we were often separated

—sometimes years at a stretch—but the books kept us united. Every morning each of us read what was going to happen to the other that day. During separations we corresponded constantly, yet never wrote a letter. The letters which we were about to write, and which were in our minds, were always in the books—put there by Satan long before. Whenever a great joy or a great sorrow came into my life I took my book and read Seppi's letter of sympathy about it. And when a joy or a sorrow came into Seppi's life I knew that he was finding a letter from me in his book concerning it. I have lost a grandchild to-day. I have his good letter of pity and condolence in my book.

But I am wandering too far from my boyhood. We often got Satan to furnish us the happenings of the town a day in advance, and this was a very good scheme, and interesting. When there was to be an event, we turned out and made bets with the other boys and bankrupted them. The time that the church was to be struck by lightning, we stripped them clean. It was a particularly good opportunity, for nothing could have made them believe that God would strike his own house; so they were an easy prey. We betted that it would happen on the morrow; they took us up and gave us the odds of two to one; we betted that it would happen in the afternoon; we got odds of four to one on that; we betted that it would happen at two minutes to three; they willingly granted us the odds of ten to one on that. They went home rejoicing, and we were not sad ourselves.

Next day it was beautiful weather; at noon it was the same. The boys began to make fun of us, and said perhaps we wanted to make some more bets, and we said no, and looked depressed, as well as we could. This was to draw them on. They offered us multiplied odds, but we declined. It made them bolder, and they followed us up, increasing the odds, and we looking ashamed and regretful, and not taking them up. This also was to draw them on. It had that effect. They still followed us around and raised the odds, and got everybody to laughing at us, and all had a good time. At a quarter past 2 we were looking cowed—which was intentional, and made them lose the rest of their judgment. They raised the odds to the bursting point, and then all of a sudden we took them up!

At first they could not believe it, and were funnier over it than ever, for still the skies were bright. But only for a quarter of an hour. Then the clouds came and a storm began to gather. It grew blacker and blacker, and the lightnings began to glimmer and the thunder to mutter. The boys stopped laughing and began to look sober; and it was time. Then we began to jeer and offer odds, but there were no takers. They grew very anxious and went drifting toward the church, so that they could see the clock. At ten minutes to 3 the thunder was booming and the lightning glaring fiercely out on the gloom every little while. We all stood in the rain, unconscious of it, saying not a word, holding our breath, gaping at the creeping minute-hand. It crept and crept, dragged and dragged—it seemed weeks to those boys, no doubt. Then at 2 minutes to 3 there was a crash and a blinding flash, and the gilt Apostle over the great door was struck down.

There was not a marble, nor a top, nor a kite, nor any useful thing left in that town that did not belong to Seppi and me. And silbergroschen galore! It was a long time before those boys' fortunes recovered from that cataclysm. And when they did recover, at last, we could not get them to bet with us. They betted with each other, but were afraid to take risks with us, thinking we might be in league with the evil spirit which was occupying Father Adolf. But little by little we drew them on once more. This was by art. By a private arrangement Seppi made bets with me, in the boys' presence, and won them every time, he jeering and I losing my temper. So then they began to bet with me and I let them win, but they would not risk a bet with Seppi. At last they were ripe, and we set our trap for them. On a Monday Simon Hirsch was going to break his leg at seven minutes after 12, noon, and as soon as Satan told us the day before, Seppi went to betting with me that it would not happen, and soon they got excited and went to betting with me themselves. By working the game judiciously I presently had them in for all they were worth; and next day, sure enough, at 7 minutes after 12 we skinned them again, and divided the take. We were not sorry, for it was wrong for them to bet on Sunday. It seemed to me that it was a plain judgment on them. And not an accident, but intentional. Seppi said it was as manifest as the fly's case. Seppi knew about judgments, for his uncle was in the ministry.

We tried to sell advance-news to the man who wrote the daily news-letter in the cathedral town ten miles up the river, but he said we were fools: "how could we know what was going to happen next day." But we had already told him; so next day he saw that we had been right; then he was ready to buy, and we furnished him the news early enough so that he could get his news-letter out a whole day before the happenings happened. His circulation was much increased, and there was an excitement. We offered to sell him news a year in advance—a century if he liked; but his faith was not strong enough for that; he said a couple of days ahead was good enough for him. The excitement increased; and presently we were able to tell him a specially good item—that inside of twenty-four hours he would be in jail as a wizard. It came near to scaring him to death, and in the jail he sent for us to come and tell him some more of his future, and how to beat it if possible. Satan said he was due to be burnt in a week, but that if he would not answer the jailor's knock at once, that night, but count five, first, it would change his career and he would live fifteen years and then be hanged; but he must be exact, for if he counted only four he would get his throat cut before the end of the year, and if he counted six he would break his neck in three months and be certainly damned besides—he could have his choice. So we went and reported, and he was very grateful, and paid us nobly, and elected to be hanged.

It was wonderful, the mastery Satan had over time and distance. For him they did not exist. He called them human inventions, and said they were mere artificialities. We often went to the most distant parts of the globe with him, and stayed weeks and months, and yet were gone only a fraction of a second, as a rule. You could prove it by the clock. One day when our people were in such awful distress because the witch-commission were afraid to proceed against Father Adolf and Father Peter's household, or against any, indeed, but the poor and the friendless, they lost patience and took to witch-hunting on their own score, and began to chase a born lady who was known to have the habit of curing people by devilish arts, such as bathing them, washing them and nourishing them, instead of bleeding them and purging them through the ministrations of a barber-surgeon in the proper way. She came flying down, with the mob after her howling and cursing, and tried to take refuge in houses, but the doors were shut in her face. They chased her more than half an hour, we following, to see it, and at last she was exhausted, and fell, and they caught her. They dragged her to a tree and threw a rope over a limb and began to make a noose in it, some holding her, meantime, and she crying and begging, and her young daughter looking on and weeping, but afraid to say or do anything.

In a way it was dreadful; still it was brave in the people, seeing they were not backed up by authority, but were willing to do their Christian duty without it, a thing which was to our Church's credit, and I said so; and said only Catholics could have this courage. But Satan said—

"No, Protestants have it also. Come with me to Scotland and I will show you that which will rebuke your pride."

So we went. The Protestants were chasing a middle-aged gentle-woman who was charged by a servant with secretly practising the papist religion. She was large and strong, and horribly frightened, and she ran like a deer, her gray hair flying out loose behind; and whenever the mob came near to overtaking her she dodged quickly off on another course and got ahead again, and it seemed as if they would never catch her. But after two hours the clergyman arrived, and he said "form a half-circle and close in on her and drive her to the sea-beach." That worked better, and I think she lost hope, then. Still, she struggled on, in her despair, and it was another half hour before they caught her, so many ingenious ways did she invent to elude them. But at last she stumbled and fell, and before she could rise they were upon her, and a great shout of triumph went up. She struggled, but some held her down while others fetched a barn door and laid it upon her and stood on it. Even dying she struggled with such power that she made the door rock and surge under their feet for a little while; then all was still, and she was dead. And sure enough, *her* daughter stood apart and saw it all, weeping, but afraid to speak or try to help her mother. Satan said—

"There—you see? You have nothing to be proud of more than these Protestants. Come back to Eseldorf."

We had been gone more than three hours, and yet were back just as they finished making the noose. We had seen them begin it, it took them only a minute to finish it; and in that little interval we had spent all that time far away across the sea in Scotland. It was wonderful. They hanged the lady, and I threw a stone at her, although in my heart I was sorry for her; but all were throwing stones and each was watching his neighbor, and if I had not done as the others did it would have been noticed and spoken of. Satan burst out laughing.

All that were near by turned upon him astonished and not pleased. It was an ill time to laugh, for his free and scoffing ways and his supernatural music had brought him under suspicion all over the town and turned many privately against him. The big blacksmith called attention to him, now, raising his voice so that all should hear, and said—

"What are you laughing at? Answer! Moreover, please explain to the company why you threw no stone."

"Are you sure I did not throw a stone?"

"Yes. You needn't try to get out of it; I had my eye on you."

"And I—I noticed you!" shouted two others.

"Three witnesses," said Satan. "Müller, the blacksmith; Klein, the butcher's man; Pfeiffer, the weaver's journeyman. Three very ordinary liars. Are there any more?"

"Never mind whether there are others or not, and never mind about what *you* consider us—three's enough to settle your matter for you. You'll prove that you threw a stone, or it shall go hard with you."

"That's so!" shouted the crowd, and surged up as closely as they could to the centre of interest.

"And first you will answer that other question," cried the blacksmith, pleased with himself for being mouthpiece to the public and hero of the occasion. "What were you laughing at?"

Satan smiled, and answered pleasantly—

"To see three cowards stoning a dying lady when they were so near to death themselves."

You could see the superstitious crowd shrink and catch their breath under the sudden shock. The blacksmith, with a show of bravado, said—

"Pooh! what do you know about it?"

"I? Everything. By profession I am a fortune-teller, and I read the hands of you three—and some others—when you lifted them to stone the woman. One of you will die to-morrow week; another of you will die to-night; the third has but five minutes to live—and yonder is the clock!"

It made a sensation. The faces of the crowd blenched, and turned mechanically toward the clock. The butcher and the weaver seemed smitten with an illness, but the blacksmith braced up and said, with spirit—

"It is not long to wait for prediction Number One. If it fails, young master, you will not live a whole minute after, I promise you that."

No one said anything; all watched the clock in a deep stillness which was impressive. When four and a half minutes were gone, the blacksmith gave a sudden gasp and clapped his hand upon his heart, saying, "Give me breath! give me room!" and began to sink down. The crowd surged back, no one offering to support him, and he fell lumbering to the ground and was dead. The people stared at him, then at Satan, then at each other, and their lips moved but no words came. Then Satan said—

"Three saw that I threw no stone. Perhaps there are others; let them speak."

It struck a kind of panic into them, and although no one answered him, many began to violently accuse each other, saying, "*You* said he didn't throw," and getting for reply, "It is a lie, and I will make you eat it!" And so in a moment they were in a raging and noisy turmoil, and beating and banging each other; and in the midst was the only indifferent one—the dead lady hanging from her rope, her troubles forgotten, her spirit at peace.

So we walked away, and I was not at ease, but was saying to myself, "He told them he was laughing at them, but it was a lie, he was laughing at me."

That made him laugh again, and he said—

"Yes, I was laughing at you, because in fear of what others might report about you, you stoned the woman when your heart revolted at the act—but I was laughing at the others, too."

"Why?"

"Because their case was yours."

"How is that?"

"Well, there were sixty-eight people there, and sixty-two of them had no more desire to throw a stone than you had."

"Satan!"

"Oh, it's true. I know your race. It is made up of sheep. It is governed by minorities, seldom or never by majorities. It suppresses its feelings and its beliefs and follows the handful that makes the most noise. Sometimes the noisy handful is right, sometimes wrong; but no matter, the crowd follows it. The vast majority of the race, whether savage or civilized, are secretly kind-hearted, and shrink from inflicting pain; but in the presence of the aggressive and pitiless minority they don't dare to assert themselves. Think of it! one kind-hearted creature spies upon another, and sees to it that he loyally helps in iniquities which revolt both of them. Speaking as an expert, I *know* that ninety-nine out of a hundred of your race were strongly against the killing of witches when that foolishness was first agitated by a handful of pious lunatics in the long ago. And I know that even to-day, after ages of transmitted prejudice and silly teaching, only one person in twenty puts any real heart into the harrying of a witch. And yet apparently *everybody* hates witches and wants them killed. Some day a handful will rise up on the other side and make the most noise—perhaps even a single daring man with a big voice and a determined front will do it—and in a week all the sheep will wheel and follow him, and witch-hunting will come to a sudden end. In fact this happened within these ten years, in a little country called New England.

"Monarchies, aristocracies and religions are all based upon that large defect in your race—the individual's distrust of his neighbor, and his desire, for safety's or comfort's sake, to stand well in his neighbor's eyes. These institutions will always remain, always flourish, and always oppress you, affront you and degrade you, because you will always be and remain slaves of minorities. There was never a country where the majority of the people were in their secret hearts loyal to either of these institutions."

I did not like to hear our race called sheep, and said I did not think they were.

"Still, it is true, lamb," said Satan. "Look at you in war—what mutton you are, and how ridiculous."

"In war? How?"

"There has never been a just one, never an honorable one—on the part of the instigator of the war. I can see a million years ahead, and this rule will never change in so many as half a dozen instances. The loud little handful—as usual—will shout for the war. The pulpit will—warily and cautiously—object—at first; the great big dull bulk of the nation will rub its sleepy eyes and try to make out why there should be a war, and will say, earnestly and indignantly, "It is unjust and dishonorable, and there is no necessity for it." Then the handful will shout louder. A few fair men on the other side will argue and reason against the war with speech and pen, and at first will have a hearing and be applauded; but it will not last long; those others will out-shout them, and presently the anti-war audiences will thin out and lose popularity. Before long you will see this curious thing: the speakers stoned from the platform and free speech strangled, by hordes of furious men who in their secret hearts are still at one with those stoned speakers,—as earlier,—but do not dare to say so! And now the whole nation—pulpit and all—will take up the war-cry, and shout itself hoarse, and mob any honest man who ventures to open his mouth; and presently such mouths will cease to open. Next, the statesmen will

invent cheap lies, putting the blame upon the nation that is attacked, and every man will be glad of those conscience-soothing
falsities, and will diligently study them, and refuse to examine any
refutations of them; and thus he will by and by convince himself
that the war *is* just, and will thank God for the better sleep he
enjoys after this process of grotesque self-deception."

"But Satan, as civilization advances—"

Of course he broke in with a laugh. He never could hear that
word without jeering at it and making fun of it. He said he had
seen thirteen of them rise in the world and decay and perish to
savagery—three of them the superiors in every way to any now
known to the histories or to be known to the histories in the next
ten thousand years—and they were all poor things: shams and
hypocrisies and tyrannies, every one.

"Two centuries from now," he said, "the Christian civilization
will reach its highest mark. Yet its kings will still be, then, what
they are now, a close corporation of land-thieves. Is that an advance? England will be prodigious and strong; she will bear the
most honorable name that ever a nation bore, and will lose it in a
single little shameful war and carry the stench of it and the blot of
it to the end of her days. To please a dozen rich adventurers her
statesmen will pick a quarrel with a couple of wee little Christian
farmer-communities, and send against that half dozen villages the
mightiest army that ever invaded any country, and will crush
those little nations and rob them of their independence and their
land. She will make a noisy pretence of being proud of these things,
but deep down in her heart she will be ashamed of them and will
grieve for her soiled flag—once the symbol of liberty and honor and
justice, now the pirate's emblem."

"Satan," I said, "this would not happen if she could have the true
religion."

"Ah, yes—the kind of treasure which you have here in Austria.
My uncle is thinking of introducing it into his dominions."

It was shocking to hear him talk so.

"Satan," I said, "it would defile it!"

He only pulled down the corner of his eye with his finger.

Chapter 10

Days and days went by, now, and no Satan. It was dull without him. But Father Adolf was around braving public opinion in his impudent way and getting a stone in the middle of his back now and then when some witch-hater got a safe chance to throw it and dodge out of sight. Meantime two influences had been working well for Marget. Satan, who was quite indifferent to her, had stopped going to her house, and this had hurt her pride and she had set herself the task of banishing him from her heart; the reports of Wilhelm Meidling's dissipation brought to her from time to time by old Ursula had touched her with remorse, she being the cause of it; and so now, these two matters working upon her together, she was getting a good profit out of the combination: her interest in Satan was steadily cooling, her interest in Wilhelm as steadily warming. All that was needed to complete her conversion was that Wilhelm should brace up and do something that should cause favorable talk and incline the public toward him again.

The opportunity came, now. Marget sent and asked him to defend her uncle in the approaching trial, and he was greatly pleased, and stopped drinking and began his preparations with diligence. With more diligence than hope, in fact, for it was not a promising case. He had many interviews in his office with Seppi and me, and thrashed out our testimony pretty thoroughly, thinking to find some valuable grains among the chaff, but the harvest was poor, of course.

If Satan would only come! That was my constant thought. *He* could invent some way to win the case; for he had said it would be won, so he necessarily knew how it could be done. But the days dragged on, and still he did not come. Of course I did not doubt that it would win, and that Father Peter would be happy for the rest of his life, since Satan had said so; yet I knew I should be much more comfortable if he would come and tell us how to manage it. It was getting high time for Father Peter to have a saving change toward happiness, for by general report he was worn out with his imprisonment and the ignominy that was burdening him, and was like to die of his miseries unless he got relief soon.

At last the trial came on, and the people gathered from all around to witness it; among them many strangers from considerable distances. Yes, everybody was there, except the accused. He was too feeble in body for the strain. But Marget was present, and keeping up her hope and her spirit the best she could.

The money was present, too. It was emptied on the table, and was handled and caressed and examined by such as were privileged.

Father Adolf was put in the witness box.

Question. You claim that this money is yours?

Answer. I do.

Q. How did you come by it?

A. I found the bag in the road when I was returning from a journey.

Q. When?

A. More than two years ago.

Q. What did you do with it?

A. I brought it home and hid it in a secret place in my study, intending to find the owner if I could.

Q. You endeavored to find him?

A. I made diligent inquiry during several months, but nothing came of it.

Q. And then?

A. I thought it not worth while to look further, and was minded to use the money in finishing the wing of the foundling asylum connected with the priory and nunnery. So I took it out of its hiding-place and counted it to see if any of it was missing. And then—

Q. Why do you stop? Proceed.

A. I am sorry to have to say this, but just as I had finished and was restoring the bag to its place, I looked up and there stood Father Peter behind me.

Several murmured, "That looks bad," but others answered, "Ah, but he is such a liar!"

Q. That made you uneasy?

A. No, I thought nothing of it at the time, for Father Peter often came in unannounced to ask for a little help in his need.

Marget blushed crimson at hearing her uncle falsely and impudently charged with begging, and was going to speak, but remembered herself in time and held her peace.

Q. Proceed.

A. In the end I was afraid to contribute the money to the foundling asylum, but elected to wait yet another year and continue my inquiries. When I heard of Father Peter's find I was glad, and no suspicions entered my mind; when I came home a day or two later and discovered that my own money was gone I still did not suspect, until three circumstances connected with Father Peter's good fortune struck me as being singular coincidences.

Q. Pray name them.

A. Father Peter had found his money in a *path*—I had found mine in a *road*. Father Peter's find consisted exclusively of gold ducats—*mine also*. Father Peter found eleven hundred and seven ducats—I *exactly the same*.

This closed his evidence; and certainly it made a strong impression on the house; one could see that.

Wilhelm Meidling asked him some questions, then called us boys, and we told our tale. It made the people laugh, and we were ashamed. We were feeling pretty badly anyhow, because Wilhelm was hopeless, and showed it. He was doing as well as he could, poor young fellow, but nothing was in his favor, and such sympathy as there was was now plainly not with his client. It might be difficult for court and people to believe Father Adolf's story, considering his character, but it was almost impossible to believe Father Peter's. We were already feeling badly enough, but when Father Adolf's lawyer said he believed he would not ask us any questions, for our story was a little delicate and it would be cruel for him to put any strain upon it, everybody tittered, and it was almost more than we could bear. Then he made a sarcastic little speech, and got so much fun out of our tale, and made it seem so ridiculous and childish and every way impossible and foolish that it made everybody laugh till the tears came; and at last Marget could not keep up her courage any longer, but broke down and cried, and I was so sorry for her.

Now I noticed something that braced me up. It was Satan, standing alongside of Wilhelm! And there was such a contrast: Satan looked so confident, had such a spirit in his eyes and face, and Wilhelm looked so depressed and despondent. We two were comfortable now, and judged that he would testify, and would persuade the bench and the people that black was white and white black, or any other color he wanted it. We glanced around to see what the strangers in the house thought of him, for he was beautiful, you know; stunning, in fact; but no one was noticing him; so we knew by that that he was invisible.

That lawyer was saying his last words; and while he was saying them Satan began to melt into Wilhelm. He melted into him and disappeared; and then there was a change, when *his* spirit began to look out of Wilhelm's eyes.

That lawyer finished quite seriously, and with dignity. He pointed to the money, and said—

"The love of it is the root of all evil. There it lies, the ancient tempter, newly red with the shame of its latest victory—the dishonor of a priest of God and of his two poor juvenile helpers in crime. If it could but speak, let us hope that it would be constrained to confess that of all its conquests this was the basest and the most pathetic."

He sat down. Wilhelm rose, and said—

"From the testimony of the reverend Father Adolf I gather that he found this money in a road more than two years ago. Correct me, sir, if I misunderstood you."

Father Adolf said his understanding of it was correct.

"And that the money so found was never out of his hands thenceforth up to a certain definite date—the last day of last year. Correct me, sir, if I am wrong."

Father Adolf nodded his head. Wilhelm turned to the bench and said—

"If I prove that this money here was not *that* money, then it is not his?"

"Certainly not; but this is irregular. If you had such a witness it was your duty to give proper notice of it and have him here to—" He broke off and began to consult with the other judges. Meantime that other lawyer got up excited and began to protest against allowing new witnesses to be brought into the case at this late stage.

The judges decided that his contention was just and must be allowed.

"But this is not a new witness," said Wilhelm. "It has already been partly examined. I speak of the coin."

"The coin? What can the coin say?"

"It can say it is not the coin that Father Adolf once possessed. It can say it was not in existence last December. By its date it can say this."

And it was so! There was the greatest excitement in the court while that lawyer, and Father Adolf and the judges were reaching for coins and examining them and exclaiming. And everybody was full of admiration of Wilhelm's brightness in happening to think of that neat idea. At last order was called and the court said—

"All of the coins but four are of the date of the present year. The court tenders its sincere sympathy to the accused, and its deep regret that he, an innocent man, should through an unfortunate mistake have suffered the undeserved humiliation of imprisonment and trial. The case is dismissed."

So the money *could* speak, after all, though that lawyer thought it couldn't. The court rose, and almost everybody came forward to shake hands with Marget and congratulate her and then to shake with Wilhelm and praise him; and Satan had stepped out of Wilhelm and was standing around looking on full of interest, and people walking through him every which way, not knowing he was there. And Wilhelm could not explain why he only thought of the date on the coins at the last moment, instead of earlier; he said it just occurred to him all of a sudden, like an inspiration, and he brought it right out without any hesitation, for although he hadn't examined the coins he seemed somehow to know it was true. That was honest of him, and like him; another would have pretended he had thought of it earlier, and was keeping it back for a surprise.

He had dulled down a little, now; not much, but still you could notice that he hadn't that luminous look in his eyes that he had while Satan was in him. He nearly got it back, though, for a moment, when Marget came and praised him and thanked him, and couldn't keep him from seeing how proud she was of him. Father Adolf went off dissatisfied and cursing, and Solomon Isaacs gathered up the money and carried it away. It was Father Peter's for good and all, now.

Satan was gone. I judged that he had spirited himself to the jail to tell the prisoner the news; and in this I was right. Marget and the rest of us hurried thither at our best speed, in a great state of rejoicing.

Well, what Satan had done was this. He had appeared before that poor prisoner exclaiming—

"The trial is over, and you stand forever disgraced as a thief—by verdict of the court!"

The shock unseated the old man's reason. When we arrived, ten minutes later, he was parading pompously up and down and delivering commands to this and that and the other constable or jailor, and calling them Grand Chamberlain, and Prince This and Prince That, and Admiral of the Fleet, and Field Marshal in Command, and all such fustian, and was as happy as a bird. He thought he was Emperor!

Marget flung herself on his breast and cried, and indeed everybody was moved, almost to heart-break. He recognised Marget, but could not understand why she should cry. He patted her on the shoulder and said—

"Don't do it, dear; remember, there are witnesses, and it is not becoming in the Crown Princess. Tell me your trouble—it shall be mended; there is nothing the Emperor cannot do." Then he looked around and saw old Ursula with her apron to her eyes. He was puzzled at that, and said, "And what is the matter with *you?*"

Through her sobs she got out words explaining that she was distressed to see him—"so." He reflected over that a moment, then muttered, as if to himself, "A singular old thing, the Dowager Duchess—means well, but is always snuffling, and never able to tell what it is about. It is because she doesn't know." His eye fell on Wilhelm. "Prince of India," he said, "I divine that it is you that the Crown Princess is concerned about. Her tears shall be dried; I will no longer stand between you; she shall share your throne; and between you, you shall inherit mine. There, little lady, have I done well? you can smile, now—isn't it so?"

He petted Marget, and kissed her, and was so contented with himself and with everybody, that he could not do enough for us all, but began to give away kingdoms and such things right and left, and the least that any of us got was a principality. And so at last being persuaded to go home, he marched in imposing state, and when the crowds along the way saw how it gratified him to be hurrah'd at, they humored him to the top of his desire, and he responded with condescending bows and gracious smiles, and often stretched out a hand and said "Bless you, my people."

As pitiful a sight as ever I saw. And Marget and old Ursula crying, all the way.

On my road home I came upon Satan, and reproached him for deceiving me with that lie. He was not embarrassed, but said, quite simply and composedly—

"Ah, you mistake—it was the truth. I said he would be happy the rest of his days, and he will. For he will always think he is the Emperor, and his pride in it and his joy in it will endure to the end. He is now, and will remain, the one utterly happy person in this Empire."

"But the method of it, Satan, the method! Couldn't you have done it without depriving him of his reason?"

It was difficult to irritate Satan, but that accomplished it.

"What an ass you are!" he said. "Are you so unobservant as not to have found out that sanity and happiness are an impossible combination? No sane man can be happy, for to him life is real, and he sees what a fearful thing it is. Only the mad can be happy, and not many of those. The few that imagine themselves kings or gods are happy, the rest are no happier than the sane. Of course no man is entirely in his right mind at any time, but I have been referring to the extreme cases. I have taken from this man that trumpery thing which the race regards as a Mind; I have replaced his tin life with a silver-gilt fiction; you see the result—and you criticise! I said I would make him permanently happy, and I have done it. I have made him happy by the only means possible to his race—and you are not satisfied!" He heaved a discouraged sigh, and said, "It seems to me that this race is hard to please."

There it was, you see. He didn't seem to know any way to do a person a favor except by killing him or making a lunatic out of him. I apologised, as well as I could; but privately I did not think much of his processes. At that time.

Satan was accustomed to say that our race lived a life of continuous and uninterrupted self-deception. It duped itself from cradle to grave with shams and delusions which it mistook for realities, and this made its entire life a sham. Of the score of fine qualities which it imagined it had, and was vain of, it really possessed hardly one. It regarded itself as gold, and was only brass. One day when he was in this vein, he mentioned a detail—the sense of humor. I cheered up, then, and took issue. I said we possessed it.

"There spoke the race!" he said; "always ready to claim what it hasn't got, and mistake its ounce of brass filings for a ton of gold dust. You have a bastard perception of humor, nothing more; a multitude of you possess that. This multitude see the comic side of a thousand low-grade and trivial things—broad incongruities, mainly; grotesqueries, absurdities, evokers of the horse-laugh. The ten thousand high-grade comicalities which exist in the world are sealed from their dull vision, they are unconscious of their presence. The ten thousand are hid from the entire race."

By request he proceeded to name some of them.

"No religion exists which is not littered with engaging and

delightful comicalities, but the race never perceives them. Nothing can be more deliciously comical than hereditary royalties and aristocracies, but none except royal families and aristocrats are aware of it."

"Are *they?*"

"Oh, *aren't* they! Often they cannot sleep for laughing at their dependents. It would surprise you to know the names they privately call them by."

"But republics and democracies see, don't they?"

"Oh, no—and never will. While they scoff with their mouths they reverence them in their hearts. That democrat will never live who will marry a democrat into his family when he can get a duke. All forms of government—including republican and democratic—are rich in funny shams and absurdities, but their supporters do not see it."

It took him an hour to list a lot of the comicalities which the race is not capable of perceiving, then he left off. He said it would take him a month to name the rest.

Intercourse with him had colored my mind, of course, he being a strong personality and I a weak one; therefore I was inclined to think his position correct, but I did not say it. I only said our race was progressing, and that in time its sense of humor would develop to a point where it would enable us to perceive many things which we cannot see now.

But he only made fun of that idea, and said—

"The race had as much humor-perception when it was created as it has now, and it will never have any more. Look at the Pope's infallibility. Does any one see the humor of that? Not a soul, except the Pope and the Conclave. Look at his loosing-and-binding authority—which is not confined to earth, but which even God on His throne is obliged to submit to—as per the claim. Does any one see the humor of that? Not a soul outside the Vatican. Heretics rage about it, but no one laughs at it. Will a day come when the race will detect the funniness of these juvenilities and laugh at them—and by laughing at them destroy them? For your race, in its poverty, has unquestionably one really effective weapon—laughter. Power,

Money, Persuasion, Supplication, Persecution—these can lift at a colossal humbug,—push it a little—crowd it a little—weaken it a little, century by century: but only Laughter can blow it to rags and atoms at a blast. Against the assault of Laughter nothing can stand. You are always fussing and fighting with your other weapons: do you ever use that one? No, you leave it lying rusting. As a race, do you ever use it at all? No—you lack sense and the courage. Once in an age a single hero lifts it, delivers his blow, and a hoary humbug goes to ruin. Before this century closes, Robert Burns, a peasant, will break the back of the Presbyterian Church with it, and set Scotland free. I ask you again: will a day come when the race will have so developed its humor-perception as to be able to detect the funniness of Papal Infallibility and God-subordinating Papal Authority?"

"I think so."

"When?"

"Well, not in my time, maybe, but in a century, anyway."

A newspaper flashed into his hand.

"Not in two centuries," he said. "I will prove it. Two centuries from now, a king of Italy will be assassinated. He will be under excommunication at the time—that is to say, damned to perdition by the Pope; and whom the Pope damns, Heaven itself is impotent to save—as per the claim. Here is a journal which will issue from the press in those days; we may cull from it some historical facts in advance of their occurrence; details that are full of hideous humor, but in that day the race will be as unconscious of it as it would be to-day. In her grief the widowed Queen will compose a prayer. What will she do with it? Prostrate herself and pour it into the ear of God? No. Being a good Catholic, she will know the forms of holy etiquette better. She will submit it to a Bishop, in the hope that through his influence she may get permission to pray it, in case it shall be found to be a proper kind of prayer—and regular. Is that funny? Your race will not suspect it. The Bishop will inspect the prayer, dissect it, analyse it, submit it to an ecclesiastical fire-assay, and will decide that it is innocuous. He will then lay it before the Pope, together with his expert-report and the mourner's supplication for permission to pray it. Now it is not good form to intrude my uncle's acquired subjects upon the Deity's attention, and the Pope will know that; but being a kind-hearted old man he will waive etiquette for charity's sake, and 'by his express sanction' the widow will get leave to say her prayer—at last. This is an utter and thorough endorsement of the prayer by an authority whose judgments are infallible and whose verdicts cannot be set aside by any Power in heaven or earth. The Pope will carry his generosity still further: he will order fifty pulpits to pump that same prayer into heaven. Why? If it is bad form to allow one person to intrude a subject of Satan upon the Deity's attention, is it better form to set fifty at it? Will the people of that day see the grotesqueness of the situation? No, they will contemplate it with petrified gravity. Next, 'the French clerical press' will 'complain that the interests of the Church are compromised by this display of Christian spirit,' and the Pope's note will be 'abruptly changed.' The official organ of the Vatican will announce that the religious services for the dead King were 'tolerated,' but that the Queen's prayer must be suppressed as 'incompatible with the Holy Liturgy.' It will be considered 'impolitic' to show Christian gentleness to a sorrowing widow, and so 'the concession which was made to her' will be 'rudely withdrawn.' This is Papal 'infallibility.' Will the humor of it be perceived? No—not by the public. Meantime the prayer has been received in heaven from fifty-one sources—and recorded. The record will be meekly expunged—by order from below. Is that funny—or isn't it? I think it is; in fact I know it is; but none of your race will find it out. Why don't you laugh?"

I said I was too much hurt to laugh. I said our religion was our stay, our solace and our hope; it was the most precious thing we had, and I could not bear to hear its sacred servants derided.

I think it touched him; for he became gentle and kind at once, and set about banishing my trouble from my mind. It did not take him long—it never did. He flashed me around the globe, stopping an hour or a week, at intervals, in one or another strange country, and doing the whole journey in a few minutes by the clock, and I was in a condition of contentment before we had covered the first stage. Satan was always good and considerate, that way. He liked to rough a person up, but he liked to smooth him down again just as well.

We stopped at a little city in India and looked on while a juggler did his tricks before a group of natives. They were wonderful, but I knew Satan could beat that game, and I begged him to show off a little, and he said he would. He changed himself into a native, in turban and breech-clout, and very considerately conferred on me a temporary knowledge of the language.

The juggler exhibited a seed, covered it with earth in a small flower-pot, then put a rag over the pot; after a minute the rag began to rise; in ten minutes it had risen a foot; then the rag was removed and a little tree was exposed, which had leaves upon it and ripe fruit. We ate the fruit, and it was good. But Satan said—

"Why do you cover the pot? Can't you grow the tree in the sunlight?"

"No," said the juggler; "no one can do that."

"You are only an apprentice; you don't know your trade. Give me seed—I will show you."

He took the seed, and said—

"What shall I raise from it?"

"It is a cherry seed; of course you will raise a cherry."

"Oh, no—that is a trifle; any novice can do it. Shall I raise an orange tree from it?"

"Oh, yes!" and the juggler laughed.

"And shall I make it bear other fruits as well as oranges?"

"If God wills!" and they all laughed.

Satan put the seed on the ground, put a handful of dust on it, and said—

"Rise!"

A tiny stem shot up and began to grow; and grew so fast that in five minutes it was a great tree and we were sitting in the shade of it. There was a murmur of wonder, then all looked up and saw a strange and pretty sight; for the branches were heavy with fruits of many kinds and colors—oranges, grapes, bananas, peaches, cherries, apricots and so on. Baskets were brought, and the unlading of the tree began; and the people crowded around Satan and kissed his hand, and praised him, calling him the prince of jugglers. The news went about the town, and everybody came running to see the wonder—and they remembered to bring baskets, too. But the tree was equal to the occasion; it put out new fruits as fast as any were removed; baskets were filled by the score and by the hundred, but always the supply remained undiminished. At last a foreigner in white linen and sun-helmet arrived, and exclaimed angrily—

"Away from here! Clear out, you dogs; the tree is on my lands, and is my property."

The natives put down their baskets and made humble obeisance. Satan made humble obeisance, too, with his fingers to his forehead, in the native way, and said—

"Please let them have their pleasure for an hour, sir—only that, and no longer. Afterward you may forbid them; and you will still have more fruit than you and the State together can consume in a year."

This made the foreigner very angry, and he cried out—

"Who are *you*, you vagabond, to tell your betters what they may do and what they mayn't!" and he struck Satan with his cane and followed this error with a kick.

The fruits rotted on the branches, and the leaves withered and fell.

The foreigner gazed at the bare limbs with the look of one who is surprised, and not gratified. Satan said—

"Take good care of the tree, for its health and yours are bound up together. It will never bear again, but if you tend it well it will live long. Water its roots once in each hour every night—and do it yourself, it must not be done by proxy, and to do it in daylight will not answer. If you fail only once in any night, the tree will die, and you likewise. Do not go home to your own country any more—you would not reach there; make no business or pleasure engagements which require you to go outside your gate at night—you cannot afford the risk; do not rent or sell this place—it would be injudicious."

The foreigner was proud, and wouldn't beg, but I thought he

looked as if he would like to. While he stood gazing at Satan, we vanished away and landed in Ceylon.

I was sorry for that man; sorry Satan hadn't been his customary self and killed him. It would have been a mercy. Satan overheard the thought, and said—

"I would have done it, but for his wife, who has not offended me. She is coming to him presently from their native land, Portugal. She is well, but has not long to live, and has been yearning to see him and persuade him to go back with her next year. She will die without knowing he can't leave that place."

"He won't tell her?"

"He? He will not trust that secret with any one; he will reflect that it could be revealed in sleep, in the hearing of some Portuguese guest's servant, some time or other."

"Did none of those natives understand what you said to him?"

"None of them understood, but he will always be afraid that some of them did. That fear will be a torture to him; for he has been a harsh master to them. In his dreams he will imagine them chopping his tree down. That will make his days uncomfortable—I have already arranged for his nights."

It grieved me, though not sharply, to see him take such a malicious satisfaction in his plans for this foreigner.

"Does he believe what you told him, Satan?"

"He thought he didn't, but our vanishing helped. The tree, where there had been no tree before—that helped. The insane and uncanny variety of fruits—the sudden withering—all these things are helps. Let him think as he may, reason as he may, one thing is certain—he will water the tree. But between this and night he will begin his changed career with a very natural precaution—for him."

"What is that?"

"He will fetch a priest to cast out the tree's devil. You are such a humorous race—and don't suspect it."

"Will he tell the priest?"

"No. He will say a juggler from Bombay created it, and that he wants the juggler's devil driven out of it, so that it will thrive and be fruitful again. The priest's incantations will fail; then the Portuguese will give up that scheme and get his watering-pot ready."

"But the priest will burn the tree. I know it; he will not allow it to remain."

"Yes, and anywhere in Europe he would burn the man, too. But in India the people are civilized, and these things will not happen. The man will drive the priest away and take care of the tree."

I reflected a little, then said—

"Satan, you have given him a hard life, I think."

"Comparatively. It must not be mistaken for a holiday."

"What is the man doing now?"

"Sorrowing. Sorrowing, and getting ready for the night. He will sit with his clothes on and an alarm-clock at his elbow. Last night he slept in a bed for the last time in this life—at night, I mean."

"Satan, it is horrible!"

"Comparatively. To-morrow he will lay in fifteen alarm-clocks; he will never trust his life to one, nor to half a dozen."

"What will he tell his wife when she comes?"

"Several quite excusable lies."

"Won't the alarm clocks disturb her, when they all go off at once?"

"Along at first, yes. They will make her jump out of bed. Eight times the first night. She will go and expostulate with her husband, and complain that her sleep is too periodical. He will explain—with lies—saying he is engaged in important scientific experiments; and he will plead with her to be patient with them and learn to love them, for his sake. And he will pet her and persuade her. But this cannot last for long."

"No, I believe it."

"The third day she will go and destroy the clocks while he is taking his sleep. He will be frightened nearly to death when he wakes and learns of his disaster; and she will be so moved by his distress that she will go and buy a new outfit of clocks herself, and will let him have his way after that."

"But she will pine away with loss of sleep, and die, Satan."

"No, she will accommodate her life to the new circumstances. She will sleep in the daytime, and sit up with him, nights. She will thus have his society and be quite content. She will never quite get the hang of his experiments, but he will make her believe that in time they will restore the tree, and make it the marvel and wonder it was at first, and people will cross the ocean to see it. Then she will be interested, and will offer to do the watering herself, but will be excused."

"Poor thing!"

"No, not she. She will be happy, and proud of her scientific husband, and hopefully expectant of his success until her latest day —and that is not far off."

"God keep her in ignorance!"

"Her husband will assist."

Chapter 11

MY APPETITE was not satisfied, it was only sharpened; I wanted to see Satan show off some more. It was a delight to me to see him astonish people; it was a private pride to me, too, and pleased my vanity, for I was envied, as being friend and comrade to so great a magician. Satan was willing to content my desire, and said there was an opportunity now, up in the hills not twenty miles away, in the palace of a native of wealth and high degree. We were there in a moment, Satan properly clothed for the occasion in silks of rich color loosely draped about his slender black figure, and on his head a handsome turban with gold stripes winding in and out among its folds. He had made his age about twenty-five. On a dais at the end of a noble hall sat the host, a blaze of gaudy silks and flashing jewels, and in front of him on oriental rugs sat forty or fifty natives in fine apparel. A magician of great renown was about to perform.

He held up a small ivory ball, so that all might see it, then gave it to a young man and told him to carry it away and hide it. The young man departed, and returned after a little time. The magician now tied a bandage over his eyes, and said he would go and find the ball. He felt his way along, with a cane, and many witnesses followed, to see if he succeeded. He wandered here and there and yonder about the great garden, not hesitating but moving with confidence, and at last he bent quickly down and apparently took the ball out from under a covering of loose moss and leaves at the root of a tree, and held it up. He and the witnesses came back and reported to the Rajah, who marveled greatly, and ordered a present of twenty gold mohurs to be given to the miracle-worker. Then Satan made a deep obeisance toward the chair of state, and said—

"I am also a magician, your Highness, and by my science I am able to perceive that this is not a wonderful thing. The young man who professed to hide the ball is the magician's confederate. He hid no ball; the magician found no ball. The confederate's ball is in his girdle, the magician's ball lies in his hand. With a confederate's help, this trick is nothing."

The magician loudly protested, and said he was not acquainted with the young man who had assisted him, and did not know he had a ball; and in any case the young man's ball had not been used. Satan asked—

"Could you tell your ball from the other if they were together?"

"Certainly."

"If your Highness will deign to give the command—"

His Highness ordered that the two balls be brought to him. He rolled them about in his hands, then held them exposed in his palm. The magician made choice promptly, saying—

"This is mine; I recognise it easily. To others they may seem alike —to me they are not so."

The Rajah wondered at his sharpness of eye, and said it was amazing. He supposed the incident closed, and was going to order some more gold mohurs, but Satan interrupted respectfully and asked the magician—

"Is your ball hollow, and is there something concealed in it?"

"Certainly not."

"Then that is not his ball, your Highness. Will your Highness be pleased to take it and unscrew its parts?"

"What is in it?"

"A diamond, your Highness."

Schoolhouse Hill

Chapter 1

I T W A S not much short of fifty years ago—and a frosty morning. Up the naked long slant of Schoolhouse Hill the boys and girls of Petersburg village were struggling from various directions against the fierce wind, and making slow and difficult progress. The wind was not the only hindrance, nor the worst; the slope was steel-clad in frozen snow, and the foothold offered was far from trustworthy. Every now and then a boy who had almost gained the schoolhouse stepped out with too much confidence, thinking himself safe, lost his footing, struck upon his back and went skimming down the hill behind his freed sled, the straggling schoolmates scrambling out of his way and applauding as he sailed by; and in a few seconds he was at the bottom with all his work to do over again. But this was fun; fun for the boy, fun for the witnesses, fun all around; for boys and girls are ignorant and do not know trouble when they see it.

Sid Sawyer, the good boy, the model boy, the cautious boy, did not lose his footing. He brought no sled, he chose his steps with care, and he arrived in safety. Tom Sawyer brought his sled and he, also, arrived without adventure, for Huck Finn was along to help, although he was not a member of the school in these days; he merely came in order to be with Tom until school "took in." Henry

Bascom arrived safely, too—Henry Bascom the new boy of last year, whose papa was a "nigger" trader and rich; a mean boy, he was, and proud of his clothes, and he had a play-slaughterhouse at home, with all the equipment, in little, of a regular slaughterhouse, and in it he slaughtered puppies and kittens exactly as beeves were done to death down at the "Point;" and he was this year's school-bully, and was dreaded and flattered by the timid and the weak and disliked by everybody. He arrived safely because his slave-boy Jake helped him up the hill and drew his sled for him; and it wasn't a home-made sled but a "store" sled, and was painted, and had iron-tyred runners, and came from St. Louis, and was the only store-sled in the village.

All the twenty-five or thirty boys and girls arrived at last, red and panting, and still cold, notwithstanding their yarn comforters and mufflers and mittens; and the girls flocked into the little school-house and the boys packed themselves together in the shelter of its lee.

It was noticed now that a new boy was present, and this was a matter of extraordinary interest, for a new boy in the village was a rarer sight than a new comet in the sky. He was apparently about fifteen; his clothes were neat and tasty above the common, he had a good and winning face, and he was surpassingly handsome—handsome beyond imagination! His eyes were deep and rich and beautiful, and there was a modesty and dignity and grace and gracious-ness and charm about him which some of the boys, with a pleased surprise, recognised at once as familiar—they had encountered it in books about fairy-tale princes and that sort. They stared at him with a trying backwoods frankness, but he was tranquil and did not seem troubled by it. After looking him over, Henry Bascom pushed forward in front of the others and began in an insolent tone to question him:

"Who are you? What's your name?"

The boy slowly shook his head, as if meaning by that that he did not understand.

"Do you hear? Answer up!"

Another slow shake.

"Answer up, I tell you, or I'll make you!"

Tom Sawyer said—

"That's no way, Henry Bascom—it's against the rules. If you want your fuss, and can't wait till recess, which is regular, go at it right and fair; put a chip on your shoulder and dare him to knock it off."

"All right; he's got to fight, and fight now, whether he answers or not; and I'm not particular about how it's got at." He put a flake of ice on his shoulder and said, "There—knock it off if you dare!"

The boy looked inquiringly from face to face, and Tom stepped up and answered by signs. He touched the boy's right hand, then flipped off the ice with his own, put it back in its place, and indicated that that was what the boy must do. The lad smiled, put out his hand, and touched the ice with his finger. Bascom launched a blow at his face which seemed to miss; the energy of it made Bascom slip on the ice, and he departed on his back for the bottom of the hill, with cordial laughter and mock applause from the boys to cheer his way.

The bell began to ring, and the little crowd swarmed into the schoolhouse and hurried to their places. The stranger found a seat apart, and was at once a target for the wondering eyes and eager whisperings of the girls. School now "began." Archibald Ferguson, the old Scotch schoolmaster, rapped upon his desk with his ruler, rose upon his dais and stood, with his hands together, and said "Let us pray." After the prayer there was a hymn, then the buzz of study began, and the multiplication class was called up. It recited, up to "twelve times twelve;" then the arithmetic class followed and exposed its slates to much censure and little commendation; next came the grammar class of parsing parrots, who knew everything about grammar except how to utilize its rules in common speech.

"Spelling class!" The schoolmaster's wandering eye now fell upon the new boy, and he countermanded that order. "Hm—a stranger? Who is it? What is your name, my boy?"

The lad rose and bowed, and said—

"Pardon, monsieur—je ne comprends pas."

Ferguson looked astonished and pleased, and said, in French—

"Ah, French—how pleasant! It is the first time I have heard that tongue in many years. I am the only person in this village who speaks it. You are very welcome; I shall be glad to renew my practice. You speak no English?"

"Not a word, sir."

"You must try to learn it."

"Gladly, sir."

"It is your purpose to attend my school regularly?"

"If I may have the privilege, sir."

"That is well. Take English only, for the present. The grammar has about thirty rules. It will be necessary to learn them by heart."

"I already know them, sir, but I do not know what the words mean."

"What is it you say? You know the rules of the grammar, and yet don't know English? How can that be? When did you learn them?"

"I heard your grammar class recite the rules before entering upon the rest of their lesson."

The teacher looked over his glasses at the boy a while, in a puzzled way, then said—

"If you know no English words, how did you know it was a grammar lesson?"

"From similarities to the French—like the word grammar itself."

"True! You have a headpiece! You will soon get the rules by heart."

"I know them by heart, sir."

"Impossible! You are speaking extravagantly; you do not know what you are saying."

The boy bowed respectfully, resumed his upright position, and said nothing. The teacher felt rebuked, and said gently—

"I should not have spoken so, and am sorry. Overlook it, my boy; recite me a rule of grammar—as well as you can—never mind the mistakes."

The boy began with the first rule and went along with his task quite simply and comfortably, dropping rule after rule unmutilated from his lips, while the teacher and the school sat with parted lips and suspended breath, listening in mute wonder. At the finish the boy bowed again, and stood, waiting. Ferguson sat silent a moment or two in his great chair, then said—

"On your honor—those rules were wholly unknown to you when you came into this house?"

"Yes, sir."

"Upon my word I believe you, on the veracity that is written in your face. No—I don't—I can't. It is beyond the reach of belief. A memory like that—an ear for pronunciation like that, is of course im— why, *no* one in the earth has such a memory as that!"

The boy bowed, and said nothing. Again the old Scot felt rebuked, and said—

"Of course I don't mean—I don't really mean—er—tell me: if you could *prove* in some way that you have never until now—for instance, if you could repeat other things which you have heard here. Will you try?"

With engaging simplicity and serenity, and with apparently no intention of being funny, the boy began on the arithmetic lesson, and faithfully put into his report everything the teacher had said and everything the pupils had said, and imitated the voices and style of all concerned—as follows:

"Well, I give you my word it's enough to drive a man back to the land of his fathers, and make him hide his head in the charitable heather and never more give out that *he* can teach the race! Five slates—five of the chiefest intelligences in the school—and look at them! Scots wha hae wi' Wallace bled—Harry Slater! *Yes, sir.* Since when, is it, that 17, and 45, and 68 and 21 make 155, ye unspeakable creature? *I—I—if you please, sir, Sally Fitch hunched me and I reckon it made me make a figure 9 when I was intending to make a—* There's not a 9 in the sum, you blockhead!—and ye'll get a black mark for the lie you've told; a foolish lie, ill wrought and clumsy in the invention; you have no talent—stick to the truth. Becky Thatcher! *Yes, sir, please.* Make the curtsy over again, and do it better. *Yes, sir.* Lower, still! *Yes, sir.* Very good. Now I'll just ask you how you make out that 58 from 156 leaves 43? *If you please, sir, I subtracted the 8 from the 6, which leaves—which leaves—I* THINK *it leaves 3—and then—* Peace! ye banks and braes o' bonny Doon but it's a rare answer and a credit to my patient teaching! Jack Stillson! *Yes, sir.* Straighten up, and don't d-r-a-w-l like that—it's a fatigue to hear ye! And what *have* you been setting down here: If a horse travel 96 feet in 4 seconds and two-tenths of a second, how much will a barrel of mackerel cost when potatoes are 22 cents a bushel? Answer—eleven dollars and forty-six cents. You incurable ass, don't you see that ye've mixed three questions into one? The gauds and vanities o' learning! Oh, here's a hand, my trusty fere, and gie's a hand o' thine, and we'll—out of my sight, ye maundering idiot!—"

The show was become unendurable. The boy had forgotten not a word, nor a tone, nor a look, nor a gesture, nor any shade or trifle of detail—he was letter-perfect, and the house could shut its eyes anywhere in the performance and know which individual was being imitated. The boy's deep gravity and sincerity made the exhibition more and more trying the longer he went on. For a time, in decorous, disciplined and heroic silence, house and teacher sat bursting to laugh, with the tears running down, the regulations requiring noiseless propriety and solemnity; but when the stranger recited the answer to the triple sum and then put his hands together and raised his despairing eyes toward heaven in exact imitation of Mr. Ferguson's manner, the teacher's face broke up; and with that concession the house let go with a crash and laughed its fill thenceforth. But the boy went tranquilly on and on, unheeding the screams and throes and explosions, clear to the finish; then made his bow and straightened up and stood, bland and waiting.

It took some time to quiet the school; then Mr. Ferguson said—

"It is the most extraordinary thing I have seen in my life. In this world there is not another talent like yours, lad; be grateful for it, and for the noble modesty with which you bear about such a treasure. How long would you be able to keep in your memory the things which you have been uttering?"

"I cannot forget anything that I see or hear, sir."

"At all?"

"No, sir."

"It seems incredible—just impossible. Let me experiment a little —for the pure joy of it. Take my English-French dictionary and sit down and study it while I go on with the school's exercises. Shall you be disturbed by us?"

"No, sir."

He took the dictionary and began to skim the pages swiftly, one after another. Evidently he dwelt upon no page, but merely gave it a lick from top to bottom with his eye and turned it over. The school-work rambled on after a fashion, but it consisted of blunders, mainly, for the fascinated eyes and minds of school and teacher were oftener on the young stranger than elsewhere. At the end of twenty minutes the boy laid the book down. Mr. Ferguson noticed this, and said, with a touch of disappointment in his tone—

"I am sorry. I saw that it did not interest you."

The boy rose and said—

"Oh, sir, on the contrary!" This in French; then in English, "I have now the words of your language, but the forms not—perhaps, how you call?—the pronunciation also."

"You have the words? How many of the words do you know?"

"All, sir."

"No—no—there are 645 octavo pages—you couldn't have examined a tenth of them in this short time. A page in two seconds?—it is impossible."

The boy bowed respectfully, and said nothing.

"There—I am in fault again. I shall learn of you—courtesy. Give me the book. Begin. Recite—recite!"

It was another miracle. The boy poured out, in a rushing stream, the words, the definitions, the accompanying illustrative phrases and sentences, the signs indicating the parts of speech—everything; he skipped nothing, he put in all the details, and he even got the pronunciations substantially right, since it was a pronouncing-dictionary. Teacher and school sat in a soundless and motionless spell of awe and admiration, unconscious of the flight of time, unconscious of everything but the beautiful stranger and his stupendous performance. After a long while the juggler interrupted his recitation to say—in rather cumbrous and booky English—

"It is of necessity—what you call 'of course,' n'est-ce pas?—that I now am enabled to apply the machinery of the rules of the grammar, since the meanings of the words which constitute them were become my possession—" Here he stopped, quoted the violated rule, corrected his sentence, then went on: "And it is of course that

I now understand the languages—language—appropriated to the lesson of arithmetic—yet not all, the dictionary being in the offensive. As for example, to-wit, 'Scots wha hae wi' Wallace bled, Sally Fitch *hunched* me, ye banks and braes o' bonny Doon, oh here's a hand my trusty fere and gie's a hand o' thine.' Some of these words are by mischance omitted from the dictionary, and thereby results confusion. Without knowledge of the signification of *hunched* one is ignorant of the nature of the explanation preferred by the mademoiselle Thatcher; and if one shall not know what a Doon is, and whether it is a financial bank or other that is involved, one is still yet again at a loss."

Silence. The master roused himself as if from a dream, and lifted his hands and said—

"It is not a parrot—it *thinks!* Boy, ye are a marvel! With listening an hour and studying half as long, you have learned the English language. You are the only person in America that knows all its words. Let it rest, where it is—the construction will come of itself. Take up the Latin, now, and the Greek, and short-hand writing, and the mathematics. Here are the books. You shall have thirty minutes to each. Then your education will be complete. But tell me! How do you manage these things? What is your method? You do not read the page, you only skim it down with your eye, as one wipes a column of sums from a slate. You understand my English?"

"Yes, master—perfectly. I have no method—meaning I have no mystery. I see what is on the page—that is all."

"But you see it at a glance."

"But is not the particulars of the page—" He stopped to apply the rule and correct the sentence: "are not the particulars of the page the same as the particulars of the school? I see all the pupils at once; do I not know, then, how each is dressed, and his attitude and expression, and the color of his eyes and hair, and the length of his nose, and if his shoes are tied or not? Why shall I glance twice?"

Margaret Stover, over in the corner, drew her untied shoe back out of sight.

"Ah, well, I have seen no one else who could individualize a thousand details with one sweep of the two eyes. Maybe the eyes of the admirable creature the dragon-fly can do it, but that is another matter—he has twelve thousand, and so the haul he makes with his multitudinous glance is a thing within reason and comprehension. Get at your Latin, lad." Then with a sigh, "We will proceed with our poor dull ploddings."

The boy took up the book and began to turn the pages, much as if he were carefully counting them. The school glanced with an evil joy at Henry Bascom, and was pleased to note that he was not happy. He was the only Latin pupil in the school, and his pride in this distinction was a thing through which his mates were made to endure much suffering.

The school droned and buzzed along, with the bulk of its mind and its interest not on its work but fixed in envy and discouragement upon the new scholar. At the end of half an hour it saw him lay down his Latin book and take up the Greek; it glanced contentedly at Henry Bascom, and a satisfied murmur dribbled down the benches. In turn the Greek and the mathematics were mastered, then "The New Short-Hand Method, called Phonography" was taken up. But the phonographic study was short-lived—it lasted but a minute and twenty seconds; then the boy played with several other books. The master noticed this, and by and by said—

"So soon done with the Phonography?"

"It is only a set of compact and simple *principles*, sir. They are applicable with ease and certainty—like the principles of the mathematics. Also, the examples assist; innumerable combinations of English words are given, and the vowels eliminated. It is admirable, this system, for precision and clarity; one could write Greek and Latin with it, making word-combinations with the vowels excised, and still be understood."

"Your English is improving by leaps and bounds, my boy."

"Yes, sir. I have been reading these English books. They have furnished me the forms of the language—the moulds in which it is cast—the idioms."

"I am past wondering! I think there is no miracle that a mind like this cannot do. Pray go to the blackboard and let me see what Greek may look like in phonographic word-combinations with the vowel-signs left out. I will read some passages."

The boy took the chalk, and the trial began. The master read very slowly; then a little faster; then faster still; then as fast as he could. The boy kept up, without apparent difficulty. Then the master threw in Latin sentences, English sentences, French ones, and now and then a hardy problem from Euclid to be ciphered out. The boy was competent, all the while.

"It is amazing, my child, amazing—stupefying! Do me one more miracle, and I strike my flag. Here is a page of columns of figures. Add them up. I have seen the famous lightning-calculator do it in three minutes and a quarter, and I know the answer. I will hold the watch. Beat him!"

The boy glanced at the page, made his bow and said,—

"The total is 4,865,493 if the blurred twenty-third figure in the fifth column is a 9; if it is a 7, the total is less by 2."

"Right, and he is beaten by incredible odds; but you hadn't time to even see the blurred figure, let alone note its place. Wait till I find it—the twenty-third, did you say? Here it is, but I can't tell which it is—it may be a 9, it may be a 7. But no matter, one of your answers is right, according to which name we give the figure. Dear me, can my watch be right? It is long past the noon recess, and everybody has forgotten his dinner. In my thirty years of school-teaching experience this has not happened before. Truly it is a day of miracles. Children, we dull moles are in no condition to further plod and grub after the excitements and bewilderments of this intellectual conflagration—school is dismissed. My wonderful scholar, tell me your name."

The school crowded forward in a body to devour the stranger at close quarters with their envying eyes; all except Bascom, who remained apart and sulked.

"Quarante-quatre, sir. Forty-four."

"Why—why—that is only a number, you know, not a name."

The boy bowed. The master dropped the subject.

"When did you arrive in our town?"

"Last night, sir."

"Have you friends or relatives among us?"

"No, sir—none. Mr. Hotchkiss allows me to lodge in his house."

"You will find the Hotchkisses good people, excellent people. Had you introductions to them?"

"No, sir."

"You see I am curious; but we are all that, in this monotonous little place, and we mean no harm. How did you make them understand what you wanted?"

"Through my signs and their compassion. It was cold, and I was a stranger."

"Good—good—and well stated, without waste of words. It describes the Hotchkisses; it's a whole biography. Whence did you come—and how?"

Forty-four bowed. The master said, affably—

"It was another indiscretion—you will not remember it against —no, I mean you will forget it, in consid— what I am trying to say is, that you will overlook it—that is it, overlook it. I am glad you are come, grateful that you are come."

"I thank you—thank you deeply, sir."

"My official character requires that I precede you in leaving this house, therefore I do it. This is an apology. Adieu."

"Adieu, my master."

The school made way, and the old gentleman marched out between the ranks with a grave dignity proper to his official state.

Chapter 2

THE GIRLS went vivaciously chattering away, eager to get home and tell of the wonders they had seen; but outside of the schoolhouse the boys grouped themselves together and waited; silent, expectant, and nervous. They paid but little attention to the bitter weather, they were apparently under the spell of a more absorbing interest. Henry Bascom stood apart from the others, in the neigh-

borhood of the door. The new boy had not come out, yet. Tom
Sawyer had halted him to give him a warning.

"Look out for him—he'll be waiting. The bully, I mean—Hen
Bascom. He's treacherous and low down."

"Waiting?"

"Yes—for you."

"What for?"

"To lick you—whip you."

"On what account?"

"Why, he's the bully this year, and you're a fresh."

"Is that a reason?"

"Plenty—yes. He's got to take your measure, and do it to-day—
he knows that."

"It's a custom, then?"

"Yes. He's got to fight you, whether he wants to or not. But he
wants to. You've knocked his Latin layout galley-west."

"Galley west? Je ne—"

"It's just a word, you know. Means you've knocked his props
from under him."

"Knocked his props from under him?"

"Yes—trumped his ace."

"Trumped his—"

"Ace. That's it—pulled his leg."

"I assure you this is an error. I have not pulled his leg."

"But you don't understand. Don't you see? You've graveled him,
and he's disgruntled."

The new boy's face expressed his despair. Tom reflected a moment, then his eye lighted with hope, and he said, with confidence—

"Now you'll get the idea. You see, he held the age on Latin—just
a lone hand, don't you know, and it made him Grand Turk and
Whoopjamboreehoo of the whole school, and he went in procession
all by himself, like Parker's hog. Well, you've walked up to the
captain's office with *your* Latin, now, and pulled in high, low, jack
and the game, and it's taken the curl out of his tail. There—that's
the idea."

The new boy hesitated, passed his hand over his forehead, and began, haltingly—

"It is still a little vague. It was but a poor dictionary—that French-English—and over-rich in omissions. Do you perhaps mean that he is jealous?"

"Score *one!* That's it. Jealous—the very word. Now then, there'll be a ring, and you'll fight. Can you box? do you know the trick of it?"

"No."

"I'll show you. You'll learn in two minutes and less; it don't *begin* with grammar for difficulties. Put up your fists—so. Now then, hit me . . . . . You notice how I turned that off with my left? Again . . . . . . See?—turned it with my right. Dance around; caper—like this. Now I'm coming for you—look sharp . . . . . . That's the ticket—I didn't arrive. Once more . . . . . . Good! You're all right. Come on. It's a cold day for Henry."

They stepped outside, now. As they walked past Bascom he suddenly thrust out his foot, to trip Forty-four. But the foot was no obstruction, it did not interrupt Forty-four's stride. Necessarily, then, Bascom was himself tripped. He fell heavily, and everybody laughed privately. He got up, all a-quiver with passion, and cried out—

"Off with your coat, Know-it-all—you're going to fight or eat dirt, one or t'other. Form a ring, fellows!"

He threw off his coat. The ring was formed.

"May I keep my coat on? Do the rules allow it?"

"Don't!" said Tom; "it's a disadvantage. Pull it off."

"Keep it on, you wax doll, if you want to," said Henry, "it won't do you any good either way. Time!"

Forty-four took position, with his fists up, and stood without moving, while the lithe and active Bascom danced about him, danced up toward him, feinted with his right, feinted with his left, danced away again, danced forward again—and so-on and so-on, Tom and others putting in frequent warnings for Forty-four: "Look out for him—look *o-u-t!*" At last Forty-four opened his guard for an instant, and in that instant Henry plunged, and let drive with all his force; but Forty-four stepped lightly aside, and Henry's impulse and a slip on the ice carried him to the ground. He got up lame but eager, and began his dance again; he presently lunged again, hit vacancy and got another fall. After that he respected the slippery ground, and lunged no more, and danced cautiously; he fought with energy, interest and smart judgment, and delivered a sparkling rain of blows, but none of them got home—some were dodged by a sideward tilt of the head, the others were neatly warded. He was getting winded with his violent exercise, but the other boy was still fresh, for he had done no dancing, he had struck no blows, and had had no exercise of consequence. Henry stopped to rest and pant, and Forty-four said—

"Let us not go on with it. What good can come of it?"

The boys murmured dissent; this was an election for Bully; they were personally interested, they had hopes, and their hopes were getting the color of certainties. Henry said—

"You'll stay where you are, Miss Nancy. You don't leave this ground till I know who wears the belt."

"Ah, but you already know—or ought to; therefore, where is the use of going on? You have not struck me, and I have no wish to strike you."

"Oh, you haven't, haven't you? How kind! Keep your benevolences to yourself till somebody asks you for them. Time!"

The new boy began to strike out, now; and every time he struck, Henry went down. Five times. There was great excitement among the boys. They recognised that they were going to lose a tyrant and perhaps get a protector in his place. In their happiness they lost their fears and began to shout—

"Give it him, Forty-four! Let him have it! Land him again! Another one! Give it him good!"

Henry was pluck. He went down time after time, but got patiently up and went at his work again, and did not give up until his strength was all gone. Then he said—

"The belt's yours—but I'll get even with you, yet, girly, you see if I don't." Then he looked around upon the crowd, and called eight of them by name, ending with Huck Finn, and said: "You're spotted, you see. *I* heard you. To-morrow I'll begin on you, and I'll lam the daylights out of you."

For the first time, a flash of temper showed in the new boy's eye. It was only a flash; it was gone in a moment; then he said, without passion—

"I will not allow that."

"*You* won't allow it! Who's asking you? Who cares what you allow and what you don't allow? To show you how much I care, I'll begin on them *now.*"

"I cannot have it. You must not be foolish. I have spared you, till now; I have struck you only lightly. If you touch one of the boys, I will hit you *hard.*"

But Henry's temper was beyond his control. He jumped at the nearest boy on his black-list, but he did not reach him; he went down under a sounding slap from the flat of the new boy's hand, and lay motionless where he fell.

"I saw it! I saw that!" This shout was from Henry's father, the nigger-trader—an unloved man, but respected for his muscle and his temper. He came running from his sleigh, with his whip in his hand and raised to strike. The boys fell back out of his way, and as he reached Forty-four he brought down the whip with an angry "*I'll* learn you!" Forty-four dodged deftly out of its course and seized the trader's wrist with his right hand. There was a sound of crackling bones and a groan, and the trader staggered away, saying—

"Name of God, my wrist is crushed!"

Henry's mamma arrived from the sleigh, now and broke into frenzies of lamentation over her collapsed son and her crippled husband, while the schoolboys looked on, dazed, and rather frightened at the woman's spectacular distress, but fascinated with the show and glad to be there and see it. It absorbed their attention so entirely that when Mrs. Bascom presently turned and demanded the extradition of Forty-four so that she might square accounts with him they found that he had disappeared without their having noticed it.

Chapter 3

WITHIN an hour afterward people began to drop in at the Hotchkiss house; ostensibly to make a friendly call, really to get sight of the miraculous boy. The news they brought soon made the Hotchkisses proud of their prize and glad that they had caught him. Mr. Hotchkiss's pride and joy were frank and simple; every new marvel that any comer added to the list of his lodger's great deeds made him a prouder and happier man than he was before, he being a person substantially without jealousies and by nature addicted to admirations. Indeed he was a broad man in many ways; hospitable to new facts and always seeking them; to new ideas, and always examining them; to new opinions and always adopting them; a man ready to meet any novelty half way and give it a friendly trial. He changed his principles with the moon, his politics with the weather, and his religion with his shirt. He was recognized as being limitlessly good-hearted, quite fairly above the village average intellectually, a diligent and enthusiastic seeker after truth, and a sincere believer in his newest belief, but a man who had missed his vocation—he should have been a weather-vane. He was tall and handsome and courteous, with winning ways, and expressive eyes, and had a white head which looked twenty years older than the rest of him.

His good Presbyterian wife was as steady as an anvil. She was not a creature of change. When she gave shelter to an opinion she did not make a transient guest of it, but a permanency. She was fond and proud of her husband, and believed he would have been great if he had had a proper chance—if he had lived in a metropolis, instead of a village; if his merits had been exposed to the world instead of being hidden under a bushel. She was patient with his excursions after the truth. She expected him to be saved—thought she knew that that would happen, in fact. It could only be as a Presbyterian, of course, but that would come—come of a certainty. All the signs indicated it. He had often been a Presbyterian; he was periodically a Presbyterian, and she had noticed with comfort that his period was almost astronomically regular. She could take the almanac and calculate its return with nearly as much confidence as other astronomers calculated an eclipse. His Mohammedan period, his Methodist period, his Buddhist period, his Baptist period, his Parsi period, his Roman Catholic period, his Atheistic period—these were all similarly regular, but she cared nothing for that. She knew there was a patient and compassionate Providence watching over him that would see to it that he died in his Presbyterian period. The latest thing in religions was the Fox-girl Rochester rappings; so he was a Spiritualist for the present.

Hannah Hotchkiss exulted in the wonders brought by the visitors, and the more they brought the happier she was in the possession of that boy; but she was very human in her make-up, and she felt a little aggravated over the fact that the news had to come from the outside; that these people should know these things about her lodger before she knew them herself; that she must sit and do the wondering and exclaiming when in all fairness she ought to be doing the telling and they the applauding; that they should be able to contribute all the marvels and she none. Finally the widow Dawson remarked upon the circumstance that all the information was being furnished from the one side; and added—

"Didn't he do anything out of the common here, sister * Hotchkiss—last night or this morning?"

Hannah was ashamed of her poverty. The only thing she was able to offer was colorless compared with the matters which she had been listening to.

"Well, no—I can't say that he did; unless you consider that we couldn't understand his language but *did* understand his signs about as easy as if they had been talk. We were astonished at it, and spoke of it afterwards."

Her young niece, Annie Fleming, spoke up and said—

"Why, auntie, that wasn't all. The dog doesn't allow a stranger to come to the door at night, but he didn't bark at the boy; he acted as

---

* "Sister" in the Methodist, or Presbyterian, or Baptist, or Campbellite church—nothing more. A common form, in those days [MT's note].

if he was ever so glad to see him. You said, yourself, that that never happened with a stranger before."

"It's true, as sure as I live; it had passed out of my mind, child."

She was happier, now. Then her husband made a contribution—

"I call to mind, now, that just as we stepped into his room to show him its arrangements I knocked my elbow against the wardrobe and the candle fell and went out, and—"

"Certainly!" exclaimed Hannah, "and the next moment he had struck a match and was lighting—"

"Not the stub I had dropped," cried Hotchkiss, "but a whole candle! Now the marvel is that there was only one whole candle in the room—"

"And it was clear on the *other side* of the room," interrupted Hannah, "and moreover only just the end of it was showing, where it lay on the top of the bookcase, and he had noticed it with that lightning eye of his—"

"Of course, of course!" exclaimed the company, with admiration.

"—and gone right to it in the dark without disturbing a chair. Why, sister Dawson, a *cat* couldn't have done it any quicker or better or surer! Just think of it!"

A chorus of rewarding astonishment broke out which made Hannah's whole constitution throb with pleasure; and when sister Dawson laid her hand impressively upon Hannah's hand, and then walled her eyes toward the ceiling, as much as to say, "it's beyond words, beyond words!" the pleasure rose to ecstasy.

"Wait!" said Mr. Hotchkiss, breaking out with the kind of laugh which in the back settlements gives notice that something humorous is coming, "I can tell you a wonder that beats that to pieces— beats anything and everything that has been told about him up to date. He paid four weeks' board in advance—cash down! Petersburg can believe the rest, but you'll never catch it taking *that* statement at par."

The joke had immense success; the laugh was hearty all around. Then Hotchkiss issued another notifying laugh, and added—

"And there's another wonder on top of that; I tell you a little at a time, so as not to overstrain you. He didn't pay in wildcat at

twenty-five discount, but in a currency you've forgotten the look of
—minted gold! Four yellow eagle-birds—and here they are, if you
don't believe me."

This was too grand and fine to be humorous; it was impressive,
almost awe-inspiring. The gold pieces were passed from hand to
hand and contemplated in mute reverence. Aunt Rachel, elderly
slave woman, was passing cracked nuts and cider. She offered a
contribution, now.

"Now, den, dat 'splain it! I uz a wonderin' 'bout dat cannel. You
is right, Miss Hannah, dey uz only one in de room, en she uz on top
er de bookcase. Well, she dah *yit*—she hain't been tetched."

"Not been touched?"

"No, m'am; she hain't been tetched. A ornery po' yaller taller
cannel, ain't she?"

"Of course."

"Yes'm. I mould' dat cannel myself. Kin we 'ford *wax* cannels—
half a dollar a pound?"

"Wax! The idea!"

"Dat new cannel's *wax!*"

"Oh, come!"

"Fo' Gawd she is. White as Miss Guthrie's store-teeth."

A delicate flattery-shot, neatly put. The widow Guthrie, 56 and
dressed for 25, was pleased, and exhibited a girlish embarrassment
that was very pretty. She was excusably vain of her false teeth, the
only ones in the town; a costly luxury, and a fine and showy
contrast with the prevailing mouth-equipment of both old and
young—the kind of sharp contrast which white-washed palings
make with a charred stump-fence.

Everybody wanted to see the wax candle; Annie Fleming was
hurried away to fetch it, and aunt Rachel resumed—

"Miss Hannah, dey's sump'n pow'ful odd 'bout our young gent-
man. In de fust place, he ain't got no baggage. Ain't dat so?"

"It hasn't come yet, but I reckon it's coming. I've been expecting
it all day, of course."

"Well, don't you give yourself no mo' trouble 'bout it, honey. In
my opinion he ain't got no baggage, en none ain't a-coming."

"What makes you think that, Rachel?"

"Caze he ain't got no use for it, Miss Hannah."

"Why?"

"I's gwyne tell you. Warn't he dress' beautiful when he come?"

"Yes." Then she added—to the company: "Plain, but of finer materials than anybody here is used to. Nicely made, too, and spick and span new."

"You's got it down 'cording to de facts. Now den, I went to his room dis mawnin to fetch his clo'es so Jeff could bresh 'em en black his boots, en dey warn't no clo'es dah. Nary a rag. En no boots en no socks, nuther. He uz soun' asleep, en I search de place all over. Tuck his breakfus after you-all uz done—didn't he?"

"Yes."

"Prim en slick en combed up nice as a cat, warn't he?"

"Yes. I think so. I had only a glimpse of him."

"Well, he was; en dey ain't no comb ner bresh ner nothing in dat room. How you reckon he done it?"

"I don't know."

"En *I* don't. But dem is de facts. Did you notice his clo'es, honey?"

"No. Only that they were neat and handsome."

"Now den, I did. *Dey warn't de same dat he come in.*"

"Why, Rachel—"

"Nemmine, I knows what I's a talkin' 'bout. Dey warn't de same. Every rag of 'em jist a little diffunt; not much, but diffunt. His overcoat uz on a cheer by him, en *it* uz *entirely* diffunt. Las' night it uz long en brown, dis mawnin' it uz short en blue; en dah he sot, wid *shoes* on, not boots—I swah to it!"

The explosions of astonishment that followed this charmed Mrs. Hotchkiss's ear; the family's shares in the wonder-market were accumulating satisfactorily.

"Now, den, Miss Hannah, dat ain't all. I fotch him some mo' batter-cakes, en whilst I uz a butterin' 'em for him I happens to look around, en dah uz ole Sanctified Sal, as Marse Oliver calls her, a loafin' along in, perfeckly comfortable. When I see dat, I says to myself, By jimminy dey's bewitchment here som'ers, en it's time for me to light out, en I done it. En I tole Jeff, en he didn't b'lieve me, so me en him slip back en peep, for to see what uz gwyne to happen. En Jeff uz a sayin' 'She'll tah de livers en lights outer him, dat's what she'll do; she ain't friendly to no stranger any time, en now she's got kittens, she won't stan' 'em nohow.' "

"Rachel, it was shame of you to leave her there; you knew perfectly well what could happen."

"I knowed it warn't right, Miss Hannah, but *I* couldn't he'p it, I uz scairt to see de cat so ca'm. But don't you worry, honey. You 'member 'bout de dog? De dog didn't fly at him, de dog uz glad to see him. Jist de same wid de cat. Me en Jeff seen it. She jump' up in his lap, en he stroke her, en she uz happy, en raise her back up en down comfortable, en wave her tail, en scrape her head along under his chin, en den jump on de table en set down, en den dey talk together."

"*Talk* together!"

"Yes'm. I wisht I may die if it ain't so."

"The foreign talk that he began with, last night?"

"No'm. Cat-talk."

"Nonsense!"

"Shore's you born. Cat-talk. Bofe of 'em talked cat-talk—sof' en petting—jist like a ole cat en a young cat—cats dat's relations. Well, she tuck a chance at de vittles, en didn't like 'em, so den he tuck truck outer his pocket en fed it to her—en you bet you she didn't go back on *dat!* No'm—'deed she didn't. She laid into it like she hain't had nothin' to eat for four years. He tuck it all outer de same pocket. Now, den, Miss Hannah, I reckon you knows how much Sanctified Sal kin hold? Well, he loaded her chock up to de chin—yes'm, till her eyes fairly bug out. She couldn't wag her tail she's so full. Look like she'd swallered a watermillion she uz dat crammed. Tuck it all outer dat one pocket. Now, den, Miss Hannah, dey ain't no pocket, en dey ain't no saddle-bags dat kin hold enough to load up Sanctified Sal, en you knows it. Well, he tuck it all outer de one pocket—I swah to it."

Everybody was impressed; there was a crackling fire of ejaculations; sister Dawson walled her eyes again, and Dr. Wheelright, that imposing oracle, nodded his head slowly up and down, as one who could deliver a weighty thought an' he would.

"Well, a mouse come a-running, en run up his leg en into his bosom, en Sanctified Sal was nodding, but she seen it en forgot she uz loaded, en made a jump for it en fell off the table, en laid there on her back a-waving her hands in the air, en waved a couple of times or so en went to sleep jist so—couldn't keep her eyes open. Den he loaded up de mouse—outer dat same pocket; en put his head down en dey talked mouse-talk together."

"Oh, stop—your imagination's running away with you."

"Fo' Gawd it's true. Me en Jeff heard 'em. Den he put de mouse down en started off, en de mouse was bound she'd foller him; so he put her in de cubberd en shet de do'; den he cler'd out de back way."

"How does it come you didn't tell us these things sooner, Rachel?"

"*Me* tell you! Hm! You reckon you'd a b'lieved me? You reckon you'd a b'lieved Jeff? *We* b'lieves in bewitchments, caze we knows dey's so; but you-all only jist laughs at 'em. Does you reckon you'd a b'lieved me, Miss Hannah?—does you?"

"Well—no."

"Den you'd a laughed at me. Does a po' nigger want to git laughed at any mo' d'n white folks? No, Miss Hannah, dey don't. We's got our feelin's, same as *you*-all, alldough we's ign'ant en black."

Her tongue was hung in the middle and was easier to start than to stop. It would have gone on wagging, now, but that the wax candle had long ago been waiting for exhibition. Annie Fleming sat with it in her hand, with one ear drinking in aunt Rachel's fairy-tales, and the other one listening for the click of the gate-latch; for she had lost her tender little inexperienced heart to the new boy without suspecting it; awake and asleep she had been dreaming of his beautiful face ever since she had had her first glimpse of it and she was longing to see it again and feel that enchanting and mysterious ecstasy which it had inspired in her before. She was a dear and sweet and pretty and guileless creature, she was just turned eighteen, she did not know she was in love, she only knew that she worshiped—worshiped as the fire-worshipers worship the sun, content to see his face and feel his warmth, unworthy of a nearer intimacy, unequal to it, unfitted for it, and not requiring it or aspiring to it. Why didn't he come? Why had he not come to dinner? The hours were so slow, the day so tedious; the longest she had known in her eighteen years. All were growing more and more impatient for his coming, but their impatience was pale beside hers; and besides, they could express it, and did, but she could not have that relief, she must hide her secret, she must put on the lie of indifference and act it the best she could.

The candle was passed from hand to hand, now, and its material admired and verified; then Annie carried it away.

It was well past mid-afternoon, and the days were short. Annie and her aunt were to sup and spend the night with sister Guthrie on the hill, a good mile distant. What should be done? Was it worth while to wait longer for the boy? The company were reluctant to go without seeing him; sister Guthrie hoped she might have the distinction of his presence in her house with the niece and the aunt, and would like to wait a little longer and invite him; so it was agreed to hold on a while.

Annie returned, now, and there was disappointment in her face and a pain at her heart, though no one detected the one nor suspected the other. She said—

"Aunty, he has been here, and is gone again."

"Then he must have come the back way. It's *too* bad. But are you sure? How do you know?"

"Because he has changed his clothes."

"Are there clothes there?"

"Yes; and not the ones he had this morning, nor the ones he wore last night."

"Dah, now, what I tell you? En dat baggage not come *yit!*"

"Can we see them?"

"Can't we see them?"

"Do let us go and look at them!"

Everybody wanted to see the clothes, everybody begged. So, sentries were posted to look out for the boy's approach and give notice—Annie to watch the front door and Rachel the back one— and the rest went up to Forty-four's chamber. The clothes were there, new and handsome. The coat lay spread upon the bed. Mrs. Hotchkiss took it by the skirts and held it up to display it—a flood of gold and silver coin began to pour out of the inverted pockets; the woman stood aghast and helpless; the coin piled higher and higher on the floor—

"Put it down!" shouted her husband; "drop it, can't you!" But she was paralysed; he snatched the coat and threw it on the bed, and the flood ceased. "Now we are in a fine fix; he can come at any moment and catch us; and we'll have to explain, if we can, how we happen to be here. Quick, all you accessories after the fact and before it—turn to; we must gather it up and put it back."

So all those chief citizens got down on their hands and knees and scrambled all around and everywhere for the coins, raking under the bed and the sofa and the wardrobe for estrays, a most undignified spectacle. The work was presently finished, but that did not restore happiness, for there was a new trouble, now: after the coat's pockets had been stuffed there was still half a peck of coin left. It was a shameful predicament. Nobody could get command of his wits for a moment or two; then sister Dawson made a suggestion—

"No real harm is done, when you come to look at it. It is natural that we should have some curiosity about the belongings of such a wonderful stranger, and if we try to satisfy it, not meaning any harm or disrespect—"

"Right," interrupted Miss Pomeroy, the school m'am; "he's only a boy, and he wouldn't mind, and he wouldn't think it anything odd if people as old as we are should take a little liberty which he mightn't like in younger folks."

"And besides," said Judge Taylor the magistrate, "he hasn't suffered any loss, and isn't going to suffer any. Let us put the whole of the money in his table drawer and close it, and lock the room door; and when he comes we will all tell him just how it was, and apologise. It will come out all right; I think we don't need to worry."

It was agreed that this was probably as good a plan as could be contrived in the difficult circumstances of the case; so the company took all the comfort from it they could, and were glad to get out of the place and clear for their homes without waiting longer for the boy, in case he shouldn't arrive before they got their wraps on. They said Hotchkiss could do the explaining and apologising, and depend upon them to indorse and stand by all his statements.

"And besides," said Mrs. Wheelright, "how do we know it is real money? He may be a juggler out of India; in that case the drawer is empty, or full of sawdust by this time."

"I am afraid it's not going to happen," said Hotchkiss; "the money was rather heavy for sawdust. The thing that mainly interests me is, that I shan't sleep very well with that pile of money in the house—I shan't sleep at all if you people are going to tell about it, and so I'll ask you to keep the secret until morning; then I will make the boy send it to the bank, and you may talk as freely as you please, then."

Annie put on her things and she and her aunt departed with the rest. Darkness was approaching; the lodger was not come. What could the matter be? Mrs. Hotchkiss said he was probably coasting with his schoolmates and paying no attention to more important things—boy-like. Rachel was told to keep his supper warm and let him take his own time about coming for it; "boys will be boys, and late by nature, nights and mornings; let them be boys while they can, it's the best of life and the shortest."

It had turned warm, and clouds were gathering fast, with a promise of snow—a promise which would be kept.

As Doctor Wheelright, the stately old First-Family Virginian and imposing Thinker of the village was going out at the front door, he unloaded a Thought. It seemed to weigh a good part of a ton, and it impressed everybody—

"It is my opinion—after much and careful reflection, sir—that the indications warrant the conjecture that in several ways this youth is an extraordinary person."

That verdict would go around. After such an endorsement, from such a source, the village would think twice before it ventured to think small potatoes of that boy.

Chapter 4

As the darkness closed down an hour later, what is to this day called the Great Storm began. It was in reality a Blizzard, but that expressive word had not then been invented. It was this storm's mission to bury the farms and villages of a long narrow strip of country for ten days, and do it as compactly and as thoroughly as the mud and ashes had buried Pompeii nearly eighteen centuries before. The Great Storm began its work modestly, deceptively. It made no display, there was no wind and no noise; whoever was abroad and crossed the lamp-glares flung from uncurtained windows noticed that the snow came straight down, and that it laid its delicate white carpet softly, smoothly, artistically, thickening the substance swiftly and equably; the passenger noticed also that this snow was of an unusual sort, it not coming in an airy cloud of great feathery flakes, but in a fog of white dust-forms—mere powder; just powder; the strangest snow imaginable. By 8 in the evening this snow-fog had become so dense that lamp-glares four steps away were not visible, and without the help of artificial light a passenger could see no object till he was near enough to touch it with his hand. Whosoever was abroad now was practically doomed, unless he could soon stumble upon somebody's house. Orientation was impossible; to be abroad was to be lost. A man could not leave his own door, walk ten steps and find his way back again.

The wind rose, now, and began to sing through this ghastly fog; momently it rose higher and higher, soon its singing had developed into roaring, howling, shrieking. It gathered up the snow from the ground and drove it in massy walls ahead of it and distributed it here and there across streets and open lots and against houses, in drifts fifteen feet deep.

There were disasters now, of course. Very few people were still out, but those few were necessarily in bad case. If they faced the wind, it caked their faces instantly with a thick mask of powder which closed their eyes in blindness and stopped their nostrils and their breath, and they fell where they were; if they tried to move with the wind they soon plunged into a drift and the on-coming wall of snow buried them. Even in that little village twenty-eight persons perished that night, some because they had heard cries of distress and went out to help, but got lost within sixty seconds, and then, seeking their own doors, went in the wrong direction and found their graves in five minutes.

At 8, just as the wind began to softly moan and whimper and wheeze, Mr. Hotchkiss laid his spiritualistic book down, snuffed the candle, threw an extra log on the fire, then parted his coat tails and stood with his back to the blaze and began to turn over in his mind some of the information which he had been gathering about the manners and customs and industries of the spirit land, and to repeat and try to admire some of the poetry which Byron had sent thence through the rapping-mediums. He did not know that there was a storm outside. He had been absorbed in his book for an hour and a half. Aunt Rachel appeared, now, with an armful of wood, which she flung in the box and said—

"Well, seh, it's de wust I ever see; and Jeff say de same."

"Worst what?"

"Storm, seh."

"Is there a storm?"

"My! didn't you know it, seh?"

"No."

"Why, it's de beatenes' storm—tain't like nothin' you ever see, Marse Oliver—so fine—like ashes a-blowin'; why, you can't see no distance scasely. Me en Jeff was at de prar meetin', en come back a little bit ago, en come mighty near miss'n de house; en when we look out, jist dis minute it's a heap wuss'n ever. Jeff he uz a sayin'—" She glanced around; an expression of fright came into her face and she exclaimed, "Why, I reckoned of cose he uz here—en he ain't!"

"Who?"

"Young Marse Fawty-fo'."

"Oh, he's playing somewhere; he'll be along presently."

"You hain't seen him, seh?"

"No."

"O, my Gawd!"

She fled away, and in five minutes was back again, sobbing and panting.

"He ain't in his room, his supper ain't tetched, he ain't anywhers; I been all over de house. O, Marse Oliver de chile's lost, we ain't never gwyne to see him no mo'."

"Oh, nonsense, you needn't be afraid—boys don't mind a storm."

Uncle Jeff arrived at this moment, and said—

"But Marse Oliver *dis* ain't no common storm—has you been to look at it?"

"No."

Hotchkiss was alarmed, at last, and ran with the others to the front door and snatched it open. The wind piped a high note, and they disappeared in a world of snow which was discharged at them as if from steam-shovels.

"Shut it, shut it!" gasped the master. It was done. A blast of wind came that rocked the house. There was a faint and choking cry outside. Hotchkiss blenched, and said, "What can we do? It's death to go out there. But we *must* do something—it may be the boy."

"Wait, Marse Oliver, I'll fetch a clo'es line, en Jeff he—" She was gone, and in a moment brought it and began to tie an end around uncle Jeff's waist. "Now, den, out wid you! me en Marse Oliver'll hole on to de yuther end."

Jeff was ready; the door was opened for the plunge, and the plunge was made; but in the same instant a suffocating assault of snow closed the eyes and took away the breath of the master and Rachel and they sank gasping to the floor and the line escaped from their hands. They threw themselves on their faces, with their feet toward the door; their breath returned, and Rachel moaned, *"He's gone, now!"* By the light from the hall lamp over the door she caught a dim vision of the new boy, coming from toward the dining room, and said "Thank de good Gawd for *dat* much—how ever did he find de back gate?"

The boy came through against the wind and shut the front door. The master and Rachel rose out of their smother of snow, and the former said, in words broken by sobs—

"I'm so grateful! I never expected to see you again."

By this time Rachel's sobs and groans and lamentations were rising above the clamors of the storm, and the boy asked what the trouble was. Hotchkiss told him about Jeff.

"I will go and fetch him, sir. Get into the parlor, and close the door."

"You will venture out? Not a step—stay where you are! I wouldn't allow—"

The boy interrupted—not with words, but only a look—and the man and the servant passed into the parlor and closed the door. Then they heard the front door close, and stood looking at each other. The storm raged on; every now and then a gust of wind burst against the house with a force which made it quake, and in the intervals it wailed like a lost soul; the listeners tallied the gusts and the intervals, losing heart all the time, and when they had counted five of each, their hopes died.

Then they opened the parlor door—to do they didn't know what —the street door sprang open at the same moment, and two snow-figures entered: the boy carrying the unconscious old negro man in his arms. He delivered his burden to Rachel, shut the door, and said—

"A man has found refuge in the open shed over yonder; a slender, tall, wild-looking man with thin sandy beard. He is groaning. It is not much of a shelter, that shed."

He said it indifferently, and Hotchkiss shuddered.

"Oh, it is awful, awful!" he said, "he will die."

"Why is it awful?" asked the boy.

"*Why?* It—it—why of *course* it's awful!"

"Perhaps it is as you say; I do not know. Shall I fetch him?"

"Great guns, no! Don't dream of such a thing—one miracle of the sort is enough."

"But if you want him— Do you want him?"

"Want him? I—why, I don't *want* him—*that* isn't it—I mean, why, don't you understand?—it's a pity he should *die,* poor fellow; but we are not in a position to—"

"I will fetch him."

"Stop, stop, are you mad!—come back!"

But the boy was gone.

"Rachel, why the devil did you let him get out? Can't you see that the lad's a rank lunatic?"

"O, Marse Oliver, gim it *to* me, I deserve it! I's so thankful to git my ole Jeff back I ain't got no sense en can't take notice of nothin'. I's so shamed, en O, my Gawd, I—"

"We had him, and now we've lost him again; and this time for good; and it's all your fault, for being a—"

The door fell open, a snow image plunged in upon the floor, the boy's voice called, "There he is—there's others, yet," and the door closed again.

"Oh, well," cried Hotchkiss with a note of despair, "we've got to give him up, there's no saving him. Rachel!" He was flapping the snow from the new take, with a "tidy." "Bless my soul, it's Crazy Meadows! Rouse up, Jeff! lend a hand, both of you—drag him to my fire." It was done. "Now, then, blankets, food, hot water, whisky—fly around! we'll save him, he isn't more than half dead, yet."

The three worked over Crazy Meadows half an hour, and brought him around. Meantime they had kept alert ears open, listening; but their listening was unblessed, no sounds came but the rumbling and blustering of the storm. Crazy Meadows gazed around confusedly, gradually got his bearings, recognized the faces, and said—

"I am saved! Hotchkiss, it seems impossible. How did it happen?"

"A boy did it—the most marvelous boy on the planet. It was lucky you had a lantern."

"Lantern? I hadn't any lantern."

"Yes, you had. *You* don't know. The boy described your build and beard."

"I *hadn't* any lantern, I tell you. There wasn't any light around."

"Marse Oliver," said Rachel, "didn't Miss Hannah say de young marster kin see in de dark?"

"Why, certainly—now that you mention it. But how could he see through that blanket of snow? My gracious, I wish he would come! Oh, but he'll never come, poor young chap, he'll never come— never any more."

"Marse Oliver, don't you worry, de good Lawd kin take care of him."

"In this storm, you old idiot? You don't know what you're talking about. Wait—I've got an idea! Quick—get around the table; now then, take hold of hands. Banish all obstructive influences—you want to be particular about that; the spirits can't do anything against doubt and incredulity. Silence, now, and concentrate your minds. Poor boy, if he is dead he will come and say so."

He glanced up, and perceived that there was a hiatus in the circle; Crazy Meadows said, without breach of slave-State politeness, and without offence to the slaves present, since they had been accustomed to the franknesses of slave-State etiquette all their lives—

"I'll go any reasonable length to prove my solicitude for the fate of my benefactor, for I am not an ungrateful man, and not a soured one, either, if the children *do* chase me and stone me for the fun they get out of it; but I've got to draw the line. I'm willing to sit at a table with niggers for just this once, for your sake, Oliver Hotchkiss, but that is as far as I can go—I'll get you to excuse me from taking them by the hand."

The gratitude of the two negroes was deep and honest; this speech promised relief for them; their situation had been a cruelly embarrassing one; they had sat down with these white men because they had been ordered to do it, and it was habit and heredity to obey, but their seats had not been more comfortable than a hot stove would have been. They hoped and expected that their master would be reasonable and rational, now, and send them away, but it didn't happen. He could manage his *seance* without Meadows, and would do it. He didn't mind holding hands with negroes, for he was a sincere and enthusiastic abolitionist; in fact had been an abolitionist for five weeks, now, and if nothing happened would be one for a fortnight longer. He had confirmed the sincerity of his new convictions in the very beginning by setting the two slaves free—a generosity which had failed only because they didn't belong to him but to his wife. As she had never been an abolitionist it was impossible that she could ever become one.

By command the slaves joined hands with their master and sat trembling and silent, for they were miserably afraid of spectres and spirits. Hotchkiss bowed his head solemnly to the table, and said in a reverent tone:

"Are there any spirits present? If so, please rap three times."

After a pause the response came—three faint raps. The negroes shrunk together till their clothes were loose upon their bodies, and begged pathetically to be released.

"Sit still! and don't let your hands shake like that."

It was Lord Byron's spirit. Byron was the most active poet on the other side of the grave in those days, and the hardest one for a medium to get rid of. He reeled off several rods of poetry now, of his usual spiritual pattern—rhymy and jingly and all that, but not good, for his mind had decayed since he died. At the end of three-quarters of an hour he went away to hunt for a word that would rhyme with silver—good luck and a long riddance, Crazy Meadows said, for there wasn't any such word. Then Napoleon came and explained Waterloo all over again and how it wasn't his fault—a thing which he was always doing in the St. Helena days, and latterly around the festive rapping-table. Crazy Meadows scoffed at him, and said he didn't even get the dates right, let alone the facts; and he laughed his wild mad laugh—a reedy and raspy and horrid explosion which had long been a fright to the village and its dogs, and had brought him many a volley of stones from the children.

Shakspeare arrived and did some rather poor things, and was followed by a throng of Roman statesmen and generals whose English was the only remarkable thing about their contributions;

then at last, about eleven o'clock, came some thundering raps which made the table and the company jump.

"Who is it, please?"

"Forty-four!"

"Ah, how sad!—we are deeply grieved, but of course we feared it and expected it. Are you happy?"

"Happy? Certainly."

"We are so glad! It is the greatest comfort to us. Where are you?"

"In hell!"

"O, de good Lawd!—please, Marse Oliver, lemme go, oh, please lemme go—oh, Marse Oliver, me en Rachel *can't* stan' it!"

"Hold still, you fool!"

"Oh, please, *please,* Marse Oliver!"

"*Will* you keep still, you puddnhead! Ah, now, if we can only persuade him to materialize! I've never seen one yet. Forty-four, dear lost lad, *would* you mind appearing to us?"

"Oh, *don't,* Marse Oliver!—please, don't!"

"Shut up! *Do* materialize! Do appear to us, if only for a moment!"

Presto! There sat the boy, in their midst! The negroes shrieked, and went over on their backs on the floor and continued to shriek. Crazy Meadows fell over backwards, too, but gathered himself up in silence and stood apart with heaving breast and flaming eyes, staring at the boy. Hotchkiss rubbed his hands together in gratitude and delight, and his face was transfigured with the glory-light of triumph.

"*Now* let the doubter doubt and the scoffer scoff if they want to —but they've had their day! Ah, Forty-four, dear Forty-four, you've done our cause a noble service."

"What cause?"

"Spiritualism. *Stop* that screeching and screaming, will you!"

The boy stooped and touched the negroes, and said—

"There—go to sleep. Now go to bed. In the morning you will think it was a dream." They got up and wandered somnambulistically away. He turned and looked at Crazy Meadows, whose lids at once sank down and hid his wild eyes. "Go and sleep in my bed; in the morning it will be a dream to you, too." Meadows drifted away like one in a trance, and followed after the vanished negroes. "What is spiritualism, sir?"

Hotchkiss eagerly explained. The boy smiled, made no comment, and changed the subject.

"Twenty-eight have perished in your village by the storm."

"Heavens! Can that be true?"

"I saw them; they are under the snow—scattered over the town."

"*Saw* them?"

The boy took no notice of the inquiry in the emphasised word.

"Yes—twenty-eight."

"What a misfortune!"

"Is it?"

"Why—how can you ask?"

"I don't know. I could have saved them if I had known it was desirable. After you wanted that man saved I gathered the idea that it was desirable, so I searched the town and saved the rest that were straggling—thirteen."

"How noble! And how beautiful it was to die in such a work. Oh, sainted spirit, I worship your memory!"

"Whose memory?"

"Yours; and I—"

"Do you take me for dead?"

"Dead? Of course. Aren't you?"

"Certainly not."

Hotchkiss's joy was without limit or measure. He poured it eloquently out until he was breathless; then paused, and added pathetically—

"It is bad for spiritualism—yes, bad, bad—but let it go—go and welcome, God knows I'm glad to have you back, even on those costly terms! And by George, we'll celebrate! I'm a teetotaler—been a teetotaler for years—months, anyway—*a* month—but at a time like this—"

The kettle was still on the fire, the bottle which had revived Meadows was still at hand, and in a couple of minutes he had brewed a pair of good punches—"anyway, good enough for a person out of practice," he said.

The boy began to sip, and said it was pleasant, and asked what it was.

"Why, bless your heart, whisky of course—can't you tell by the smell of it? And we'll have a smoke, too. I don't smoke—haven't for years—I *think* it's years—because I'm president of the Anti-Smoking League—but at a time like this—" He jumped up and threw a log on the fire, punched the pile into a roaring blaze, then filled a couple of cob pipes and brought them. "There, now, ain't it cosy, ain't it comfortable?—and just *hear* the storm! My, but she's booming! But snug here?—it's no name for it!"

The boy was inspecting his pipe with interest.

"What shall I do with it, sir?"

"*Do* with it? Do you mean to say you don't smoke? I never saw such a boy. Next you'll say you don't break the Sabbath."

"But what is the material?"

"That? Tobacco—of course."

"Oh, I see. Sir Walter Raleigh discovered it among the Indians; I read about it in the school. Yes, I understand now."

He applied the candle and began to smoke, Hotchkiss gazing at him puzzled.

"You've *read* about it! Upon my word! Now that I come to think about it, you don't seem to know anything except what you've read about in that school. Why how in the world could you be born and raised in the State of Missouri and never—"

"But I wasn't. I am a foreigner."

"You don't say!—and speak just like an educated native—not even an accent. Where *were* you raised?"

The boy answered naïvely—

"Partly in heaven, partly in hell."

Hotchkiss's glass fell from one hand, his pipe from the other, and he sat staring stupidly at the boy, and breathing short. Presently he murmured dubiously—

"I reckon the punch—out of practice, you know—maybe both of us—and—" He paused, and continued to gaze and blink; then

shook his thoughts together and said, "Can't tell anything about it
—it is too undeveloped for me; but it's all right, we'll make a night
of it. It's my opinion, speaking as a prohibitionist—" He stooped
and picked up his glass and his pipe, and went rambling on in a
broken and incoherent way while he filled them, glancing furtively
at the boy now and then out of the corner of his eye and trying to
settle his disturbed and startled mind and get his bearings again.
But the boy was not disturbed; he smoked and sipped in peace, and
quiet, and manifest contentment. He took a book out of his pocket,
and began to turn the pages swiftly; Hotchkiss sat down, stirring
his new punch, and keeping a wistful and uneasy eye upon him.
After a minute or two the book was laid upon the table.

"Now I know all about it," said the boy. "It is all here—tobacco,
and liquors, and such things. Champagne is placed at the head of
everything; and Cuban tobacco at the head of the tobaccos."

"Oh, yes, they are the gems of the planet in those lines. Why—I
don't recognise this book; did you bring it in to-night?"

"Yes."

"Where from?"

"The British Museum."

Hotchkiss began to blink again, and look uneasy.

"It is a new work," added the boy. "Published yesterday."

The blinking continued. Hotchkiss started to take a sip of punch,
but reconsidered the motion; shook his head and put the glass
down. Upon pretext of examining the print and the binding, he
opened the book; then closed it at once and pushed it away. He had
seen the Museum stamp—bearing date of the preceding day. He
fussed nervously at his pipe a moment; then held it to the candle
with a hand that trembled and made some of the tobacco spill out,
then asked timidly—

"How did you get the book?"

"I went after it myself."

"Your—self. Mercy! When?"

"While you were stooping for your pipe and glass."

Hotchkiss moaned.

"Why do you make that noise?"

"Be—because I—I am afraid."

The boy reached out and touched the trembling hand and said gently—

"There—it is gone."

The troubled look passed from the old prohibitionist's face, and he said, in a sort of soft ecstasy of relief and contentment—

"It tingles all through me—all through me. De—licious! Every fibre—the root of every hair—it is enchantment! Oh magician of the magicians, talk to me—talk! tell me everything."

"Certainly, if you like."

"Now, that is lovely! First I will rout out old Rachel and we'll have a bite and be comfortable and freshen up; I am pretty sharp-set after all these hours, and I reckon you are, too."

"Wait. It is not necessary. I will order something."

Smoking dishes began to descend upon the table; it was covered in a moment.

"It's the Arabian Nights come again! And I am not scared, now. I don't know why—it was that magic touch, I think. But you didn't fetch them yourself, this time; I was noticing, and you didn't go away."

"No, I sent my servants."

"I didn't see them."

"You can if you wish."

"I'd give anything!"

The servants became visible; all the room was crowded with them. Trim and shapely little fellows they were; velvety little red fellows, with short horns on their heads and spiked tails at the other end; and those that stood, stood in metal plates, and those that sat—on chairs, in a row upon settees, and on top of the bookcase with their legs dangling—had metal plates under them—"to keep from scorching the furniture," the boy quietly explained, "these have come but this moment, and of course are hot, yet."

Hotchkiss asked, a little timidly—

"Are they little devils?"

"Yes."

"Real ones?"

"Oh, yes—quite."

"They—are they safe?"

"Perfectly."

"I don't need to be afraid?"

"Oh, not at all."

"Then I won't be. I think they are charming. Do they understand English?"

"No, only French. But they could be taught it in a few minutes."

"It is wonderful. Are they—you won't mind my asking—relatives?"

"Of mine? No; sons of my father's subordinates. You are dismissed, young gentlemen, for the present."

The little fiends vanished.

"Your father is—er—"

"Satan!"

"Good land!"

Chapter 5

HOTCHKISS sank into his chair weak and limp, and began to pour out broken words and disjointed sentences whose meanings were not always clear but whose general idea was comprehensible. To this effect: from custom bred of his upbringing and his associations he had often talked about Satan with a freedom which was regrettable, but it was really only talk, mere idle talk, he didn't mean anything by it; in fact there were many points about Satan's character which he greatly admired, and although he hadn't said so, publicly, it was an oversight and not intentional—but from this out he meant to open his mouth boldly, let people say what they might and think what they chose—

The boy interrupted him, gently and quietly—

"*I* don't admire him."

Hotchkiss was hard aground, now; his mouth was open, and remained so, but no words came; he couldn't think of anything judicious to say. Presently he ventured to throw out a feeler—cautiously, tentatively, feelingly, persuasively:

"You see—well, you know—it would be only natural, if I was a devil—a good, kind, honorable devil, I mean—and my father was a good, kind, honorable devil against whom narrow and perhaps wrongful or at least exaggerated prejudices—"

"But I am not a devil," said the boy, tranquilly.

Hotchkiss was badly confused, but profoundly relieved.

"I—er—I—well, you know, I suspected as much, I—I—indeed I hadn't a doubt of it; and—although it—on the whole—oh, good land, I can't understand it, of course, but I give you my word of honor I like you all the better for it, I do indeed! I feel good, now—good, and comfortable, and in fact happy. Join me—take something! I wish to drink your health; and—and your family's."

"With pleasure. Now eat—refresh yourself. I will smoke, if you don't mind. I like it."

"Certainly; but eat, too; aren't you hungry?"

"No, I do not get hungry."

"Is that actually so?"

"Yes."

"Ever? Never?"

"No."

"Ah, it is a pity. You miss a great deal. Now tell me about yourself, won't you?"

"I shall be glad to do it, for I have a purpose in coming to the earth, and if you should find the matter interesting, you can be useful to me."

Then the talking and eating began, simultaneously.

"I was born before Adam's fall—"

"Wh-at!"

"It seems to surprise you. Why?"

"Because it caught me unprepared. And because it is six thousand years ago, and you look to be only about fifteen years old."

"True—that is my age, within a fraction."

"Only fifteen, and yet—"

"Counting by *our* system of measurement, I mean—not yours."

"How is that?"

"A day, with us, is as a thousand years with you."

Hotchkiss was awed. A seriousness which was near to solemnity settled upon his face. After a meditative pause he said—

"Surely it cannot be that you really and not figuratively mean—"

"Yes—really, not figuratively. A minute of our time is 41⅔ years of yours. By our system of measurement I am fifteen years old; but by yours I am five million, lacking twenty thousand years."

Hotchkiss was stunned. He shook his head in a hopeless way, and said, resignedly—

"Go on—I can't realize it—it is astronomy to me."

"Of course you cannot realize these things, but do not be troubled; measurements of time and eternity are merely conveniences, they are not of much importance. It is about a week ago that Adam fell—"

"A week?—Ah, yes, *your* week. It is awful—that compression of time! Go on."

"I was in heaven; I had always lived in heaven, of course; until a week ago, my father had always lived there. But I saw this little world created. I was interested; we were all interested. There is much more interest attaching to the creation of a planet than attaches to the creation of a sun, on account of the life that is going to inhabit it. I have seen many suns created—many indeed, that you are not yet acquainted with, they being so remotely situated in the deeps of space that their light will not reach here for a long time yet; but the planets—I cared the most for them; we all did; I have seen millions of them made, and the Tree planted in the Garden, and the man and the woman placed in its shade, with the animals about them. I saw your Adam and Eve only once; they were happy, then, and innocent. This could have continued forever, but for my father's conduct. I read it all in the Bible in Mr. Ferguson's school. As it turned out, Adam's happiness lasted less than a day—"

"Less than one day?"

"By our reckoning, I mean; by yours he lived nine hundred and twenty years—the bulk of it unhappily."

"I see; yes, it is true."

"It was my father's fault. Then hell was created, in order that Adam's race might have a place to go to, after death—"

"They could go to heaven, too."

"That was later. Two days ago. Through the sacrifice made for them by the son of God, the Savior."

"Is hell so new?"

"It was not needed before. No Adam in any of the millions of other planets had ever disobeyed and eaten of the forbidden fruit."

"It is strange."

"No—for the others were not tempted."

"How was that?"

"There was no tempter until my father ate of the fruit himself and became one. Then he tempted other angels and they ate of it also; then Adam and the woman."

"How did your father come to eat of it this time?"

"I did not know at the time."

"Why didn't you?"

"Because I was away when it happened; I was away some days, and did not hear of it at all and of the disaster to my father until I got back; then I went to my father's place to speak with him of it; but his trouble was so new, and so severe, and so amazing to him that he could do nothing but grieve and lament—he could not bear to talk about the details; I merely gathered that when he made the venture it was because his idea of the nature of the fruit was a most erroneous one."

"Erroneous?"

"Quite erroneous."

"You do not know in what way it was erroneous?"

"Yes, I think I know now. He probably—in fact unquestionably —supposed that the nature of the fruit was to reveal to human beings the knowledge of good and evil—that, and nothing more; but not to Satan the great angel; he had that knowledge before. We always had it—always. Now why he was moved to taste it himself is not clear; I shall never know until he tells me. But his error was—"

"Yes, what was his error?"

"His error was in supposing that a knowledge of the difference between good and evil was *all* that the fruit could confer."

"Did it confer more than that?"

"Consider the passage which says *man is prone to evil as the sparks to fly upward.* Is that true? Is that really the nature of man? —I mean your man—the man of this planet?"

"Indeed it is—nothing could be truer."

"It is not true of the men of any other planet. It explains the mystery. My father's error stands revealed in all its nakedness. The fruit's office was not confined to conferring the mere knowledge of good and evil, it conferred also the passionate and eager and hungry *disposition to* DO *evil.* Prone as sparks to fly upward; in other words, prone as water to run down hill—a powerful figure, and means that man's disposition is wholly evil, uncompromisingly evil, inveterately evil, and that he is as undisposed to do good as water is undisposed to run *up* hill. Ah, my father's error brought a colossal disaster upon the men of this planet. It *poisoned* the men of this planet—poisoned them in mind and body. I see it, plainly."

"It brought death, too."

"Yes—whatever that may be. I do not quite understand it. It seems to be a sleep. You do not seem to mind sleep. By my reading I gather that you are not conscious of either death *or* sleep; that nevertheless you fear the one and do not fear the other. It is very stupid. Illogical."

Hotchkiss put down his knife and fork and explained the difference between sleep and death; and how a person was not sorry when asleep, but sorry when dead, because—because—

He found it was not so easy to explain why as he had supposed it was going to be; he floundered a while, then broke down. But presently he tried again, and said that death *was* only a sleep, but that the objection to it was that it was so *long*; then he remembered that time stands still when one sleeps, and so the difference between a night and a thousand years is really no difference at all so far as the sleeper is personally affected.

However, the boy was thinking, profoundly, and heard none of it; so nothing was lost. By and by the boy said, earnestly—

"The fundamental change wrought in man's nature by my father's conduct must remain—it is permanent; but a part of its burden of evil consequences can be lifted from your race, and I will undertake it. Will you help?"

He was applying in the right quarter. Lifting burdens from a whole race was a fine and large enterprise, and suited Oliver Hotchkiss's size and gifts better than any contract he had ever taken hold of yet. He gave in his adhesion with promptness and enthusiasm, and wanted the scheme charted out at once. Privately he was immeasurably proud to be connected in business with an actual angel and son of a devil, but did what he could to keep his exultation from showing. The boy said—

"I cannot map out a definite plan yet; I must first study this race. Its poisoned condition and prominent disposition to do evil differentiate it radically from any men whom I have known before, therefore it is a new race to me and must be exhaustively studied before I shall know where and how to begin. Indefinitely speaking, our plan will be confined to ameliorating the condition of the race in some ways in *this* life; we are not called upon to concern ourselves with its future fate; that is in abler hands than ours."

"I hope you will begin your studies right away."

"I shall. Go to bed, and take your rest. During the rest of the night and to-morrow I will travel about the globe and personally examine some of the nationalities, and learn languages and read the world's books in the several tongues, and to-morrow night we will talk together here. Meantime the storm has made you a prisoner. Will you have one of my servants to wait on you?"

A genuine little devil all for his own! It was a lovely idea, and swelled Hotchkiss's vanity to the bursting point. He was lavish with his thanks.

"But he won't understand what I say to him."

"He will learn in five minutes. Would you like any particular one?"

"If I could have the cunning little rascal that sat down in the fire after he got cooled off—"

There was a flash of scarlet and the little fiend was present and smiling; and he had with him some books from the school; among them the French-English dictionary and the phonographic shorthand system.

"There. Use him night and day. He knows what he is here for. If he needs help he will provide it. He requires no lights; take them, and go to bed; leave him to study his books. In five minutes he will be able to talk broken English in case you want him. He will read twelve or fifteen of your books in an hour and learn shorthand besides; then he will be a capable secretary. He will be visible or invisible according to your orders. Give him a name—he has one already, and so have I, but you would not be able to pronounce either of them. Good-bye."

He vanished.

Hotchkiss stood smiling all sorts of pleasant smiles of intricate and variegated pattern at his little devil, with the idea of making him understand how welcome he was; and he said to himself, "It's a bitter climate for him, poor little rascal, the fire will go down and he will freeze; I wish I knew how to tell him to run home and warm himself whenever he wants to."

He brought blankets and made signs to him that these were for him to wrap up in; then he began to pile wood on the fire, but the red stranger took that work promptly off his hands, and did the work like an expert—which he was. Then he sat down on the fire and began to study his book, and his new master took the candle and went away to bed, meditating a name for him. "He is a dear little devil," he said, "and must have a nice one." So he named him Edward Nicholson Hotchkiss—after a brother that was dead.

Chapter 6

IN THE MORNING the world was still invisible, for the powdery snow was still sifting thickly down—noiselessly, now, for the wind had ceased to blow. The new devil appeared in the kitchen and scared aunt Rachel and uncle Jeff out of it, and they fled to the master's room with the tale. Hotchkiss explained the situation and told them there was no harm in this devil, but a great deal of good; and that he was the property of the wonderful boy, who had strongly recommended him.

"Is he a slave, Marse Oliver?" asked Rachel.

"Yes."

"Well, den, dey oughtn't to be much harm in him, I reckon; but is he a *real* devil?"

"Yes, genuine."

"Den how kin he be good?"

"Well, he is, anyway. We have been misinformed about devils. There's a great deal of ignorant prejudice around, concerning them. I want you to be friends with this one."

"But how kin we, Marse Oliver?" asked uncle Jeff; "we's afraid of him. We'd *like* to be friends wid him, *becase* we's afraid of him, en if he stays on de place, 'course we gwyne to do de bes' we kin; but when he come a skippin' into de kitchen all red hot like a stack of fire-coals, bless you *I* didn't want nothin' to do wid him. Still, if *he's* willin' to be friends it ain't gwyne to answer for *us* to hold back, for Gawd on'y knows what he might do."

"S'pose things don't go to suit him, Marse Oliver," said Rachel, "What he gwyne do *den?*"

"Really, you needn't worry, Rachel, he has a kind disposition, and moreover he wants to be useful—I know it."

"Why, Marse Oliver, he'll take en tear up all de hymn-books en—"

"No he won't; he's perfectly civil and obliging, and he'll do anything he is asked to do."

"Is dat so?"

"I know it."

"But what *kin* he do, Marse Oliver? he's so little, en den he don't know our ways."

"Oh, he can do anything—shovel snow, for instance."

"My! kin he do dat?" asked Jeff. "If he'll do dat, *I*'s his friend, for one—right on de spot!"

"Yes, and he can run errands—any errand you want, Rachel."

"Dat 'ud come mighty handy, Marse Oliver," said Rachel, relenting; "he can't run none now, 'course, but if de snow 'uz gone—"

"He'll run them for you, I know he will; I wish he were here, I—"

Edward Nicholson Hotchkiss appeared in their midst, and the negroes scrambled for the door, but he was there first and barred the way. He smiled an eager and fiery smile, and said—

"I've been listening. I want to be friends—don't be afraid. Give me an errand—I'll show you."

Rachel's teeth chattered a little, and her breath came short and she was as pale as bronze; but she found her tongue, and said—

"I's yo' friend—I is, I swah it. Be good to me en ole Jeff, honey—don't hurt us; don't do us no harm, for yo' ma's sake."

"Hurt you?—no. Give me an errand—I'll show you."

"But chile, dey ain't no errand; de snow's so deep, en you'd catch cold, anyway, de way you's been raised. But sakes, if you'd been here yistiddy evenin'—Marse Oliver I clean forgot de cream, en dey ain't a drop for yo' breakfast."

"I'll fetch it," said Edward, "Go down—you'll find it on the table."

He disappeared. The negroes were troubled, and did not know what to make of this. They were afraid of him again; he must be off his balance, for he could not run errands in this weather. Hotchkiss smoothed away their fears with persuasive speeches, and they presently went below, where they found the new servant trying to tame the cat and not succeeding; but the cream was there, and their respect for Edward and his abilities received a great impulse.

No. 44, The Mysterious Stranger

Chapter 1

IT WAS IN 1490—winter. Austria was far away from the world, and asleep; it was still the Middle Ages in Austria, and promised to remain so forever. Some even set it away back centuries upon centuries and said that by the mental and spiritual clock it was still the Age of Faith in Austria. But they meant it as a compliment, not a slur, and it was so taken, and we were all proud of it. I remember it well, although I was only a boy; and I remember, too, the pleasure it gave me.

Yes, Austria was far from the world, and asleep, and our village was in the middle of that sleep, being in the middle of Austria. It drowsed in peace in the deep privacy of a hilly and woodsy solitude where news from the world hardly ever came to disturb its dreams, and was infinitely content. At its front flowed the tranquil river, its surface painted with cloud-forms and the reflections of drifting arks and stone-boats; behind it rose the woody steeps to the base of the lofty precipice; from the top of the precipice frowned the vast castle of Rosenfeld, its long stretch of towers and bastions mailed in vines; beyond the river, a league to the left, was a tumbled expanse of forest-clothed hills cloven by winding gorges where the sun never penetrated; and to the right, a precipice overlooked the river, and between it and the hills just spoken of lay a far-reaching plain dotted with little homesteads nested among orchards and shade-trees.

The whole region for leagues around was the hereditary property of prince Rosenfeld, whose servants kept the castle always in perfect condition for occupancy, but neither he nor his family came there oftener than once in five years. When they came it was as if the lord of the world had arrived, and had brought all the glories of its kingdoms along; and when they went they left a calm behind which was like the deep sleep which follows an orgy.

Eseldorf was a paradise for us boys. We were not overmuch pestered with schooling. Mainly we were trained to be good Catholics; to revere the Virgin, the Church and the saints above everything; to hold the Monarch in awful reverence, speak of him with bated breath, uncover before his picture, regard him as the gracious provider of our daily bread and of all our earthly blessings, and ourselves as being sent into the world with the one only mission, to labor for him, bleed for him, die for him, when necessary. Beyond these matters we were not required to know much; and in fact, not allowed to. The priests said that knowledge was not good for the common people, and could make them discontented with the lot which God had appointed for them, and God would not endure discontentment with His plans. This was true, for the priests got it of the Bishop.

It was discontentment that came so near to being the ruin of Gretel Marx the dairyman's widow, who had two horses and a cart, and carried milk to the market town. A Hussite woman named Adler came to Eseldorf and went slyly about, and began to persuade some of the ignorant and foolish to come privately by night to her house and hear "God's *real* message," as she called it. She was a cunning woman, and sought out only those few who could read— flattering them by saying it showed their intelligence, and that only the intelligent could understand her doctrine. She gradually got ten together, and these she poisoned nightly with her heresies in her house. And she gave them Hussite sermons, all written out, to keep for their own, and persuaded them that it was no sin to read them.

One day Father Adolf came along and found the widow sitting in the shade of the horse-chestnut that stood by her house, reading these iniquities. He was a very loud and zealous and strenuous priest, and was always working to get more reputation, hoping to be a Bishop some day; and he was always spying around and keeping a sharp lookout on other people's flocks as well as his own; and he was dissolute and profane and malicious, but otherwise a good enough man, it was generally thought. And he certainly had talent; he was a most fluent and chirpy speaker, and could say the cuttingest things and the wittiest, though a little coarse, maybe—however it was only his enemies who said that, and it really wasn't any truer of him than of others; but he belonged to the village council, and lorded it there, and played smart dodges that carried his projects through, and of course that nettled the others; and in their resentment they gave him nicknames privately, and called him the "Town Bull," and "Hell's Delight," and all sorts of things; which was natural, for when you are in politics you are in the wasp's nest with a short shirt-tail, as the saying is.

He was rolling along down the road, pretty full and feeling good, and braying "We'll sing the wine-cup and the lass" in his thundering bass, when he caught sight of the widow reading her book. He came to a stop before her and stood swaying there, leering down at her with his fishy eyes, and his purple fat face working and grimacing, and said—

"What is it you've got there, Frau Marx? What are you reading?"

She let him see. He bent down and took one glance, then he knocked the writings out of her hand and said angrily—

"Burn them, burn them, you fool! Don't you know it's a sin to read them? Do you want to damn your soul? Where did you get them?"

She told him, and he said—

"By God I expected it. I will attend to that woman; I will make this place sultry for her. You go to her meetings, do you? What does she teach you—to worship the Virgin?"

"No—only God."

"I thought it. You are on your road to hell. The Virgin will punish you for this—you mark my words." Frau Marx was getting frightened; and was going to try to excuse herself for her conduct, but Father Adolf shut her up and went on storming at her and telling her what the Virgin would do with her, until she was ready to swoon with fear. She went on her knees and begged him to tell her what to do to appease the Virgin. He put a heavy penance on her, scolded her some more, then took up his song where he had left off, and went rolling and zigzagging away.

But Frau Marx fell again, within the week, and went back to Frau Adler's meeting one night. Just four days afterward both of her horses died! She flew to Father Adolf, full of repentance and despair, and cried and sobbed, and said she was ruined and must starve; for how could she market her milk now? What *must* she do? tell her what to do. He said—

"I told you the Virgin would punish you—didn't I tell you that? Hell's bells! did you think I was lying? You'll pay attention next time, I reckon."

Then he told her what to do. She must have a picture of the horses painted, and walk on pilgrimage to the Church of Our Lady of the Dumb Creatures, and hang it up there, and make her offerings; then go home and sell the skins of her horses and buy a lottery ticket bearing the number of the date of their death, and then wait in patience for the Virgin's answer. In a week it came, when Frau Marx was almost perishing with despair—her ticket drew fifteen hundred ducats!

That is the way the Virgin rewards a real repentance. Frau Marx did not fall again. In her gratitude she went to those other women and told them her experience and showed them how sinful and foolish they were and how dangerously they were acting; and they all burned their sermons and returned repentant to the bosom of the Church, and Frau Adler had to carry her poisons to some other market. It was the best lesson and the wholesomest our village ever had. It never allowed another Hussite to come there; and for reward the Virgin watched over it and took care of it personally, and made it fortunate and prosperous always.

It was in conducting funerals that Father Adolf was at his best, if he hadn't too much of a load on, but only about enough to make him properly appreciate the sacredness of his office. It was fine to see him march his procession through the village, between the kneeling ranks, keeping one eye on the candles blinking yellow in the sun to see that the acolytes walked stiff and held them straight, and the other watching out for any dull oaf that might forget himself and stand staring and covered when the Host was carried past. He would snatch that oaf's broad hat from his head, hit him a staggering whack in the face with it and growl out in a low snarl—

"Where's your manners, you beast?—and the Lord God passing by!"

Whenever there was a suicide he was active. He was on hand to see that the government did its duty and turned the family out into the road, and confiscated its small belongings and didn't smouch any of the Church's share; and he was on hand again at midnight when the corpse was buried at the cross-roads—not to do any religious office, for of course that was not allowable—but to see, for himself, that the stake was driven through the body in a right and permanent and workmanlike way.

It was grand to see him make procession through the village in plague-time, with our saint's relics in their jeweled casket, and trade prayers and candles to the Virgin for her help in abolishing the pest.

And he was always on hand at the bridge-head on the 9th of December, at the Assuaging of the Devil. Ours was a beautiful and massive stone bridge of five arches, and was seven hundred years old. It was built by the Devil in a single night. The prior of the monastery hired him to do it, and had trouble to persuade him, for the Devil said he had built bridges for priests all over Europe, and had always got cheated out of his wages; and this was the last time he would trust a Christian if he got cheated now. Always before, when he built a bridge, he was to have for his pay the first passenger that crossed it—everybody knowing he meant a Christian, of course. But no matter, he didn't *say* it, so they always sent a jackass or a chicken or some other undamnable passenger across first, and so got the best of him. This time he *said* Christian, and wrote it in the bond himself, so there couldn't be any misunderstanding. And that isn't tradition, it is history, for I have seen that bond myself, many a time; it is always brought out on Assuaging Day, and goes to the bridge-head with the procession; and anybody who pays ten groschen can see it and get remission of thirty-three sins besides, times being easier for every one then than they are now, and sins much cheaper; so much cheaper that all except the very poorest could afford them. Those were good days, but they are gone and will not come any more, so every one says.

Yes, he put it in the bond, and the prior said he didn't want the bridge built yet, but would soon appoint a day—perhaps in about a week. There was an old monk wavering along between life and death, and the prior told the watchers to keep a sharp eye out and let him know as soon as they saw that the monk was actually dying. Towards midnight the 9th of December the watchers brought him word, and he summoned the Devil and the bridge was begun. All the rest of the night the prior and the Brotherhood sat up and prayed that the dying one might be given strength to rise up and walk across the bridge at dawn—strength enough, but not too much. The prayer was heard, and it made great excitement in heaven; insomuch that all the heavenly host got up before dawn and came down to see; and there they were, clouds and clouds of angels filling all the air above the bridge; and the dying monk tottered across, and just had strength to get over; then he fell dead just as the Devil was reaching for him, and as his soul escaped the angels swooped down and caught it and flew up to heaven with it, laughing and jeering, and Satan found he hadn't anything but a useless carcase.

He was very angry, and charged the prior with cheating him, and said "*this* isn't a Christian," but the prior said "Yes it is, it's a *dead* one." Then the prior and all the monks went through with a great lot of mock ceremonies, pretending it was to assuage the Devil and reconcile him, but really it was only to make fun of him and stir up his bile more than ever. So at last he gave them all a solid good cursing, they laughing at him all the time. Then he raised a black

storm of thunder and lightning and wind and flew away in it; and
as he went the spike on the end of his tail caught on a capstone and
tore it away; and there it always lay, throughout the centuries, as
proof of what he had done. I have seen it myself, a thousand times.
Such things speak louder than written records; for written records
can lie, unless they are set down by a priest. The mock Assuaging is
repeated every 9th of December, to this day, in memory of that holy
thought of the prior's which rescued an imperiled Christian soul
from the odious Enemy of mankind.

There have been better priests, in some ways, than Father Adolf,
for he had his failings, but there was never one in our commune
who was held in more solemn and awful respect. This was because
he had absolutely no fear of the Devil. He was the only Christian I
have ever known of whom that could be truly said. People stood in
deep dread of him, on that account; for they thought there must be
something supernatural about him, else he could not be so bold and
so confident. All men speak in bitter disapproval of the Devil, but
they do it reverently, not flippantly; but Father Adolf's way was
very different; he called him by every vile and putrid name he
could lay his tongue to, and it made every one shudder that heard
him; and often he would even speak of him scornfully and scoffingly; then the people crossed themselves and went quickly out of
his presence, fearing that something fearful might happen; and this
was natural, for after all is said and done Satan is a sacred character,
being mentioned in the Bible, and it cannot be proper to utter
lightly the sacred names, lest heaven itself should resent it.

Father Adolf had actually met Satan face to face, more than
once, and defied him. This was known to be so. Father Adolf said it
himself. He never made any secret of it, but spoke it right out. And
that he was speaking true, there was proof, in at least one instance;
for on that occasion he quarreled with the Enemy, and intrepidly
threw his bottle at him, and there, upon the wall of his study was
the ruddy splotch where it struck and broke.

The priest that we all loved best and were sorriest for, was Father
Peter. But the Bishop suspended him for talking around in conversation that God was all goodness and would find a way to save *all*

his poor human children. It was a horrible thing to say, but there was never any absolute proof that Father Peter said it; and it was out of character for him to say it, too, for he was always good and gentle and truthful, and a good Catholic, and always teaching in the pulpit just what the Church required, and nothing else. But there it was, you see: he wasn't charged with saying it in the pulpit, where all the congregation could hear and testify, but only outside, in talk; and it is easy for enemies to manufacture *that*. Father Peter denied it; but no matter, Father Adolf wanted his place, and he told the Bishop, and swore to it, that he overheard Father Peter say it; heard Father Peter say it to his niece, when Father Adolf was behind the door listening—for he was suspicious of Father Peter's soundness, he said, and the interests of religion required that he be watched.

The niece, Gretchen, denied it, and implored the Bishop to believe her and spare her old uncle from poverty and disgrace; but Father Adolf had been poisoning the Bishop against the old man a long time privately, and he wouldn't listen; for he had a deep admiration of Father Adolf's bravery toward the Devil, and an awe of him on account of his having met the Devil face to face; and so he was a slave to Father Adolf's influence. He suspended Father Peter, indefinitely, though he wouldn't go so far as to excommunicate him on the evidence of only one witness; and now Father Peter had been out a couple of years, and Father Adolf had his flock.

Those had been hard years for the old priest and Gretchen. They had been favorites, but of course that changed when they came under the shadow of the Bishop's frown. Many of their friends fell away entirely, and the rest became cool and distant. Gretchen was a lovely girl of eighteen, when the trouble came, and she had the best head in the village, and the most in it. She taught the harp, and earned all her clothes and pocket money by her own industry. But her scholars fell off one by one, now; she was forgotten when there were dances and parties among the youth of the village; the young fellows stopped coming to the house, all except Wilhelm Meidling —and he could have been spared; she and her uncle were sad and forlorn in their neglect and disgrace, and the sunshine was gone out of their lives. Matters went worse and worse, all through the two years. Clothes were wearing out, bread was harder and harder to get. And now at last, the very end was come. Solomon Isaacs had lent all the money he was willing to put on the house, and gave notice that to-morrow he should foreclose.

Chapter 2

I HAD BEEN familiar with that village life, but now for as much as a year I had been out of it, and was busy learning a trade. I was more curiously than pleasantly situated. I have spoken of Castle Rosenfeld; I have also mentioned a precipice which overlooked the river. Well, along this precipice stretched the towered and battle-mented mass of a similar castle—prodigious, vine-clad, stately and beautiful, but mouldering to ruin. The great line that had possessed it and made it their chief home during four or five centuries was extinct, and no scion of it had lived in it now for a hundred years. It was a stanch old pile, and the greater part of it was still habitable. Inside, the ravages of time and neglect were less evident than they were outside. As a rule the spacious chambers and the vast corri-dors, ballrooms, banqueting halls and rooms of state were bare and melancholy and cobwebbed, it is true, but the walls and floors were in tolerable condition, and they could have been lived in. In some of the rooms the decayed and ancient furniture still remained, but if the empty ones were pathetic to the view, these were sadder still.

This old castle was not wholly destitute of life. By grace of the Prince over the river, who owned it, my master, with his little household, had for many years been occupying a small portion of it, near the centre of the mass. The castle could have housed a thou-sand persons; consequently, as you may say, this handful was lost in it, like a swallow's nest in a cliff.

My master was a printer. His was a new art, being only thirty or forty years old, and almost unknown in Austria. Very few persons in our secluded region had ever seen a printed page, few had any very clear idea about the art of printing, and perhaps still fewer had any curiosity concerning it or felt any interest in it. Yet we had to conduct our business with some degree of privacy, on account of the Church. The Church was opposed to the cheapening of books and the indiscriminate dissemination of knowledge. Our villagers did not trouble themselves about our work, and had no commerce in it; we published nothing there, and printed nothing that they could have read, they being ignorant of abstruse sciences and the dead languages.

We were a mixed family. My master, Heinrich Stein, was portly, and of a grave and dignified carriage, with a large and benevolent face and calm deep eyes—a patient man whose temper could stand much before it broke. His head was bald, with a valance of silky white hair hanging around it, his face was clean shaven, his raiment was good and fine, but not rich. He was a scholar, and a dreamer or a thinker, and loved learning and study, and would have submerged his mind all the days and nights in his books and been pleasantly and peacefully unconscious of his surroundings, if God had been willing. His complexion was younger than his hair; he was four or five years short of sixty.

A large part of his surroundings consisted of his wife. She was well along in life, and was long and lean and flat-breasted, and had an active and vicious tongue and a diligent and devilish spirit, and more religion than was good for her, considering the quality of it. She hungered for money, and believed there was a treasure hid in the black deeps of the castle somewhere; and between fretting and sweating about that and trying to bring sinners nearer to God when any fell in her way she was able to fill up her time and save her life from getting uninteresting and her soul from getting mouldy. There was old tradition for the treasure, and the word of Balthasar Hoffman thereto. He had come from a long way off, and had brought a great reputation with him, which he concealed in our family the best he could, for he had no more ambition to be burnt by the Church than another. He lived with us on light salary and board, and worked the constellations for the treasure. He had an easy berth and was not likely to lose his job if the constellations held out, for it was Frau Stein that hired him; and her faith in him, as in all things she had at heart, was of the staying kind. Inside the walls, where was safety, he clothed himself as Egyptians and magicians should, and moved stately, robed in black velvet starred and mooned and cometed and sun'd with the symbols of his trade done in silver, and on his head a conical tower with like symbols glinting from it. When he at intervals went outside he left his business suit behind, with good discretion, and went dressed like anybody else and looking the Christian with such cunning art that St. Peter would have let him in quite as a matter of course, and probably asked him to take something. Very naturally we were all afraid of him—abjectly so, I suppose I may say—though Ernest Wasserman professed that he wasn't. Not that he did it publicly; no, he didn't; for, with all his talk, Ernest Wasserman had a judgment in choosing the right place for it that never forsook him. He wasn't even afraid of ghosts, if you let him tell it; and not only that but didn't believe in them. That is to say, he *said* he didn't believe in them. The truth is, he would say any foolish thing that he thought would make him conspicuous.

To return to Frau Stein. This masterly devil was the master's second wife, and before that she had been the widow Vogel. She had brought into the family a young thing by her first marriage, and this girl was now seventeen and a blister, so to speak; for she was a second edition of her mother—just plain galley-proof, neither revised nor corrected, full of turned letters, wrong fonts, outs and doubles, as we say in the printing-shop—in a word, *pi*, if you want to put it remorselessly strong and yet not strain the facts. Yet if it ever would be fair to strain facts it would be fair in her case, for she was not loath to strain them herself when so minded. Moses Haas said that whenever she took up an en-quad fact, just watch her and you would see her try to cram it in where there wasn't breathing-room for a 4-m space; and she'd do it, too, if she had to take the sheep-foot to it. Isn't it neat! Doesn't it describe it to a dot? Well, he could say such things, Moses could—as malicious a devil as we had on the place, but as bright as a lightning-bug and as sudden, when he was in the humor. He had a talent for getting himself hated, and always had it out at usury. That daughter kept the name she was born to—Maria Vogel; it was her mother's preference and her own. Both were proud of it, without any reason, except reasons which they invented, themselves, from time to time, as a market offered. Some of the Vogels may have been distinguished, by not getting hanged, Moses thought, but no one attached much importance to what the mother and daughter claimed for them. Maria had plenty of energy and vivacity and tongue, and was shapely enough but not pretty, barring her eyes, which had all kinds of fire in them, according to the mood of the moment—opal-fire, fox-fire, hell-fire, and the rest. She hadn't any fear, broadly speaking. Perhaps she had none at all, except for Satan, and ghosts, and witches and the priest and the magician, and a sort of fear of God in the dark, and of the lightning when she had been blaspheming and hadn't time to get in *aves* enough to square up and cash-in. She despised Marget Regen, the master's niece, along with Marget's mother, Frau Regen, who was the master's sister and a dependent and bedridden widow. She loved Gustav Fischer, the big and blonde and handsome and good-hearted journeyman, and detested the rest of the tribe impartially, I think. Gustav did not reciprocate.

Marget Regen was Maria's age—seventeen. She was lithe and graceful and trim-built as a fish, and she was a blue-eyed blonde, and soft and sweet and innocent and shrinking and winning and gentle and beautiful; just a vision for the eyes, worshipful, adorable, enchanting; but that wasn't the hive for her. She was a kitten in a menagerie.

She was a second edition of what her mother had been at her age; but struck from the standing forms and needing no revising, as one says in the printing-shop. That poor meek mother! yonder she had lain, partially paralysed, ever since her brother my master had brought her eagerly there a dear and lovely young widow with her little child fifteen years before; the pair had been welcome, and had forgotten their poverty and poor-relation estate and been happy during three whole years. Then came the new wife with her five-year brat, and a change began. The new wife was never able to root out the master's love for his sister, nor to drive sister and child from under the roof, but she accomplished the rest: as soon as she had gotten her lord properly trained to harness, she shortened his visits to his sister and made them infrequent. But she made up for this by going frequently herself and roasting the widow, as the saying is.

Next was old Katrina. She was cook and housekeeper; her forbears had served the master's people and none else for three or four generations; she was sixty, and had served the master all his life, from the time when she was a little girl and he was a swaddled baby. She was erect, straight, six feet high, with the port and stride of a soldier; she was independent and masterful, and her fears were limited to the supernatural. She believed she could whip anybody on the place, and would have considered an invitation a favor. As far as her allegiance stretched, she paid it with affection and reverence, but it did not extend beyond "her family"—the master, his sister, and Marget. She regarded Frau Vogel and Maria as aliens and intruders, and was frank about saying so.

She had under her two strapping young wenches—Sara and Duffles (a nickname), and a manservant, Jacob, and a porter, Fritz.

Next, we have the printing force.

Adam Binks, sixty years old, learnèd bachelor, proof-reader, poor, disappointed, surly.

Hans Katzenyammer, 36, printer, huge, strong, freckled, red-headed, rough. When drunk, quarrelsome. Drunk when opportunity offered.

Moses Haas, 28, printer; a looker-out for himself; liable to say acid things about people and to people; take him all around, not a pleasant character.

Barty Langbein, 15; cripple; general-utility lad; sunny spirit; affectionate; could play the fiddle.

Ernest Wasserman, 17, apprentice; braggart, malicious, hateful, coward, liar, cruel, underhanded, treacherous. He and Moses had a sort of half fondness for each other, which was natural, they having one or more traits in common, down among the lower grades of traits.

Gustav Fischer, 27, printer; large, well built, shapely and muscular; quiet, brave, kindly, a good disposition, just and fair; a slow temper to ignite, but a reliable burner when well going. He was about as much out of place as was Marget. He was the best man of them all, and deserved to be in better company.

Last of all comes August Feldner, 16, 'prentice. This is myself.

Chapter 3

O F SEVERAL conveniences there was no lack; among them, fire-wood and room. There was no end of room, we had it to waste. Big or little chambers for all—suit yourself, and change when you liked. For a kitchen we used a spacious room which was high up over the massive and frowning gateway of the castle and looked down the woody steeps and southward over the receding plain.

It opened into a great room with the same outlook, and this we used as dining room, drinking room, quarreling room—in a word, family room. Above its vast fire-place, which was flanked with fluted columns, rose the wide granite mantel, heavily carved, to the high ceiling. With a cart-load of logs blazing here within and a snow-tempest howling and whirling outside, it was a heaven of a place for comfort and contentment and cosiness, and the exchange of injurious personalities. Especially after supper, with the lamps going and the day's work done. It was not the tribe's custom to hurry to bed.

The apartments occupied by the Steins were beyond this room to the east, on the same front; those occupied by Frau Regen and Marget were on the same front also, but to the west, beyond the kitchen. The rooms of the rest of the herd were on the same floor, but on the other side of the principal great interior court—away over in the north front, which rose high in air above precipice and river.

The printing-shop was remote, and hidden in an upper section of a round tower. Visitors were not wanted there; and if they had tried to hunt their way to it without a guide they would have concluded to give it up and call another time before they got through.

One cold day, when the noon meal was about finished, a most forlorn looking youth, apparently sixteen or seventeen years old, appeared in the door, and stopped there, timid and humble, venturing no further. His clothes were coarse and old, ragged, and lightly powdered with snow, and for shoes he had nothing but some old serge remnants wrapped about his feet and ancles and tied with strings. The war of talk stopped at once and all eyes were turned upon the apparition; those of the master, and Marget, and Gustav Fischer, and Barty Langbein, in pity and kindness, those of Frau Stein and the rest in varying shades of contempt and hostility.

"What do you want here?" said the Frau, sharply.

The youth seemed to wince under that. He did not raise his head, but with eyes still bent upon the floor and shyly fumbling his ruin of a cap which he had removed from his head, answered meekly—

"I am friendless, gracious lady, and am so—*so* hungry!"

"*So* hungry, are you?"—mimicking him. "Who invited you? How did you get in? Take yourself out of this!"

She half rose, as if minded to help him out with her hands. Marget started to rise at the same moment, with her plate in her hands and an appeal on her lips: "May I, madam?"

"No! Sit down!" commanded the Frau. The master, his face all pity, had opened his lips—no doubt to say the kind word—but he closed them now, discouraged. Old Katrina emerged from the kitchen, and stood towering in the door. She took in the situation, and just as the boy was turning sorrowfully away, she hailed him:

"Come back, child, there's room in my kitchen, and plenty to eat, too!"

"Shut your mouth you hussy, and mind your own affairs and keep to your own place!" screamed the Frau, rising and turning toward Katrina, who, seeing that the boy was afraid to move, was coming to fetch him. Katrina, answering no word, came striding on. "Command her, Heinrich Stein! will you allow your own wife to be defied by a servant?"

The master said "It isn't the first time," and did not seem ungratified.

Katrina came on, undisturbed; she swung unheeding past her mistress, took the boy by the hand, and led him back to her fortress, saying, as she crossed its threshold,

"If any of you wants this boy, you come and get him, that's all!"

Apparently no one wanted him at that expense, so no one followed. The talk opened up briskly, straightway. Frau Stein wanted the boy turned out as soon as might be; she was willing he should be fed, if he was so hungry as he had said he was, which was probably a lie, for he had the look of a liar, she said, but shelter he could have none, for in her opinion he had the look of a murderer and a thief; and she asked Maria if it wasn't so. Maria confirmed it, and then the Frau asked for the general table's judgment. Opinions came freely: negatives from the master and from Marget and Fischer, affirmatives from the rest; and then war broke out. Presently, as one could easily see, the master was beginning to lose patience. He was likely to assert himself when that sign appeared. He suddenly broke in upon the wrangle, and said,

"Stop! This is a great to-do about nothing. The boy is not necessarily *bad* because he is unfortunate. And if he *is* bad, what of it? A bad person can be as hungry as a good one, and hunger is always respectable. And so is weariness. The boy is worn and tired, any one can see it. If he wants rest and shelter, *that* is no crime; let him say it and have it, be he bad or good—there's room enough."

That settled it. Frau Stein was opening her mouth to try and unsettle it again when Katrina brought the boy in and stood him before the master and said, encouragingly,

"Don't be afraid, the master's a just man. Master, he's a plenty good enough boy, for all he looks such a singed cat. He's out of luck, there's nothing else the matter with him. Look at his face, look at his eye. He's not a beggar for love of it. He wants work."

"Work!" scoffed Frau Stein; "that tramp?" And "work!" sneered this and that and the other one. But the master looked interested, and not unpleased. He said,

"Work, is it? What kind of work are you willing to do, lad?"

"He's willing to do any kind, sir," interrupted Katrina, eagerly, "and he don't want any pay."

"What, no pay?"

"No sir, nothing but food to eat and shelter for his head, poor lad."

"Not even clothes?"

"He shan't go naked, sir, if you'll keep him, my wage is bail for that."

There was an affectionate light in the boy's eye as he glanced gratefully up at his majestic new friend—a light which the master noted.

"Do you think you could do rough work—rough, hard drudgery?"

"Yes, sir, I could, if you will try me; I am strong."

"Carry fire-logs up these long stairways?"

"Yes, sir."

"And scrub, like the maids; and build fires in the rooms; and carry up water to the chambers; and split wood; and help in the laundry and the kitchen; and take care of the dog?"

"Yes, sir, all those things, if you will let me try."

"All for food and shelter? Well, I don't see how a body is going to refu—"

"Heinrich Stein, wait! If you think you are going to nest this vermin in this place without ever so much as a by-your-leave to me, I can tell you you are very much mis—"

"Be quiet!" said the husband, sternly. "Now, then, you have all expressed your opinions about this boy, but there is one vote which you have not counted. I value that one above some of the others— above any of the others, in fact. On that vote by itself I would give him a trial. That is my decision. You can discuss some other subject, now—this one is finished. Take him along, Katrina, and give him a room and let him get some rest."

Katrina stiffened with pride and satisfaction in her triumph. The boy's eyes looked his gratitude, and he said,

"I would like to go to work *now*, if I may, sir."

Before an answer could come, Frau Stein interrupted:

"I want to *know*. Whose vote was it that wasn't counted? I'm not hard of hearing, and I don't know of any."

"The dog's."

Everybody showed surprise. But there it was: the dog hadn't made a motion when the boy came in. Nobody but the master had noticed it, but it was the fact. It was the first time that that demon had ever treated a stranger with civil indifference. He was chained in the corner, and had a bone between his paws and was gnawing it; and not even growling, which was not his usual way. Frau Stein's eyes beamed with a vicious pleasure, and she called out,

"You want work, do you? Well, there it is, cut out for you. Take the dog out and give him an airing!"

Even some of the hardest hearts there felt the cruelty of it, and their horror showed in their faces when the boy stepped innocently forward to obey.

"Stop!" shouted the master, and Katrina, flushing with anger, sprang after the youth and halted him.

"Shame!" she said; and the master turned his indignation loose and gave his wife a dressing down that astonished her. Then he said to the stranger,

"You are free to rest, lad, if you like, but if you would rather work, Katrina will see what she can find for you. What is your name?"

The boy answered, quietly,

"Number 44, New Series 864,962."

Everybody's eyes came open in a stare. Of course. The master thought perhaps he hadn't heard aright; so he asked again, and the boy answered the same as before,

"Number 44, New Series 864,962."

"What a hell of a name!" ejaculated Hans Katzenyammer, piously.

"Jail-number, likely," suggested Moses Haas, searchingly examining the boy with his rat eyes, and unconsciously twisting and stroking his silky and scanty moustache with his fingers, a way he had when his cogitations were concentrated upon a thing.

"It's a strange name," said the master, with a barely noticeable touch of suspicion in his tone, "where did you get it?"

"I don't know, sir," said No. 44, tranquilly, "I've always had it."

The master forbore to pursue the matter further, probably fearing that the ice was thin, but Maria Vogel chirped up and asked,

"Have you ever been in jail?"

The master burst in with—

"There, that's enough of that! You needn't answer, my boy, unless you want to." He paused—hopeful, maybe—but 44 did not seize the opportunity to testify for himself. He stood still and said nothing. Satirical smiles flitted here and there, down the table, and the master looked annoyed and disappointed, though he tried to conceal it. "Take him along, Katrina." He said it as kindly as he could, but there was just a trifle of a chill in his manner, and it delighted those creatures.

Katrina marched out with 44.

Out of a wise respect for the temper the master was in, there was no outspoken comment, but a low buzz skimmed along down the table, whose burden was, "That silence was a confession—the chap's a Jail-Bird."

It was a bad start for 44. Everybody recognized it. Marget was troubled, and asked Gustav Fischer if he believed the boy was what these people were calling him. Fischer replied, with regret in his tone,

"Well, you know, Fräulein, he could have denied it, and he didn't do it."

"Yes, I know, but think what a good face he has. And pure, too; and beautiful."

"True, quite true. And it's astonishing. But there it is, you see—he didn't deny it. In fact he didn't even seem greatly interested in the matter."

"I know it. It is unaccountable. What do you make out of it?"

"The fact that he didn't see the gravity of the situation marks him for a fool. But it isn't the face of a fool. That he could be silent at such a time is constructive evidence that he is a Jail-Bird—with

that face! which is impossible. I can't solve you that riddle, Fräulein
—it's beyond my depth."

Forty-Four entered, straining under a heavy load of logs, which
he dumped into a great locker and went briskly out again. He was
quickly back with a similar load; and another, and still another.

"There," said the master, rising and starting away, "that will do;
you are not required to kill yourself."

"One more—just one more," said the boy, as if asking a favor.

"Very well, but let that be the last," said the master, as if
granting one; and he left the room.

Forty-Four brought the final load, then stood, apparently waiting
for orders. None coming, he asked for them. It was Frau Stein's
chance. She gave him a joyfully malicious glance out of her yellow
eyes, and snapped out—

"Take the dog for an airing!"

Outraged, friend and foe alike rose at her! They surged forward to
save the boy, but they were too late; he was already on his knees
loosing the chain, his face and the dog's almost in contact. And now
the people surged back to save themselves; but the boy rose and
went, with the chain in his hand, and the dog trotted after him
happy and content.

Chapter 4

D ID IT make a stir? Oh, on your life! For nearly two minutes
the herd were speechless; and if I may judge by myself, they
quaked, and felt pale; then they all broke out at once, and discussed
it with animation and most of them said what an astonishing thing
it was—and unbelievable, too, if they hadn't seen it with their own
eyes. With Marget and Fischer and Barty the note was admiration.
With Frau Stein, Maria, Katzenyammer and Binks it was wonder,
but wonder mixed with maledictions—maledictions upon the devil
that possessed the Jail-Bird—they averring that no stranger unpro-
tected by a familiar spirit could touch that dog and come away but

in fragments; and so, in their opinion the house was in a much more serious plight, now, than it was before when it only had a thief in it. Then there were three silent ones: Ernest and Moses indicated by their cynical manner and mocking smiles that they had but a small opinion of the exploit, it wasn't a matter to make such a fuss about; the other silent one—the magician—was so massively silent, so weightily silent, that it presently attracted attention. Then a light began to dawn upon some of the tribe; they turned reverent and marveling eyes upon the great man, and Maria Vogel said with the happy exultation of a discoverer—

"There he stands, and let him deny it if he can! He put power upon that boy with his magic. I just suspected it, and now I know it! Ah, you are caught, you can't escape—own up, you wonder of the ages!"

The magician smiled a simpering smile, a detected and convicted smile, and several cried out—

"There, he *is* caught—he's trying to deny it, and he can't! Come, be fair, be good, confess!" and Frau Stein and Maria took hold of his great sleeves, peering worshipingly up in his face and tried to detain him; but he gently disengaged himself and fled from the room, apparently vastly embarrassed. So that settled the matter. It was such a manifest confession that not a doubter was left, every individual was convinced; and the praises that that man got would have gone far to satisfy a god. He was great before, he was held in awe before, but that was as nothing to the towering repute to which he had soared now. Frau Stein was in the clouds. She said that this was the most astonishing exhibition of magic power Europe had ever seen, and that the person who could doubt, after this, that he could work any miracle he wanted to would justly take rank as a fool. They all agreed that that was so, none denying it or doubting; and Frau Stein, taking her departure with the other ladies, declared that hereafter the magician should occupy her end of the table and she would move to a humbler place at his right, where she belonged.

All this was gall and vinegar to that jealous reptile Ernest Wasserman, who could not endure to hear anybody praised, and he began to cast about to turn the subject. Just then Fischer opened the way by remarking upon the Jail-Bird's strength, as shown in the wood-carrying. He said he judged that the Jail-Bird would be an ugly customer in a rough stand-up fight with a youth of his own age.

"*Him!*" scoffed Ernest, "I'm of his age, and I'll bet I'd make him sorry if he was to tackle me!"

This was Moses's chance. He said, with mock solicitude,

"Don't. Think of your mother. Don't make trouble with him, he might hurt you badly."

"Never you mind worrying about me, Moses Haas. Let him look out for himself if he meddles with me, that's all."

"Oh," said Moses, apparently relieved, "I was afraid you were going to meddle with *him*. I see he is not in any danger." After a pause, "Nor you," he added carelessly.

The taunt had the intended effect.

"Do you think I'm afraid to meddle with him? I'm not afraid of fifty of him. *I'll* show him!"

Forty-Four entered with the dog, and while he was chaining him Ernest began to edge toward the door.

"Oh," simpered Moses, "good-bye, ta-ta, I thought you were going to meddle with the Jail-Bird."

"What, to-day—and him all tired out and not at his best? I'd be ashamed of myself."

"Haw-haw-haw!" guffawed that lumbering ox, Hans Katzenyammer, "hear the noble-hearted poltroon!"

A whirlwind of derisive laughter and sarcastic remarks followed, and Ernest, stung to the quick, threw discretion to the winds and marched upon the Jail-Bird, and planted himself in front of him, crying out,

"Square off! Stand up like a man, and defend yourself."

"Defend myself?" said the boy, seeming not to understand. "From what?"

"From me—do you hear?"

"From you? I have not injured you; why should you wish to hurt me?"

The spectators were disgusted—and disappointed. Ernest's courage came up with a bound. He said fiercely,

"Haven't you any sense? Don't you know anything? You've got to fight me—do you understand that?"

"But I cannot fight you; I have nothing against you."

Ernest, mocking: "Afraid of *hurting* me, I suppose."

The Jail-Bird answered quite simply,

"No, there is no danger of that. I have nothing to hurt you for, and I shall not hurt you."

"Oh, thanks—how kind. Take that!"

But the blow did not arrive. The stranger caught both of Ernest's wrists and held them fast. Our apprentice tugged and struggled and perspired and swore, while the men stood around in a ring and laughed, and shouted, and made fun of Ernest and called him all sorts of outrageous pet names; and still the stranger held him in that grip, and did it quite easily and without puffing or blowing, whereas Ernest was gasping like a fish; and at last, when he was worn out and couldn't struggle any more, he snarled out,

"I give in—let go!" and 44 let go and said gently, "if you will let me I will stroke your arms for you and get the stiffness and the pain out;" but Ernest said "You go to hell," and went grumbling away and shaking his head and saying what he would do to the Jail-Bird one of these days, he needn't think it's over yet, he'd better look out or he'll find he's been fooling with the wrong customer; and so flourished out of the place and left the men jeering and yelling, and the Jail-Bird standing there looking as if it was all a puzzle to him and he couldn't make it out.

Chapter 5

THINGS were against that poor waif. He had maintained silence when he had had an opportunity to deny that he was a Jail-Bird, and that was bad for him. It got him that name, and he was likely to keep it. The men considered him a milksop because he spared

Ernest Wasserman when it was evident that he could have whipped him. Privately my heart bled for the boy, and I wanted to be his friend, and longed to tell him so, but I had not the courage, for I was made as most people are made, and was afraid to follow my own instincts when they ran counter to other people's. The best of us would rather be popular than right. I found that out a good while ago. Katrina remained the boy's fearless friend, but she was alone in this. The master used him kindly, and protected him when he saw him ill treated, but further than this it was not in his nature to go except when he was roused, the current being so strong against him.

As to the clothes, Katrina kept her word. She sat up late, that very first night, and made him a coarse and cheap, but neat and serviceable doublet and hose with her own old hands; and she properly shod him, too. And she had her reward, for he was a graceful and beautiful creature, with the most wonderful eyes, and these facts all showed up, now, and filled her with pride. Daily he grew in her favor. Her old hungry heart was fed, she was a mother at last, with a child to love,—a child who returned her love in full measure, and to whom she was the salt of the earth.

As the days went along, everybody talked about 44, everybody observed him, everybody puzzled over him and his ways; but it was not discoverable that he ever concerned himself in the least degree about this or was in any way interested in what people thought of him or said about him. This indifference irritated the herd, but the boy did not seem aware of it.

The most ingenious and promising attempts to ruffle his temper and break up his calm went for nothing. Things flung at him struck him on the head or the back, and fell at his feet unnoticed; now and then a leg was shoved out and he tripped over it and went heavily down amid delighted laughter, but he picked himself up and went on without remark; often when he had brought a couple of twenty-pound cans of water up two long flights of stairs from the well in the court, they were seized and their winter-cold contents poured over him, but he went back unmurmuring for more; more than once, when the master was not present, Frau Stein made him share the dog's dinner in the corner, but he was content and offered no protest. The most of these persecutions were devised by Moses and Katzenyammer, but as a rule were carried out by that shabby poor coward, Ernest.

You see, now, how I was situated. I should have been despised if I had befriended him; and I should have been treated as he was, too. It is not everybody that can be as brave as Katrina was. More than once she caught Moses devising those tricks and Ernest carrying them out, and gave both of them an awful hiding; and once when Hans Katzenyammer interfered she beat that big ruffian till he went on his knees and begged.

What a devil to work the boy was! The earliest person up found him at it by lantern-light, the latest person up found him still at it long past midnight. It was the heaviest manual labor, but if he was ever tired it was not perceptible. He always moved with energy, and seemed to find a high joy in putting forth his strange and enduring strength.

He made reputation for the magician right along; no matter what unusual thing he did, the magician got the credit of it; at first the magician was cautious, when accused, and contented himself with silences which rather confessed than denied the soft impeachment, but he soon felt safe to throw that policy aside and frankly take the credit, and he did it. One day 44 unchained the dog and said "Now behave yourself, Felix, and don't hurt any one," and turned him loose, to the consternation of the herd, but the magician sweetly smiled and said,

"Do not fear. It is a little caprice of mine. My spirit is upon him, he cannot hurt you."

They were filled with adoring wonder and admiration, those people. They kissed the hem of the magician's robe, and beamed unutterable things upon him. Then the boy said to the dog,

"Go and thank your master for this great favor which he has granted you."

Well, it was an astonishing thing that happened, then. That ignorant and malignant vast animal, which had never been taught language or manners or religion or any other valuable thing, and could not be expected to understand a dandy speech like that, went and stood straight up on its hind feet before the magician, with its nose on a level with his face, and curved its paws and ducked its head piously, and said

"Yap-yap!—yap-yap!—yap-yap!" most reverently, and just as a Christian might at prayers.

Then it got down on all fours, and the boy said,

"Salute the master, and retire as from the presence of royalty."

The dog bowed very solemnly, then backed away stern-first to his corner—not with grace it is true, but well enough for a dog that hadn't had any practice of that kind and had never heard of royalty before nor its customs and etiquettes.

Did that episode take those people's breath away? You will not doubt it. They actually went on their knees to the magician, Frau Stein leading, the rest following. I know, for I was there and saw it. I was amazed at such degraded idolatry and hypocrisy—at least servility—but I knelt, too, to avert remark.

Life was become very interesting. Every few days there was a fresh novelty, some strange new thing done by the boy, something to wonder at; and so the magician's reputation was augmenting all the time. To be envied is the secret longing of pretty much all human beings—let us say *all*; to be envied makes them happy. The magician was happy, for never was a man so envied; he lived in the clouds.

I passionately longed to know 44, now. The truth is, he was being envied himself! Spite of all his shames and insults and persecutions. For, there is no denying it, it was an enviable conspicuousness and glory to be the instrument of such a dreaded and extraordinary magician as that and have people staring at you and holding their breath with awe while you did the miracles he devised. It is not for me to deny that I was one of 44's enviers. If I hadn't been, I should have been no natural boy. But I *was* a natural boy, and I longed to be conspicuous, and wondered at and talked about. Of course the case was the same with Ernest and Barty, though they did as I did—concealed it. I was always throwing myself in the magician's way whenever I could, in the hope that he would do miracles through me, too, but I could not get his attention. He never seemed to see me when he was preparing a prodigy.

At last I thought of a plan that I hoped might work. I would seek 44 privately and tell him how I was feeling and see if he would help me attain my desire. So I hunted up his room, and slipped up there clandestinely one night after the herd were in bed, and waited. After midnight an hour or two he came, and when the light of his lantern fell upon me he set it quickly down, and took me by both of my hands and beamed his gladness from his eyes, and there was no need to say a word.

Chapter 6

H E CLOSED the door, and we sat down and began to talk, and he said it was good and generous of me to come and see him, and he hoped I would be his friend, for he was lonely and so wanted companionship. His words made me ashamed—so ashamed, and I felt so shabby and mean, that I almost had courage enough to come out and tell him how ignoble my errand was and how selfish. He smiled most kindly and winningly, and put out his hand and patted me on the knee, and said,

"Don't mind it."

I did not know what he was referring to, but the remark puzzled me, and so, in order not to let on, I thought I would throw out an observation—anything that came into my head; but nothing came but the weather, so I was dumb. He said,

"Do you care for it?"

"Care for what?"

"The weather."

I was puzzled again; in fact astonished; and said to myself "This is uncanny; I'm afraid of him."

He said cheerfully,

"Oh, you needn't be. Don't you be uneasy on my account."

I got up trembling, and said,

"I—I am not feeling well, and if you don't mind, I think I will excuse myself, and—"

"Oh, don't," he said, appealingly, "don't go. Stay with me a little. Let me do something to relieve you—I shall be so glad."

"You are so kind, so good," I said, "and I wish I could stay, but I will come another time. I—well, I—you see, it is cold, and I seem to have caught a little chill, and I think it will soon pass if I go down and cover up warm in bed—"

"Oh, a hot drink is a hundred times better, a hundred times!— that is what you really want. Now isn't it so?"

"Why yes; but in the circumstances—"

"Name it!" he said, all eager to help me. "Mulled claret, blazing hot—isn't that it?"

"Yes, indeed; but as we haven't any way to—"

"Here—take it as hot as you can bear it. You'll soon be all right."

He was holding a tumbler to me—fine, heavy cut-glass, and the steam was rising from it. I took it, and dropped into my chair again, for I was faint with fright, and the glass trembled in my hand. I drank. It was delicious; yes, and a surprise to my ignorant palate.

"Drink!" he said. "Go on—drain it. It will set you right, never fear. But this is unsociable; I'll drink with you."

A smoking glass was in his hand; I was not quick enough to see where it came from. Before my glass was empty he gave me a full one in its place and said heartily,

"Go right on, it will do you good. You are feeling better already, now aren't you?"

"Better?" said I to myself; "as to temperature, yes, but I'm scared to rags."

He laughed a pleasant little laugh and said,

"Oh, I give you my word there's no occasion for that. You couldn't be safer in my good old Mother Katrina's protection. Come, drink another."

I couldn't resist; it was nectar. I indulged myself. But I was miserably frightened and uneasy, and I couldn't stay; I didn't know what might happen next. So I said I must go. He wanted me to sleep in his bed, and said he didn't need it, he should be going to work pretty soon; but I shuddered at the idea, and got out of it by saying I should rest better in my own, because I was accustomed to it. So then he stepped outside the door with me, earnestly thanking me over and over again for coming to see him, and generously forbearing to notice how pale I was and how I was quaking; and he made me promise to come again the next night, I saying to myself that I should break that promise if I died for it. Then he said good-bye, with a most cordial shake of the hand, and I stepped feebly into the black gloom—and found myself in my own bed, with my door closed, my candle blinking on the table, and a welcome great fire flaming up the throat of the chimney!

It made me gasp! But no matter, I presently sank deliciously off to sleep, with that noble wine weltering in my head, and my last expiring effort at cerebration hit me with a cold shock:

"Did he *overhear* that thought when it passed through my mind —when I said I would break that promise if I died for it?"

Chapter 7

To my astonishment I got up thoroughly refreshed when called at sunrise. There was not a suggestion of wine or its effects in my head.

"It was all a dream," I said, gratefully. "I can get along without the mate to it."

By and by, on a stairway I met 44 coming up with a great load of wood, and he said, beseechingly,

"You *will* come again to-night, won't you?"

"Lord! I thought it was a dream," I said, startled.

"Oh, no, it was not a dream. I should be sorry, for it was a pleasant night for me, and I was *so* grateful."

There was something so pathetic in his way of saying it that a great pity rose up in me and I said impulsively,

"I'll come if I die for it!"

He looked as pleased as a child, and said,

"It's the same phrase, but I like it better this time." Then he said, with delicate consideration for me, "Treat me just as usual when others are around; it would injure you to befriend me in public, and I shall understand and not feel hurt."

"You are just lovely!" I said, "and I honor you, and would brave them all if I had been born with any spirit—which I wasn't."

He opened his big wondering eyes upon me and said,

"Why do you reproach yourself? You did not make yourself; how then are you to blame?"

How perfectly sane and sensible that was—yet I had never thought of it before, nor had ever heard even the wisest of the professionally wise people say it—nor anything half so intelligent and unassailable, for that matter. It seemed an odd thing to get it from a boy, and he a vagabond landstreicher at that. At this juncture a proposition framed itself in my head, but I suppressed it, judging that there could be no impropriety in my acting upon it without permission if I chose. He gave me a bright glance and said,

"Ah, you couldn't if you tried!"

"Couldn't what?"

"Tell what happened last night."

"Couldn't I?"

"No. Because I don't wish it. What I don't wish, doesn't happen. I'm going to tell you various secrets by and by, one of these days. You'll keep them."

"I'm sure I'll try to."

"Oh, tell them if you think you *can!* Mind, I don't say you shan't, I only say you can't."

"Well, then, I shan't try."

Then Ernest came whistling gaily along, and when he saw 44 he cried out,

"Come, hump yourself with that wood, you lazy beggar!"

I opened my mouth to call him the hardest name in my stock, but nothing would come. I said to myself, jokingly, "Maybe it's because 44 disapproves."

Forty-Four looked back at me over his shoulder and said,

"Yes, that is it."

These things were dreadfully uncanny, but interesting. I went musing away, saying to myself, "he must have read my thoughts when I was minded to ask him if I might tell what happened last night." He called back from far up the stairs,

"I did!"

Breakfast was nearing a finish. The master had been silent all through it. There was something on his mind; all could see it. When he looked like that, it meant that he was putting the sections of an important and perhaps risky resolution together, and bracing up to pull it off and stand by it. Conversation had died out; everybody was curious, everybody was waiting for the outcome.

Forty-Four was putting a log on the fire. The master called him. The general curiosity rose higher still, now. The boy came and stood respectfully before the master, who said,

"Forty-Four, I have noticed—Forty-Four is correct, I believe?—"

The boy inclined his head and added gravely,

"New Series 864,962."

"We will not go into that," said the master with delicacy, "that is your affair and I conceive that into it charity forbids us to pry. I have noticed, as I was saying, that you are diligent and willing, and have borne a hard lot these several weeks with exemplary patience. There is much to your credit, nothing to your discredit."

The boy bent his head respectfully, the master glanced down the table, noted the displeasure along the line, then went on.

"You have earned friends, and it is not your fault that you haven't them. You haven't one in the castle, except Katrina. It is not fair. I am going to be your friend myself."

The boy's eyes glowed with happiness, Maria and her mother tossed their heads and sniffed, but there was no other applause. The master continued.

"You deserve promotion, and you shall have it. Here and now I raise you to the honorable rank of apprentice to the printer's art, which is the noblest and the most puissant of all arts, and destined in the ages to come to promote the others and preserve them."

And he rose and solemnly laid his hand upon the lad's shoulder like a king delivering the accolade. Every man jumped to his feet excited and affronted, to protest against this outrage, this admission of a pauper and tramp without name or family to the gate leading to the proud privileges and distinctions and immunities of their great order; but the master's temper was up, and he said he would turn adrift any man that opened his mouth; and he commanded them to sit down, and they obeyed, grumbling, and pretty nearly strangled with wrath. Then the master sat down himself, and began to question the new dignitary.

"This is one of the learned professions. Have you studied the Latin, Forty-Four?"

"No, sir."

Everybody laughed, but not aloud.

"The Greek?"

"No, sir."

Another clandestine laugh; and this same attention greeted all the answers, one after the other. But the boy did not blush, nor look confused or embarrassed; on the contrary he looked provokingly contented and happy and innocent. I was ashamed of him, and felt for him; and that showed me that I was liking him very deeply.

"The Hebrew?"

"No, sir."

"Any of the sciences?—the mathematics? astrology? astronomy? chemistry? medicine? geography?"

As each in turn was mentioned, the youth shook his untroubled head and answered "No, sir," and at the end said,

"None of them, sir."

The amusement of the herd was almost irrepressible by this time; and on his side the master's annoyance had risen very nearly to the bursting point. He put in a moment or two crowding it down, then asked,

"Have you ever studied *anything*?"

"No, sir," replied the boy, as innocently and idiotically as ever.

The master's project stood defeated all along the line! It was a critical moment. Everybody's mouth flew open to let go a triumphant shout; but the master, choking with rage, rose to the emergency, and it was his voice that got the innings:

"By the splendor of God I'll teach you myself!"

It was just grand! But it was a mistake. It was all I could do to keep from raising a hurrah for the generous old chief. But I held in. From the apprentices' table in the corner I could see every face, and I knew the master had made a mistake. I knew those men. They could stand a good deal, but the master had played the limit, as the saying is, and I knew it. He had struck at their order, the apple of their eye, their pride, the darling of their hearts, their dearest possession, their nobility—as they ranked it and regarded it—and had degraded it. They would not forgive that. They would seek revenge, and find it. This thing that we had witnessed, and which had had the form and aspect of a comedy, was a tragedy. It was a turning point. There would be consequences. In ordinary cases where there was matter for contention and dispute, there had always been chatter and noise and jaw, and a general row; but now the faces were black and ugly, and not a word was said. It was an omen.

We three humble ones sat at our small table staring; and thinking thoughts. Barty looked pale and sick. Ernest searched my face with his evil eyes, and said,

"I caught you talking with the Jail-Bird on the stairs. You needn't try to lie out of it, I saw you."

All the blood seemed to sink out of my veins, and a cold terror crept through me. In my heart I cursed the luck that had brought upon me that exposure. What should I do? What could I do? What could I say in my defence? I could think of nothing; I had no words, I was dumb—and that creature's merciless eyes still boring into me. He said,

"Say—you are that animal's *friend*. Now deny it if you can."

I was in a bad scrape. He would tell the men, and I should be an outcast, and they would make my life a misery to me. I was afraid enough of the men, and wished there was a way out, but I saw there was none, and that if I did not want to complete my disaster I must pluck up some heart and not let this brute put me under his feet. I wasn't afraid of *him,* at any rate; even *my* timidity had its limitations. So I pulled myself together and said,

"It's a lie. I did talk with him, and I'll do it again if I want to, but that's no proof that I'm his friend."

"Oho, so you don't deny it! That's enough. I wouldn't be in your shoes for a good deal. When the men find it out you'll catch it, I can tell you that."

That distressed Barty, and he begged Ernest not to tell on me, and tried his best to persuade him; but it was of no use. He said he would tell if he died for it.

"Well, then," I said, "go ahead and do it; it's just like your sort, anyway. Who cares?"

"Oh, you don't care, don't you? Well, we'll see if you won't. And I'll tell them you're his friend, too."

If that should happen! The terror of it roused me up, and I said, "Take that back, or I'll stick this dirk into you!"

He was badly scared, but pretended he wasn't, and laughed a sickly laugh and said he was only funning. That ended the discussion, for just then the master rose to go, and we had to rise, too, and look to our etiquette. I was sufficiently depressed and unhappy, for I knew there was sorrow in store for me. Still, there was one comfort: I should not be charged with being poor 44's friend, I hoped and believed; so matters were not quite so calamitous for me as they might have been.

We filed up to the printing rooms in the usual order of precedence, I following after the last man, Ernest following after me, and Barty after him. Then came 44.

Forty-Four would have to do his studying after hours. During hours he would now fill Barty's former place and put in a good deal of his time in drudgery and dirty work; and snatch such chances as he could, in the intervals, to learn the first steps of the divine art—composition, distribution and the like.

Certain ceremonies were Forty-Four's due when as an accredited apprentice he crossed the printing-shop's threshold for the first time. He should have been invested with a dagger, for he was now privileged to bear minor arms—foretaste and reminder of the future still prouder day when as a journeyman he would take the rank of a gentleman and be entitled to wear a sword. And a red chevron should have been placed upon his left sleeve to certify to the world his honorable new dignity of printer's apprentice. These courtesies were denied him, and omitted. He entered unaccosted and unwelcomed.

The youngest apprentice should now have taken him in charge and begun to instruct him in the rudimentary duties of his position. Honest little Barty was commencing this service, but Katzenyammer the foreman stopped him, and said roughly,

"Get to your case!"

So 44 was left standing alone in the middle of the place. He looked about him wistfully, mutely appealing to all faces but mine, but no one noticed him, no one glanced in his direction, or seemed aware that he was there. In the corner old Binks was bowed over a proof-slip; Katzenyammer was bending over the imposing-stone making up a form; Ernest, with ink-ball and coarse brush was proving a galley; I was overrunning a page of Haas's to correct an out; Fischer, with paste-pot and brown linen, was new-covering the tympan; Moses was setting type, pulling down his guide for every line, weaving right and left, bobbing over his case with every type he picked up, fetching the box-partition a wipe with it as he brought it away, making two false motions before he put it in the stick and a third one with a click on his rule, justifying like a rail fence, spacing like an old witch's teeth—hair-spaces and m-quads turn about—just a living allegory of falseness and pretence from his green silk eye-shade down to his lifting and sinking heels, making show and bustle enough for 3,000 an hour, yet never good for 600 on a fat take and double-leaded at that. It was inscrutable that God would endure a comp like that, and lightning so cheap.

It was pitiful to see that friendless boy standing there forlorn in that hostile stillness. I did wish somebody would relent and say a kind word and tell him something to do. But it could not happen; they were all waiting to see trouble come to him, all expecting it, all tremulously alert for it, all knowing it was preparing for him, and

wondering whence it would come, and in what form, and who
would invent the occasion. Presently they knew. Katzenyammer
had placed his pages, separated them with reglets, removed the
strings from around them, arranged his bearers; the chase was on,
the sheep-foot was in his hand, he was ready to lock up. He slowly
turned his head and fixed an inquiring scowl upon the boy. He
stood so, several seconds, then he stormed out,

"Well, are you going to fetch me some quoins, or *not?*"

Cruel! How could *he* know what the strange word meant? He
begged for the needed information with his eloquent eyes—the
men were watching and exulting—Katzenyammer began to move
toward him with his big hand spread for cuffing—ah, my God, I
mustn't venture to speak, was there no way to save him? Then I
had a lightning thought; would he gather it from my brain?—
"Forty-Four, that's the quoin-box, under the stone table!"

In an instant he had it out and on the imposing-stone! He was
saved. Katzenyammer and everybody looked amazed. And deeply
disappointed.

For a while Katzenyammer seemed to be puzzling over it and
trying to understand it; then he turned slowly to his work and
selected some quoins and drove them home. The form was ready.
He set that inquiring gaze upon the boy again. Forty-Four was
watching with all his eyes, but it wasn't any use; how was he to
guess what was wanted of him? Katzenyammer's face began to
work, and he spat dry a couple of times, spitefully; then he shouted,

"Am *I* to do it—or *who?*"

I was ready this time. I said to myself, "Forty-Four, raise it
carefully on its edge, get it under your right arm, carry it to that
machine yonder, which is the press, and lay it gently down flat on
that stone, which is called the bed of the press."

He went tranquilly to work, and did the whole thing as right as
nails—did it like an old hand! It was just astonishing. There wasn't
another untaught and unpractised person in all Europe who could
have carried that great and delicate feat half-way through without
piing the form. I was so carried away that I wanted to shout. But I
held in.

Of course the thing happened, now, that was to be expected. The men took Forty-Four for an old apprentice, a refugee flying from a hard master. They could not ask him, as to that, custom prohibiting it; but they could ask him other questions which could be awkward. They could be depended upon to do that. The men all left their work and gathered around him, and their ugly looks promised trouble. They looked him over silently—arranging their game, no doubt—he standing in the midst, waiting, with his eyes cast down. I was dreadfully sorry for him. I knew what was coming, and I saw no possibility of his getting out of the hole he was in. The very first question would be unanswerable, and quite out of range of help from me. Presently that sneering Moses Haas asked it:

"So you are an experienced apprentice to this art, and yet don't know the Latin!"

There it was! I knew it. But—oh, well, the boy was just an ever-fresh and competent mystery! He raised his innocent eyes and placidly replied,

"Who—I? Why yes, I know it."

They gazed at him puzzled—stupefied, as you might say. Then Katzenyammer said,

"Then what did you tell the master that lie for?"

"I? I didn't know I told him a lie; I didn't mean to."

"Didn't mean to? Idiot! he asked you if you knew the Latin, and you said no."

"Oh, no," said the youth, earnestly, "it was quite different. He asked me if I had *studied* it—meaning in a school or with a teacher, as I judged. Of course I said no, for I had only picked it up—from books—by myself."

"Well, upon my soul, you *are* a purist, when it comes to cast-iron exactness of statement," said Katzenyammer, exasperated. "Nobody knows how to take you or what to make of you; every time a person puts his finger on you you're not there. Can't you do *anything* but the unexpected? If you belonged to me, damned if I wouldn't drown you."

"Look here, my boy," said Fischer, not unkindly, "do you know

—as required—the rudiments of all those things the master asked
you about?"

"Yes, sir."

"Picked them up?"

"Yes, sir."

I wished he hadn't made that confession. Moses saw a chance
straightway:

"Honest people don't get into this profession on picked-up cul-
ture; they don't get in on odds and ends, they have to *know* the
initial stages of the sciences and things. You sneaked in without an
examination, but you'll pass one now, or out you go."

It was a lucky idea, and they all applauded. I felt more comfortable, now, for if he could take the answers from my head I could
send him through safe. Adam Binks was appointed inquisitor, but I
soon saw that 44 had no use for me. He was away up. I would have
shown off if I had been in his place and equipped as he was. But he
didn't. In knowledge Binks was a child to him—that was soon
apparent. He wasn't competent to examine 44; 44 took him out of
his depth on every language and art and science, and if erudition
had been water he would have been drowned. The men had to
laugh, they couldn't help it; and if they had been manly men they
would have softened toward their prey, but they weren't and they
didn't. Their laughter made Binks ridiculous, and he lost his temper; but instead of venting it on the laughers he let drive at the boy,
the shameless creature, and would have felled him if Fischer hadn't
caught his arm. Fischer got no thanks for that, and the men would
have resented his interference, only it was not quite safe and they
didn't want to drive him from their clique, anyway. They could see
that he was at best only lukewarm on their side, and they didn't
want to cool his temperature any more.

The examination-scheme was a bad failure—a regular collapse,
in fact,—and the men hated the boy for being the cause of it,
whereas they had brought it upon themselves. That is just like
human beings. The foreman spoke up sharply, now, and told them
to get to work; and said that if they fooled away any more of the

shop's time he would dock them. Then he ordered 44 to stop idling around and get about his business. No one watched 44 now; they all thought he knew his duties, and where to begin. But it was plain to me that he didn't; so I prompted him out of my mind, and couldn't keep my attention on my work, it was so interesting and so wonderful to see him perform.

Under my unspoken instructions he picked up all the good type and broken type from about the men's feet and put the one sort in the pi pile and the other in the hell-box; turpentined the inking-balls and cleaned them; started up the ley-hopper; washed a form in the sink, and did it well; removed last week's stiff black towel from the roller and put a clean one in its place; made paste; dusted out several cases with a bellows; made glue for the bindery; oiled the platen-springs and the countersunk rails of the press; put on a paper apron and inked the form while Katzenyammer worked off a token of signature 16 of a Latin Bible, and came out of the job as black as a chimney-sweep from hair to heels; set up pi; struck galley-proofs; tied up dead matter like an artist, and set it away on the standing galley without an accident; brought the quads when the men jeff'd for takes, and restored them whence they came when the lucky comps were done chuckling over their fat and the others done damning their lean; and would have gone innocently to the village saddler's after strap-oil and *got* it—on his rear—if it had occurred to the men to start him on the errand—a thing they didn't think of, they supposing he knew that sell by memorable experience; and so they lost the best chance they had in the whole day to expose him as an impostor who had never seen a printing-outfit before.

A marvelous creature; and he went through without a break; but by consequence of my having to watch over him so persistently I set a proof that had the smallpox, and the foreman made me distribute his case for him after hours as a "lesson" to me. He was not a stingy man with that kind of tuition.

I had saved 44, unsuspected and without damage or danger to myself, and it made me lean toward him more than ever. That was natural.

Then, when the day was finished, and the men were washing up and I was feeling good and fine and proud, Ernest Wasserman came out and told on me!

Chapter 8

I SLIPPED out and fled. It was wise, for in this way I escaped the first heat of their passion, or I should have gotten not merely insults but kicks and cuffs added. I hid deep down and far away, in an unvisited part of the castle among a maze of dark passages and corridors. Of course I had no thought of keeping my promise to visit 44; but in the circumstances he would not expect it—I knew that. I had to lose my supper, and that was hard lines for a growing lad. And I was like to freeze, too, in that damp and frosty place. Of sleep little was to be had, because of the cold and the rats and the ghosts. Not that I saw any ghosts, but I was expecting them all the time, and quite naturally, too, for that historic old ruin was lousy with them, so to speak, for it had had a tough career through all the centuries of its youth and manhood—a career filled with romance and sodden with crime—and it is my experience that between the misery of watching and listening for ghosts and the fright of seeing them there is not much choice. In truth I was not sorry sleep was chary, for I did not wish to sleep. I was in trouble, and more was preparing for me, and I wanted to pray for help, for therein lay my best hope and my surest. I had moments of sleep now and then, being a young creature and full of warm blood, but in the long intervals I prayed persistently and fervently and sincerely. But I knew I needed more powerful prayers than my own—prayers of the pure and the holy—prayers of the consecrated—prayers certain to be heard, whereas mine might not be. I wanted the prayers of the Sisters of Perpetual Adoration. They could be had for 50 silver groschen. In time of threatened and imminent trouble, trouble which promised to be continuous, one valued their championship far above that of any priest, for his prayers would ascend at regularly appointed times only, with nothing to protect you in the exposed intervals between, büt theirs were perpetual—hence their name—there were no intervals, night or day: when two of the Sisters rose from before the altar two others knelt at once in their place and the supplications went on unbroken. Their convent was on the other side of the river, beyond the village, but Katrina would get the money to them for me. They would take special pains for any of us in the castle, too, for our Prince had been doing them a valuable favor lately, to appease God on account of a murder he had done on an elder brother of his, a great Prince in Bohemia and head of the house. He had repaired and renovated and sumptuously fitted up the ancient chapel of our castle, to be used by them while their convent, which had been struck by lightning again and much damaged, was undergoing reparations. They would be coming over for Sunday, and the usual service would be greatly augmented, in fact doubled: the Sacred Host would be exposed in the monstrance, and four Sisters instead of two would hold the hours of adoration; yet if you sent your 50 groschen in time you would be entitled to the advantage of this, which is getting in on the ground floor, as the saying is.

Our Prince not only did for them what I have mentioned, but was paying for one-third of those repairs on their convent besides. Hence we were in great favor. That dear and honest old Father Peter would conduct the service for them. Father Adolf was not willing, for there was no money in it for the priest, the money all going to the support of a little house of homeless orphans whom the good Sisters took care of.

At last the rats stopped scampering over me, and I knew the long night was about at an end; so I groped my way out of my refuge. When I reached Katrina's kitchen she was at work by candle-light, and when she heard my tale she was full of pity for me and maledictions for Ernest, and promised him a piece of her mind, with foot-notes and illustrations; and she bustled around and hurried up a hot breakfast for me, and sat down and talked and gossiped, and enjoyed my voracity, as a good cook naturally would, and indeed I was fairly famished. And it was good to hear her rage at those rascals for persecuting her boy, and scoff at them for that they couldn't produce one individual manly enough to stand up for him and the master. And she burst out and said she wished to God Doangivadam was here, and I just jumped up and flung my arms around her old neck and hugged her for the thought! Then she went gently down on her knees before the little shrine of the Blessed Virgin, I doing the same of course, and she prayed for help for us all out of her fervent and faithful heart, and rose up refreshed and strengthened and gave our enemies as red-hot and competent a damning as ever came by natural gift from uncultured lips in my experience.

The dawn was breaking, now, and I told her my project concerning the Sisters of the Perpetual Adoration, and she praised me and blest me for my piety and right-heartedness, and said she would send the money for me and have it arranged. I had to ask would she lend me two groschen, for my savings lacked that much of being fifty, and she said promptly—

"Will I? and you in this trouble for being good to my boy? That I will; and I'd do it if it was five you wanted!"

And the tears came in her eyes and she gave me a hug; then I hasted to my room and shut the door and locked it, and fished my hoard out of its hiding-place and counted the coins, and there were *fifty*. I couldn't understand it. I counted them again—twice; but there was no error, there were two there that didn't belong. So I didn't have to go into debt, after all. I gave the money to Katrina and told her the marvel, and she counted it herself and was astonished, and couldn't understand it any more than I could. Then came sudden comprehension! and she sank down on her knees before the shrine and poured out her thanks to the Blessed Virgin for this swift and miraculous answer.

She rose up the proudest woman in all that region; and she was justified in feeling so. She said—and tried to say it humbly—

"To think She would do it for me, a poor lowly servant, dust of the earth: There's crowned monarchs She wouldn't do it for!" and her eyes blazed up in spite of her.

It was all over the castle in an hour, and wheresoever she went, there they made reverence and gave her honor as she passed by.

It was a bad day that had dawned for 44 and me, this wretched Tuesday. The men were sour and ugly. They snarled at me whenever they could find so much as half an occasion, they sneered at me and made jokes about me; and when Katzenyammer wittily called me by an unprintable name they shouted with laughter, and sawed their boxes with their composing-rules, which is a comp's way of expressing sarcastic applause. The laughter was praise of the foreman's wit, the sarcasm was for me. You must choose your man when you saw your box; not every man will put up with it. It is the most capable and eloquent expression of derision that human beings have ever invented. It is an urgent and strenuous and hideous sound, and when an expert makes it it shrieks out like the braying of a jackass. I have seen a comp draw his sword for that. As for that name the foreman gave me, it stung me and embittered me more than any of the other hurts and humiliations that were put upon me; and I was girl-boy enough to cry about it, which delighted the men beyond belief, and they rubbed their hands and shrieked with delight. Yet there was no point in that name when applied to a person of my shape, therefore it was entirely witless. It was the slang name (imported from England), used by printers to describe a certain kind of type. All types taper slightly, and are narrower at the letter than at the base of the shank; but in some fonts this spread is so pronounced that you can almost detect it with the eye, loose and exaggerative talkers asserting that it was exactly the taper of a leather bottle. Hence that odious name: and now they had fastened it upon me. If I knew anything about printers, it would stick. Within the hour they had added it to my slug! Think of that. Added it to my number, by initials, and there you could read it in the list above the take-file: "Slug 4, B.-A." It may seem a small thing; but I can tell you that not all seemingly small things are small to a boy. That one shamed me as few things have done since.

The men were persistently hard on poor unmurmuring 44.

Every time he had to turn his back and cross the room they rained quoins and 3-m quads after him, which struck his head and bounded off in a kind of fountain-shower. Whenever he was bending down at any kind of work that required that attitude, the nearest man would hit him a blistering whack on his southern elevation with the flat of a galley, and then apologise and say,

"Oh, was it you? I'm sorry; I thought it was the master."

Then they would all shriek again.

And so on and so on. They insulted and afflicted him in every way they could think of—and did it far more for the master's sake than for his own. It was their purpose to provoke a retort out of 44, then they would thrash him. But they failed, and considered the day lost.

Wednesday they came loaded with new inventions, and expected to have better luck. They crept behind him and slipped cakes of ice down his back; they started a fire under the sink, and when he discovered it and ran to put it out they swarmed there in artificial excitement with buckets of water and emptied them on him instead of on the fire, and abused him for getting in the way and defeating their efforts; while he was inking for Katzenyammer, this creature continually tried to catch him on the head with the frisket before he could get out of the way, and at last fetched it down so prematurely that it failed to get home, but struck the bearers and got itself bent like a bow—and he got a cursing for it, as if it had been his fault.

They led him a dog's life all the forenoon—but they failed again. In the afternoon they gave him a Latin Bible-take that took him till evening to set up; and after he had proved it and was carrying away the galley, Moses tripped him and he fell sprawling, galley and all. The foreman raged and fumed over his clumsiness, putting all the blame on him and none on Moses, and finished with a peculiarly mean piece of cruelty: ordering him to come back after supper and set up the take again, by candle-light, if it took him all night.

This was a little too much for Fischer's stomach, and he began to remonstrate; but Katzenyammer told him to mind his own business;

and the others moved up with threatenings in their eyes, and so Fischer had to stand down and close his mouth. He had occasion to be sorry he had tried to do the boy a kindness, for it gave the foreman an excuse to double-up the punishment. He turned on Fischer and said,

"You think you've got some influence here, don't you? I'll give you a little lesson that'll teach you that the best way for you to get this Jail-Bird into trouble is to come meddling around here trying to get him out of it."

Then he told 44 he must set up the pi'd matter and distribute it before he began on the take!

An all-night job!—and that poor friendless creature hadn't done a thing to deserve it. Did the master know of these outrages? Yes, and was privately boiling over them; but he had to swallow his wrath, and not let on. The men had him in their power, and knew it. He was under heavy bonds to finish a formidable piece of work for the University of Prague—it was almost done, a few days more would finish it, to fall short of completion would mean ruin. He must see nothing, hear nothing, of these wickednesses: if his men should strike—and they only wanted an excuse and were playing for it—where would he get others? Venice? Frankfort? Paris? London? Why, these places were weeks away!

The men went to bed exultant that Wednesday night, and I sore-hearted.

But lord, how premature we were: the boy's little job was all right in the morning! Ah, he *was* the most astonishing creature!

Then the disaster fell: the men gave it up and struck! The poor master, when he heard the news, staggered to his bed, worn out with worry and wounded pride and despair, to toss there in fever and delirium and gabble distressful incoherencies to his grieving nurses, Marget and Katrina. The men struck in the forenoon of Thursday, and sent the master word. Then they discussed and discussed—trying to frame their grounds. Finally the document was ready, and they sent it to the master. He was in no condition to read it, and Marget laid it away. It was very simple and direct. It said that the Jail-Bird was a trial to them, and an unendurable aggravation; and that they would not go back to work again until he was sent away.

They knew the master couldn't send the lad away. It would break his sword and degrade him from his guild, for he could prove no offence against the apprentice. If he did not send 44 away work would stand still, he would fail to complete his costly printing-contract and be ruined.

So the men were happy; the master was their meat, as they expressed it, no matter which move he made, and he had but the two.

Chapter 9

It was a black and mournful time, that Friday morning that the works stood idle for the first time in their history. There was no hope. As usual the men went over to early mass in the village, like the rest of us, but they did not come back for breakfast—naturally. They came an hour later, and idled about and put in the dull time the best they could, with dreary chat, and gossip, and prophecies, and cards. They were holding the fort, you see; a quite unnecessary service, since there was none to take it. It would not have been safe for any one to set a type there.

No, there was no hope. By and by Katrina was passing by a group of the strikers, when Moses, observing the sadness in her face, could not forbear a gibe:

"I wouldn't look so disconsolate, Katrina, prayer can pull off anything, you know. Toss up a hint to your friend the Virgin."

You would have thought, by the sudden and happy change in her aspect, that he had uttered something very much pleasanter than a coarse blasphemy. She retorted,

"Thanky, dog, for the idea. I'll do it!" and she picked up her feet and moved off briskly.

I followed her, for that remark had given me an idea, too. It was this: to cheer up, on our side, and stop despairing and get down to work—bring to our help every supernatural force that could be had for love or money: the Blessed Mother, Balthasar the magician, and the Sisters of the Perpetual Adoration. It was a splendid inspiration, and she was astonished at my smartness in thinking of it. She was electrified with hope and she praised me till I blushed; and indeed I was worthy of some praise, on another count: for I told her to withdraw my former "intention," (you have to name your desire— called "intention"—when you apply to the P. A.,) and tell the Sisters not to pray for my relief, but leave me quite out and throw all their strength into praying that Doangivadam might come to the master's rescue—an exhibition of self-sacrifice on my part which Katrina said was noble and beautiful and God would remember it and requite it to me; and indeed I had thought of that already, for it would be but right and customary.

At my suggestion she said she would get 44 to implore his overlord the magician to exert his dread powers in the master's favor. So now our spirits had a great uplift; our clouds began to pass, and the sun to shine for us again. Nothing could be more judicious than the arrangement we had arrived at; by it we were pooling our stock, not scattering it; by it we had our money on three cards instead of one, and stood to win on one turn or another. Katrina said she would have all these great forces at work within the hour, and keep them at it without intermission until the winner's flag went up.

I went from Katrina's presence walking on air, as the saying is. Privately I was afraid we had one card that was doubtful—the magician. I was entirely certain that he could bring victory to our flag if he chose, but would he choose? He probably would if Maria and her mother asked him, but who was to ask them to ask him? Katrina? They would not want the master ruined, since that would be their own ruin; but they were in the dark, by persuasion of the strikers, who had made them believe that no one's ruin was really going to result except 44's. As for 44 having any influence with his mighty master, I did not take much stock in that; one might as well expect a poor lackey to have the ear and favor of a sovereign.

I expected a good deal of Katrina's card, and as to my own I hadn't the least doubt. It would fetch Doangivadam, let him be where he might; of that I felt quite sure. What he might be able to accomplish when he arrived—well, that was another matter. One thing could be depended upon, anyway—he would take the side of the under dog in the fight, be that dog in the right or in the wrong, and what man could do he would do—and up to the limit, too.

He was a wandering comp. Nobody knew his name, it had long ago sunk into oblivion under that nickname, which described him to a dot. Hamper him as you might, obstruct him as you might, make things as desperate for him as you pleased, he didn't give a damn, and said so. He was always gay and breezy and cheerful, always kind and good and generous and friendly and careless and wasteful, and couldn't keep a copper, and never tried. But let his fortune be up or down you never could catch him other than handsomely dressed, for he was a dandy from the cradle, and a flirt. He was a beauty, trim and graceful as Satan, and was a born masher and knew it. He was not afraid of anything or anybody, and was a fighter by instinct and partiality. All printers were pretty good swordsmen, but he was a past master in the art, and as agile as a cat and as quick. He was very learned, and could have occupied with credit the sanctum sanctorum, as the den of a book-editor was called, in the irreverent slang of the profession. He had a baritone voice of great power and richness, he had a scientific knowledge of music, was a capable player upon instruments, was possessed of a wide knowledge of the arts in general, and could swear in nine languages. He was a good son of the Church, faithful to his religious duties, and the most pleasant and companionable friend and comrade a person could have.

But you never could get him to stay in a place, he was always wandering, always drifting about Europe. If ever there was a perpetual sub, he was the one. He could have had a case anywhere for the asking, but if he had ever had one, the fact had passed from the memory of man. He was sure to turn up with us several times a year, and the same in Frankfort, Venice, Paris, London, and so on, but he was as sure to flit again after a week or two or three—that is to say, as soon as he had earned enough to give the boys a rouse and have enough left over to carry him to the next front-stoop on his milk-route, as the saying is.

Here we were, standing still, and so much to do! So much to do, and so little time to do it in: it must be finished by next Monday; those commissioners from Prague would arrive then, and demand their two hundred Bibles—the sheets, that is, we were not to bind them. Half of our force had been drudging away on that great job for eight months; 30,000 ems would finish the composition; but for our trouble, we could turn on our whole strength and do it in a day of 14 hours, then print the final couple of signatures in a couple of hours more and be far within contract-time—and here we were, idle, and ruin coming on!

All Friday and Saturday I stumped nervously back and forth between the Owl Tower and the kitchen—watching from the one, in hope of seeing Doangivadam come climbing up the winding road; seeking Katrina in the other for consultation and news. But when night shut down, Saturday, nothing definite had happened, uncertainty was still our portion, and we did not know where we were at, as the saying is. The magician had treated 44 to an exceedingly prompt snub and closed out his usefulness as an ambassador; then Katrina had scared Maria and her mother into a realization of their danger and they had tried *their* hands with Balthasar. He was very gracious, very sympathetic, quite willing to oblige, but pretty non-committal. He said that these printers were not the originators of this trouble, and were acting in opposition to their own volition; they were only unwitting tools—tools of three of the most malignant and powerful demons in hell, demons whom he named, and whom he had battled with once before, overcoming them, but at cost of his life almost. They were not conspiring against the master, that was only a blind—he, the magician, was the prey they were after, and he could not as yet foresee how the struggle would come out; but he was consulting the stars, and should do his best. He believed that three other strong demons were in the conspiracy, and he was working spells to find out as to this; if it should turn out to be so, he should have to command the

presence and aid of the very Prince of Darkness himself! The result
would necessarily be terrible, for many innocent persons would be
frightened to death by his thunders and lightnings and his awful
aspect; still, if the ladies desired it—

But the ladies didn't! nor any one else, for that matter. So there it
stood. If the three extra fiends didn't join the game, we might
expect Balthasar to go in and win it and make everything comfortable again for the master; but if they joined, the game was blocked,
of course, since no one was willing to have Lucifer go to the bat. It
was a momentous uncertainty; there was nothing for it but to wait
and see what those extras would elect to do.

Meantime Balthasar was doing his possible—we could see that.
He was working his incantations right along, and sprinkling pow-
ders, and lizards, and newts, and human fat, and all sorts of puissant things into his caldron, and enveloping himself in clouds of
smoke and raising a composite stink that made the castle next to
unendurable, and could be smelt in heaven.

I clung to my hope, and stuck to the Owl Tower till night closed
down and veiled the road and the valley in a silvery mist of
moonlight, but Doangivadam did not come, and my heart was very
heavy.

But in the morrow was promise; the service in our chapel would
have double strength, because four Sisters would be on duty before
the altar, whereas two was the custom. That thought lifted my
hope again.

Apparently all times are meet for love, sad ones as well as bright
and cheerful ones. Down on the castle roof I could see two couples
doing overtime—Fischer and Marget, and Moses and Maria. I did
not care for Maria, but if I had been older, and Fischer had wanted
to put on a sub—but it was long ago, long ago, and such things do
not interest me now. She was a beautiful girl, Marget.

Chapter 10

IT WAS a lovely Sunday, calm and peaceful and holy, and bright
with sunshine. It seemed strange that there could be jarrings and
enmities in so beautiful a world. As the forenoon advanced the
household began to appear, one after another, and all in their best;
the women in their comeliest gowns, the men in velvets and laces,
with snug-fitting hose that gave the tendons and muscles of their
legs a chance to show their quality. The master and his sister were
brought to the chapel on couches, that they might have the benefit
of the prayers—he pale and drowsing and not yet really at himself;
then the rest of us (except 44 and the magician) followed and took
our places. It was not a proper place for sorcerers and their tools.
The villagers had come over, and the seats were full.

The chapel was fine and sumptuous in its new paint and gilding;
and there was the organ, in full view, an invention of recent date,
and hardly any in the congregation had ever seen one before.
Presently it began to softly rumble and moan, and the people held
their breath for wonder at the adorable sounds, and their faces were
alight with ecstasy. And I—I had never heard anything so plaintive, so sweet, so charged with the deep and consoling spirit of
religion. And oh, so dreamily it moaned, and wept, and sighed and
sang, on and on, gently rising, gently falling, fading and fainting,
retreating to dim distances and reviving and returning, healing our
hurts, soothing our griefs, steeping us deeper and deeper in its
unutterable peace—then suddenly it burst into breath-taking rich
thunders of triumph and rejoicing, and the consecrated ones came
filing in! You will believe that all worldly thoughts, all ungentle
thoughts, were gone from that place, now; you will believe that
these uplifted and yearning souls were as a garden thirsting for the
fructifying dew of truth, and prepared to receive it and hold it
precious and give it husbandry.

Father Peter's face seemed to deliver hope and blessing and grace
upon us just by the benignity and love that was in it and beaming
from it. It was good to look at him, that true man. He described to

us the origin of the Perpetual Adoration, which was a seed planted
in the heart of the Blessed Margaret Alacoque by Our Lord himself, what time he complained to her of the neglect of his worship
by the people, after all he had done for men. And Father Peter said,

"The aim of the Perpetual Adoration is to give joy to Our Lord,
and to make at least some compensation by its atonement for the
ingratitude of mankind. It keeps guard day and night before the
Most Holy, to render to the forgotten and unknown Eucharistic
God acts of praise and thanksgiving, of adoration and reparation. It
is not deterred by the summer's heat nor the winter's cold. It knows
no rest, no ceasing, night or day. What a sublime vocation! After
the sacerdotal dignity, one more sublime can hardly be imagined. A
priestly virgin should the adorer be, who raises her spotless hands
and pure heart in supplication toward heaven imploring mercy,
who continually prays for the welfare of her fellow creatures, and
in particular for those who have recommended themselves to her
prayers."

Father Peter spoke of the blessings both material and spiritual
that would descend upon all who gave of their substance toward
the repairing of the convent of the Sisters of the Adoration and its
new chapel, and said,

"In our new chapel the Blessed Sacrament will be solemnly
exposed for adoration during the greater part of the year. It is our
hearts' desire to erect for Our Lord and Savior a beautiful altar, to
place Him on a magnificent throne, to surround Him with splendor
and a sea of light; for," continued he, "Our Lord said again to his
servant Margaret Alacoque: 'I have a burning thirst to be honored
by men, in the Blessed Sacrament—I wish to be treated as king in a
royal palace.' You have therefore His own warrant and word: it is
Our Lord's desire to dwell in a royal palace and to be treated as a
king."

Many among us, recognizing the reasonableness of this ambition,
rose and went forward and contributed money, and I would have
done likewise, and gladly, but I had already given all I possessed.
Continuing, Father Peter said, referring to testimonies of the supernatural origin and manifold endorsements of the Adoration,

"Miracles not contained in Holy Scripture are not articles of faith, and are only to be believed when proved by trustworthy witnesses."

"But," he added, "God permits such miracles from time to time, in order to strengthen our faith or to convert sinners." Then most earnestly he warned us to be on our guard against accepting miracles, or what seemed to be miracles, upon our own judgment and without the educated and penetrating help of a priest or a bishop. He said that an occurrence could be extraordinary without necessarily being miraculous; that indeed a true miracle was usually not merely extraordinary, it was also a thing likely to happen. Likely, for the reason that it happened in circumstances where it manifestly had a service to perform—circumstances which showed that it was not idly sent, but for a solemn and sufficient purpose. He illustrated this with several most interesting instances where both the likelihood of the events and their unusual nature were strikingly perceptible; and not to cultured perceptions alone perhaps, but possibly to even untrained intelligences. One of these he called "The miracle of Turin," and this he told in these words:

"In the year 1453 a church in Isiglo was robbed and among other things a precious monstrance was stolen which still contained the Sacred Host. The monstrance was put in a large sack and a beast of burden carried the booty of the robbers. On the 6th of June the thieves were passing through the streets of Turin with their spoil, when suddenly the animal became furious and no matter how much it was beaten could not be forced from the spot. At once the cords with which the burden was fastened to the ass's back broke, the sack opened of itself, the monstrance appeared, rose on high, and miraculously remained standing in the air to the astonishment of the many spectators. The news of this wonderful event was quickly spread through the city. Bishop Louis appeared with the chapter of his cathedral and the clergy of the city. But behold, a new prodigy! The Sacred Host leaves the case in which it was enclosed, the monstrance lowers itself to the ground, but the Sacred Host remains immovable and majestic in the air, shining like the sun and sending forth in all directions rays of dazzling splendor.

The astonished multitude loudly expressed its joy and admiration, and prostrated itself weeping and adoring before the divine Savior, who displayed His glory here in such a visible manner. The bishop too on his knees implored our Lord to descend into the chalice which he raised up to Him. Thereupon the Sacred Host slowly descended and was carried to the church of St. John amid the inexpressible exultation of the people. The city of Turin had a grand basilica built on the spot where the miracle took place."

He observed that here we had two unchallengeable testimonies to the genuineness of the miracle: that of the bishop, who would not deceive, and that of the ass, who could not. Many in the congregation who had thitherto been able to restrain themselves, now went forward and contributed. Continuing, Father Peter said,

"But now let us hear how our dear Lord, in order to call His people to repentance, once showed something of His majesty in the city of Marseilles, in France. It was A.D. 1218 that the Blessed Sacrament was exposed for adoration in the convent church of the Cordeliers for the forty hours devotion. Many devout persons were assisting at the divine service, when suddenly the sacramental species disappeared and the people beheld the King of Glory in person. His countenance shone with brightness, His look was at once severe and mild, so that no one could bear His gaze. The faithful were motionless with fear, for they soon comprehended what this august apparition meant. Bishop Belsune had more than sixty persons witness to this fact, upon oath."

Yet notwithstanding this the people continued in sin, and had to be again admonished. As Father Peter pointed out:

"At the same time it was revealed to two saintly persons that our Lord would soon visit the city with a terrible punishment if it would not be converted. After two years a pestilence really came and carried off a great part of the inhabitants."

Father Peter told how, two centuries before, in France, Beelzebub and another devil had occupied a woman, and refused to come forth at the command of the bishop, but fled from her, blaspheming, when the Sacred Host was exposed, "this being witnessed by more than 150,000 persons;" he also told how a picture of the

Sacred Host, being painted in the great window of a church that was habitually being struck by lightning, protected it afterward; then he used that opportunity to explain that churches are not struck by lightning by accident, but for a worthy and intelligent purpose:

"Four times our chapel has been struck by lightning. Now some might ask: why did God not turn away the lightning? God has in all things his most wise design, and we are not permitted to search into it. But certain it is, that if our chapel had not been visited in this way, we would not have called on the kindness and charity of the devout lovers of the Holy Eucharist. We would have remained hidden and would have been happy in our obscurity. Perhaps just *this* was His loving design."

Some who had never contributed since the chapel was first struck, on account of not understanding the idea of it before, went forward cheerfully, now, and gave money; but others, like the brewer Hummel, ever hard-headed and without sentiment, said it was an extravagant way to advertise, and God the Father would do well to leave such things to persons in the business, practical persons who had had experience; so Hummel and his like gave nothing. Father Peter told one more miracle, and all were sorry it was the last, for we could have listened hours, with profit, to these moving and convincing wonders:

"On the afternoon of February 3d, 1322, the following incident took place in the Loretto Chapel at Bordeaux. The learned priest, Dr. Delort, professor of theology in Bordeaux, exposed the Blessed Sacrament for adoration. After the Pange lingua had been chanted the sacristan suddenly arises, taps the priest on the shoulder and says: 'God appears in the Sacred Host.' Dr. Delort raises his eyes, looks at the Sacred Host and perceives the apparition. Thinking it might be a mere effect of the light he changes his position in order to be able to see better. He now sees that the Sacred Host had, so to say, separated into two parts, in order to make room in the middle for the form of a young man of wondrous beauty. The breast of Jesus projected beyond the circle of the monstrance, and He graciously moved His head whilst with His right hand He blessed the assembly.

His left hand rested on His heart. The sacristan, several children, and many adults saw the apparition, which lasted during the entire time of the exposition. With superhuman strength the priest then took the monstrance—and constantly gazing at the divine countenance—he gave the final benediction. The commemoration of this apparition is celebrated every year in this convent."

There was not a dry eye in the house.

At this moment the lightning struck the chapel once more and emptied it in a moment, everybody fleeing from it in a frenzy of terror.

This was clearly another miracle, for there was not a cloud in the sky. Proof being afterward collected and avouched by Father Peter, it was accepted and consecrated at Rome, and our chapel became celebrated by reason of it, and a resort for pilgrims.

Chapter 11

To KATRINA and me the miracle meant that my card had turned up, and we were full of joy and confidence. Doangivadam was coming, we were sure of it. I hurried to the Owl Tower and resumed my watch.

But it was another disappointment. The day wasted away, hour by hour, the night closed down, the moon rose, and still he did not come. At eleven I gave it up and came down heavy-hearted and stiff with the cold. We could not understand it. We talked it over, we turned it this way and that, it was of no use, the thing was incomprehensible. At last Katrina had a thought that seemed to throw light, and she uttered it, saying,

"Sometimes such things are delayed, for a wise purpose, a purpose hidden from us, and which it is not meet for us to inquire into: to punish Marseilles and convert it, the cholera was promised, by a revelation—but it did not come for two years."

"Ah, dear, that is it," I said, "I see it now. He will come in two years, but then it will be too late. The poor master! nothing can save him, he is lost. Before sunset to-morrow the strikers will have triumphed, and he will be a ruined man. I will go to bed; I wish I might never wake again."

About nine the next morning, Doangivadam arrived! Ah, if he could only have come a few short days before! I was all girl-boy again, I couldn't keep the tears back. At his leisure he had strolled over from the village inn, and he marched in among us, gay and jovial, plumed and gorgeous, and took everybody by surprise. Here he was in the midst, scattering salutations all around. He chucked old Frau Stein under the chin and said,

"Beautiful as ever, symbol of perpetual youth!" And he called Katrina his heart's desire and snatched a kiss; and fell into raptures over Maria, and said she was just dazzling and lit up the mouldy castle like the sun; then he came flourishing in where the men were at their early beer and their rascal plans, now at the threshold of success; and he started to burst out with some more cordialities there, but not a man rose nor gave him a look of welcome, for they knew him, and that as soon as he found out how things stood he would side with the under dog in the fight, from nature and habit. He glanced about him, and his face sobered. He backed against an unoccupied table, and half-sitting upon its edge, crossed his ancles, and continued his examination of the faces. Presently he said, gravely,

"There's something the matter, here; what is it?"

The men sat glum and ugly, and no one answered. He looked toward me, and said,

"Tell me about it, lad."

I was proud of his notice, and it so lifted my poor courage that although I dreaded the men and was trembling inside, I actually opened my mouth to begin; but before I could say anything 44 interposed and said, meekly,

"If you please, sir, it would get him into trouble with the men, and he is not the cause of the difficulty, but only I. If I may be allowed to explain it—"

Everybody was astonished to see poor 44 making so hardy a

venture, but Katzenyammer glanced at him contemptuously and cut him short:

"Shut your mouth, if you please, and look to it that you don't open it again."

"Suppose *I* ask him to open it," said Doangivadam; "what will you do about it?"

"*Close* it for him—that's what."

A steely light began to play in Doangivadam's eyes, and he called 44 to his side and said,

"Stand there. I'll take care of you. Now go on."

The men stirred in their chairs and straightened up, their faces hardening—a sort of suggestion of preparation, of clearing for action, so to speak. There was a moment's pause, then the boy said in a level and colorless voice, like one who is not aware of the weight of his words,

"I am the new apprentice. Out of unmerited disapproval of me, and for no other or honorable reason, these cowardly men conspired to ruin the master."

The astonished men, their indignant eyes fixed upon the boy, began slowly to rise; said Doangivadam,

"They did, did they?"

"Yes," said the boy.

"The—*sons* of bitches!" and every sword was out of its sheath in an instant, and the men on their feet.

"Come on!" shouted Doangivadam, fetching his long rapier up with a whiz and falling into position.

But the men hesitated, wavered, gave back, and that was the friend of the under dog's opportunity—he was on them like a cat. They recovered, and braced up for a moment, but they could not stand against the man's impetuous assault, and had to give way before it and fall back, one sword after another parting from their hands with a wrench and flying, till only two of the enemy remained armed—Katzenyammer and Binks—then the champion slipped and fell, and they jumped for him to impale him, and I turned sick at the sight; but 44 sprang forward and gripped their necks with his small hands and they sank to the floor limp and gasping. Doangivadam was up and on guard in a moment, but the battle was over. The men formally surrendered—except the two that lay there. It was as much as ten minutes before they recovered; then they sat up, looking weak and dazed and uncertain, and maybe thinking the lightning had struck again; but the fight was all out of them and they did not need to surrender; they only felt of their necks and reflected.

We victors stood looking down upon them, the prisoners of war stood grouped apart and sullen.

"How was that done?" said Doangivadam, wondering; "what was it done with?"

"He did it with his hands," I said.

"With his hands? Let me see them, lad . . . . Why, they are soft and plump—just a girl's. Come, there's no strength in these paddies; what is the secret of this thing?"

So I explained:

"It isn't his own strength, sir; his master gives it him by magic—Balthasar the enchanter."

So then he understood it.

He noticed that the men had fallen apart and were picking up their swords, and he ordered 44 to take the swords away from them and bring them to him. And he chuckled at the thought of what the boy had done, and said,

"If they resist, try those persuaders of yours again."

But they did not resist. When 44 brought him the swords he piled them on the table and said,

"Boy, you were not in the conspiracy; with that talent of yours, why didn't you make a stand?"

"There was no one to back me, sir."

"There's something in that. But I'm here, now. It's backing enough, isn't it? You'll enlist for the war?"

"Yes, sir."

"That settles it. I'll be the right wing of the army, and you'll be the left. We will concentrate on the conspiracy here and now. What is your name?"

The boy replied with his customary simplicity,

"No. 44, New Series 864,962."

Doangivadam, who was inserting the point of his rapier into its sheath, suspended the operation where it was, and after a moment asked,

"What did I understand you to say?"

"No. 44, New Series 864,962."

"Is—is that your *name?*"

"Yes, sir."

"My—word, but it's a daisy! In the hurry of going to press, let's dock it to Forty-Four and put the rest on the standing-galley and let it go for left-over at half rates. Will that do?"

"Yes, sir."

"Come, now—range up, men, and plant yourselves! Forty-Four is going to resume his account of the conspiracy. Now go on, 44, and speak as frankly as you please."

Forty-Four told the story, and was not interrupted. When it was finished Doangivadam was looking sober enough, for he recognized that the situation was of a seriousness beyond anything he had guessed—in fact it had a clearly hopeless look, so far as he could at the moment see. The men had the game in their hands; how could he, or any other, save the master from the ruin they had planned? That was his thought. The men read it in his face, and they looked the taunts which they judged it injudicious to put into words while their weapons were out of their reach. Doangivadam noted the looks and felt the sting of them as he sat trying to think out a course. He finished his thinkings, then spoke:

"The case stands like this. If the master dismisses 44—but he can't lawfully do it; that way out is blocked. If 44 remains, you refuse to work, and the master cannot fulfill his contract. That is ruin for him. You hold all the cards, that is evident.

Having conceded this, he began to reason upon the matter, and to plead for the master, the just master, the kind and blameless master, the generous master, now so sorely bested, a master who had never wronged any one, a master who would be compassionate if he were in their place and they in his . . . . .

It was time to interrupt him, lest his speech begin to produce effects, presently; and Katzenyammer did it.

"That's enough of that taffy—shut it off!" he said. "We stand solid; the man that weakens—let him look to himself!"

The war-light began to rise in Doangivadam's eyes, and he said—

"You refuse to work. Very well, I can't make you, and I can't persuade you—but starvation can! I'll lock you into the shop, and put guards over you, and the man that breaks out shall have his reward."

The men realized that the tables had been turned; they knew their man—he would keep his word; he had their swords, he was master of the situation. Even Katzenyammer's face went blank with the suddenness of the checkmate, and his handy tongue found nothing at the moment to say. By order the men moved by in single file and took up their march for the shop, followed by 44 and Doangivadam, who carried swords and maintained peace and order. Presently—

"Halt!" cried the commander. "There's a man missing. Where is Ernest Wasserman?"

It was found that he had slipped out while 44 was telling his story. But all right, he was heard coming, now. He came swaying and tottering in, sank into a chair, looking snow white, and said, "O, Lord!"

Everybody forgot the march, and crowded around him, eager to find out what dreadful thing had happened. But he couldn't answer questions, he could only moan and shiver and say—

"Don't ask *me!* I've been to the shop! O, *lordy*-lord, oh, *lordy*-lord!"

They couldn't get a thing out of him but that, he was that used up and gone to pieces. Then there was a break for the shop, Doangivadam in the lead, and the rest clattering after him through the dim and musty corridors. When we arrived we saw a sight to turn a person to stone: there before our eyes the press was whirling out printed sheets faster than a person could count them—just *snowing* them onto the pile, as you may say—yet *there wasn't a human creature in sight anywhere!*

And that wasn't all, nor the half. All the *other* printing-shop work was going briskly on—yet nobody there, not a living thing to be seen! You would see a sponge get up and dip itself in a basin of water; see it sail along through the air; see it halt an inch above a galley of dead matter and squeeze itself and drench the galley, then toss itself aside; then an invisible expert would flirt the leads out of that matter so fast they fairly seemed to rain onto the imposing-stone, and you would see the matter contract and shrink together under the process; next you would see as much as five inches of that matter separate itself from the mass and rise in the air and stand upright; see it settle itself upon that invisible expert's ring-finger as upon a seat; see it move across the room and pause above a case and go to scattering itself like lightning into the boxes—raining again? yes, it was like that. And in half or three-quarters of no time you would see that five inches of matter scatter itself out and another five come and take its place; and in another minute or two there would be a mountain of wet type in every box and the job finished.

At other cases you would see "sticks" hovering in the air above the space-box; see a line set, spaced, justified and the rule slipped over in the time it takes a person to snap his fingers; next minute the stick is full! next moment it is emptied into the galley! and in ten minutes the *galley's* full and the case empty! It made you dizzy to see these incredible things, these impossible things.

Yes, all the different kinds of work were racing along like Sam Hill—*and all in a sepulchral stillness.* The way the press was carrying on, you would think it was making noise enough for an insurrection, but in a minute you would find it was only your fancy, it wasn't producing a sound—then you would have that sick and chilly feeling a person always has when he recognizes that he is in the presence of creatures and forces not of this world. The invisibles were making up forms, locking up forms, unlocking forms, carrying new signatures to the press and removing the old: abundance of movement, you see, plenty of tramping to and fro, yet you couldn't hear a footfall; there wasn't a spoken word, there wasn't a whisper, there wasn't a sigh—oh, the saddest, uncanniest silence that ever was.

But at last I noticed that there really was one industry lacking—a couple of them: no proofs were taken, no proofs were read! Oh, these *were* experts, sure enough! When *they* did a thing, they did it right, apparently, and it hadn't any occasion to be corrected.

Frightened? We were paralyzed; we couldn't move a limb to get away, we couldn't even cross ourselves, we were so nerveless. And we couldn't look away, the spectacle of those familiar objects drifting about in the air unsupported, and doing their complex and beautiful work without visible help, was so terrifyingly fascinating that we had to look and keep on looking, we couldn't help it.

At the end of half an hour the distribution stopped, and the composing. In turn, one industry after another ceased. Last of all, the churning and fluttering press's tremendous energies came to a stand-still; invisible hands removed the form and washed it, invisible hands scraped the bed and oiled it, invisible hands hung the frisket on its hook. Not anywhere in the place was any motion, any movement, now; there was nothing there but a soundless emptiness, a ghostly hush. This lasted during a few clammy moments, then came a sound from the furthest case—soft, subdued, but harsh, gritty, mocking, sarcastic: the scraping of a rule on a box-partition! and with it came half a dozen dim and muffled spectral chuckles, the dry and crackly laughter of the dead, as it seemed to me.

In about a minute something cold passed by. Not wind, just cold. I felt it on my cheek. It was one of those ghosts; I did not need any one to tell me that; it had that damp, tomby feel which you do not get from any live person. We all shrank together, so as not to obstruct the others. They straggled along by at their leisure, and we counted the frosts as they passed: eight.

Chapter 12

WE ARRIVED back to our beer-and-chess room troubled and miserable. Our adventure went the rounds of the castle, and soon the ladies and the servants came, pale and frightened, and when they heard the facts it knocked them dumb for one while, which was not a bad thing.

But the men were not dumb. They boldly proposed to denounce the magician to the Church and get him burnt, for this thing was a little *too* much, they said. And just then the magician appeared, and when he heard those awful words, fire and the Church, he was that scared he couldn't stand; the bones fairly melted in his legs and he squshed down in a chair alongside of Frau Stein and Maria, and began to beg and beseech. His airy pride and self-sufficiency had all gone out of him, and he pretended with all his might that he hadn't brought those spectres and hadn't had anything to do with it. He seemed so earnest that a body could hardly keep from believing him, and so distressed that I had to pity him though I had no love for him, but only admiration.

But Katzenyammer pressed him hard, and so did Binks and Moses Haas, and when Maria and her mother tried to put in a word for him they convinced nobody and did him no good. Doangivadam put the climax to the poor man's trouble and hit the nail on the head with a remark which everybody recognized as the wisest and tellingest thing that had been said yet. He said—

"Balthasar Hoffman, such things don't happen by accident—you know that very well, and we all do. You are the only person in the castle that has the power to do a miracle like that. Now then—firstly, it *happened;* secondly, it didn't happen by itself; thirdly, *you are here.* What would anybody but a fool conclude?"

Several shouted—

"He's *got* him! got him where he can't budge!"

Another shouted—

"He doesn't answer, and he can't—the stake's the place for him!"

The poor old thing began to cry. The men rose against him in a fury; they were going to seize him and hale him before the authorities, but Doangivadam interposed some more wisdom, good and sound. He said—

"Wait. It isn't the best way. He will leave the enchantment on, for revenge. We want it taken off, don't we?"

Everybody agreed, by acclamation. Doangivadam certainly had a wonderful head, and full of talent.

"Very well, then. Now Balthasar Hoffman, you've got a chance for your life. It has suited you to deny, in the most barefaced way, that you put that enchantment on—let that pass, it doesn't signify.

What we want to know now, is, if we let you alone, do you promise it shan't happen again?"

It brought up his spirits like raising the dead, he was so glad and grateful.

"I do, I do!" he said; "on my honor it shan't happen again."

It made the greatest change. Everybody was pleased, and the awful shadow of that fear vanished from all faces, and they were as doomed men that had been saved. Doangivadam made the magician give his honor that he would not try to leave the castle, but would stand by, and be a safeguard; and went on to say—

"That enchantment had malice back of it. It is my opinion that those invisible creatures have been setting up and printing mere rubbish, in order to use up the paper-supply and defeat the master's contract and ruin him. I want somebody to go and see. Who will volunteer?"

There was a large silence; enough of it to spread a foot deep over four acres. It spread further and further, and got thicker and thicker. Finally Moses Haas said, in his mean way—

"Why don't *you* go?"

They all had to smile at that, for it was a good hit. Doangivadam managed to work up a smile, too, but you could see it didn't taste good; then he said—

"I'll be frank about it. I don't go because I am afraid to. Who is the bravest person here?"

Nearly everybody nominated Ernest Wasserman, and laughed, and Doangivadam ordered him to go and see, but he spoke out with disgust and indignation and said—

"See you in hell, first, and *then* I wouldn't!"

Then old Katrina spoke up proud and high, and said—

"There's my boy, there. I lay he's not afraid. Go 'long and look, child."

They thought 44 wouldn't, but I thought he would, and I was right, for he started right along, and Doangivadam patted him on the head and praised his pluck as he went by. It annoyed Ernest Wasserman and made him jealous, and he pursed up his lips and said—

"I wasn't *afraid* to go, but I'm no slave and I wasn't going to do it on any random unclassified Tom-Dick-and-Harry's orders."

Not a person laughed or said a word, but every man got out his composing rule and scraped wood, and the noise of it was like a concert of jackasses. That is a thing that will take the stiffening out of the conceitedest donkey you can start, and it squelched Ernest Wasserman, and he didn't pipe up any more. Forty-Four came back with an astonisher. He said—

"The invisibles have finished the job, and it's perfect. The contract is saved."

"Carry that news to the master!" shouted Doangivadam, and Marget got right up and started on that mission; and when she delivered it and her uncle saw he was saved in purse and honor and everything, it was medicine for him, and he was a well man again or next to it before he was an hour older.

Well, the men looked that disgusted, you can't think—at least those that had gotten up the strike. It was a good deal of a pill, and Katzenyammer said so; and said—

"We've got to take it—but there'll be sugar on it. We've lost the game, but I'll not call off the strike nor let a man go to work till we've been paid *waiting*-wages."

The men applauded.

"What's waiting-wages?" inquired Doangivadam.

"Full wages for the time we've lost during the strike."

"M-y—word! Well, if that isn't cheek! You're to be paid for time lost in trying to ruin the master! Meantime, where does *he* come in? Who pays him *his* waiting-time?"

The leaders tossed their heads contemptuously, and Binks said he wasn't interested in irrelevances.

So there we were, you see—at a stand-still. There was plenty of work on hand, and the "takes" were on the hooks in the shop, but the men stood out; they said they wouldn't go near the place till their waiting-wages had been paid and the shop spiritually disinfected by the priest. The master was as firm; he said he would never submit to that extortion.

It seemed to be a sort of drawn battle, after all. The master had won the biggest end of the game, but the rest of it remained in the men's hands. This was exasperating and humiliating, but it was a fact just the same, and the men did a proper amount of crowing over it.

About this time Katzenyammer had a thought which perhaps had occurred to others, but he was the first to utter it. He said, with a sneer—

"A lot is being taken for granted—on not even respectable *evidence,* let alone proof. How do *we* know the contract has been completed and saved?"

It certainly was a hit, everybody recognized that; in fact you could call it a sockdolajer, and not be any out of the way. The prejudice against 44 was pretty strong, you know. Doangivadam was jostled—you could see it. He didn't know what to say—you could see that, too. Everybody had an expression on his face, now—a very exultant one on the rebel side, a very uncomfortable one on the other—with two exceptions: Katrina and 44; 44 hadn't any expression at all—his face was wood; but Katrina's eyes were snapping. She said—

"I know what you mean, you ornery beer-jug, you Katzenyammer; you mean he's a liar. Well, then, why don't you go and see for yourself? Answer me that—why *don't* you?"

"I don't *need* to, if you want to know. It's nothing to me—*I* don't care what becomes of the contract."

"Well, then, keep your mouth shut and mind your own business. You *dasn't* go, and you know it. Why, you great big mean coward, to call a poor friendless boy a liar, and then ain't man enough to go and prove it!"

"Look here, woman, if you—"

"Don't you call *me* woman, you scum of the earth!" and she strode to him and stood over him; "say it again and I'll tear you to rags!"

The bully murmured—

"I take it back," which made many laugh.

Katrina faced about and challenged the house to go and see. There was a visible shrinkage all around. No answer. Katrina looked at Doangivadam. He slowly shook his head, and said—

"I'll not deny it—I lack the grit."

Then Katrina stretched herself away up in the air and said—

"I'm under the protection of the Queen of Heaven, and I'll go myself! Come along, 44."

They were gone a considerable time. When they returned Katrina said—

"He showed me everything and explained it all, and it's just exactly as he told you." She searched the house, face by face, with her eyes, then settled them upon Katzenyammer and finished: "Is there any polecat here that's got the sand to doubt it *now?*"

Nobody showed up. Several of our side laughed, and Doangivadam he laughed too, and fetched his fist down with a bang on the table like the Lord Chief Justice delivering an opinion, and said—

"That settles it!"

Chapter 13

N EXT DAY was pretty dreary. The men wouldn't go to work, but loafed around moody and sour and uncomfortable. There was not much talk; what there was was mumbled, in the main, by pairs. There was no general conversation. At meals silence was the rule. At night there was no jollity, and before ten all had disappeared to their rooms and the castle was a dim and grim solitude.

The day after, the same. Wherever 44 came he got ugly looks, threatening looks, and I was afraid for him and wanted to show sympathy but was too timid. I tried to think I avoided him for his own good, but did not succeed to my satisfaction. As usual, he did not seem to know he was being so scowled at and hated. He certainly could be inconceivably stupid at times, for all he was so capable at others. Marget pitied him and said kind things to him, and Doangivadam was cordial and handsome to him, and whenever Doangivadam saw one of those scowls he insulted the man that exhibited it and invited him to exhibit it again, which he didn't. Of course Katrina was 44's friend right along. But the friendliness was confined to those three, at least as far as any open show of it went.

So things drifted along, till the contract-gentlemen came for the goods. They brought a freight wagon along, and it waited in the great court. There was an embarrassment, now. Who would box-up the goods? Our men? Indeed, no. They refused, and said they wouldn't allow any outsider to do it, either. And Katzenyammer said to Doangivadam, while he was pleading—

"Save your breath—the contract has failed, after all!"

It made Doangivadam mad, and he said—

"It hasn't failed, either. I'll box the things myself, and Katrina and I will load them into the wagon. Rather than see you people win, I'll chance death by ghost and fright. I reckon Katrina's Virgin can protect the two of us. Perhaps you boys will interfere. I have my doubts."

The men chuckled, furtively. They knew he had spoken rashly. They knew he had not taken into account the size and weight of those boxes.

He hurried away and had a private word with the master, saying—

"It's all arranged, sir. Now if you—"

"Excellent! and most unexpected. Are the men—"

"No, but no matter, it's arranged. If you can feed and wine and otherwise sumptuously and satisfactorily entertain your guests three hours, I'll have the goods in the wagon then."

"Oh, many, many thanks—I'll make them stay all night."

Doangivadam came to the kitchen, then, and told Katrina and 44 all this, and I was there just at that time and heard it; and Katrina said all right, she would protect him to the shop, now, and leave him in the care of the Virgin while he did the packing, and in two hours and a half dinner would be down to the wine and nuts and then she would come and help carry the boxes. Then he left with her, but I stayed, for no striker would be likely to venture into the kitchen, therefore I could be in 44's company without danger. When Katrina got back, she said—

"That Doangivadam's a gem of the ocean—he's a *man,* that's what he is, not a waxwork, like that Katzenyammer. I wasn't going to discourage him, but *we* can't carry the boxes. There's five, and each of them a barrow-load; and besides, there has to be four carriers to the barrow. And then—"

Forty-Four interrupted:

"There's two of you, and I'll be the other two. You two will carry one end, and I'll carry the other. I am plenty strong enough."

"Child, you'll just stay out of sight, that's what you'll do. Do you want to provoke the men every way you can think of, you foolish little numskull? Ain't they down on you a plenty, just the way it is?"

"But you see, you two *can't* carry the boxes, and if you'll only let me help—"

"You'll not budge a step—do you hear me?" She stood stern and resolute, with her knuckles in her hips. The boy looked disappointed and grieved, and that touched her. She dropped on her knees where he sat, and took his face between her hands, and said, "Kiss your old mother, and forgive"—which he did, and the tears came into her eyes, which a moment before were so stormy. "Ain't you all I've got in the world? and don't I love the ground you walk on, and can I bear to see you getting into more and more danger all the time, and no need of it? Here, bless your heart," and she jumped up and brought a pie, "You and August sample *that,* and be good. It ain't the kind you get outside of this kitchen, that you can't tell from plate-mail when you bite it in the dark."

We began on the pie with relish, and of course conversation failed for a time. By and by 44 said, softly—

"Mother, he gave his word, you know."

Katrina was hit. She had to suspend work and think that over. She seated herself against the kitchen table, with her legs aslant and braced, and her arms folded and her chin down, and muttered several times, "Yes, that's so, he did." Finally she unlimbered and reached for the butcher-knife, which she fell to sharpening with energy on a brick. Then she lightly tested its edge with the ball of her thumb, and said—

"I know it—we've got to have two more. Doangivadam will force one, and I bet I'll persuade the other."

"*Now* I'm content," said 44, fervently, which made Katrina beam with pleasure.

We stayed there in the comfortable kitchen and chatted and played checkers, intending to be asked by Katrina to take our dinner with her, for she was the friendliest and best table-company *we* had. As time drew on, it became jolly in the master's private dining-room where it was his custom to feed guests of honor and distinction, and whenever a waiter came in or went out we could hear the distant bursts of merriment, and by and by bursts of song, also, showing that the heavy part of the feeding had been accomplished. Then we had our dinner with Katrina, and about the time we had finished, Doangivadam arrived hungry and pretty well tired out and said he had packed every box; but he wouldn't take a bite, he said, until his job was finished up and the wagon loaded. So Katrina told him her plan for securing extra help by compulsion and persuasion, and he liked it and they started. Doangivadam said he hadn't seen any of the men in sight, therefore he judged they must be lying in wait somewhere about the great court so as to interrupt any scheme of bribing the two porters of the freight wagon to help carry the boxes; so it was his idea to go there and see.

Katrina ordered us to stay behind, which we didn't do, after they were out of sight. We went down by secret passages and reached the court ahead of them, and hid. We were near the wagon. The driver and porters had been given their supper, and had been to the stalls to feed and water the horses, and now they were walking up and down chatting and waiting to receive the freight. Our two friends arrived now, and in low voices began to ask these men if they had seen any men of the castle around about there, but before they could answer, something happened: we saw some dim big bulks emerge from our side of the court about fifty yards away and come in procession in our direction. Swiftly they grew more and more distinct under the stars and by the dim lamps, and they turned out to be men, and each of them was drooping under one of our big freight boxes. The idea—carrying it all alone! And another surprising thing was, that when the first man passed us it turned out to be Katzenyammer! Doangivadam was delighted out of his senses, almost, and said some splendid words of praise about his change of heart, but Katzenyammer could only grunt and growl, he was strained so by his burden.

And the next man was Binks! and there was more praise and more grunts. And next came Moses Haas—think of it! And then Gustav Fischer! And after him, the end of the procession—Ernest Wasserman! Why, Doangivadam could hardly believe it, and said he *didn't* believe it, and *couldn't;* and said "*Is* it you, Ernest?" and Ernest told him to go to hell, and then Doangivadam was satisfied and said "that settles it."

For that was Ernest's common word, and you could know him by it in the dark.

Katrina couldn't say a word, she just stood there dazed. She saw the boxes stowed in the wagon, she saw the gang file back and disappear, and still she couldn't get her voice till then; and even then all she could say, was—

"Well, it beats the band!"

Doangivadam followed them a little way, and wanted to have a supper and a night of it, but they answered him roughly and he had to give it up.

Chapter 14

THE FREIGHT wagon left at dawn; the honored guests had a late breakfast, paid down the money on the contract, then after a good-bye bottle they departed in their carriage. About ten the master, full of happiness and forgiveness and benevolent feeling, had the men assembled in the beer-and-chess room, and began a speech that was full of praises of the generous way they had thrown ill-will to the winds at the last moment and loaded the wagon last night and saved the honor and the life of his house—and went on and on, like that, with the water in his eyes and his voice trembling; and there the men sat and stared at one another, and at the master, with their mouths open and their breath standing still; till at last Katzenyammer burst out with—

"What in the nation *are* you mooning about? Have you lost your mind? *We've* saved you nothing; *we've* carried no boxes"—here he rose excited and banged the table—"and what's more, we've arranged that nobody *else* shall carry a box or load that wagon till our waiting-time's paid!"

Well, think of it! The master was so astonished that for a moment or two he couldn't pull his language; then he turned sadly and uncertainly to Doangivadam and said—

"I could not have dreamed it. Surely you told me that they—"

"Certainly I did. I told you they brought down the boxes—"

"*Listen* at him!" cried Binks, springing to his feet.

"—those five *there*—Katzenyammer at the head, Wasserman at the tail—"

"As sure as my name's Was—"

"—each with a box on his shoulders—"

All were on their feet, now, and they drowned out the speaker with a perfect deluge of derisive laughter, out of the midst of which burst Katzenyammer's bull-voice shouting—

"Oh, listen to the maniac! *Each* carrying a box weighing *five— hundred—pounds!*"

Everybody took up that telling refrain and screamed it and yelled it with all his might. Doangivadam saw the killing force of the argument, and began to look very foolish—which the men saw, and they roared at him, challenging him to get up and purge his soul and trim his imagination. He was caught in a difficult place, and he did not try to let on that he was in easy circumstances. He got up and said, quietly, and almost humbly—

"I don't understand it, I can't explain it. I realize that no man here could carry one of those boxes; and yet as sure as I am alive I saw it done, just as I have said. Katrina saw it too. We were awake, and not dreaming. I spoke to every one of the five. I saw them load the boxes into the wagon. I—"

Moses Haas interrupted:

"Excuse me, nobody loaded any boxes into the wagon. It wouldn't have been allowed. We've kept the wagon under watch." Then he said, ironically, "Next, the gentleman will work his imagination up to saying the wagon is gone and the master paid."

It was good sarcasm, and they all laughed; but the master said, gravely, "Yes, I have been paid," and Doangivadam said, "Certainly the wagon is gone."

"Oh, come!" said Moses, leaving his seat, "this is going a little *too* far; it's a trifle *too* brazen; come out and say it to the wagon's face. If you've got the cheek to do it, follow me."

He moved ahead, and everybody swarmed after him, eager to see what would happen. I was getting worried; nearly half convinced, too; so it was a relief to me when I saw that the court was empty. Moses said—

"Now then, what do you call *that?* Is it the wagon, or isn't it?"

Doangivadam's face took on the light of a restored confidence and a great satisfaction, and he said—

"I see no wagon."

"What!" in a general chorus.

"No—I don't see any wagon."

"Oh, great guns! perhaps the master will say *he* doesn't see a wagon."

"Indeed I see none," said the master.

"Wel-l, well, *well!"* said Moses, and was plumb nonplussed. Then he had an idea, and said, "Come, Doangivadam, you seem to be near-sighted—please to follow me and *touch* the wagon, and see if you'll have the hardihood to go on with this cheap comedy."

They walked briskly out a piece, then Moses turned pale and stopped.

"By God, it's gone!" he said.

There was more than one startled face in the crowd. They crept out, silent and looking scared; then they stopped, and sort of moaned—

"It *is* gone; it was a ghost-wagon."

Then they walked right over the place where it had been, and crossed themselves and muttered prayers. Next they broke into a fury, and went storming back to the chess-room, and sent for the magician, and charged him with breaking his pledge, and swore the Church should have him now; and the more he begged the more they scared him, till at last they grabbed him to carry him off—then he broke down, and said that if they would spare his life he would confess. They told him to go ahead, and said if his confession was not satisfactory it would be the worse for him. He said—

"I hate to say it—I wish I could be spared it—oh, the shame of it, the ingratitude of it! But—pity me, pity me!—I have been nourishing a viper in my bosom. That boy, that pupil whom I have so loved —in my foolish fondness I taught him several of my enchantments, and now he is using them for your hurt and my ruin!"

It turned me sick and faint, the way the men plunged at 44, crying "Kill him, kill him!" but the master and Doangivadam jumped in and stood them off and saved him. Then Doangivadam talked some wisdom and reasonableness into the gang which had good effect. He said—

"What is the use to kill the boy? He isn't the *source;* whatever power he has, he gets from his master, this magician here. Don't you believe that if the magician wants to, he can put a spell on the boy that will abolish his power and make him harmless?"

Of course that was so, and everybody saw it and said so. So then Doangivadam worked some more wisdom: instead of letting on to know it all himself, he gave the others a chance to seem to know a little of what was left. He asked them to assist him in this difficult case and suggest some wise and practical way to meet this emergency. It flattered them, and they unloaded the suggestion that the magician be put under bond to shut off the boy's enchantments, on pain of being delivered to the Church if anything happened again.

Doangivadam said it was the very thing; and praised the idea, and let on to think it was wonderfully intelligent, whereas it was only what he had suggested himself, and what anybody would have thought of and suggested, including the cat, there being no other way with any sense in it.

So they bonded the magician, and he didn't lose any time in furnishing the pledge and getting a new lease on his hide. Then he turned on the boy and reproached him for his ingratitude, and then he fired up on his subject and turned his tongue and his temper loose, and most certainly he did give him down the banks and roll Jordan roll! I never felt so sorry for a person, and I think others were sorry for him, too, though they would have said that as long as he deserved it he couldn't expect to be treated any gentler, and it would be a valuable lesson to him anyway, and save him future trouble, and worse. The way the magician finished, was awful; it made your blood run cold. He walked majestically across the room with his solemn professional stride, which meant that something was going to happen. He stopped in the door and faced around, everybody holding their breath, and said, slow and distinct, and pointing his long finger—

"Look at him, there where he sits—and remember my words, and the doom they are laden with. I have put him under my spells; if he thinks he can dissolve them and do you further harm, let him try. But I make this pledge and compact: on the day that he succeeds I will put an enchantment upon him, here in this room, which shall slowly consume him to ashes before your eyes!"

Then he departed. Dear me, but it was a startled crowd! Their faces were that white—and they couldn't seem to say a word. But there was one good thing to see—there was pity in every face of them! That was human nature, wasn't it—when your enemy is in awful trouble, to be sorry for him, even when your pride won't let you go and say it to him before company? But the master and Doangivadam went and comforted him and begged him to be careful and work no spells and run no risks; and even Gustav Fischer ventured to go by, and heave out a kindly word in passing; and pretty soon the news had gone about the castle, and Marget and Katrina came; *they* begged him, too, and both got to crying, and that made him so conspicuous and heroic, that Ernest Wasserman was bursting with jealousy, and you could see he wished *he* was advertised for roasting, too, if this was what you get for it.

Katrina had sassed the magician more than once and had not seemed to be afraid of him, but this time her heart was concerned and her pluck was all gone. She went to him, with the crowd at her heels, and went on her knees and begged him to be good to her boy, and stay his hand from practising enchantments, and be his guardian and protector and save him from the fire. Everybody was moved. Except the boy. It was one of his times to be an ass and a wooden-head. He certainly could choose them with the worst judgment I ever saw. Katrina was alarmed; she was afraid his seeming lack of interest would have a bad effect with the magician, so she did his manners for him and conveyed his homage and his pledges of good behavior, and hurried him out of the presence.

Well, to my mind there is nothing that makes a person interesting like his being about to get burnt up. We had to take 44 to the sick lady's room and let her gaze at him, and shudder, and shrivel, and wonder how he would look when he was done; she hadn't had such a stirring up for years, and it acted on her kidneys and her spine and her livers and all those things and her other works, and started up her flywheel and her circulation, and she said, herself, it had done her more good than any bucketful of medicine she had taken that week. And begged him to come again, and he promised he would if he could. Also said if he couldn't he would send her some of the ashes; for he certainly was a good boy at bottom, and thoughtful.

They all wanted to see him, even people that had taken hardly any interest in him before—like Sara and Duffles and the other maids, and Fritz and Jacob and the other men-servants. And they were all tender toward him, and ever so gentle and kind, and gave him little things out of their poverty, and were ever so sorry, and showed it by the tears in their eyes. But not a tear out of *him*, you might have squeezed him in the hydraulic press and you wouldn't have got dampness enough to cloud a razor, it being one of his blamed wooden times, you know.

Why, even Frau Stein and Maria were full of interest in him, and gazed at him, and asked him how it felt—in prospect, you know—and said a lot of things to him that came nearer being kind, than anything they were used to saying, by a good deal. It was surprising how popular he was, all of a sudden, now that he was in such awful danger if he didn't behave himself. And although I was around with him I never got a sour look from the men, and so I hadn't a twinge of fear the whole time. And then the supper we had that night in the kitchen!—Katrina laid out her whole strength on it, and cried all over it, and it was wonderfully good and salty.

Katrina told us to go and pray all night that God would not lead 44 into temptation, and she would do the same. I was ready and anxious to begin, and we went to my room.

Chapter 15

B<small>UT WHEN</small> we got there I saw that 44 was not minded to pray, but was full of other and temporal interests. I was shocked, and deeply concerned; for I felt rising in me with urgency a suspicion which had troubled me several times before, but which I had ungently put from me each time—that he was indifferent to religion. I questioned him—he confessed it! I leave my distress and consternation to be imagined, I cannot describe them.

In that paralysing moment my life changed, and I was a different being; I resolved to devote my life, with all the affections and forces and talents which God had given me to the rescuing of this endangered soul. Then all my spirit was invaded and suffused with a blessed feeling, a divine sensation, which I recognized as the approval of God. I knew by that sign, as surely as if He had spoken to me, that I was His appointed instrument for this great work. I knew that He would help me in it; I knew that whenever I should need light and leading I could seek it in prayer, and have it; I knew—

"I get the idea," said 44, breaking lightly in upon my thought, "it will be a Firm, with its headquarters up there and its hindquarters down here. There's a duplicate of it in every congregation—in every family, in fact. Wherever you find a warty little devotee who isn't in partnership with God—as *he* thinks—on a speculation to save some little warty soul that's no more worth saving than his own, stuff him and put him in the museum, it is where he belongs."

"Oh, don't say such things, I beseech you! They are so shocking, and so awful. And so unjust; for in the sight of God all souls are precious, there is no soul that is not worth saving."

But the words had no effect. He was in one of his frivolous moods, and when these were upon him one could not interest him in serious things. For all answer to what I had been saying, he said in a kindly but quite unconcerned way that we would discuss this trifle at another time, but not now. That was the very word he used; and plainly he used it without any sense of its gross impropriety. Then he added this strange remark—

"For the moment, I am not living in the present century, but in one which interests me more, for the time being. *You* pray, if you like—never mind me, I will amuse myself with a curious toy if it won't disturb you."

He got a little steel thing out of his pocket and set it between his teeth, remarking "it's a jew's-harp—the niggers use it"—and began to buffet out of it a most urgent and strenuous and vibrant and exceedingly gay and inspiriting kind of music, and at the same time he went violently springing and capering and swooping and swirling all up and down the room in a way to banish prayer and make a person dizzy to look at him; and now and then he would utter the excess of his joy in a wild whoop, and at other times he would leap into the air and spin there head over heels for as much as a minute like a wheel, and so frightfully fast that he was all webbed together and you could hear him buzz. And he kept perfect time to his music all the while. It was a most extravagant and stirring and heathen performance.

Instead of being fatigued by it he was only refreshed. He came and sat down by me and rested his hand on my knee in his winning way, and smiled his beautiful smile, and asked me how I liked it. It was so evident that he was expecting a compliment, that I was obliged to furnish it. I had not the heart to hurt him, and he so innocently proud of his insane exhibition. I could not expose to him how undignified it was, and how degrading, and how difficult it had been for me to stand it through; I forced myself to say it was "ideal—*more* than ideal;" which was of course a perfectly meaningless phrase, but he was just hungry enough for a compliment to

make him think this was one, and also make him overlook what was
going on in my mind; so his face was fairly radiant with thanks and
happiness, and he impulsively hugged me and said—

"It's lovely of you to like it so. I'll do it again!"

And at it he went, God assoil him, like a tempest. I couldn't say
anything, it was my own fault. Yet I was not really to blame, for I
could not foresee that he would take that uninflamed compliment
for an invitation to do the fiendish orgy over again. He kept it up
and kept it up until my heart was broken and all my body and spirit
so worn and tired and desperate that I could not hold in any longer,
I *had* to speak out and beg him to stop, and not tire himself so. It
was another mistake; damnation, he thought I was suffering on *his*
account! so he piped out cheerily, as he whizzed by—

"Don't worry about *me*; sit right where you are and enjoy it, I
can do it all night."

I thought I would go out and find a good place to die, and was
starting, when he called out in a grieved and disappointed tone—

"Ah, you are not going, are you?"

"Yes."

"What for? Don't go—please don't."

"Are you going to keep still? Because I am not going to stay here
and see you tire yourself to death."

"Oh, it doesn't tire me in the least, I give you my word. *Do* stay."

Of course I wanted to stay, but not unless he would sit down and
act civilized, and give me a rest. For a time he could *not* seem to get
the situation through his head—for he certainly could be the dull-
est animal that ever was, at times—but at last he looked up with a
wounded expression in his big soft eyes, and said—

"August, I believe you do not *want* any more."

Of course that broke me all down and made me ashamed of
myself, and in my anxiety to heal the hurt I had given and see him
happy again I came within a hair's breadth of throwing all judgment and discretion to the winds and saying I *did* want more. But I
did not do it; the dread and terror of what would certainly follow,
tied my tongue and saved my life. I adroitly avoided a direct answer
to what he had said, by suddenly crying "ouch!" and grabbing at an

imaginary spider inside my collar, whereupon he forgot his troubles at once in his concern for me. He plunged his hand in and raked it around my neck and fetched out three spiders—real ones, whereas I had supposed there was none there but imaginary ones. It was quite unusual for any but imaginary ones to be around at that time of the year, which was February.

We had a pleasant time together, but no religious conversation, for whenever I began to frame a remark of that color he saw it in my mind and squelched it with that curious power of his whereby he barred from utterance any thought of mine it happened to suit him to bar. It was an interesting time, of course, for it was the nature of 44 to be interesting. Pretty soon I noticed that we were not in my room, but in his. The change had taken place without my knowing when it happened. It was beautiful magic, but it made me feel uneasy. Forty-Four said—

"It is because you think I am traveling toward temptation."

"I am sure you are, 44. Indeed you are already arrived there, for you are doing things of a sort which the magician has prohibited."

"Oh, that's nothing! I don't obey him except when it suits me. I mean to use his enchantments whenever I can get any entertainment out of them, and whenever I can annoy him. I know every trick he knows, and some that he doesn't know. Tricks of my own —for I bought them; bought them from a bigger expert than he is. When I play my own, he is a puzzled man, for he thinks I do it by his inspiration and command, and inasmuch as he can't remember furnishing either the order or the inspiration, he is puzzled and bothered, and thinks there is something the matter with his head. He has to father everything I do, because he has begun it and can't get out of it now, and so between working his magic and my own I mean to build him up a reputation that will leave all other second-class magicians in the shade."

"It's a curious idea. Why don't you build it up for yourself?"

"I don't want it. At home we don't care for a small vanity like that, and I shouldn't value it here."

"Where is your ho—"

It got barred before I could finish. I wished in my heart I could have that gorgeous reputation which he so despised! But he paid no attention to the thought; so I sighed, and did not pursue it. Presently I got to worrying again, and said—

"Forty-Four, I foresee that before you get far with the magician's reputation you will bring a tragedy upon yourself. And you are so unprepared. You ought to prepare, 44, you ought indeed; every moment is precious. I do wish you would become a Christian; won't you try?"

He shook his head, and said—

"I should be too lonesome."

"Lonesome? How?"

"I should be the only one."

I thought it an ill jest, and said so. But he said it was not a jest—some time he would go into the matter and prove that he had spoken the truth; at present he was busy with a thing of "importance"—and added, placidly, "I must jack-up the magician's reputation, first." Then he said in his kindest manner—

"You have a quality which I do not possess—fear. You are afraid of Katzenyammer and his pals, and it keeps you from being with me as much as you would like and as I would like. That can be remedied, in a quite simple way. I will teach you how to become invisible, whenever you please. I will give you a magic word. Utter it in your mind, for you can't do it with your tongue, though I can. Say it when you wish to disappear, and say it again when you wish to be visible again."

He uttered the word, and vanished. I was so startled and so pleased and so grateful that I did not know where I was, for a moment, nor which end of me was up; then I perceived that I was sitting by the fire in my own room, but I did not know how I got there.

Being a boy, I did what another boy would have done: as long as I could keep awake I did nothing but appear and disappear, and enjoy myself. I was very proud, and considered myself the superior of any boy in the land; and that was foolish, for I did not invent the art, it was a gift, and no merit to me that I could exercise it. Another boy with the same luck would be just as superior as I was. But these were not my thoughts, I got them later, and at second hand—where all thoughts are acquired, 44 used to say. Finally I disappeared and went to sleep happy and content, without saying one prayer for 44, and he in such danger. I never thought of it.

Chapter 16

Forty-four, by grace of his right to wear a sword, was legally a gentleman. It suited his whim, now, to come out dressed as one. He was clever, but ill balanced; and whenever he saw a particularly good chance to be a fool, pie couldn't persuade him to let it go by; he had to sample it, he couldn't seem to help it. He was as unpopular as he could be, but the hostile feeling, the intense bitterness, had been softening little by little for twenty-four hours, on account of the awful danger his life was in, so of course he must go and choose *this* time of all times, to flaunt in the faces of the comps the offensive fact that he was their social equal. And not only did he appear in the dress of a gentleman, but the quality and splendor of it surpassed even Doangivadam's best, and as for the others they were mere lilies of the valley to his Solomon. Embroidered buskins, with red heels; pink silk tights; pale blue satin trunks; cloth of gold doublet; short satin cape, of a blinding red; lace collar fit for a queen; the cunningest little blue velvet cap, with a slender long feather standing up out of a fastening of clustered diamonds; dress sword in a gold sheath, jeweled hilt. That was his outfit; and he carried himself like a princeling "doing a cake-walk," as he described it. He was as beautiful as a picture, and as satisfied with himself as if he owned the earth. He had a lace handkerchief in his hand, and now and then he would give his nose a dainty little dab or two with it, the way a duchess does. It was evident that he thought he was going to be admired, and it was pitiful to see his disappointment when the men broke out on him with insults and ridicule and called him offensive names, and asked him where he had stolen his clothes.

He defended himself the best he could, but he was so near to crying that he could hardly control his voice. He said he had come by the clothes honestly, through the generosity of his teacher the good magician, who created them instantly out of nothing just by uttering a single magic word; and said the magician was a far mightier enchanter than they supposed; that he hadn't shown the world the half of the wonders he could do, and he wished he was here now, he would not like it to have his humble servant abused so when he wasn't doing any harm; said he believed if he was here he would do Katzenyammer a hurt for calling his servant a thief and threatening to slap his face.

"He would, would he? Well, there he comes—let's *see* if he loves his poor dear servant so much," said Katzenyammer, and gave the boy a cruel slap that you could have heard a hundred yards.

The slap spun Forty-Four around, and as soon as he saw the magician he cried out eagerly and supplicatingly—

"Oh, noble master, oh greatest and sublimest of magicians, I read your command in your eyes, and I must obey if it is your will, but I pray you, I beseech you spare me the office, do it yourself with your own just hand!"

The magician stood still and looked steadily and mutely at Forty-Four as much as half a minute, we waiting and gazing and holding our breath; then at last 44 made a reverent bow, saying, "You are master, your will is law, and I obey," and turned to Katzenyammer and said—

"In not very many hours you will discover what you have brought upon yourself and the others. You will see that it is not well to offend the master."

You have seen a cloud-shadow sweep along and sober a sunlit field; just so, that darkling vague threat was a cloud-shadow to those faces there. There is nothing that is more depressing and demoralizing than the promise of an indefinite calamity when one is dealing with a powerful and malicious necromancer. It starts large, plenty large enough, but it does not stop there, the imagination goes on spreading it, till at last it covers all the space you've got, and takes away your appetite, and fills you with dreads and miseries, and you start at every noise and are afraid of your own shadow.

Old Katrina was sent by the women to beg 44 to tell what was going to happen so that they could get relieved of a part of the crushing burden of suspense, but she could not find him, nor the magician either. Neither of them was seen, the rest of the day. At supper there was but little talk, and no mention of *the* subject. In the chess-room after supper there was some private and unsociable drinking, and much deep sighing, and much getting up and walking the floor unconsciously and nervously a little while, then sitting down again unconsciously; and now and then a tortured ejaculation broke out involuntarily. At ten o'clock nobody moved to go to bed; apparently each troubled spirit found a sort of help and solace in the near presence of its kind, and dreaded to separate itself from companionship. At half past ten no one had stirred. At eleven the same. It was most melancholy to be there like this, in the dim light of unquiet and flickering candles and in a stillness that was broken by but few sounds and was all the more impressive because of the moaning of the wintry wind about the towers and battlements.

It was at half past eleven that it happened. Everybody was sitting steeped in musings, absorbed in thought, listening to that dirge the wind was chanting—Katzenyammer like the rest. A heavy step was heard, all glanced up nervously, and yonder in the door appeared a *duplicate Katzenyammer!* There was one general gasping intake of breath that nearly sucked the candles out, then the house sat paralyzed and gazing. This creature was in shop-costume, and had a "take" in its hand. It was the exact reproduction of the other Katzenyammer to the last shade and detail, a mirror couldn't have told them apart. It came marching up the room with the only gait that could be proper to it—aggressive, decided, insolent—and held out the "take" to its twin and said—

"Here! how do you want that set, leaded, or solid?"

For about a moment the original Katzenyammer was surprised out of himself; but the next moment he was all there, and jumped up shouting—

"You bastard of black magic, I'll"—he finished with his fist, delivering a blow on the twin's jaw that would have broken anybody else's, but this jaw stood it uncrushed; then the pair danced about the place hammering, banging, ramming each other like battering machines, everybody looking on with wonder and awe and admiration, and hoping neither of them would survive. They fought half an hour, then sat down panting, exhausted, and streaming with blood—they hadn't strength to go on.

The pair sat glaring at each other a while, then the original said—

"Look here, my man, who *are* you, anyway? Answer up!"

"I'm Katzenyammer, foreman of the shop. That's who I am, if you want to know."

"It's a lie. Have you been setting type in there?"

"Yes, I have."

"The hell you have! who told you you could?"

"I told myself. That's sufficient."

"Not on your life! Do you belong to the union?"

"No, I don't."

"Then you're a scab. Boys, up and at him!"

Which they did, with a will, fuming and cursing and swearing in a way which it was an education to listen to. In another minute there would not have been anything left of that Duplicate, I reckon, but he promptly set up a ringing shout of "Help, boys, help!" and in the same moment perfect Duplicates of all the *rest* of us came swarming in and plunged into the battle!

But it was another draw. It had to be, for each Duplicate fought his own mate and was his exact match, and neither could whip the other. Then they tried the issue with swords, but it was a draw once more. The parties drew apart, now, and acrimoniously discussed the situation. The Duplicates refused to join the union, neither would they throw up their job; they were stubbornly deaf to both threats and persuasion. So there it was—just a deadlock! If the Duplicates remained, the Originals were without a living—why, they couldn't even collect their waiting-time, now! Their impregnable position, which they had been so proud of and so arrogant about had turned to air and vacancy. These were very grave and serious facts, cold and clammy ones; and the deeper they sank down into the consciousness of the ousted men the colder and clammier they became.

It was a hard situation, and pitiful. A person may say that the men had only gotten what they deserved, but when that is said is all said? I think not. They were only human beings, they had been foolish, they deserved some punishment, but to take their very bread was surely a punishment beyond the measure of their fault. But there it was—the disaster was come, the calamity had fallen, and no man could see a way out of the difficulty. The more one examined it the more perplexing and baffling and irremediable it seemed. And all so unjust, so unfair; for in the talk it came out that the Duplicates did not need to eat or drink or sleep, so long as the Originals did those things—there was enough for both; but when a *Duplicate* did them, by George, his Original got no benefit out of it! Then look at that other thing: the Originals were out of work and wageless, yet they would be supporting these intruding scabs, out of *their* food and drink, and by gracious not even a thank-you for it! It came out that the scabs got no pay for their work in the shop, and didn't care for it and wouldn't ask for it. Doangivadam finally hit upon a fair and honorable compromise, as he thought, and the boys came up a little out of their droop to listen. Doangivadam's idea was, for the Duplicates to do the work, and for the Originals to take the pay, and fairly and honorably eat and sleep enough for both. It looked bright and hopeful for a moment, but then the clouds settled down again: the plan wouldn't answer; it would not be lawful for unions and scabs to have dealings together. So that idea had to be given up, and everybody was gloomier than ever. Meantime Katzenyammer had been drinking hard, to drown his exasperations, but it was not effective, he couldn't seem to hold enough, and yet he was full. He was only half drunk; the trouble was, that his Duplicate had gotten the other half of the dividend, and was just as drunk, and as insufficiently drunk, as *he* was. When he realized this he was deeply hurt, and said reproachfully to his Duplicate, who sat there blinking and suffused with a divine contentment—

"Nobody *asked* you to partake; such conduct is grossly ill-bred; no gentleman would do such a thing."

Some were sorry for the Duplicate, for he was not to blame, but several of the Originals were evidently not sorry for him, but offended at him and ashamed of him. But the Duplicate was not affected, he did not say anything, but just blinked and looked drowsy and grateful, the same as before.

The talk went on, but it arrived nowhere, of course. The situation remained despairingly incurable and desperate. Then the talk turned upon the magician and 44, and quickly became bitter and vengeful. When it was at its sharpest, the magician came mooning in; and when he saw all those Duplicates he was either thunderstruck with amazement or he played it well. The men were vexed to see him act so, and they said, indignantly—

"It's your own fiendish work and you needn't be pretending surprise."

He was frightened at their looks and their manner, and hastened to deny, with energy and apparent earnestness, that *this* was any work of his; he said he had given a quite different command, and he only wished 44 were here, he would keep his word and burn him to ashes for misusing his enchantments; he said he would go and find him; and was starting away, but they jumped in front of him and barred his way, and Katzenyammer-original was furious, and said—

"You are trying to escape, but you'll not! You don't have to stir out of your tracks to produce that limb of perdition, and you know it and we know it. Summon him—summon him and destroy him, or I give my honor I will denounce you to the Holy Office!"

That was a plenty. The poor old man got white and shaky, and put up his hand and mumbled some strange words, and in an instant, *bang!* went a thunderclap, and there stood 44 in the midst, dainty and gay in his butterfly clothes!

All sprang up with horror in their faces to protest, for at bottom no one really wanted the boy destroyed, they only *believed* they did; there was a scream, and Katrina came flying, with her gray hair streaming behind her; for one moment a blot of black darkness fell upon the place and extinguished us all; the next moment in our midst stood that slender figure transformed to a core of dazzling white fire; in the succeeding moment it crumbled to ashes and we were blotted out in the black darkness again. Out of it rose an adoring cry—broken in the middle by a pause and a sob—

"The Lord gave, the Lord hath taken away . . . . blessed be the name of the Lord!"

It was Katrina; it was the faithful Christian parting with its all, yet still adoring the smiting hand.

Chapter 17

I WENT invisible the most of the next day, for I had no heart to talk about common matters, and had rather a shrinking from talking about the matter which was uppermost in all minds. I was full of sorrow, and also of remorse, which is the way with us in the first days of a bereavement, and at such times we wish to be alone with our trouble and our bitter recallings of failings of loyalty or love toward the comrade who is gone. There were more of these sins to my charge than I could have believed; they rose up and accused me at every turn, and kept me saying with heart-wearing iteration, "Oh, if he were only back again, how true I would be, and how differently I would act." I remembered so many times when I could perhaps have led him toward the life eternal, and had let the chance go by; and now he was lost and I to blame, and where was I to find comfort?

I always came back to that, I could not long persuade myself to other and less torturing thoughts—such, for instance, as wonderings over his yielding to the temptation to overstep the bounds of the magician's prohibition when he knew so well that it could cost him his life. Over that, of a surety, I might and did wonder in vain, quite in vain; there was no understanding it. He was volatile, and lacking in prudence, I knew that; but I had not dreamed that he was *entirely* destitute of prudence, I had not dreamed that he could actually risk his life to gratify a whim. Well, and what was I trying to get out of these reasonings? This—and I had to confess it: I was trying to excuse myself for my desertion of him in his sore need; when my promised prayers, which might have saved him, were withheld, and neglected, and even forgotten. I turned here and there and yonder for solace, but in every path stood an accusing spirit and barred the way; solace for me there was none.

No one of the household was indifferent to Katrina's grief, and the most of them went to her and tried to comfort her. I was not of these, I could not have borne it if she had asked me if I had prayed as I had said I would, or if she had thanked me for my prayers, taking for granted that I had kept my word. But I sat invisible while the others offered their comforting words; and every sob that came from her broken heart was another reproach and gave me a guilty pang. But her misery could not be abated. She moaned and wept, saying over and over again that if the magician had only shown a little mercy, which could have cost him nothing, and had granted time for a priest to come and give her boy absolution, all would have been well, and now he would be happy in heaven and she in the earth—but no! he had cruelly sent the lad unassoiled to judgment and the eternal fires of hell, and so had doomed her also to the pains of hell forevermore, for in heaven she should feel them all the days of eternity, looking down upon him suffering there and she powerless to assuage his thirst with one poor drop of water!

There was another thing which wrung her heart, and she could not speak of it without new floods of tears: her boy had died unreconciled to the Church, and his ashes could not be buried in holy ground; no priest could be present, no prayer uttered above them by consecrated lips, they were as the ashes of the beasts that perish, and fit only to lie in a dishonored grave.

And now and then, with a new outburst of love and grief she would paint the graces of his form, and the beauty of his young face, and his tenderness for her, and tell this and that and the other little thing that he had done or said, so dear and fond, so prized at the time, so sacred now forevermore!

I could not endure it; and I floated from the place upon the unrevealing air, and went wandering here and there disconsolate and finding everywhere reminders of him, and a new heartbreak with each.

By reason of the strange and uncanny tragedy, all the household were in a subdued and timorous state, and full of vague and formless and depressing apprehensions and boding terrors, and they went wandering about, aimless, comfortless and forlorn; and such talking together as there was, was of the disjointed and rambling sort that indicates preoccupation. However, if the Duplicates were properly of the household, what I have just been saying does not include them. They were not affected, they did not seem interested. They stuck industriously to their work, and one met them going to it or coming from it, but they did not speak except when spoken to. They did not go to the table, nor to the chess-room; they did not seem to avoid us, they took no pains about that, they merely did not seek us. But we avoided them, which was natural. Every time I met myself unexpectedly I got a shock and caught my breath, and was as irritated for being startled as a person is when he runs up against himself in a mirror which he didn't know was there.

Of course the destruction of a youth by supernatural flames summoned unlawfully from hell was not an event that could be hidden. The news of it went quickly all about and made a great and terrifying excitement in the village and the region, and at once a summons came for the magician to appear before a commission of the Holy Office. He could not be found. Then a second summons was posted, admonishing him to appear within twenty-four hours or remain subject to the pains and penalties attaching to contumacy. It did not seem to us likely that he would accept either of these invitations, if he could get out of it.

All day long, things went as I have described—a dreary time. Next day it was the same, with the added gloom of the preparations for the burial. This took place at midnight, in accordance with the law in such cases, and was attended by all the occupants of the castle except the sick lady and the Duplicates. We buried the ashes in waste ground half a mile from the castle, without prayer or blessing, unless the tears of Katrina and our sorrow were in some sense a blessing. It was a gusty night, with flurries of snow, and a black sky with ragged cloud-rack driving across it. We came on foot, bearing flaring and unsteady torches; and when all was over, we inverted the torches and thrust them into the soft mould of the grave and so left them, sole and perishable memorial and remembrancer of him who was gone.

Home again, it was with a burdened and desolate weight at my heart that I entered my room. There sat the corpse!

Chapter 18

My senses forsook me and I should have fallen, but it put up its hand and flipped its fingers toward me and this brought an influence of some kind which banished my faint and restored me; yes, more than that, for I was fresher and finer now than I had been before the fatigues of the funeral. I started away at once and with such haste as I could command, for I had never seen the day that I was not afraid of a ghost or would stay where one was if there was another place convenient. But I was stopped by a word, in a voice which I knew and which was music to my ears—

"Come back! I am alive again, it is not a ghost."

I returned, but I was not comfortable, for I could not at once realize that he was really and solidly alive again, although I knew he was, for the fact was plain enough, the cat could have recognized it. As indeed the cat did; he came loafing in, waving his tail in greeting and satisfaction, and when he saw 44 he roached his back and inflated his tail and dropped a pious word and started away on urgent business; but 44 laughed, and called him back and explained to him in the cat language, and stroked him and petted him and sent him away to the other animals with the news; and in a minute here they came, padding and pattering from all directions, and they piled themselves all over him in their joy, nearly hiding him from sight, and all talking at once, each in his own tongue, and 44 answering in the language of each; and finally he fed them liberally with all sorts of palatable things from my cupboard (where there hadn't been a thing before), and sent them away convinced and happy.

By this time my tremors were gone and I was at rest, there was nothing in my mind or heart but thankfulness to have him back again, except wonder as to how it could be, and whether he had really been dead or had only seemed to perish in a magic-show and illusion; but he answered the thought while fetching a hot supper from my empty cupboard, saying—

"It wasn't an illusion, I died;" and added indifferently, "it is nothing, I have done it many a time!"

It was a hardy statement, and I did not strain myself with trying to believe it, but of course I did not say so. His supper was beyond praise for toothsomeness, but I was not acquainted with any of the dishes. He said they were all foreign, from various corners of the globe. An amazing thing, I thought, yet it seemed to me it must be true. There was a very rare-done bird that was peculiarly heavenly; it seemed to be a kind of duck.

"Canvas-back," he said, "hot from America!"

"What is America?"

"It's a country."

"A country?"

"Yes."

"Where?"

"Oh, away off. It hasn't been discovered yet. Not quite. Next fall."

"Have you—"

"Been there? Yes; in the past, in the present, in the future. You should see it four or five centuries from now! This duck is of that period. How do you like the Duplicates?"

It was his common way, the way of a boy, and most provoking: careless, capricious, unstable, never sticking to a subject, forever flitting and sampling here and there and yonder, like a bee; always, just as he was on the point of becoming interesting, he changed the subject. I was annoyed, but concealed it as well as I could, and answered—

"Oh, well, they are well enough, but they are not popular. They won't join the union, they work for nothing, the men resent their intrusion. There you have the situation: the men dislike them, and they are bitter upon the magician for sending them."

It seemed to give 44 an evil delight. He rubbed his hands vigorously together, and said—

"They were a good idea, the Duplicates; judiciously handled, they will make a lot of trouble! Do you know, those creatures are not uninteresting, all things considered, for they are not *real* persons."

"Heavens, what are they, then!"

"I will explain. Move up to the fire."

We left the table and its savory wreckage, and took comfortable seats, each at his own customary side of the fire, which blazed up briskly now, as if in a voluntary welcome of us. Then 44 reached up and took from the mantelpiece some things which I had not noticed there before: a slender reed stem with a small red-clay cup at the end of it, and a dry and dark-colored leaf, of a breed unknown to me. Chatting along,—I watching curiously—he crushed the crisp leaf in his palm, and filled that little cup with it; then he put the stem in his mouth and touched the cup with his finger, which instantly set fire to the vegetable matter and sent up a column of smoke and I dived under the bed, thinking something might happen. But nothing did, and so upon persuasion I returned to my chair but moved it a little further, for 44 was tilting his head far back and shooting ring after ring of blue smoke toward the ceiling —delicate gauzy revolving circlets, beautiful to see; and always each new ring took enlargement and 44 fired the next one through it with a good aim and happy art, and he *did* seem to enjoy it so; but not I, for I believed his entrails were on fire, and could perhaps explode and hurt some one, and most likely the wrong person, just as happens at riots and such things.

But nothing occurred, and I grew partially reconciled to the conditions, although the odor of the smoke was nauseating and a little difficult to stand. It seemed strange that he could endure it, and stranger still that he should seem to enjoy it. I turned the mystery over in my mind and concluded it was most likely a pagan religious service, and therefore I took my cap off, not in reverence but as a matter of discretion. But he said—

"No, it is only a vice, merely a vice, but not a religious one. It originated in Mexico."

"What is Mexico?"

"It's a country."

"A country?"

"Yes."

"Where is it?"

"Away off. It hasn't been discovered yet."

"Have you ever—"

"Been there? Yes, many times. In the past, in the present, and in the future. No, the Duplicates are not real, they are fictions. I will explain about them."

I sighed, but said nothing. He was always disappointing; I wanted to hear about Mexico.

"The way of it is this," he said. "You know, of course, that you are not one person, but two. One is your Workaday-Self, and 'tends to business, the other is your Dream-Self, and has no responsibilities, and cares only for romance and excursions and adventure. It sleeps when your other self is awake; when your other self sleeps, your Dream-Self has full control, and does as it pleases. It has far more imagination than has the Workaday-Self, therefore its pains and pleasures are far more real and intense than are those of the other self, and its adventures correspondingly picturesque and extraordinary. As a rule, when a party of Dream-Selves—whether comrades or strangers—get together and flit abroad in the globe, they have a tremendous time. But you understand, they have no substance, they are only spirits. The Workaday-Self has a harder lot and a duller time; it can't get away from the flesh, and is clogged and hindered by it; and also by the low grade of its own imagination."

"But 44, these Duplicates are solid enough!"

"So they are, apparently, but it is only fictitious flesh and bone, put upon them by the magician and me. We pulled them out of the Originals and gave them this independent life."

"Why, 44, they fight and bleed, like anybody!"

"Yes, and they *feel,* too. It is not a bad job, in the solidifying line, I've never seen better flesh put together by enchantment; but no matter, it is a pretty airy fabric, and if we should remove the spell they would vanish like blowing out a candle. Ah, they are a capable lot, with their measureless imaginations! If they imagine there is a mystic clog upon them and it takes them a couple of hours to set a couple of lines, that is what happens; but on the contrary, if they imagine it takes them but half a second to set a whole galleyful of matter, *that* is what happens! A dandy lot is that handful of Duplicates, and the easy match of a thousand real printers! Handled judiciously, they'll make plenty of trouble."

"But why should you *want* them to make trouble, 44?"

"Oh, merely to build up the magician's reputation. If they once get their imaginations started . . . . . oh, the consuming intensity and effectiveness of it!" He pondered a while, then said, indolently, "Those Originals are in love with these women and are not making any headway; now then, if we arrange it so that the Duplicates . . . . . lad, it's getting late—for you; time does not exist, for me. August, that is a nice table-service—you may have it. Good-night!" and he vanished.

It was heavy silver, and ornate, and on one great piece was engraved "America Cup;" on the others were chased these words, which had no meaning for me: "New York Yacht Club, 1903."

I sighed, and said to myself, "It may be that he is not honest." After some days I obliterated the words and dates, and sold the service at a good price.

Chapter 19

D AY AFTER day went by, and Father Adolf was a busy man, for he was the head of the Commission charged with trying and punishing the magician; but he had no luck, he could come upon no trace of the necromancer. He was disappointed and exasperated, and he swore hard and drank hard, but nothing came of it, he made no progress in his hunt. So, as a vent for his wrath he turned upon the poor Duplicates, declaring them to be evil spirits, wandering devils, and condemned them to the stake on his own arbitrary authority, but 44 told me he (44,) wouldn't allow them to be hurt, they being useful in the building up of the magician's reputation. Whether 44 was really their protector or not, no matter, they certainly had protection, for every time Father Adolf chained them to the stake they vanished and left the stake empty before the fire could be applied, and straightway they would be found at work in the shop and not in any way frightened or disturbed. After several failures Father Adolf gave it up in a rage, for he was becoming ridiculous and a butt for everybody's private laughter. To cover his chagrin he pretended that he had not really tried to burn them, he only wanted to scare them; and said he was only postponing the roasting, and that it would take place presently, when he should find that the right time had come. But not many believed him, and Doangivadam, to show how little he cared for Adolf's pretensions, took out a fire insurance policy upon his Duplicate. It was an impudent thing to do, and most irreverent, and made Father Adolf very angry, but he pretended that he did not mind it.

As 44 had expected, the Duplicates fell to making love to the young women, and in such strenuous fashion that they soon cut out the Originals and left them out in the cold; which made bad blood, and constant quarrels and fights resulted. Soon the castle was no better than a lunatic asylum. It was a cat-and-dog's life all around, but there was no helping it. The master loved peace, and he tried his best to reconcile the parties and make them friendly to each other, but it was not possible, the brawling and fighting went on in spite of all he could do. Forty-Four and I went about, visible to each other but to no one else, and we witnessed these affrays, and 44 enjoyed them and was perfectly charmed with them. Well, he had his own tastes. I was not always invisible, of course, for that would have caused remark; I showed up often enough to prevent that.

Whenever I thought I saw a good opportunity I tried to interest 44 in the life eternal, but the innate frivolity of his nature contin-

ually defeated my efforts, he could not seem to care for anything
but building up the magician's reputation. He said he was interested in that, and in one other thing, *the human race.* He had
nettled me more than once by seeming to speak slightingly of the
human race. Finally, one day, being annoyed once more by some
such remark, I said, acidly—

"You don't seem to think much of the human race; it's a pity you
have to belong to it."

He looked a moment or two upon me, apparently in gentle
wonder, then answered—

"What makes you think I belong to it?"

The bland audacity of it so mixed my emotions that it was a
question which would get first expression, anger or mirth; but
mirth got precedence, and I laughed. Expecting him to laugh, too,
in response; but he did not. He looked a little hurt at my levity, and
said, as in mild reproach—

"I think the human race is well enough, in its way, all things
considered, but surely, August, I have never intimated that I belonged to it. Reflect. Now have I?"

It was difficult to know what to say; I seemed to be a little
stunned. Presently I said, wonderingly—

"It makes me dizzy; I don't quite know where I am; it is as if I
had had a knock on the head. I have had no such confusing and
bewildering and catastrophical experience as this before. It is a new
and strange and fearful idea: a person who is a person and yet *not a
human being.* I cannot grasp it, I do not know how it can be, I have
never dreamed of so tremendous a thing, so amazing a thing! Since
you are not a human being, what *are* you?"

"Ah," he said, "now we have arrived at a point where words are
useless; words cannot even convey *human* thought capably, and
they can do nothing at all with thoughts whose realm and orbit are
outside the human solar system, so to speak. I will use the language
of my country, where words are not known. During half a moment
my spirit shall speak to yours and tell you something about me. Not
much, for it is not much of me that you would be able to understand, with your limited human mentality."

While he was speaking, my head was illuminated by a single sudden flash as of lightning, and I recognised that it had conveyed to me some knowledge of him; enough to fill me with awe. Envy, too—I do not mind confessing it. He continued—

"Now then, things which have puzzled you heretofore are not a mystery to you any more, for you are now aware that there is nothing I cannot do—and lay it on the magician and increase his reputation; and you are also now aware that the difference between a human being and me is as the difference between a drop of water and the sea, a rushlight and the sun, the difference between the infinitely trivial and the infinitely sublime! I say—we'll be comrades, and have scandalous good times!" and he slapped me on the shoulder, and his face was all alight with good-fellowship.

I said I was in awe of him, and was more moved to pay him reverence than to—

"Reverence!" he mocked; "put it away; the sun doesn't care for the rushlight's reverence, put it away. Come, we'll be boys together and comrades! Is it agreed?"

I said I was too much wounded, just now, to have any heart in levities, I must wait a little and get somewhat over this hurt; that I would rather beseech and persuade him to put all light things aside for a season and seriously and thoughtfully study my unjustly disesteemed race, whereby I was sure he would presently come to estimate it at its right and true value, and worthy of the sublime rank it had always held, undisputed, as the noblest work of God.

He was evidently touched, and said he was willing, and would do according to my desire, putting light things aside and taking up this small study in all heartiness and candor.

I was deeply pleased; so pleased that I would not allow his thoughtless characterization of it as a "small" study to greatly mar my pleasure; and to this end admonishing myself to remember that he was speaking a foreign language and must not be expected to perceive nice distinctions in the values of words. He sat musing a little while, then he said in his kindest and thoughtfulest manner—

"I am sure I can say with truth that I have no prejudices against the human race or other bugs, and no aversions, no malignities. I have known the race a long time, and out of my heart I can say that I have always felt more sorry for it than ashamed of it."

He said it with the gratified look of a person who has uttered a graceful and flattering thing. By God, I think he expected thanks! He did not get them; I said not a word. That made a pause, and was a little awkward for him for the moment; then he went on—

"I have often visited this world—often. It shows that I felt an interest in this race; it is proof, proof absolute, that I felt an interest in it." He paused, then looked up with one of those inane self-approving smiles on his face that are so trying, and added, "there is nothing just like it in any other world, it is a race by itself, and in many ways amusing."

He evidently thought he had said another handsome thing; he had the satisfied look of a person who thought he was oozing compliments at every pore. I retorted, with bitter sarcasm—I couldn't help it—

"As 'amusing' as a basket of monkeys, no doubt!"

It clean failed! He didn't know it was sarcasm.

"Yes," he said, serenely, "as amusing as those—and even more so, it may be claimed; for monkeys, in their mental and moral freaks show not so great variety, and therefore are the less entertaining."

This was too much. I asked, coldly—

But he was gone.

Chapter 20

A week passed.

Meantime, where was he? what was become of him? I had gone often to his room, but had always found it vacant. I was missing him sorely. Ah, he was so interesting! there was none that could approach him for that. And there could not be a more engaging mystery than he. He was always doing and saying strange and curious things, and then leaving them but half explained or not explained at all. Who was he? what was he? where was he from? I wished I knew. Could he be converted? could he be saved? Ah, if only this could happen, and I be in some humble way a helper toward it!

While I was thus cogitating about him, he appeared—gay, of course, and even more gaily clad than he was that day that the magician burnt him. He said he had been "home." I pricked up my ears hopefully, but was disappointed: with that mere touch he left the subject, just as if because it had no interest for him it couldn't have any for others. A chuckle-headed idea, certainly. He was handy about disparaging other people's reasoning powers, but it never seemed to occur to him to look nearer home. He smacked me on the thigh and said,

"Come, you need an outing, you've been shut up here quite long enough. I'll do the handsome thing by you, now—I'll show you something creditable to your race."

That pleased me, and I said so; and said it was very kind and courteous of him to find *something* to its credit, and be good enough to mention it.

"Oh, yes," he said, lightly, and paying no attention to my sarcasm, "I'll show you a really creditable thing. At the same time I'll have to show you something discreditable, too, but that's nothing —that's merely human, you know. Make yourself invisible."

I did so, and he did the like. We were presently floating away, high in the air, over the frosty fields and hills.

"We shall go to a small town fifty miles removed," he said. "Thirty years ago Father Adolf was priest there, and was thirty years old. Johann Brinker, twenty years old, resided there, with his widowed mother and his four sisters—three younger than himself, and one a couple of years older, and marriageable. He was a rising young artist. Indeed one might say that he had already risen, for he had exhibited a picture in Vienna which had brought him great praise, and made him at once a celebrity. The family had been very poor, but now his pictures were wanted, and he sold all of his little stock at fine prices, and took orders for as many more as he could paint in two or three years. It was a happy family! and was suddenly become courted, caressed and—envied, of course, for that is human. To be envied is the human being's chiefest joy.

"Then a thing happened. On a winter's morning Johann was skating, when he heard a choking cry for help, and saw that a man had broken through the ice and was struggling; he flew to the spot, and recognised Father Adolf, who was becoming exhausted by the cold and by his unwise strugglings, for he was not a swimmer. There was but one way to do, in the circumstances, and that was, to plunge in and keep the priest's head up until further help should come—which was on the way. Both men were quickly rescued by the people. Within the hour Father Adolf was as good as new, but it was not so with Johann. He had been perspiring freely, from energetic skating, and the icy water had consequences for him. Here is his small house, we will go in and see him."

We stood in the bedroom and looked about us. An elderly woman with a profoundly melancholy face sat at the fireside with her hands folded in her lap, and her head bowed, as with age-long weariness—that pathetic attitude which says so much! Without audible words the spirit of 44 explained to me—

"The marriageable sister. There was no marriage."

On a bed, half reclining and propped with pillows and swathed in wraps was a grizzled man of apparently great age, with hollow cheeks, and with features drawn by immemorial pains; and now and then he stirred a little, and softly moaned—whereat a faint spasm flitted across the sister's face, and it was as if that moan had carried a pain to her heart. The spirit of 44 breathed upon me again:

"Since that day it has been like this—thirty years!—"

"My God!"

"It is true. Thirty years. He has his wits—the worse for him— the cruelty of it! He cannot speak, he cannot hear, he cannot see, he is wholly helpless, the half of him is paralysed, the other half is but a house of entertainment for bodily miseries. At risk of his life he saved a fellow-being. It has cost him ten thousand deaths!"

Another sad-faced woman entered. She brought a bowl of gruel with her, and she fed it to the man with a spoon, the other woman helping.

"August, the four sisters have stood watches over this bed day and night for thirty years, ministering to this poor wreck. Marriage, and homes and families of their own was not for them; they gave up all their hopeful young dreams and suffered the ruin of their lives, in order to ameliorate as well as they might the miseries of their brother. They laid him upon this bed in the bright morning of his youth and in the golden glory of his new-born fame—and look at him now! His mother's heart broke, and she went mad. Add up the sum: one broken heart, five blighted and blasted young lives. All this it costs to save a priest for a life-long career of vice and all forms of shameless rascality! Come, come, let us go, before these enticing rewards for well-doing unbalance my judgment and persuade me to become a human being myself!"

In our flight homeward I was depressed and silent, there was a heavy weight upon my spirit; then presently came a slight uplift and a glimmer of cheer, and I said—

"Those poor people will be richly requited for all they have sacrificed and suffered."

"Oh, perhaps," he said, indifferently.

"It is my belief," I retorted. "And certainly a large mercy has been shown the poor mother, in granting her a blessed mental oblivion and thus emancipating her from miseries which the others, being younger, were better able to bear."

"The madness was a mercy, you think?"

"With the broken heart, yes; for without doubt death resulted quickly and she was at rest from her troubles."

A faint spiritual cackle fell upon my ear. After a moment 44 said—

"At dawn in the morning I will show you something."

Chapter 21

I spent a wearying and troubled night, for in my dreams I was a member of that ruined family and suffering with it through a dragging long stretch of years; and the infamous priest whose life had been saved at cost of these pains and sorrows seemed always present and drunk and mocking. At last I woke. In the dimmest of cold gray dawns I made out a figure sitting by my bed—an old and white-headed man in the coarse dress of a peasant.

"Ah," I said, "who are you, good man?"

It was 44. He said, in a wheezy old voice, that he was merely showing himself to me so that I would recognize him when I saw him later. Then he disappeared, and I did the same, by his order. Soon we were sailing over the village in the frosty air, and presently we came to earth in an open space behind the monastery. It was a solitude, except that a thinly and rustily clad old woman was there, sitting on the frozen ground and fastened to a post by a chain around her waist. She could hardly hold her head up for drowsiness and the chill in her bones. A pitiful spectacle she was, in the vague dawn and the stillness, with the faint winds whispering around her and the powdery snow-whorls frisking and playing and chasing each other over the black ground. Forty-Four made himself visible, and stood by, looking down upon her. She raised her old head wearily, and when she saw that it was a kindly face that was before her she said appealingly—

"Have pity on me—I am *so* tired and so cold, and the night has been so long, so long! light the fire and put me out of my misery!"

"Ah, poor soul, I am not the executioner, but tell me if I can serve you, and I will."

She pointed to a pile of fagots, and said,

"They are for me, a few can be spared to warm me, they will not be missed, there will be enough left to burn me with, oh, much more than enough, for this old body is sapless and dry. Be good to me!"

"You shall have your wish," said 44, and placed a fagot before her and lit it with a touch of his finger.

The flame flashed crackling up, and the woman stretched her lean hands over it, and out of her eyes she looked the gratitude that was too deep for words. It was weird and pathetic to see her getting comfort and happiness out of that fuel that had been provided to inflict upon her an awful death! Presently she looked up wistfully and said—

"You are good to me, you are very good to me, and I have no friends. I am not bad—you must not think I am bad, I am only poor and old, and smitten in my wits these many many years. They think I am a witch; it is the priest, Adolf, that caught me, and it is he that has condemned me. But I am not that—no, God forbid! You do not believe I am a witch?—say you do not believe that of me."

"Indeed I do not."

"Thank you for that kind word! . . . . . How long it is that I have wandered homeless—oh, many years, many! . . . . Once I had a home—I do not know where it was; and four sweet girls and a son—how dear they were! The name . . . . . the name . . . . . but I have forgotten the name. All dead, now, poor things, these many years . . . . . . If you could have seen my son! ah, so good he was, and a painter . . . . oh, such pictures he painted! . . . . Once he saved a man's life . . . . . or it could have been a woman's . . . . . . a person drowning in the ice—"

She lost her way in a tangle of vague memories, and fell to nodding her head and mumbling and muttering to herself, and I whispered anxiously in the ear of 44—

"You will save her? You will get the word to the priest, and when he knows who she is he will set her free and we will restore her to her family, God be praised!"

"No," answered 44.

"No? Why?"

"She was appointed from the beginning of time to die at the stake this day."

"How do *you* know?"

He made no reply. I waited a moment, in growing distress, then said—

"At least *I* will speak! I will tell her story. I will make myself visible, and I—"

"It is not so written," he said; "that which is not foreordained will not happen."

He was bringing a fresh fagot. A burly man suddenly appeared, from the monastery, and ran toward him and struck the fagot from his hand, saying roughly—

"You meddling old fool, mind what you are about! Pick it up and carry it back."

"And if I don't—what then?"

In his fury at being so addressed by so mean and humble a person the man struck a blow at 44's jaw with his formidable fist, but 44 caught the fist in his hand and crushed it; it was sickening to hear the bones crunch. The man staggered away, groaning and cursing, and 44 picked up the fagot and renewed the old woman's fire with it. I whispered—

"Quick—disappear, and let us get away from here; that man will soon—"

"Yes, I know," said 44, "he is summoning his underlings; they will arrest me."

"Then come—come along!"

"What good would it do? It is written. What is written must happen. But it is of no consequence, nothing will come of it."

They came running—half a dozen—and seized him and dragged him away, cuffing him with fists and beating him with sticks till he was red with his own blood. I followed, of course, but I was merely a substanceless spirit, and there was nothing that I could do in his defence. They chained him in a dim chamber under the monastery and locked the doors and departed, promising him further attentions when they should be through with burning the witch. I was troubled beyond measure, but he was not. He said he would use this opportunity to increase the magician's reputation: he would spread the report that the aged hand-crusher was the magician in disguise.

"They will find nothing here but the prisoner's clothes when they come," he said, "then they will believe."

He vanished out of the clothes, and they slumped down in a pile. He could certainly do some wonderful things, feather-headed and frivolous as he was! There was no way of accounting for 44. We soared out through the thick walls as if they had been made of air, and followed a procession of chanting monks to the place of the burning. People were gathering, and soon they came flocking in crowds, men, women, youths, maidens; and there were even children in arms.

There was a half hour of preparation: a rope ring was widely drawn around the stake to keep the crowd at a distance; within this a platform was placed for the use of the preacher—Adolf. When all was ready he came, imposingly attended, and was escorted with proper solemnity and ceremony to this pulpit. He began his sermon at once and with business-like energy. He was very bitter upon witches, "familiars of the Fiend, enemies of God, abandoned of the angels, foredoomed to hell;" and in closing he denounced this present one unsparingly, and forbade any to pity her.

It was all lost upon the prisoner; she was warm, she was comfortable, she was worn out with fatigue and sorrow and privation, her gray head was bowed upon her breast, she was asleep. The executioners moved forward and raised her upon her feet and drew her chains tight, around her breast. She looked drowsily around upon the people while the fagots were being piled, then her head drooped again, and again she slept.

The fire was applied and the executioners stepped aside, their mission accomplished. A hush spread everywhere: there was no movement, there was not a sound, the massed people gazed, with lips apart and hardly breathing, their faces petrified in a common expression, partly of pity, mainly of horror. During more than a minute that strange and impressive absence of motion and movement continued, then it was broken in a way to make any being with a heart in his breast shudder—a man lifted his little child and sat her upon his shoulder, that she might see the better!

The blue smoke curled up about the slumberer and trailed away upon the chilly air; a red glow began to show at the base of the fagots; this increased in size and intensity and a sharp crackling sound broke upon the stillness; suddenly a sheet of flame burst upward and swept the face of the sleeper, setting her hair on fire, she uttered an agonizing shriek which was answered by a horrified groan from the crowd, then she cried out "Thou art merciful and good to Thy sinful servant, blessed be Thy holy Name—sweet Jesus receive my spirit!"

Then the flames swallowed her up and hid her from sight. Adolf stood sternly gazing upon his work. There was now a sudden movement upon the outskirts of the crowd, and a monk came plowing his way through and delivered a message to the priest—evidently a pleasant one to the receiver of it, if signs go for anything. Adolf cried out—

"Remain, everybody! It is reported to me that that arch malignant the magician, that son of Satan, is caught, and lies a chained
prisoner under the monastery, disguised as an aged peasant. He is
already condemned to the flames, no preliminaries are needed, his
time is come. Cast the witch's ashes to the winds, clear the stake!
Go—you, and you, and you—bring the sorcerer!"

The crowd woke up! this was a show to their taste. Five minutes
passed—ten. What might the matter be? Adolf was growing
fiercely impatient. Then the messengers returned, crestfallen. They
said the magician was gone—gone, through the bolted doors and
the massive walls; nothing was left of him but his peasant clothes!
And they held them up for all to see.

The crowd stood amazed, wondering, speechless—and disappointed. Adolf began to storm and curse. Forty-Four whispered—

"The opportunity is come. I will personate the magician and
make some more reputation for him. Oh, just watch me raise the
limit!"

So the next moment there was a commotion in the midst of the
crowd, which fell apart in terror exposing to view the supposed
magician in his glittering oriental robes; and his face was white
with fright, and he was trying to escape. But there was no escape
for him, for there was one there whose boast it was that he feared
neither Satan nor his servants—this being Adolf the admired.
Others fell back cowed, but not he; he plunged after the sorcerer,
he chased him, gained upon him, shouted, "Yield—in His Name I
command!"

An awful summons! Under the blasting might of it the spurious
magician reeled and fell as if he had been smitten by a bolt from
the sky. I grieved for him with all my heart and in the deepest
sincerity, and yet I rejoiced for that at last he had learned the power
of that Name at which he had so often and so recklessly scoffed.
And all too late, too late, forever and ever too late—ah, why had he
not listened to me!

There were no cowards there, now! Everybody was brave, everybody was eager to help drag the victim to the stake, they swarmed
about him like raging wolves; they jerked him this way and that,
they beat him and reviled him, they cuffed him and kicked him, he

wailing, sobbing, begging for pity, the conquering priest exulting, scoffing, boasting, laughing. Briskly they bound him to the stake and piled the fagots around him and applied the fire; and there the forlorn creature stood weeping and sniffling and pleading in his fantastic robes, a sorry contrast to that poor humble Christian who but a little while before had faced death there so bravely. Adolf lifted his hand and pronounced with impressive solemnity the words—

"Depart, damned soul, to the regions of eternal woe!"

Whereat the weeping magician laughed sardonically in his face and vanished away, leaving his robes empty and hanging collapsed in the chains! There was a whisper at my ear—

"Come, August, let us to breakfast and leave these animals to gape and stare while Adolf explains to them the unexplainable—a job just in his line. By the time I have finished with the sorcerer he will have a dandy reputation—don't you think?"

So all his pretence of being struck down by the Name was a blasphemous jest. And I had taken it so seriously, so confidingly, innocently, exultantly. I was ashamed. Ashamed of him, ashamed of myself. Oh, manifestly nothing was serious to him, levity was the blood and marrow of him, death was a joke; his ghastly fright, his moving tears, his frenzied supplications—by God, it was all just coarse and vulgar horse-play! The only thing he was capable of being interested in, was his damned magician's reputation! I was too disgusted to talk, I answered him nothing, but left him to chatter over his degraded performance unobstructed, and rehearse it and chuckle over it and glorify it up to his taste.

Chapter 22

I T WAS in my room. He brought it—the breakfast—dish after dish, smoking hot, from my empty cupboard, and briskly set the table, talking all the while—ah, yes, and pleasantly, fascinatingly, winningly; and not about that so-recent episode, but about these fragrant refreshments and the far countries he had summoned them from—Cathay, India, and everywhere; and as I was famishing, this talk was pleasing, indeed captivating, and under its influence my sour mood presently passed from me. Yes, and it was healing to my bruised spirit to look upon the rich and costly table-service—quaint of shape and pattern, delicate, ornate, exquisite, beautiful!—and presently quite likely to be mine, you see.

"Hot corn-pone from Arkansas—split it, butter it, close your eyes and enjoy! Fried spring chicken—milk-and-flour gravy—from Alabama. Try it, and grieve for the angels, for they have it not! Cream-smothered strawberries, with the prairie-dew still on them —let them melt in your mouth, and don't try to say what you feel! Coffee from Vienna—fluffed cream—two pellets of saccharin— drink, and have compassion for the Olympian gods that know only nectar!"

I ate, I drank, I reveled in these alien wonders; truly I was in Paradise!

"It is intoxication," I said, "it is delirium!"

"It's a jag!" he responded.

I inquired about some of the refreshments that had outlandish names. Again that weird detail: they were non-existent as yet, they were products of the unborn *future!* Understand it? How could I? Nobody could. The mere *trying* muddled the head. And yet it was a pleasure to turn those curious names over on the tongue and taste them: Corn-pone! Arkansas! Alabama! Prairie! Coffee! Saccharin! Forty-Four answered my thought with a stingy word of explanation—

"Corn-pone is made from maize. Maize is known only in America. America is not discovered yet. Arkansas and Alabama will be States, and will get their names two or three centuries hence. Prairie—a future French-American term for a meadow like an ocean. Coffee: they have it in the Orient, they will have it here in Austria two centuries from now. Saccharin—concentrated sugar, 500 to 1; as it were, the sweetness of five hundred pretty maids concentrated in a young fellow's sweetheart. Saccharin is not due yet for nearly four hundred years; I am furnishing you several advance-privileges, you see."

"Tell me a little, *little* more, 44—please! You starve me so! and I am so hungry to know how you find out these strange marvels, these impossible things."

He reflected a while, then he said he was in a mood to enlighten me, and would like to do it, but did not know how to go about it, because of my mental limitations and the general meanness and poverty of my construction and qualities. He said this in a most casual and taken-for-granted way, just as an archbishop might say it to a cat, never suspecting that the cat could have any feelings about it or take a different view of the matter. My face flushed, and I said with dignity and a touch of heat—

"I must remind you that I am made in the image of God."

"Yes," he said carelessly, but did not seem greatly impressed by it, certainly not crushed, not overpowered. I was more indignant than ever, but remained mute, coldly rebuking him by my silence. But it was wasted on him; he did not see it, he was thinking. Presently he said—

"It is difficult. Perhaps impossible, unless I should make you over again." He glanced up with a yearningly explanatory and apologetic look in his eyes, and added, "For you are an animal, you see—you understand that?"

I could have slapped him for it, but I austerely held my peace, and answered with cutting indifference—

"Quite so. It happens to happen that all of us are that."

Of course I was including him, but it was only another waste—he didn't perceive the inclusion. He said, as one might whose way has been cleared of an embarrassing obstruction—

"Yes, that is just the trouble! It makes it ever so difficult. With my race it is different; we have no limits of any kind, we comprehend all things. You see, for your race there is such a thing as *time* —you cut it up and measure it; to your race there is a past, a present and a future—out of one and the same thing you make *three;* and to your race there is also such a thing as *distance*—and hang it, you measure *that,* too! . . . . . Let me see: if I could only . . . . if I . . . . oh, no, it is of no use—there is no such thing as enlightening that kind of a mind!" He turned upon me despairingly, pathetically, adding, "If it only had *some* capacity, some depth, or breadth, or—or—but you see it doesn't *hold* anything; one cannot pour the starred and shoreless expanses of the universe into a jug!"

I made no reply; I sat in frozen and insulted silence; I would not have said a word to save his life. But again he was not aware of what was happening—he was thinking. Presently he said—

"Well, it is *so* difficult! If I only had a starting-point, a basis to proceed from—but I can't find any. If—look here: *can't* you extinguish time? *can't* you comprehend eternity? can't you conceive of a thing like that—a thing with *no* beginning—a thing that *always* was? Try it!"

"Don't! I've tried it a hundred times," I said, "It makes my brain whirl just to think of it!"

He was in despair again.

"Dear me—to think that there can be an ostensible Mind that cannot conceive of so simple a trifle as that! . . . . Look here, August: there are really no divisions of time—none at all. The past is always present when I want it—the *real* past, not an image of it; I can summon it, and there it *is*. The same with the future: I can summon it out of the unborn ages, and there it is, before my eyes, alive and real, not a fancy, an image, a creation of the imagination. Ah, these troublesome limitations of yours!—they hamper me. Your race cannot even conceive of something being made out of nothing —I am aware of it, your learned men and philosophers are always confessing it. They say there had to be *something* to start with— meaning a solid, a substance—to build the world out of. Man, it is perfectly simple—it was built out of *thought*. Can't you comprehend that?"

"No, I can't! *Thought!* There is no substance to thought; then how is a material thing going to be constructed out of it?"

"But August, I don't mean *your* kind of thought, I mean my kind, and the kind that the gods exercise."

"Come, what is the difference? Isn't thought just *thought*, and all said?"

"No. A man *originates* nothing in his head, he merely observes exterior things, and *combines* them in his head—puts several observed things together and draws a conclusion. His mind is merely a machine, that is all—an *automatic* one, and he has no control over it; it cannot conceive of a *new* thing, an original thing, it can only gather material from the outside and combine it into new *forms* and patterns. But it always has to have the *materials* from the *outside,* for it can't make them itself. That is to say, a man's mind cannot *create*—a god's can, and my race can. That is the difference. *We* need no contributed materials, we *create* them—out of thought. All things that exist were made out of thought—and out of nothing else."

It seemed to me charitable, also polite, to take him at his word and not require proof, and I said so. He was not offended. He only said—

"Your automatic mind has performed its function—its sole function—and without help from you. That is to say, it has listened, it has observed, it has put this and that together, and drawn a conclusion—the conclusion that my statement was a doubtful one. It is now privately beginning to wish for a test. Is that true?"

"Well, yes," I said, "I won't deny it, though for courtesy's sake I would have concealed it if I could have had my way."

"Your mind is automatically suggesting that I offer a specific proof—that I create a dozen gold coins out of nothing; that is to say, out of *thought.* Open your hand—they are there."

And so they were! I wondered; and yet I was not very greatly astonished, for in my private heart I judged—and not for the first time—that he was using magic learned from the magician, and that he had no gifts in this line that did not come from that source. But was this so? I dearly wanted to ask this question, and I started to do it. But the words refused to leave my tongue, and I realized that he had applied that mysterious check which had so often shut off a question which I wanted to ask. He seemed to be musing. Presently he ejaculated—

"That poor old soul!"

It gave me a pang, and brought back the stake, the flames and the death-cry; and I said—

"It was a shame and a pity that she wasn't rescued."

"Why a pity?"

"*Why?* How can you ask, 44?"

"What would she have gained?"

"An extension of life, for instance; is that nothing?"

"Oh, there spoke the human! He is always pretending that the eternal bliss of heaven is such a priceless boon! Yes, and always keeping out of heaven just as long as he can! At bottom, you see, he is far from being certain about heaven."

I was annoyed at my carelessness in giving him that chance. But I allowed it to stand at that, and said nothing; it could not help the matter to go into it further. Then, to get away from it I observed that there was at least one gain that the woman could have had if she had been saved: she might have entered heaven by a less cruel death.

"She isn't going there," said 44, placidly.

It gave me a shock, and also it angered me, and I said with some heat—

"You seem to know a good deal about it—*how* do you know?"

He was not affected by my warmth, neither did he trouble to answer my question; he only said—

"The woman could have gained nothing worth considering—certainly nothing worth measuring by your curious methods. What are ten years, subtracted from ten billion years? It is the ten-thousandth part of a second—that is to say, it is nothing at all. Very well, she is in hell now, she will remain there forever. Ten years subtracted from it wouldn't count. Her bodily pain at the stake lasted six minutes—to save her from *that* would not have been worthwhile. That poor creature is in hell; see for yourself!"

Before I could beg him to spare me, the red billows were sweeping by, and she was there among the lost.

The next moment the crimson sea was gone, with its evoker, and I was alone.

Chapter 23

Young as I was—I was barely seventeen—my days were now sodden with depressions, there was little or no rebound. My interest in the affairs of the castle and of its occupants faded out and disappeared; I kept to myself and took little or no note of the daily happenings; my Duplicate performed all my duties, and I had nothing to do but wander aimlessly about and be unhappy.

Thus the days wore heavily by, and meantime I was missing something; missing something, and growing more and more conscious of it. I hardly had the daring to acknowledge to myself what it was. It was the master's niece—Marget! I was a secret worshipper; I had been that a long time; I had worshipped her face and her form with my eyes, but to go further would have been quite beyond my courage. It was not for me to aspire so high; not yet, certainly; not in my timid and callow youth. Every time she had blessed me with a passing remark, the thrill of it, the bliss of it had tingled through me and swept along every nerve and fibre of me with a sort of celestial ecstasy and given me a wakeful night which was better than sleep. These casual and unconsidered remarks, unvalued by her were treasures to me, and I hoarded them in my memory, and knew when it was that she had uttered each of them, and the occasion and the circumstance that had produced each one, and the tone of her voice and the look of her face and the light in her eye; and there was not a night that I did not pass them through my mind caressingly, and turn them over and pet them and play with them, just as a poor girl possessed of half a dozen cheap seed-pearls might do with her small hoard. But that Marget should ever give me an actual thought—any word or notice above what she might give the cat—ah, I never dreamed of it! As a rule she had never been conscious of my presence at all; as a rule she gave me merely a glance of recognition and nothing more when she passed me by in hall or corridor.

As I was saying, I had been missing her, a number of days. It was because her mother's malady was grown a trifle worse and Marget was spending all her time in the sick room. I recognized, now, that I was famishing to see her, and be near that gracious presence once more. Suddenly, not twenty steps away, she rose upon my sight—a fairy vision! That sweet young face, that dainty figure, that subtle exquisite something that makes seventeen the perfect year and its bloom the perfect bloom—oh, there it all was, and I stood transfixed and adoring! She was coming toward me, walking slowly, musing, dreaming, heeding nothing, absorbed, unconscious. As she drew near I stepped directly in her way; and as she passed through me the contact invaded my blood as with a delicious fire! She stopped, with a startled look, the rich blood rose in her face, her breath came quick and short through her parted lips, and she gazed wonderingly about her, saying twice, in a voice hardly above a whisper—

"What could it have been?"

I stood devouring her with my eyes, she remained as she was, without moving, as much as a minute, perhaps more; then she said in that same low soliloquising voice, "I was surely asleep—it was a dream—it must have been that—why did I wake?" and saying this, she moved slowly away, down the great corridor.

Nothing can describe my joy. I believed she loved me, and had been keeping her secret, as maidens will; but now I would persuade it out of her; I would be bold, brave, and speak! I made myself visible, and in a minute had overtaken her and was at her side. Excited, happy, confident, I touched her arm, and the warm words began to leap from my mouth—

"Dear Marget! oh, my own, my dar—"

She turned upon me a look of gentle but most chilly and dignified rebuke, allowed it a proper time to freeze where it struck, then moved on, without a word, and left me there. I did not feel inspired to follow.

No, I could not follow, I was petrified with astonishment. Why should she act like that? Why should she be glad to dream of me and not glad to meet me awake? It was a mystery; there was something very strange about this; I could make nothing out of it. I went on puzzling and puzzling over the enigma for a little while, still gazing after her and half crying for shame that I had been so fresh and had gotten such a blistering lesson for it, when I saw her stop. Dear me, she might turn back! I was invisible in half an instant—I wouldn't have faced her again for a province.

Sure enough, she did turn back. I stepped to the wall, and gave her the road. I wanted to fly, but I had no power to do that, the sight of her was a spell that I could not resist; I had to stay, and gaze, and worship. She came slowly along in that same absorbed and dreamy way, again; and just as she was passing by me she stopped, and stood quite still a moment—two or three moments, in fact—then moving on, she said, with a sigh, "I was mistaken, but I thought I faintly felt it again."

Was she sorry it was a mistake? It certainly sounded like that. It put me in a sort of ecstasy of hope, it filled me with a burning desire to test the hope, and I could hardly refrain from stepping out and barring her way again, to see what would happen; but that rebuff was too recent, its smart was still too fresh, and I hadn't the pluck to do it.

But I could feast my eyes upon her loveliness, at any rate, and in safety, and I would not deny myself that delight. I followed her at a distance, I followed all her wanderings; and when at last she entered her apartment and closed the door, I went to my own place and to my solitude, desolate. But the fever born of that marvelous first contact came back upon me and there was no rest for me. Hour after hour I fought it, but still it prevailed. Night came, and dragged along, there was no abatement. At ten the castle was asleep and still, but I could not sleep. I left my room and went wandering here and there, and presently I was floating through the great corridor again. In the vague light I saw a figure standing motionless in that memorable spot. I recognized it—even less light would have answered for that. I could not help approaching it, it drew me like a magnet. I came eagerly on; but when I was within two or three steps of it I remembered, with a chill, who I was, and stopped. No matter: To be so near to Marget was happiness enough, riches enough! With a quick movement she lifted her head and poised it in the attitude of one who listens—listens with a tense and wistful and breathless interest; it was a happy and longing face that I saw in the dim light; and out of it, as through a veil, looked darkling and humid the eyes I loved so well. I caught a whisper: "I cannot hear anything—no, there is no sound—but it is near, I know it is near, and the dream is come again!" My passion rose and overpowered me and I floated to her like a breath and put my arms about her and drew her to my breast and put my lips to hers, unrebuked, and drew intoxication from them! She closed her eyes, and with a sigh which seemed born of measureless content, she said dreamily, "I love you so—and have so longed for you!"

Her body trembled with each kiss received and repaid, and by the power and volume of the emotions that surged through me I realized that the sensations I knew in my fleshly estate were cold and weak by contrast with those which a spirit feels.

I was invisible, impalpable, substanceless, I was as transparent as the air, and yet I seemed to support the girl's weight and bear it up. No, it was more than seeming, it was an actuality. This was new; I had not been aware that my spirit possessed this force. I must exploit this valuable power, I must examine it, test it, make experiments. I said—

"When I press your hand, dear, do you feel it?"

"Why, of course."

"And when I kiss you?"

"Indeed yes!" and she laughed.

"And do you *feel* my arms about you when I clasp you in them?"

"Why, certainly. What strange questions!"

"Oh, well, it's only to make talk, so that I can hear your voice. It is such music to me, Marget, that I—"

"Marget? Marget? Why do you call me that?"

"Oh, you little stickler for the conventions and proprieties! Have I got to call you Miss Regen? Dear me, I thought we were further along than that!"

She seemed puzzled, and said—

"But why should you call me *that?*"

It was my turn to be puzzled.

"Why should I? I don't know any really good reason, except that it's your name, dear."

"My name, indeed!" and she gave her comely head a toss. "I've never heard it before!"

I took her face between my hands and looked into her eyes to see if she were jesting, but there was nothing there but sweet sincerity. I did not quite know what to say, so at a venture I said—

"Any name that will be satisfactory to you will be lovely to me, you unspeakably adorable creature! Mention it! What shall I call you?"

"Oh, what a time you do have, to make talk, as you call it! What shall you *call* me? Why, call me by my own name—my *first* name —and don't put any Miss to it!"

I was still in the fog, but that was no matter—the longer it might take to work out of it the pleasanter and the better. So I made a start:

"Your first name . . . . your first name . . . . . how annoying, I've forgotten it! What is it, dear?"

The music of her laugh broke out rich and clear, like a bird-song, and she gave me a light box on the ear, and said—

"Forgotten it?—oh, no, that won't do! You are playing some kind of a game—I don't know what it is, but you are not going to catch me. You want me to say it, and then—then—why then you are going to spring a trap or a joke or something and make me feel foolish. Is that it? What *is* it you are going to do if I say it, dearheart?"

"*I'll* tell you," I said, sternly, "I am going to bend your head back and cradle your neck in the hollow of my left arm,—so—and squeeze you close—so—and the moment you say it I am going to kiss you on the mouth."

She gazed up from the cradling arm with the proper play-acting humility and resignation, and whispered—

"Lisabet!" and took her punishment without a protest.

"You have been a very good girl," I said, and patted her cheek approvingly. "There wasn't any trap, Lisabet—at least none but this: I pretended that forgetfulness because when the sweetest of all names comes from the sweetest of all lips it is sweeter then than ever, and I wanted to hear you say it."

"Oh, you dear thing! I'll say the rest of it at the same price!"

"Done!"

"Elisabeth von Arnim!"

"One—two—three: a kiss for each component!"

I was out of the fog, I had the name. It was a triumph of diplomacy, and I was proud of it. I repeated the name several times, partly for the pleasure of hearing it and partly to nail it in my memory, then I said I wished we had some more things to trade between us on the same delicious basis. She caught at that, and said—

"We can do *your* name, Martin."

Martin! It made me jump. Whence had she gathered this batch of thitherto unheard-of names? What was the secret of this mystery, the how of it, the why of it, the explanation of it? It was too deep for me, much too deep. However, this was no time to be puzzling over it, I ought to be resuming trade and finding out the rest of my name; so I said—

"Martin is a poor name, except when you say it. Say it again, sweetheart."

"Martin. Pay me!"

Which I did.

"Go on, Betty dear; more music—say the rest of it."

"Martin von Giesbach. I wish there was more of it. Pay!"

I did, and added interest.

Boom-m-m-m! from the solemn great bell in the main tower.

"Half-past eleven—oh, what will mother say! I did not dream it was so late, did you Martin?"

"No, it seemed only fifteen minutes."

"Come, let us hurry," she said, and we hurried—at least after a sort of fashion—with my left arm around her waist and the hollow of her right hand cupped upon my left shoulder by way of having a support. Several times she murmured dreamily, "How happy I am, how happy, happy, happy!" and seemed to lose herself in that thought and be conscious of nothing else. By and by I had a rare start—my Duplicate stepped suddenly out from a bunch of shadows, just as we were passing by! He said, reproachfully—

"Ah, Marget, I waited so long by your door, and you broke your promise! Is this kind of you? is it affectionate?"

Oh, jealousy—I felt the pang of it for the first time.

To my surprise—and joy—the girl took no more notice of him than if he had not been there. She walked right on, she did not seem to see him nor hear him. He was astonished, and stopped still and turned, following her with his eyes. He muttered something, then in a more definite voice he said—

"What a queer attitude—to be holding her hand up in the air like that! . . . . . Why, she's walking in her sleep!"

He began to follow, a few steps behind us. Arrived at Marget's door, I took her—no, Lisbet's!—peachy face between my hands and kissed the eyes and the lips, her delicate hands resting upon my shoulders the while; then she said "Good-night—good-night and blessed dreams," and passed within. I turned toward my Duplicate. He was standing near by, staring at the vacancy where the girl had been. For a time he did only that. Then he spoke up and said joyfully—

"I've been a jealous fool! That was a kiss—and it was for me! She was dreaming of me. I understand it all, now. And that loving good-night—it was for me, too. Ah, it makes all the difference!" He went to the door and knelt down and kissed the place where she had stood.

I could not endure it. I flew at him and with all my spirit-strength I fetched him an open-handed slat on the jaw that sent him lumbering and spinning and floundering over and over along the stone floor till the wall stopped him. He was greatly surprised. He got up rubbing his bruises and looking admiringly about him for a minute or two, then went limping away, saying—

"I wonder what in hell *that* was!"

Chapter 24

I FLOATED off to my room through the unresisting air, and stirred up my fire and sat down to enjoy my happiness and study over the enigma of those names. By ferreting out of my memory certain scraps and shreds of information garnered from 44's talks I presently untangled the matter, and arrived at an explanation— which was this: the presence of my flesh-and-blood personality was not a circumstance of any interest to Marget Regen, but my presence as a spirit acted upon her hypnotically—as 44 termed it—and plunged her into the somnambulic sleep. This removed her Day-Self from command and from consciousness, and gave the command to her Dream-Self for the time being. Her Dream-Self was a quite definite and independent personality, and for reasons of its own it had chosen to name itself Elisabeth von Arnim. It was entirely unacquainted with Marget Regen, did not even know she existed, and had no knowledge of her affairs, her feelings, her opinions, her religion, her history, nor of any other matter concerning her. On the other hand, Marget was entirely unacquainted with Elisabeth and wholly ignorant of her existence and of all other matters concerning her, including her name.

Marget knew me as August Feldner, her Dream-Self knew me as Martin von Giesbach—*why,* was a matter beyond guessing. Awake, the girl cared nothing for me; steeped in the hypnotic sleep, I was the idol of her heart.

There was another thing which I had learned from 44, and that was this: each human being contains not merely two independent entities, but three—the Waking-Self, the Dream-Self, and the Soul. This last is immortal, the others are functioned by the brain and the nerves, and are physical and mortal; they are not functionable when the brain and nerves are paralysed by a temporary hurt or stupefied by narcotics; and when the man dies *they* die, since their life, their energy and their existence depend solely upon physical sustenance, and they cannot get that from dead nerves and a dead brain. When I was invisible the whole of my physical make-up was gone, nothing connected with it or depending upon it was left. My soul—my immortal spirit—alone remained. Freed from the encumbering flesh, it was able to exhibit forces, passions and emotions of a quite tremendously effective character.

It seemed to me that I had now ciphered the matter out correctly, and unpuzzled the puzzle. I was right, as I found out afterward.

And now a sorrowful thought came to me: all three of my Selves were in love with the one girl, and how could we all be happy? It made me miserable to think of it, the situation was so involved in difficulties, perplexities and unavoidable heart-burnings and resentments.

Always before, I had been tranquilly unconcerned about my Duplicate. To me he was merely a stranger, no more no less; to him I was a stranger; in all our lives we had never chanced to meet until 44 had put flesh upon him; we could not have met if we had wanted to, because whenever one of us was awake and in command of our common brain and nerves the other was of necessity asleep and unconscious. All our lives we had been what 44 called Box and Cox lodgers in the one chamber: aware of each other's existence but not interested in each other's affairs, and never encountering each other save for a dim and hazy and sleepy half-moment on the threshold, when one was coming in and the other going out, and never in any case halting to make a bow or pass a greeting.

And so it was not until my Dream-Self's fleshing that he and I met and spoke. There was no heartiness; we began as mere acquaintances, and so remained. Although we had been born together, at the same moment and of the same womb, there was no spiritual kinship between us; spiritually we were a couple of distinctly independent and unrelated individuals, with equal rights in a common fleshly property, and we cared no more for each other than we cared for any other stranger. My fleshed Duplicate did not even bear my name, but called himself Emil Schwarz.

I was always courteous to my Duplicate, but I avoided him. This was natural, perhaps, for he was my superior. My imagination, compared with his splendid dream-equipment, was as a lightning bug to the lightning; in matters of our trade he could do more with his hands in five minutes than I could do in a day; he did all my work in the shop, and found it but a trifle; in the arts and graces of beguilement and persuasion I was a pauper and he a Croesus; in passion, feeling, emotion, sensation—whether of pain or pleasure—I was phosphorus, he was fire. In a word he had all the intensities one suffers or enjoys in a dream!

This was the creature that had chosen to make love to Marget! In my coarse dull human form, what chance was there for me? Oh, none in the world, none! I knew it, I realized it, and the heartbreak of it was unbearable.

But my Soul, stripped of its vulgar flesh—what was my Duplicate in competition with *that?* Nothing, and less than nothing. The conditions were reversed, as regarded passions, emotions, sensations, and the arts and graces of persuasion. Lisbet was mine, and I could hold her against the world—but only when she was Lisbet, only when her Dream-Self was in command of her person! when she was Marget she was her Waking-Self, and the slave of that reptile! Ah, there could be no help for this, no way out of this fiendish complication. I could have only half of her; the other half, no less dear to me, must remain the possession of another. She was mine, she was his, turn-about.

These desolating thoughts kept racing and chasing and scorching and blistering through my brain without rest or halt, and I could find no peace, no comfort, no healing for the tortures they brought. Lisbet's love, so limitlessly dear and precious to me, was almost lost sight of because I couldn't have Marget's too. By this sign I perceived that I was still a human being; that is to say, a person who wants the earth, and cannot be satisfied unless he can have the whole of it. Well, we are made so; even the humblest of us has the voracity of an emperor.

At early mass the next morning my happiness came back to me, for Marget was there, and the sight of her cured all my sorrows. For a time! She took no notice of me, and I was not expecting she would, therefore I was not troubled about that, and was content to look at her, and breathe the same air with her, and note and admire everything she did and everything she didn't do, and bless myself in these privileges; but when I found she had over-many occasions to glance casually and fleetingly around to her left I was moved to glance around, myself, and see if there was anything particular there. Sure enough there was. It was Emil Schwarz. He was already become a revolting object to me, and I now so detested him that I could hardly look at anything else during the rest of the service; except, of course, Marget.

When the service was over, I lingered outside, and made myself invisible, purposing to follow Marget and resume the wooing. But she did not come. Everybody came out but two,—*those* two. After a little, Marget put her head out and looked around to see if any one was in sight, then she glanced back, with a slight nod, and moved swiftly away. That saddened me, for I interpreted it to mean that the other wooing was to have first place. Next came Schwarz, and him I followed—upward, always upward, by dim and narrow stairways seldom used; and so, to a lofty apartment in the south tower, the luxurious quarters of the departed magician. He entered, and closed the door, but I followed straight through the heavy panels, without waiting, and halted just on the inside. There was a great fire of logs at the other end of the room, and Marget was there! She came briskly to meet this odious Dream-stuff, and flung herself into his arms, and kissed him—and he her, and she him again, and he her again, and so on, and so on, and so on, till it was most unpleasant to look at. But I bore it, for I wanted to know all my misfortune, the full magnitude of it and the particulars. Next, they went arm-in-arm and sat down and cuddled up together on a sofa, and did that all over again—over and over and over and over—the most offensive spectacle I had ever seen, as it seemed to me. Then Schwarz tilted up that beautiful face, using his profane forefinger as a fulcrum under the chin that should have been sacred to me, and looked down into the luminous eyes which should have been wholly mine by rights, and said, archly—

"Little traitor!"

"Traitor? I? How, Emil?"

"You didn't keep your tryst last night."

"Why, Emil, I did!"

"Oh, not you! Come—what did we do? where did we go? For a ducat you can't tell!"

Marget looked surprised—then nonplussed—then a little frightened.

"It is very strange," she said, "very strange . . . . . unaccountable. I seem to have forgotten everything. But I know I was out; I was out till near midnight; I know it because my mother chided me, and tried her best to make me confess what had kept me out so late; and she was very uneasy, and I was cruelly afraid she would suspect the truth. I remember nothing at all of what happened before. Isn't it strange!"

Then the devil Schwarz laughed gaily and said that for a kiss he would unriddle the riddle. So he told her how he had encountered her, and how she was walking in her sleep, and how she was dreaming of him, and how happy it made him to see her kiss the air, imagining she was kissing him. And then they both laughed at the odd incident, and dropped the trifle out of their minds, and fell to trading caresses and endearments again, and thought no more about it.

They talked of the "happy day!"—a phrase that scorched me like a coal. They would win over the mother and the uncle presently—yes, they were quite sure of it. Then they built their future—built it out of sunshine and rainbows and rapture; and went on adding and adding to its golden ecstasies until they were so intoxicated with the prospect that words were no longer adequate to express what they were foreseeing and pre-enjoying, and so died upon their lips and gave place to love's true and richer language, wordless soul-communion: the heaving breast, the deep sigh, the unrelaxing embrace, the shoulder-pillowed head, the bliss-dimmed eyes, the lingering kiss . . . .

By God, my reason was leaving me! I swept forward and enveloped them as with a viewless cloud! In an instant Marget was Lisbet again; and as she sprang to her feet divinely aflame with passion for me I stepped back, and back, and back, she following, then I stopped and she fell panting in my arms, murmuring—

"Oh, my own, my idol, how wearily the time has dragged—do not leave me again!"

That Dream-mush rose astonished, and stared stupidly, his mouth working, but fetching out no words. Then he thought he understood, and started toward us, saying—

"Walking in her sleep again—how suddenly it takes her! . . . . . I wonder how she can lean over like that without falling?"

He arrived and put his arms through me and around her to support her, saying tenderly—

"Wake, dearheart, shake it off, I cannot bear to see you so!"

Lisbet freed herself from his arms and bent a stare of astonishment and wounded dignity upon him, accompanied by words to match—

"Mr. Schwarz, you forget yourself!"

It knocked the reptile stupid for a moment; then he got his bearings and said—

"Oh, please come to yourself, dear, it is so hard to see you like this. But if you can't wake, do come to the divan and sleep it off, and I will so lovingly watch over you, my darling, and protect you from intrusion and discovery. Come, Marget—do!"

"*Marget!*" Lisbet's eyes kindled, as at a new affront. "*What* Marget, please? Whom do you take me for? And why do you venture these familiarities?" She softened a little then, seeing how dazed and how pitiably distressed he looked, and added, "I have always treated you with courtesy, Mr. Schwarz, and it is very unkind of you to insult me in this wanton way."

In his miserable confusion he did not know what to say, and so he said the wrong thing—

"Oh, my poor afflicted child, shake it off, be your sweet self again, and let us steep our souls once more in dreams of our happy marriage day and—"

It was too much. She would not let him finish, but broke wrathfully into the midst of his sentence.

"Go away!" she said; "your mind is disordered, you have been drinking. Go—go at once! I cannot bear the sight of you!"

He crept humbly away and out at the door, mopping his eyes with his handkerchief and muttering "Poor afflicted thing, it breaks my heart to see her so!"

Dear Lisbet, she was just a girl—alternate sunshine and shower, peremptory soldier one minute, crying the next. Sobbing, she took refuge on my breast, saying—

"Love me, oh my precious one, give me peace, heal my hurts, charm away the memory of the shame this odious creature has put upon me!"

During half an hour we re-enacted that sofa-scene where it had so lately been played before, detail by detail, kiss for kiss, dream for dream, and the bliss of it was beyond words. But with an important difference: in Marget's case there was a mamma to be pacified and persuaded, but Lisbet von Arnim had no such incumbrances; if she had a relative in the world she was not aware of it; she was free and independent, she could marry whom she pleased and when she pleased. And so, with the dearest and sweetest naivety she suggested that to-day and now was as good a time as any! The suddenness of it, the unexpectedness of it, would have taken my breath if I had had any. As it was, it swept through me like a delicious wind and set my whole fabric waving and fluttering. For a moment I was gravely embarrassed. Would it be right, would it be honorable, would it not be treason to let this confiding young creature marry herself to a viewless detail of the atmosphere? I knew how to accomplish it, and was burning to do it, but would it be fair? Ought I not to at least tell her my condition, and let her decide for herself? Ah . . . . . She might decide the wrong way!

No, I couldn't bring myself to it, I couldn't run the risk. I must think—think—think. I must hunt out a good and righteous reason for the marriage without the revelation. That is the way we are made; when we badly want a thing, we go to hunting for good and righteous reasons for it; we give it that fine name to comfort our consciences, whereas we privately know we are only hunting for plausible ones.

I seemed to find what I was seeking, and I urgently pretended to myself that it hadn't a defect in it. Forty-Four was my friend; no doubt I could persuade him to return my Dream-Self into my body and lock it up there for good. Schwarz being thus put out of the way, wouldn't my wife's Waking-Self presently lose interest in him and cease from loving him? That looked plausible. Next, by throwing *my* Waking-Self in the way of *her* Waking-Self a good deal and using tact and art, would not a time come when . . . . . oh, it was all as clear as a bell! Certainly. It wouldn't be long, it couldn't be long, before I could retire my Soul into my body, then both Lisbet and Marget being widows and longing for solace and tender companionship, would yield to the faithful beseechings and supplications of my poor inferior Waking-Self and marry *him*. Oh, the scheme was perfect, it was flawless, and my enthusiasm over it was without measure or limit. Lisbet caught that enthusiasm from my face and cried out—

"I know what it is! It is going to be *now!*"

I began to volley the necessary "suggestions" into her head as fast as I could load and fire—for by "suggestion," as 44 had told me, you make the hypnotised subject see and do and feel whatever you please: see people and things that are not there, hear words that are not spoken, eat salt for sugar, drink vinegar for wine, find the rose's sweetness in a stench, carry out all suggested acts—and forget the whole of it when he wakes, and remember the whole of it again whenever the hypnotic sleep returns!

In obedience to suggestion, Lisbet clothed herself as a bride; by suggestion she made obeisance to imaginary altar and priest, and smiled upon imaginary wedding-guests; made the solemn responses; received the ring, bent her dear little head to the benediction, put up her lips for the marriage kiss, and blushed as a new-made wife should before people!

Then, by suggestion altar and priest and friends passed away and we were alone—alone, immeasurably content, the happiest pair in the Duchy of Austria!

Ah . . . . . footsteps! some one coming! I fled to the middle of the room, to emancipate Lisbet from the embarrassment of the hypnotic sleep and be Marget again and ready for emergencies. She began to gaze around and about, surprised, wondering, also a little frightened, I thought.

"Why, where is Emil?" she said. "How strange; I did not see him go. How could he go and I not see him? . . . . Emil! . . . . No answer! Surely this magician's den is bewitched. But we've been here many times, and nothing happened."

At that moment Emil slipped in, closed the door, and said, apologetically and in a tone and manner charged with the most respectful formality—

"Forgive me, Miss Regen, but I was afraid for you and have stood guard—it would not do for you to be found in this place, and asleep. Your mother is fretting about your absence—her nurse is looking for you everywhere—I have misdirected her . . . . . pardon, what is the matter?"

Marget was gazing at him in a sort of stupefaction, with the tears beginning to trickle down her face. She began to sob in her hands, and said—

"If I have been asleep it was cruel of you to leave me. Oh, Emil, how could you desert me at such a time, if you love me?"

The astonished and happy bullfrog had her in his arms in a minute and was blistering her with kisses, which she paid back as fast as she could register them, and she not cold yet from her marriage-oath! A man—and such a man as that—hugging my wife before my eyes, and she getting a gross and voracious satisfaction out of it!—I could not endure the shameful sight. I rose and winged my way thence, intending to kick a couple of his teeth out as I passed over, but his mouth was employed and I could not get at it.

Chapter 25

T HAT NIGHT I had a terrible misfortune. The way it came about was this. I was so unutterably happy and so unspeakably unhappy that my life was become an enchanted ecstasy and a crushing burden. I did not know what to do, and took to drink. Merely for that evening. It was by Doangivadam's suggestion that I did this. He did not know what the matter was, and I did not tell him; but he could see that something *was* the matter and wanted regulating, and in his judgment it would be well to try drink, for it might do good and couldn't do harm. He was ready to do any kindness for me, because I had been 44's friend; and he loved to have me talk about 44, and mourn with him over his burning. I couldn't tell him 44 was alive again, for the mysterious check fell upon my tongue whenever I tried to. Very well; we were drinking and mourning together, and I took a shade too much and it biased my judgment. I was not what one could call at all far gone, but I had reached the heedless stage, the unwatchful stage, when we parted, and I forgot to make myself invisible! And so, eager and unafraid, I entered the boudoir of my bride confident of the glad welcome which would of course have been mine if I had come as Martin von Giesbach, whom she loved, instead of as August Feldner, whom she cared nothing about. The boudoir was dark, but the bedroom door was standing open, and through it I saw an enchanting picture and stopped to contemplate it and enjoy it. It was Marget. She was sitting before a pier glass, snowily arrayed in her dainty nightie, with her left side toward me; and upon her delicate profile and her shining cataract of dark red hair streaming unvexed to the floor a strong light was falling. Her maid was busily grooming her with brush and comb, and gossiping, and now and then Marget smiled up at her and she smiled back, and I smiled at both in sympathy and good-fellowship out of the dusk, and altogether it was a gracious and contenting condition of things, and my heart sang with happiness. But the picture was not quite complete, not wholly perfect—there was a pair of lovely blue eyes that persistently failed to turn my way. I thought I would go nearer and correct that defect. Supposing that I was invisible I tranquilly stepped just within the room and stood there; at the same moment Marget's mother appeared in the further door; and also at the same moment the three indignant women discovered me and began to shriek and scream in the one breath!

I fled the place. I went to my quarters, resumed my flesh, and sat mournfully down to wait for trouble. It was not long coming. I expected the master to call, and was not disappointed. He came in anger—which was natural,—but to my relief and surprise I soon found that his denunciations were not for me! What an uplift it was! No, they were all for my Duplicate—all that the master wanted from me was a denial that I was the person who had profaned the sanctity of his niece's bedchamber. When he said *that* . . . . well, it took the most of the buoyancy out of the uplift. If he had stopped there and challenged me to testify, I—but he didn't. He went right on recounting and re-recounting the details of the exasperating episode, never suspecting that they were not news to me, and all the while he freely lashed the Duplicate and took quite for granted that he was the criminal and that my character placed me above suspicion. This was all so pleasant to my ear that I was glad to let him continue: indeed the more he abused Schwarz the better I liked it, and soon I was feeling grateful that he had neglected to ask for my testimony. He was very bitter, and when I perceived that he was minded to handle my detestable rival with severity I rejoiced exceedingly in my secret heart. Also I became evilly eager to keep him in that mind, and hoped for chances to that end.

It appeared that both the mother and the maid were positive that the Duplicate was the offender. The master kept dwelling upon that, and never referring to Marget as a witness, a thing that seemed so strange to me that at last I ventured to call his attention to the omission.

"Oh, her unsupported opinion is of no consequence!" he said, indifferently. "She says it was you—which is nonsense, in the face of the other evidence and your denial. She is only a child—how can *she* know one of you from the other? To satisfy her I said I would bring your denial; as for Emil Schwarz's testimony I don't want it and shouldn't value it. These Duplicates are ready to say anything that comes into their dreamy heads. This one is a good enough fellow, there's no deliberate harm in him, but—oh, as a witness he is not to be considered. He has made a blunder—in another person it would have been a crime—and by consequence my niece is compromised, for sure, for the maid can't keep the secret; poor thing, she's like all her kind—a secret, in a lady's-maid, is water in a basket. Oh, yes, it's true that this Duplicate has merely committed a blunder, but all the same my mind is made up as to one thing . . . . . the bell is tolling midnight, it marks a change for him . . . . . when I am through with him to-day, let him blunder as much as he likes he'll not compromise my niece again!"

I suppose it was wicked to feel such joy as I felt, but I couldn't help it. To have that hated rival put summarily out of my way and my road left free—the thought was intoxicating! The master asked me—as a formality—to deny that I was the person who had invaded Marget's chamber.

I promptly furnished the denial. It had always cost me shame to tell an injurious lie before, but I told this one without a pang, so eager was I to ruin the creature that stood between me and my worshipped little wife. The master took his leave, then, saying—

"It is sufficient. It is all I wanted. He shall marry the girl before the sun sets!"

Good heavens! in trying to ruin the Duplicate, I had only ruined myself.

Chapter 26

I was so miserable! A whole endless hour dragged along. Oh, why didn't he come, *why* didn't he come! wouldn't he *ever* come, and I so in need of his help and comfort!

It was awfully still and solemn and midnighty, and this made me feel creepy and shivery and afraid of ghosts; and that was natural, for the place was foggy with them, as Ernest Wasserman said, who was the most unexact person in his language in the whole castle, foggy being a noun of multitude and not applicable to ghosts, for they seldom appear in large companies, but mostly by ones and twos, and then—oh, then, when they go flitting by in the gloom like forms made of delicate smoke, and you see the furniture through them—

My, what is that! . . . . I heard it again! . . . . I was quaking like a jelly, and my heart was *so* cold and scared! Such a dry, bony noise, such a kl—lackety klackclack, kl—lackety klackclack!—dull, muffled, far away down the distant caverns and corridors—but approaching! oh, dear, approaching! It shriveled me up like a spider in a candle-flame, and I sat scrunched together and quivering, the way the spider does in his death-agony, and I said to myself, "skeletons a-coming, oh, what *shall* I do!"

Do? Shut my door, of course! if I had the strength to get to it—which I wouldn't have, on my legs, I knew it well; but I collapsed to the floor and crawled to the door, and panted there and listened, to see if the noise was certainly coming my way—which it was!—and I took a look; and away down the murky hall a long square of moonlight lay across the floor, and a tall figure was capering across it, with both hands held aloft and violently agitated and clacking out that clatter—and next moment the figure was across and blotted out in the darkness, but not the racket, which was getting loud and sharp, now—then I pushed the door to, and crept back a piece and lay exhausted and gasping.

It came, and came,—that dreadful noise—straight to my door, then that figure capered in and slammed the door to, and went on capering gaily all around me and everywhere about the room; and it was not a skeleton; no, it was a tall man, clothed in the loudest and most clownish and outlandish costume, with a vast white collar that stood above its ears, and a battered hat like a bucket, tipped gallusly to one side, and betwixt the fingers of the violent hands were curved fragments of dry bone which smote together and made that terrible clacking; and the man's mouth reached clear across his face and was unnaturally red, and had extraordinarily thick lips, and the teeth showed intensely white between them, and the face was as black as midnight. It was a terrible and ferocious spectre, and would bound as high as the ceiling, and crack its heels together, and yah-yah-yah! like a fiend, and keep the bones going, and soon it broke into a song in a sort of bastard English,

> "Buffalo gals can't you come out to-night,
> Can't you come out to-night,

>   Can't you come out to-night,
>   O, Buffalo gals can't you come out to-night—
>   A-n-d *dance* by de light er de moon!"

And then it burst out with a tremendous clatter of laughter, and
flung itself furiously over and over in the air like the wings of a
windmill in a gale, and landed with a whack! on its feet alongside
of me and looked down at me and shouted most cheerfully—

"*Now* den, Misto' Johnsing, how does yo' corporsosity seem to
segashuate!"

I gasped out—

"Oh, dread being, have pity, oh—if—if—"

"Bress yo' soul, honey, *I* ain' no dread being, I's Cunnel Bludso's
nigger fum Souf C'yarlina, en I's heah th'ee hund'd en fifty year
ahead o' time, caze you's down in de mouf en I got to 'muse you wid
de banjo en make you feel all right en comfy agin. So you jist lay
whah you is, boss, en listen to de music; I gwineter sing to you,
honey, de way de po' slave-niggers sings when dey's sol' away fum
dey home en is homesick en down in de mouf."

Then out of nowhere he got that thing that he called a banjo,
and sat down and propped his left ancle on his right knee, and
canted his bucket-hat a little further and more gallusly over his ear,
and rested the banjo in his lap, and set the grip of his left fingers on
the neck of it high up, and fetched a brisk and most thrilling rake
across the strings low down, giving his head a toss of satisfaction, as
much as to say "I reckon *that* gets in to where you live, oh I guess
not!" Then he canted his head affectionately toward the strings,
and twisted the pegs at the top and tuned the thing up with a
musical plunkety-plunk or so; then he re-settled himself in his chair
and lifted up his black face toward the ceiling, grave, far-away, kind
of pathetic, and began to strum soft and low—and then! Why
then his voice began to tremble out and float away toward heaven
—such a sweet voice, such a divine voice, and so touching—

>   "Way down upon de Swanee river,
>   Far, far away,
>   Dah's whah my heart is turnin' ever,
>   Dah's whah de ole folks stay."

And so on, verse after verse, sketching his humble lost home, and the joys of his childhood, and the black faces that had been dear to him, and which he would look upon no more—and there he sat lost in it, with his face lifted up that way, and there was never anything so beautiful, never anything so heart-breaking, oh, never any music like it below the skies! and by the magic of it that uncouth figure lost its uncouthness and became lovely like the song, because it so fitted the song, so belonged to it, and was such a part *of* it, so helped to body forth the feeling of it and make it visible, as it were, whereas a silken dress and a white face and white graces would have profaned it, and cheapened its noble pathos.

I closed my eyes, to try if I could picture to myself that lost home; and when the last notes were dying away, and apparently receding into the distance, I opened them again: the singer was gone, my room was gone, but afar off the home was there, a cabin of logs nestling under spreading trees, a soft vision steeped in a mellow summer twilight—and steeped in that music, too, which was dying, dying, fading, fading; and with it faded the vision, like a dream, and passed away; and as it faded and passed, my room and my furniture began to dimly reappear—spectrally, with the perishing home showing vaguely, through it, as through a veil; and when the transformation was accomplished my room was its old self again, my lights were burning, and in the black man's place sat Forty-Four beaming a self-complimenting smile. He said—

"Your eyes are wet; it's the right applause. But it's nothing, I could fetch that effect if they were glass. Glass? I could do it if they were knot-holes. Get up, and let's feed."

I *was* so glad to see him again! The very sight of him was enough to drive away my terrors and despairs and make me forget my deplorable situation. And then there was that mysterious soul-refreshment, too, that always charged the atmosphere as with wine and set one's spirits a-buzzing whenever he came about, and made you perceive that he was come, whether he was visible or not.

***When we had finished feeding, he lit his smoke-factory and we drew up to the fire to discuss my unfortunate situation and see what could be done about it. We examined it all around, and I said it seemed to me that the first and most urgent thing to be done was to stop the lady's-maid's gossiping mouth and keep her from compromising Marget; I said the master hadn't a doubt that she would spread the fact of the unpleasant incident of an hour or two ago. Next, I thought we ought to stop that marriage, if possible. I concluded with—

"Now, 44, the case is full of intolerable difficulties, as you see, but do try and think of some way out of them, won't you?"

To my grief I soon saw that he was settling down into one of his leather-headed moods. Ah, how often they came upon him when there was a crisis and his very brightest intelligence was needed!

He said he saw no particular difficulties in the situation if I was right about it: the first and main necessity was to silence the maid and stop Schwarz from proceeding with his marriage—and then blandly proposed that we *kill* both of them!

It almost made me jump out of my clothes. I said it was a perfectly insane idea, and if he was actually in earnest—

He stopped me there, and the argument-lust rose in his dull eye. It always made me feel depressed to see that look, because he loved to get a chance to show off how he could argue, and it was so dreary to listen to him—dreary and irritating, for when he was in one of his muddy-minded moods he couldn't argue any more than a clam. He said, big-eyed and asinine—

"What makes you think it insane, August?"

What a hopeless question! what could a person answer to such a foolishness as that?

"Oh, dear, me," I said, "can't you *see* that it's insane?"

He looked surprised, puzzled, pathetically mystified for a little while, then said—

"Why, *I* don't see how you make it out, August. We don't need those people, you know. No one needs them, so far as I can see. There's a plenty of them around, you can get as many as you want. Why, August, you don't seem to have any practical ideas—business ideas. You stay shut up here, and you don't know about these things. There's dozens and dozens of those people. I can turn out and in a couple of hours I can fetch a whole swarm of—"

"Oh, wait, 44! Dear me, is supplying their places the whole thing? is it the important thing? Don't you suppose *they* would like to have something to say about it?"

That simple aspect of it did seem to work its way into his head—after boring and tugging a moment or two—and he said, as one who had received light—

"Oh, I didn't think of that. Yes—yes, I see now." Then he brightened, and said, "but you know, they've got to die anyway, and so the *when* isn't any matter. Human beings aren't of any particular consequence; there's plenty more, plenty. Now then, after we've got them killed—"

"Damnation, we are not *going* to kill them!—now don't say another word about it; it's a perfectly atrocious idea; I should think you would be ashamed of it; and ashamed to hang to it and stick to it the way you do, and be so reluctant to give it up. Why, you act as if it was a child, and the first one you ever had."

He was crushed, and looked it. It hurt me to see him look cowed, that way; it made me feel mean, and as if I had struck a dumb animal that had been doing the best it knew how, and not meaning any harm; and at bottom I was vexed at myself for being so rough with him at such a time; for *I* know at a glance when he has a leather-headed mood on, and that he is not responsible when his brains have gone mushy; but I just *couldn't* pull myself together right off and say the gentle word and pet away the hurt I had given. I had to take time to it and work down to it gradually. But I managed it, and by and by his smiles came back, and his cheer, and then he was all right again, and as grateful as a child to see me friends with him once more.

Then he went zealously to work on the problem again, and soon evolved another scheme. The idea this time was to turn the maid into a cat, and make some *more* Schwarzes, then Marget would not be able to tell t'other from which, and couldn't choose the right one, and it wouldn't be lawful for her to marry the whole harem. That would postpone the wedding, he thought.

It certainly had the look of it! Any blind person could see that. So I gave praise, and was glad of the chance to do it and make up for bygones. He was as pleased as could be. In about ten minutes or so we heard a plaintive sound of meyow-yowing wandering around and about, away off somewhere, and 44 rubbed his hands joyfully and said—

"There she is, now!"

"Who?"

"The lady's-maid."

"No! Have you already transmuted her?"

"Yes. She was sitting up waiting for her room-mate to come, so she could tell her. Waiting for her mate to come from larking with the porter's new yunker. In a minute or two it would have been too late. Set the door ajar; she'll come when she sees the light, and we'll see what she has to say about the matter. She mustn't recognize me; I'll change to the magician. It will give him some more reputation. Would you like me to make you able to understand what she says?"

"Oh, *do,* 44, do, please!"

"All right. Here she is."

It was the magician's voice, exactly counterfeited; and there he stood, the magician's duplicate, official robes and all. I went invisible; I did not want to be seen in the condemned enchanter's company, even by a cat.

She came sauntering sadly in, a very pretty cat. But when she saw the necromancer her tail spread and her back went up and she let fly a spit or two and would have scurried away, but I flew over her head and shut the door in time. She backed into the corner and fixed her glassy eyes on 44, and said—

"It was you who did this, and it was mean of you. I never did you any harm."

"No matter, you brought it on yourself."

"How did I bring it on myself?"

"You were going to tell about Schwarz; you would have compromised your young mistress."

"It's not so; I wish I may never die if—"

"Nonsense! Don't talk so. You were waiting up to tell. I know all about it."

The cat looked convicted. She concluded not to argue the case.

After thinking a moment or two she said, with a kind of sigh—

"Will they treat me well, do you think?"

"Yes."

"Do you know they will?"

"Yes, I know it."

After a pause and another sigh—

"I would rather be a cat than a servant—a slave, that has to smile, and look cheerful, and pretend to be happy, when you are scolded for every little thing, the way Frau Stein and her daughter do, and be sneered at and insulted, and they haven't any right to, *they* didn't pay my wage, I wasn't *their* slave—a hateful life, an odious life! I'd rather be a cat. Yes, I would. Will everybody treat me well?"

"Yes, everybody."

"Frau Stein, too, and the daughter?"

"Yes."

"Will *you* see that they do?"

"I will. It's a promise."

"Then I thank you. They are all afraid of you, and the most of them hate you. And it was the same with me—but not now. You seem different to me now. You have the same voice and the same clothes, but you seem different. You seem kind; I don't know why, but you do; you seem kind and good, and I trust you; I think you will protect me."

"I will keep my promise."

"I believe it. And keep me as I am. It was a bitter life. You would think those Steins would not have been harsh with me, seeing I was a poor girl, with not a friend, nor anybody that was mine, and I never did them any harm. I *was* going to tell. Yes, I was. To get revenge. Because the family said I was bribed to let Schwarz in there—and it was a lie! Even Miss Marget believed that lie—I could see it, and she—well, she tried to defend me, but she let them convince her. Yes, I was going to tell. I was hot to tell. I was angry. But I am glad I didn't get the chance, for I am not angry any more; cats do not carry anger, I see. Don't change me back, leave me as I am. Christians go—I know where they go; some to the one place some to the other; but I think cats—where do *you* think cats go?"

"Nowhere. After they die."

"Leave me as I am, then; don't change me back. Could I have these leavings?"

"And welcome—yes."

"Our supper was there, in our room, but the other maid was frightened of me because I was a strange cat, and drove me out, and I didn't get any. This is wonderful food, I wonder how it got to this room? there's never been anything like it in this castle before. Is it enchanted food?"

"Yes."

"I just guessed it was. Safe?"

"Perfectly."

"Do you have it here a good deal?"

"Always—day and night."

"How gaudy! But this isn't your room?"

"No, but I'm here a great deal, and the food is here all the time. Would you like to do your feeding here?"

"Too good to be true!"

"Well, you can. Come whenever you like, and speak at the door."

"How dear and lovely! I've had a narrow escape—I can see it now."

"From what?"

"From not getting to be a cat. It was just an accident that that idiot came blundering in there drunk; if I hadn't been there—but I *was*, and never shall I get done being thankful. This is amazing good food; there's never been anything like it in this castle before —not in my time, I can tell you. I am thankful I may come here when I'm hungry."

"Come whenever you like."

"I'll do what I can for pay. I've never caught a mouse, but I feel it in me that I could do it, and I will keep a lookout here. I'm not so sad, now; no, things look very different; but I was pretty sad when I came. Could I room here, do you think? Would you mind?"

"Not at all. Make yourself quite at home. There'll be a special bed for you. I'll see to it."

"What larks! I never knew what nuts it was to be a cat before."

"It has its advantages."

"Oh, I should smile! I'll step out, now, and browse around a little, and see if there's anything doing in my line. Au revoir, and many many thanks for all you have done for me. I'll be back before long."

And so she went out, waving her tail, which meant satisfaction.

"There, now," said 44, "that part of the plan has come out all right, and no harm done."

"No, indeed," I said, resuming my visible form, "we've done her a favor. And in her place I should feel about it just as she does. Forty-Four, it was beautiful to hear that strange language and understand it—I understood every word. Could I learn to speak it, do you think?"

"You won't have to learn it, I'll put it *into* you."

"Good. When?"

"Now. You've already got it. Try! Speak out—do The Boy Stood on the Burning Deck—in catapult, or cataplasm, or whatever one might call that tongue."

"The Boy—what was it you said?"

"It's a poem. It hasn't been written yet, but it's very pretty and stirring. It's English. But I'll empty it into you, where you stand, in cataplasm. Now you've got it. Go ahead—recite."

I did it, and never missed a wail. It was certainly beautiful in that tongue, and quaint and touching; 44 said if it was done on a back fence, by moonlight, it would make people cry—especially a quartette would. I was proud; he was not always so complimentary. I said I was glad to have the cat, particularly now that I could talk to her; and she would be happy with me, didn't he think? Yes, he said, she would. I said—

"It's a good night's work we've done for that poor little blonde-haired lady's-maid, and I believe, as you do, that quite soon she is going to be contented and happy."

"As soon as she has kittens," he said, "and it won't be long."

Then we began to think out a name for her, but he said—
"Leave that, for the present, you'd better have a nap."

He gave a wave of his hand, and that was sufficient; before the wave was completed I was asleep.

Chapter 27

I woke up fresh and fine and vigorous, and found I had been asleep a little more than six minutes. The sleeps which he furnished had no dependence upon time, no connection with it, no relation to it; sometimes they did their work in one interval, sometimes in another, sometimes in half a second, sometimes in half a day, according to whether there was an interruption or wasn't; but let the interval be long or short, the result was the same: that is to say, the reinvigoration was perfect, the physical and mental refreshment complete.

There had been an interruption, a voice had spoken. I glanced up, and saw myself standing there, within the half-open door. That is to say, I saw Emil Schwarz, my Duplicate. My conscience gave me a little prod, for his face was sad. Had he found out what had been happening at midnight, and had he come at three in the morning to reproach me?

Reproach me? What for? For getting him falsely saddled with a vulgar indiscretion? What of it? Who was the loser by it? Plainly, I, myself—I had lost the girl. And who was the gainer? He himself, and none other—he had acquired her. Ah, very well, then—let him reproach me; if he was dissatisfied, let him trade places: he wouldn't find me objecting. Having reached solid ground by these logical reasonings, I advised my conscience to go take a tonic, and leave me to deal with this situation as a healthy person should.

Meantime, during these few seconds, I was looking at myself, standing there—and for once, I was admiring. Just because I had been doing a very handsome thing by this Duplicate, I was softening toward him, my prejudices were losing strength. I hadn't intended to do the handsome thing, but no matter, it had happened, and it was natural for me to take the credit of it and feel a little proud of it, for I was human. Being human accounts for a good many insanities, according to 44—upwards of a thousand a day was his estimate.

It is actually the truth that I had never looked this Duplicate over before. I never could bear the sight of him. I wouldn't look at him when I could help it; and until this moment I *couldn't* look at him dispassionately and with fairness. But now I could, for I had done him a great and creditable kindness, and it quite changed his aspects.

In those days there were several things which I didn't know. For instance I didn't know that my voice was not the same voice to me that it was to others; but when 44 made me talk into the thing which he brought in, one day, when he had arrived home from one of his plundering-raids among the unborn centuries, and then reversed the machine and allowed me to listen to my voice as other people were used to hearing it, I recognized that it had so little resemblance to the voice *I* was accustomed to hearing that I should have said it was not my voice at all if the proof had not been present that it was.

Also, I had been used to supposing that the person I saw in the mirror was the person others saw when they looked at me—whereas that was not the case. For once, when 44 had come back from robbing the future he brought a camera and made some photographs of me—those were the names which he gave the things, names which he invented out of his head for the occasion, no doubt, for that was his habit, on account of his not having any principles—and *always* the pictures which were like me as I saw myself in the glass he pronounced poor, and those which I thought exceedingly bad, he pronounced almost supernaturally good.

And here it was again. In the figure standing by the door I was now seeing myself as others saw me, but the resemblance to the self which I was familiar with in the glass was *merely* a resemblance, nothing more; not approaching the common resemblance of brother to brother, but reaching only as far as the resemblance which a person usually bears to his brother-in-law. Often one does not notice that, at all, until it is pointed out; and sometimes, even then, the resemblance owes as much to imagination as to fact. It's like a cloud which resembles a horse after some one has pointed out the resemblance. You perceive it, then, though I have often seen a cloud that didn't. Clouds often have nothing more than a brother-in-law resemblance. I wouldn't say this to everybody, but I believe it to be true, nevertheless. For I myself have seen clouds which looked like a brother-in-law, whereas I knew very well they didn't. Nearly all such are hallucinations, in my opinion.

Well, there he stood, with the strong white electric light flooding him, (more plunder,) and he hardly even reached the brother-in-law standard. I realized that I had never really seen this youth before. Of course I could recognize the general pattern, I don't deny it, but that was only because I knew who the creature was; but if I had met him in another country, the most that could have happened would have been this: that I would turn and look after him and say "I wonder if I have seen him somewhere before?" and then I would drop the matter out of my mind, as being only a fancy.

Well, there he was; that is to say, there *I* was. And I was interested; interested at last. He was distinctly handsome, distinctly trim and shapely, and his attitude was easy, and well-bred and graceful. Complexion—what it should be at seventeen, with a blonde ancestry: peachy, bloomy, fresh, wholesome. Clothes—precisely like mine, to a button—or the lack of it.

I was well satisfied with this front view. I had never seen my back; I was curious to see it. I said, very courteously—

"Would you please turn around for a moment?—only a moment? . . . Thank you."

Well, well, how little we know what our backs are like! This one was all right, I hadn't a fault to find with it, but it was all new to me, it was the back of a stranger—hair-aspects and all. If I had seen it walking up the street in front of me it would not have occurred to me that I could be in any personal way interested in it.

"Turn again, please, if you will be so good . . . . Thank you kindly."

I was to inspect the final detail, now—mentality. I had put it last, for I was reluctant, afraid, doubtful. Of course one glance was enough—I was expecting that. It saddened me: he was of a loftier world than I, he moved in regions where I could not tread, with my earth-shod feet. I wished I had left that detail alone.

"Come and sit down," I said, "and tell me what it is. You wish to speak with me about something?"

"Yes," he said, seating himself, "if you will kindly listen."

I gave a moment's thought to my defence, as regards the impending reproach, and was ready. He began, in a voice and manner which were in accord with the sadness which sat upon his young face—

"The master has been to me and has charged me with profaning the sanctity of his niece's chamber."

It was a strange place to stop, but there he stopped, and looked wistfully at me, just as a person might stop in a dream, and wait for another person to take up the matter there, without any definite text to talk to. I had to say something, and so for lack of anything better to offer, I said—

"I am truly sorry, and I hope you will be able to convince him that he is mistaken. You can, can't you?"

"Convince him?" he answered, looking at me quite vacantly, "Why should I wish to convince him?"

I felt pretty vacant myself, now. It was a most unlooked-for question. If I had guessed a week I should not have hit upon that one. I said—and it was the only thing a body would ever think of saying—

"But you do, don't you?"

The look he gave me was a look of compassion, if I know the signs. It seemed to say, gently, kindly, but clearly, "alas, this poor creature doesn't know anything." Then he uttered his answer—

"Wh-y, no, I do not see that I have that wish. It—why, you see, it isn't any matter."

"Good heavens! It isn't any matter whether you stand disgraced or not?"

He shook his head, and said quite simply—

"No, it isn't any matter, it is of no consequence."

It was difficult to believe my ears. I said—

"Well, then, if disgrace is nothing to you, consider *this* point. If the report gets around, it can mean disgrace for the young *lady*."

It had no effect that I could see! He said—

"Can it?" just as an idiot child might have said it.

"*Can* it? Why of course it can! You wouldn't want *that* to happen, would you?"

"We-ll," (reflectively), "I don't know. I don't see the bearing of it."

"Oh, great guns, this infantile stu—this—this—why, it's perfectly disheartening! You love her, and yet you don't care whether her good name is ruined or not?"

"Love her?" and he had the discouraged aspect of a person who is trying to look through a fog and is not succeeding, "why, I don't love her; what makes you think I do?"

"Well, I must say! Well, certainly this is too many for *me*. Why, hang it, *I* know you've been courting her."

"Yes—oh, yes, that is true."

"Oh, it is, is it! Very well, then, how is it that you were courting her and yet didn't love her?"

"No, it isn't that way. No, I loved her."

"Oh—go on, I'll take a breath or two—I don't know where I am, I'm all at sea."

He said, placidly—

"Yes, I remember about that. I loved her. It had escaped me. No —it hadn't escaped me; it was not important, and I was thinking of something else."

"Tell me," I said, "is *anything* important to you?"

"Oh, yes!" he responded, with animation and a brightening face; then the animation and the brightness passed, and he added, wearily, "but not these things."

Somehow, it touched me; it was like the moan of an exile. We were silent a while, thinking, ruminating, then I said—

"Schwarz, I'm not able to make it out. It is a sweet young girl, you certainly did love her, and—"

"Yes," he said, tranquilly, "it is quite true. I believe it was yesterday . . . . yes, I think it was yesterday."

"Oh, you *think* it was! But of course it's not important. Dear me, why should it be?—a little thing like that. Now then, something has changed it. What was it? What has happened?"

"Happened? Nothing, I think. Nothing that I know of."

"Well, then, why the devil . . . . oh, great Scott, I'll never get my wits back again! Why, look here, Schwarz, you wanted to *marry* her!"

"Yes. Quite true. I think . . . . yesterday? Yes, I think it was yesterday. I am to marry her to-day. I think it's to-day; anyway, it is pretty soon. The master requires it. He has told me so."

"Well . . . . upon my word!"

"What is the matter?"

"Why, you are as indifferent about this as you are about everything else. You show no feeling whatever, you don't even show interest. Come! surely you've got a heart hidden away somewhere; open it up; give it air; show at least some little corner of it. Land, I wish I were in your place! Don't you *care* whether you marry her or not?"

"Care? Why, *no*, of course I don't. You do ask the *strangest* questions! I wander, wander, wander! I try to make you out, I try to understand you, but it's all fog, fog, fog—you're just a riddle, nobody *can* understand you!"

Oh, the idea! the impudence of it! this to *me!*—from this frantic chaos of unimaginable incomprehensibilities, who couldn't by any chance utter so much as half a sentence that Satan himself could make head or tail of!

"Oh, I like *that!*" I cried, flying out at him. "*You* can't understand *me!* Oh, but that *is* good! It's immortal! Why, look here, when you came, I thought I knew what you came for—I thought I knew all about it—I would have said you were coming to reproach me for—for—"

I found it difficult to get it out, and so I left it in, and after a pause, added—

"Why, Schwarz, you certainly had something on your mind when you came—I could see it in your face—but if ever you've got to it I've not discovered it—oh, not even a sign of it! You *haven't* got to it, *have* you?"

"*Oh*, no!" he answered, with an outburst of very real energy. "These things were of no sort of consequence. *May* I tell it now? Oh, *will* you be good and hear me? I shall be so grateful, if you will!"

"Why, certainly, and glad to! Come, *now* you're waking up, at last! You've got a heart in you, sure enough, and plenty of feeling —why, it burns in your eye like a star! Go ahead—I'm all interest, all sympathy."

Oh, well, he was a different creature, now. All the fogs and puzzlings and perplexities were gone from his face, and had left it clear and full of life. He said—

"It was no idle errand that brought me. No, far from it! I came with my heart in my mouth, I came to beg, to plead, to pray—to beseech you, to implore you, to have mercy upon me!"

"Mercy—upon *you?*"

"Yes, mercy. Have mercy, oh, be merciful, and set me free!"

"Why, I—I—Schwarz, I don't understand. You say, yourself, that if they want you to marry, you are quite indif—"

"Oh, not *that!* I care nothing for that—it is these bonds"— stretching his arms aloft—"oh, free me from *them;* these bonds of flesh—this decaying vile matter, this foul weight, and clog, and burden, this loathsome sack of corruption in which my spirit is imprisoned, her white wings bruised and soiled—oh, be merciful and set her free! Plead for me with that malicious magic-monger— he has been here—I saw him issue from this door—he will come again—say you will be my friend, as well as brother! for brothers indeed we are; the same womb was mother to us both, I live by you, I perish when you die—brother, be my friend! plead with him to take away this rotting flesh and set my spirit free! Oh, this human life, this earthy life, this weary life! It is so groveling, and so mean; its ambitions are so paltry, its prides so trivial, its vanities so child-ish; and the glories that it values and applauds—lord, how empty! Oh, here I am a servant!—I who never served before; here I am a slave—slave among little mean kings and emperors made of clothes, the kings and emperors slaves themselves, to mud-built carrion that are *their* slaves!

"To think you should think I came here concerned about those other things—those inconsequentials! Why should they concern me, a spirit of air, habitant of the august Empire of Dreams? *We* have no morals; the angels have none; morals are for the impure; we have no principles, those chains are for men. We love the lovely whom we meet in dreams, we forget them the next day, and meet and love their like. They are dream-creatures—no others are real. Disgrace? We care nothing for disgrace, we do not know what it is. Crime? we commit it every night, while you sleep; it is nothing to us. We have no character, no *one* character, we have *all* characters; we are honest in one dream, dishonest in the next; we fight in one battle and flee from the next. We wear no chains, we cannot abide them; we have no home, no prison, the universe is our province; we do not know time, we do not know space—we live, and love, and labor, and enjoy, fifty years in an hour, while you are sleeping, snoring, repairing your crazy tissues; we circumnavigate your little globe while you wink; we are not tied within horizons, like a dog with cattle to mind, an emperor with human sheep to watch—we visit hell, we roam in heaven, our playgrounds are the constellations and the Milky Way. Oh, help, help! be my friend and brother in my need—beseech the magician, beg him, plead with him; he will listen, he will be moved, he will release me from this odious flesh!"

I was powerfully stirred—so moved, indeed, that in my pity for him I brushed aside unheeded or but half-heeded the scoffs and slurs which he had flung at my despised race, and jumped up and seized him by both hands and wrung them passionately, declaring that with all my heart and soul I would plead for him with the magician, and would not rest from these labors until my prayers should succeed or their continuance be peremptorily forbidden.

Chapter 28

He could not speak, for emotion; for the same cause my voice forsook me; and so, in silence we grasped hands again; and that grip, strong and warm, said for us what our tongues could not utter. At that moment the cat entered, and stood looking at us. Under her grave gaze a shame-faced discomfort, a sense of embarrassment, began to steal over me, just as would have been the case if she had been a human being who had caught me in that gushy and sentimental situation, and I felt myself blushing. Was it because I was aware that she had lately been that kind of a being? It annoyed me to see that my brother was not similarly affected. And yet, why mind it? didn't I already know that no human intelligence could guess what occurrence would affect *him* and what event would leave him cold? With an uncomfortable feeling of being critically watched by the cat, I pressed him with clumsy courtesy into his seat again, and slumped into my own.

The cat sat down. Still looking at us in that disconcerting way, she tilted her head first to one side and then the other, inquiringly and cogitatively, the way a cat does when she has struck the unexpected and can't quite make out what she had better do about it. Next she washed one side of her face, making such an awkward and unscientific job of it that almost anybody would have seen that she was either out of practice or didn't know how. She stopped with the one side, and looked bored, and as if she had only been doing it to put in the time, and wished she could think of something else to do to put in some more time. She sat a while, blinking drowsily, then she hit an idea, and looked as if she wondered she hadn't thought of it earlier. She got up and went visiting around among the furniture and belongings, sniffing at each and every article, and elaborately examining it. If it was a chair, she examined it all around, then jumped up in it and sniffed all over its seat and its back; if it was any other thing she could examine all around, she examined it all around; if it was a chest and there was room for her between it and the wall, she crowded herself in behind there and gave it a thorough overhauling; if it was a tall thing, like a washstand, she would stand on her hind toes and stretch up as high as she could, and reach across and paw at the toilet things and try to rake them to where she could smell them; if it was the cupboard, she stood on her toes and reached up and pawed the knob; if it was the table she would squat, and measure the distance, and make a leap, and land in the wrong place, owing to newness to the business; and, part of her going too far and sliding over the edge, she would scramble, and claw at things desperately, and save herself and make good; then she would smell everything on the table, and archly and daintily paw everything around that was movable, and finally paw something off, and skip cheerfully down and paw it some more, throwing herself into the prettiest attitudes, rising on her hind feet and curving her front paws and flirting her head this way and that and glancing down cunningly at the object, then pouncing on it and spatting it half the length of the room, and chasing it up and spatting it again, and again, and racing after it and fetching it another smack—and so on and so on; and suddenly she would tire of it and try to find some way to get to the top of the cupboard or the wardrobe, and if she couldn't she would look troubled and disappointed; and toward the last, when you could see she was getting her bearings well lodged in her head and was satisfied with the place and the arrangements, she relaxed her intensities, and got to purring a little to herself, and praisefully waving her tail between inspections—and at last she was done—done, and everything satisfactory and to her taste.

Being fond of cats, and acquainted with their ways, if I had been a stranger and a person had told me that this cat had spent half an hour in that room before, but hadn't happened to think to examine it until now, I should have been able to say with conviction, "Keep an eye on her, that's no orthodox cat, she's an imitation, there's a flaw in her make-up, you'll find she's born out of wedlock or some other arrested-development accident has happened, she's no true Christian cat, if *I* know the signs."

She couldn't think of anything further to do, now, so she thought she would wash the other side of her face, but she couldn't remember which one it was, so she gave it up, and sat down and went to nodding and blinking; and between nods she would jerk herself together and make remarks. I heard her say—

"One of them's the Duplicate, the other's the Original, but I can't tell t'other from which, and I don't suppose *they* can. I am sure I couldn't if I were them. The missuses said it was the Duplicate that broke in there last night, and I voted with the majority for policy's sake, which is a servant's only protection from trouble, but I would like to know how *they* knew. *I* don't believe they could tell them apart if they were stripped. Now my idea is—"

I interrupted, and intoned musingly, as if to myself,—

> "The boy stood on the burning deck,
> Whence all but him had fled—"

and stopped there, and seemed to sink into a reverie.

It gave her a start! She muttered—

"*That's* the Duplicate. Duplicates know languages—everything, sometimes, and then again they don't know anything at all. That is what Fischer says, though of course it could have been his Duplicate that said it, there's never any telling, in this bewitched place, whether you are talking to a person himself, or only to his heathen image. And Fischer says they haven't any morals nor any principles —though of course it could have been his Duplicate that said it—one never knows. Half the time when you say to a person *he* said so-and-so, he says he didn't—so then you recognize it was the other one. As between living in such a place as this and being crazy, you don't know *which* it is, the most of the time. I would rather be a cat and not have any Duplicate, then I always know which one I am. Otherwise, not. If they haven't any principles, it was this Duplicate that broke in there, though of course, being drunk he wouldn't know which one he was, and so it could be the other without him suspecting it, which leaves the matter where it was before—not certain enough to be certain, and just uncertain enough to be *un*certain. So I don't see that anything's decided. In fact I know it isn't. Still, I think this one that wailed is the Duplicate, because sometimes they know all languages a minute, and next minute they don't know their own, if they've got one, whereas a *man* doesn't. Doesn't, and can't even *learn* it—can't learn cat-language, anyway. It's what Fischer says—Fischer or his Duplicate. So this is the one—*that's* decided. He couldn't talk cataract, nor ever learn it, either, if it was the Christian one . . . . . I'm awful tired!"

I didn't let on, but pretended to be dozing; my brother was a little further along than that—he was softly snoring. I wanted to wait and see, if I could, what was troubling the cat, for it seemed plain to me that she had something on her mind, she certainly was not at her ease. By and by she cleared her throat, and I stirred up and looked at her, as much as to say, "well, I'm listening—proceed." Then she said, with studied politeness—

"It is very late. I am sorry to disturb you gentlemen, but I am very tired, and would like to go to bed."

"Oh, dear me," I said, "don't wait up on our account I beg of you. Turn right in!"

She looked astonished.

"With you present?" she said.

So then I was astonished myself, but did not reveal it.

"Do you mind it?" I asked.

"Do I *mind* it! You will grant, I make no doubt, that so extraordinary a question is hardly entitled to the courtesy of an answer from one of my sex. You are offensive, sir; I beg that you will relieve me of your company at once, and take your friend with you."

"Remove him? I could not do that. He is my guest, and it is his place to make the first move. This is my room."

I said it with a submerged chuckle, as knowing quite well, that soft-spoken as it was, it would knock some of the starch out of her. As indeed it did.

"Your room! Oh, I beg a thousand pardons, I am ashamed of my rude conduct, and will go at once. I assure you sir, I was the innocent victim of a mistake: I thought it was my room."

"And so it is. There has been no mistake. Don't you see?—there is your bed."

She looked whither I was pointing, and said with surprise—

"How strange that is! it wasn't there five seconds ago. Oh, *isn't* it a love!"

She made a spring for it—cat-like, forgetting the old interest in the new one; and feminine-like, eager to feast her native appetite for pretty things upon its elegancies and daintinesses. And really it *was* a daisy! It was a canopied four-poster, of rare wood, richly carved, with bed twenty inches wide and thirty long, sumptuously bepillowed and belaced and beruffled and besatined and all that; and when she had petted it and patted it and searched it and sniffed it all over, she cried out in an agony of delight and longing—

"Oh, I would just *love* to stretch out on that!"

The enthusiasm of it melted me, and I said heartily—

"Turn right in, Mary Florence Fortescue Baker G. Nightingale, and make yourself at home—that is the magician's own present to you, and it shows you he's no imitation-friend, but the true thing!"

"Oh, what a pretty name!" she cried; "is it mine for sure enough, and may I keep it? Where *did* you get it?"

"I don't know—the magician hooked it from somewhere, he is always at that, and it just happened to come into my mind at the psychological moment, and I'm glad it did, for your sake, for it's a dandy! Turn in, now, Baker G., and make yourself entirely at home."

"You are *so* good, dear Duplicate, and I am just as grateful as I can be, but—but—well, you see how it is. I have never roomed with any person not of my own sex, and—"

"You will be perfectly safe here, Mary, I assure you, and—"

"I should be an ingrate to doubt it, and I do not doubt it, be sure of that; but at this particular time—at this time of all others—er—well, you know, for a smaller matter than this, Miss Marget is already compromised beyond repair, I fear, and if I—"

"Say no more, Mary Florence, you are perfectly right, perfectly. My dressing-room is large and comfortable, I can get along quite well without it, and I will carry your bed in there. Come along . . . Now then, there you are! Snug and nice and all right, isn't it? Contemplate that! Satisfactory?—yes?"

She cordially confessed that it was. So I sat down and chatted along while she went around and examined *that* place all over, and pawed everything and sampled the smell of each separate detail, like an old hand, for she was getting the hang of her trade by now; then she made a final and special examination of the button on our communicating-door, and stretched herself up on her hind-toes and fingered it till she got the trick of buttoning-out inquisitives and undesirables down fine and ship-shape, then she thanked me handsomely for fetching the bed and taking so much trouble; and gave me good-night, and when I asked if it would disturb her if I talked a while with my guest, she said no, talk as much as we pleased, she was tired enough to sleep through thunderstorms and earthquakes. So I said, right cordially—

"Good-night, Mary G., und schlafen Sie wohl!" and passed out and left her to her slumbers. As delicate-minded a cat as ever I've struck, and I've known a many of them.

Chapter 29

I stirred my brother up, and we talked the time away while waiting for the magician to come. I said his coming was a most uncertain thing, for he was irregular, and not at all likely to come when wanted, but Schwarz was anxious to stay and take the chances; so we did as I have said—talked and waited. He told me a great deal about his life and ways as a dream-sprite, and did it in a skipping and disconnected fashion proper to his species. He would side-track a subject right in the middle of a sentence if another subject attracted him, and he did this without apology or explanation—well, just as a dream would, you know. His talk was scatteringly seasoned with strange words and phrases, picked up in a thousand worlds, for he had been everywhere. Sometimes he could tell me their meaning and where he got them, but not always; in fact not very often, the dream-memory being pretty capricious, he said—sometimes good, oftener bad, and always flighty. "Side-track," for instance. He was not able to remember where he had picked that up, but thought it was in a star in the belt of Orion where he had spent a summer one night with some excursionists from Sirius whom he had met in space. That was as far as he could remember with anything like certainty; as to *when* it was, that was a blank with him; perhaps it was in the past, maybe it was in the future, he couldn't tell which it was, and probably didn't know, at the time it happened. *Couldn't* know, in fact, for Past and Future were human terms and not comprehendable by him, past and future being all one thing to a dream-sprite, and not distinguishable the one from the other. "And not important, anyway." How natural that sounded, coming from him! His notions of the important were just simply elementary, as you may say.

He often dropped phrases which had clear meanings to him, but which he labored in vain to make comprehensible by me. It was because they came from countries where none of the conditions resembled the conditions I had been used to; some from comets where nothing was solid, and nobody had legs; some from our sun, where nobody was comfortable except when white-hot, and where you needn't talk to people about cold and darkness, for you would not be able to explain the words so that they could understand what you were talking about; some from invisible black planets swimming in eternal midnight and thick-armored in perpetual ice, where the people have no eyes, nor any use for them, and where you might wear yourself out trying to make them understand what you meant by such words as warmth and light, you wouldn't ever succeed; and some from *general space*—that sea of ether which has no shores, and stretches on, and on, and arrives nowhere; which is a waste of black gloom and thick darkness through which you may rush forever at thought-speed, encountering at weary long intervals spirit-cheering archipelagoes of suns which rise sparkling far in front of you, and swiftly grow and swell, and burst into blinding glories of light, apparently measureless in extent, but you plunge through and in a moment they are far behind, a twinkling archipelago again, and in another moment they are blotted out in darkness; constellations, these? yes; and the earliest of them the property of your own solar system; the rest of that unending flight is through solar systems not known to men.

And he said that in that flight one came across *such* interesting dream-sprites! coming from a billion worlds, bound for a billion others; always friendly, always glad to meet up with you, always full of where they'd been and what they'd seen, and dying to tell you about it; doing it in a million foreign languages, which some-times you understood and sometimes you didn't, and the tongue you understood to-day you forgot to-morrow, there being *nothing* permanent about a dream-sprite's character, constitution, beliefs, opinions, intentions, likes, dislikes, or anything else; all he cares for is to travel, and talk, and see wonderful things and have a good time. Schwarz said dream-sprites are well-disposed toward their fleshly brothers, and did what they could to make them partakers of the wonders of their travels, but it couldn't be managed except on a poor and not-worth-while scale, because they had to communicate through the flesh-brothers' Waking-Self imagination, and *that* medi-um—oh, well, it was like "emptying rainbows down a rat-hole."

His tone was not offensive. I think his tone was never that, and was never meant to be that; *it* was all right enough, but his phrasing was often hurtful, on account of the ideal frankness of it. He said he was once out on an excursion to Jupiter with some fellows about a million years ago, when—

I stopped him there, and said—

"I am only seventeen, and you said you were born with me."

"Yes," he said, "I've been with you only about two million years, I believe—counting as you count; *we* don't measure time at all. Many a time I've been abroad five or ten or twenty thousand years in a single night; I'm always abroad when you are asleep; I always leave, the moment you fall asleep, and I never return until you wake up. You are dreaming all the time I am gone, but you get little or nothing of what I see—never more than some cheap odds and ends, such as your groping Mortal Mind is competent to perceive—and sometimes there's nothing for you at all, in a whole night's adventures, covering many centuries; it's all above your dull Mortal Mind's reach."

Then he dropped into his "chances." That is to say, he went to discussing my health—as coldly as if I had been a piece of mere property that he was commercially interested in, and which ought to be thoughtfully and prudently taken care of for *his* sake. And he even went into particulars, by gracious! advising me to be very careful about my diet, and to take a good deal of exercise, and keep regular hours, and avoid dissipation and religion, and not get married, because a family brought love, and distributed it among many objects, and intensified it, and this engendered wearing cares and anxieties, and when the objects suffered or died the miseries and anxieties multiplied and broke the heart and shortened life; whereas if I took good care of myself and avoided these indiscretions, there was no reason why he should not live ten million years and be hap—

I broke in and changed the subject, so as to keep from getting inhospitable and saying language; for really I was a good deal tried. I started him on the heavens, for he had been to a good many of them and liked ours the best, on account of there not being any Sunday there. They kept Saturday, and it was very pleasant: plenty of rest for the tired, and plenty of innocent good times for the others. But no Sunday, he said; the Sunday-Sabbath was a commercial invention and quite local, having been devised by Constantine to equalize prosperities in this world between the Jews and the Christians. The government statistics of that period showed that a Jew could make as much money in five days as a Christian could in six; and so Constantine saw that at this rate the Jews would by and by have all the wealth and the Christians all the poverty. There was nothing fair nor right about this, a righteous government should have equal laws for all, and take just as much care of the incompetent as of the competent—more, if anything. So he added the Sunday-Sabbath, and it worked just right, because it equalized the prosperities. After that, the Jew had to lie idle 104 days in the year, the Christian only 52, and this enabled the Christian to catch up. But my brother said there was now talk among Constantine and other early Christians up there, of some more equalizing; because, in looking forward a few centuries they could notice that along in the twentieth century somewhere it was going to be necessary to furnish the Jews another Sabbath to keep, so as to save what might be left of Christian property at that time. Schwarz said he had been down into the first quarter of the twentieth century lately, and it looked so to him.

Then he "side-tracked" in his abrupt way, and looked avidly at

my head and said he did wish he was back in my skull, he would
sail out the first time I fell asleep and have a scandalous good time!
—wasn't that magician *ever* coming back?

"And oh," he said, "what wouldn't I see! wonders, spectacles,
splendors which your fleshly eyes couldn't endure; and what
wouldn't I hear! the music of the spheres—no mortal could live
through five minutes of *that* ecstasy! If he would only come! If he
. . . ." He stopped, with his lips parted and his eyes fixed, like one
rapt. After a moment he whispered, *"do you feel that?"*

I recognized it; it was that life-giving, refreshing, mysterious
something which invaded the air when 44 was around. But I
dissembled, and said—

"What is it?"

"It's the magician; he's coming. He doesn't always let that influence go out from him, and so we dream-sprites took him for an
ordinary necromancer for a while; but when he burnt 44 we were
all there and close by, and he let it out then, and in an instant we
knew what he was! We knew he was a . . . we knew he was a
. . . . a . . . a . . . how curious!—my tongue won't *say* it!"

Yes, you see, 44 wouldn't let him say it—and I so near to getting
that secret at last! It was a sorrowful disappointment.

Forty-Four entered, still in the disguise of the magician, and
Schwarz flung himself on his knees and began to beg passionately
for release, and I put in my voice and helped. Schwarz said—

"Oh, mighty one, you imprisoned me, you can set me free, and no
other can. You have the power; you possess *all* the powers, all the
forces that defy Nature, nothing is impossible to you, for you are a
. . . a . . ."

So there it was again—he couldn't say it. I was that close to it a
second time, you see; 44 wouldn't let him say that word, and I
would have given anything in the world to hear it. It's the way we
are made, you know: if we can get a thing, we don't want it, but if
we can't get it, why—well, it changes the whole aspect of it, you
see.

Forty-Four was very good about it. He said he would let this one
go—Schwarz was hugging him around the knees and lifting up the

hem of his robe and kissing it and kissing it before he could get any further with his remark—yes, he would let this one go, and make some fresh ones for the wedding, the family could get along very well that way. So he told Schwarz to stand up and melt. Schwarz did it, and it was very pretty. First, his clothes thinned out so you could see him through them, then they floated off like shreds of vapor, leaving him naked, then the cat looked in, but scrambled out again; next, the flesh fell to thinning, and you could see the skeleton through it, very neat and trim, a good skeleton; next the bones disappeared and nothing was left but the empty form—just a statue, perfect and beautiful, made out of the delicatest soap-bubble stuff, with rainbow-hues dreaming around over it and the furniture showing through it the same as it would through a bubble; then— poof! and it was gone!

Chapter 30

THE CAT walked in, waving her tail, then gathered it up in her right arm, as she might a train, and minced her way to the middle of the room, where she faced the magician and rose up and bent low and spread her hands wide apart, as if it was a gown she was spreading, then sank her body grandly rearward—certainly the neatest thing you ever saw, considering the limitedness of the materials. I think a curtsy is the very prettiest thing a woman ever does, and I think a lady's-maid's curtsy is prettier than any one else's; which is because they get more practice than the others, on account of being at it all the time when there's nobody looking. When she had finished her work of art she smiled quite Cheshirely (my dream-brother's word, he knew it was foreign and thought it was future, he couldn't be sure), and said, very engagingly—

"Do you think I could have a bite now, without waiting for the second table, there'll be *such* goings-on this morning, and I would just give a whole basket of rats to be in it! and if I—"

At that moment the wee-wee'est little bright-eyed mousie you ever saw went scrabbling across the floor, and Baker G. gave a skip and let out a scream and landed in the highest chair in the room and gathered up her imaginary skirts and stood there trembling. Also at that moment her breakfast came floating out of the cupboard on a silver tray, and she asked that it come to the chair, which it did, and she took a hurried bite or two to stay her stomach, then rushed away to get her share of the excitements, saying she would like the rest of her breakfast to be kept for her till she got back.

"Now then, draw up to the table," said 44. "We'll have Vienna coffee of two centuries hence—it is the best in the world—buckwheat cakes from Missouri, vintage of 1845, French eggs of last century, and deviled breakfast-whale of the post-pliocene, when he was whitebait size, and just *too* delicious!"

By now I was used to these alien meals, raked up from countries I had never heard of and out of seasons a million years apart, and was getting indifferent about their age and nationalities, seeing that they always turned out to be fresh and good. At first I couldn't stand eggs a hundred years old and canned manna of Moses's time, but that effect came from habit and prejudiced imagination, and I soon got by it, and enjoyed what came, asking few or no questions. At first I would not have touched whale, the very thought of it would have turned my stomach, but now I ate a hundred and sixty of them and never turned a hair. As we chatted along during breakfast, 44 talked reminiscently of dream-sprites, and said they used to be important in the carrying of messages where secrecy and dispatch were a desideratum. He said they took a pride in doing their work well, in old times; that they conveyed messages with perfect verbal accuracy, and that in the matter of celerity they were up to the telephone and away beyond the telegraph. He instanced the Joseph-dreams, and gave it as his opinion that if they had gone per Western Union the lean kine would all have starved to death before the telegrams arrived. He said the business went to pot in Roman times, but that was the fault of the interpreters, not of the dream-sprites, and remarked—

"You can easily see that accurate interpreting was as necessary as accurate wording. For instance, suppose the Founder sends a telegram in the Christian Silence dialect, what are you going to do? Why, there's nothing to do but *guess* the best you can, and take the chances, because there isn't anybody in heaven or earth that can understand *both* ends of it, and so, there you are, you see! Up a stump."

"Up a which?"

"Stump. American phrase. Not discovered yet. It means defeated. You are bound to misinterpret the end you do not understand, and so the matter which was to have been accomplished by the message miscarries, fails, and vast damage is done. Take a specific example, then you will get my meaning. Here is a telegram from the Founder to her disciples. Date, June 27, four hundred and thirteen years hence; it's in the paper—Boston paper—I fetched it this morning."

"What is a Boston paper?"

"It can't be described in just a mouthful of words—pictures, scare-heads and all. You wait, I'll tell you all about it another time; I want to read the telegram, now."

"Hear, O Israel, the Lord God is one Lord.

"I now request that the members of my Church cease special prayer for the peace of nations, and cease in full faith that God does not hear our prayers only because of oft speaking; but that He will bless all the inhabitants of the earth, and 'none can stay His hand nor say unto Him what doest thou.' Out of His allness He must bless all with His own truth and love.

"MARY BAKER G. EDDY."

"Pleasant View, Concord, N.H., June 27, 1905."

"You see? Down to the word 'nations' anybody can understand it. There's been a prodigious war going on for about seventeen months, with destruction of whole fleets and armies, and in seventeen words she indicates certain things, to-wit: I believed we could squelch the war with prayer, therefore I ordered it; it was an error of Mortal Mind, whereas I had supposed it was an inspiration; I now order you to cease from praying for peace and take hold of something nearer our size, such as strikes and insurrections. The rest seems to mean—seems to mean . . . . Let me study it a minute. It seems to mean that He does not listen to our prayers any more because we pester Him too much. This carries us to the phrase 'oft-speaking.' At that point the fog shuts down, black and impenetrable, it solidifies into uninterpretable irrelevancies. Now then, you add up, and get these results: the praying must be stopped—which is clear and definite; the reason for the stoppage is—well, uncertain. Don't you know that the incomprehensible and uninterpretable remaining half of the message may be of *actual* importance? we may be even sure of it, I think, because the first half wasn't; then what are we confronted with? what is the world confronted with? Why, possible disaster—isn't it so? Possible disaster, absolutely impossible to avoid; and all because one cannot get at the meaning of the words intended to describe it and tell how to prevent it. You now understand how important is the interpreter's share in these matters. If you put part of the message in school-girl and the rest in Choctaw, the interpreter is going to be defeated, and colossal harm can come of it."

"I am sure it is true. What is His allness?"

"I pass."

"You which?"

"Pass. Theological expression. It probably means that she entered the game because she thought only His halfness was in it and would need help; then perceiving that His allness was there and playing on the other side, she considered it best to cash-in and draw out. I think that that must be it; it looks reasonable, you see, because in seventeen months she hadn't put up a single chip and got it back again, and so in the circumstances it would be natural for her to want to go out and see a friend. In Roman times the business went to pot through bad interpreting, as I told you before. Here in Suetonius is an instance. He is speaking of Atia, the mother of Augustus Caesar:

" 'Before her delivery she dreamed that her bowels stretched to the stars, and expanded through the whole circuit of heaven and earth.'

"Now how would you interpret that, August?"

"Who—me? I do not think I could interpret it at all, but I do wish I could have seen it, it must have been magnificent."

"Oh, yes, like enough; but doesn't it suggest anything to you?"

"Why, n-no, I can't see that it does. What would *you* think—that there had been an accident?"

"Of course not! It wasn't real, it was only a dream. It was sent to inform her that she was going to be delivered of something remarkable. What should you think it was?"

"I—why, I don't know."

"Guess."

"Do you think—well, would it be a slaughter-house?"

"Sho, you've no talent for interpretation. But that is a striking instance of what the interpreter had to deal with, in that day. The dream-messages had become loose and rickety and indefinite, like the Founder's telegram, and soon the natural thing happened: the interpreters became loose and careless and discouraged, and got to guessing instead of interpreting, and the business went to ruin. Rome had to give up dream-messages, and the Romans took to entrails for prophetic information."

"Why, then, these ones must have come good, 44, don't you think?"

"I mean *bird* entrails—entrails of chickens."

"I would stake my money on the others; what does a chicken know about the future?"

"Sho, you don't get the idea, August. It isn't what the chicken knows; a chicken doesn't know anything, but by examining the condition of its entrails when it was slaughtered, the augurs could find out a good deal about what was going to happen to emperors, that being the way the Roman gods had invented to communicate with them when dream-transportation went out and Western Union hadn't come in yet. It was a good idea, too, because often a chicken's entrails knew more than a Roman god did, if he was drunk, and he generally was."

"Forty-Four, aren't you afraid to speak like that about a god?"

"No. Why?"

"Because it's irreverent."

"No, it isn't."

"Why isn't it? What do you *call* irreverence?"

"Irreverence is *another person's* disrespect to *your* god; there isn't any word that tells what your disrespect to *his* god is."

I studied it over and saw that it was the truth, but I hadn't ever happened to look at it in that way before.

"Now then, August, to come back to Atia's dream. It beat every soothsayer. None of them got it right. The real meaning of it was—"

The cat dashed in, excited, and said, "I heard Katzenyammer say there's hell to pay down below!" and out she dashed again. I jumped up, but 44 said—

"Sit down. Keep your head. There's no hurry. Things are working; I think we can have a good time. I have shut down the prophecy-works and prepared for it."

"The prophecy-works?"

"Yes. Where I come from, we—"

"*Where* do you co—"

It was as far as I could get. My jaw caught, there, and he gave me a look and went on as if nothing had happened:

"Where I come from we have a gift which we get tired of, now and then. We foresee everything that is going to happen, and so when it happens there's nothing *to* it, don't you see? we don't get any surprises. We can't shut down the prophecy-works there, but we can here. That is one of the main reasons that I come here so much. I do love surprises! I'm only a youth, and it's natural. I love shows and spectacles, and stunning dramatics, and I love to astonish people, and show off, and be and do all the gaudy things a boy loves to be and do; and whenever I'm here and have got matters worked up to where there is a good prospect to the fore, I shut down the works and have a time! I've shut them down now, two hours ago, and I don't know a thing that's ahead, any more than you do. That's all—now we'll go. I wanted to tell you that. I had plans, but I've thrown them aside. I haven't any now. I will let things go their own way, and act as circumstances suggest. Then there will be surprises.

They may be small ones, and nothing to you, because you are used to them; but even the littlest ones are grand to me!"

The cat came racing in, greatly excited, and said—

"Oh, I'm so glad I'm in time! Shut the door—there's people everywhere—don't let them see in. Dear magician, get a disguise, you are in greater danger now than ever before. You have been seen, and everybody knows it, everybody is watching for you, it was most imprudent in you to show yourself. Do put on a disguise and come with me, I know a place in the castle where they'll never find you. Oh, please, please hurry! don't you hear the distant noises? they're hunting for you—do *please* hurry!"

Forty-Four was that gratified, you can't think! He said—

"There it is, you see! I hadn't any idea of it, any more than you! And there'll be more—I just feel it."

"Oh, please don't stop to talk, but get the disguise! you don't know what may happen any moment. Everybody is searching for me, and for you, too, Duplicate, and for your Original; they've been at it some time, and are coming to think all three of us is murdered—"

"*Now* I know what I'll do!" cried 44; "oh but we'll have the gayest time! go on with your news!"

"—and Katrina is wild to get a chance at you because you burnt up 44, which was the idol of her heart, and she's got a carving knife three times as long as my tail, and is ambushed behind a marble column in the great hall, and it's awful to see how savagely she rakes it and whets it up and down that column and makes the sparks fly, and darts her head out, with her eyes glaring, to see if she can see you—oh, *do* get the disguise and come with me, quick! and laws bless me, there's a conspiracy, and—"

"Oh, it's grand, August, it's just grand! and I didn't know a thing about it, any more than you. *What* conspiracy are you talking about, pussy?"

"It's the strikers, going to kill the Duplicates—I sat in Fischer's lap and heard them talk the whole thing in whispers; and they've got signs and grips and passwords and all that, so't they can tell which is themselves and which is other people, though I hope to goodness if *I* can, not if I had a thousand such; *do* get the disguise and come, I'm just ready to cry!"

"Oh, bother the disguise, I'm going just so, and if they offer to do anything to me I will give them a piece of my mind."

And so he opened the door and started away, Mary following him, with the tears running down, and saying—

"Oh, *they* won't care for your piece of mind—why *will* you be so imprudent and throw your life away, and you *know* they'll abuse me and bang me when you are gone!"

I became invisible and joined them.

Chapter 31

I T WAS a dark, sour, gloomy morning, and bleak and cold, with a slanting veil of powdery snow driving along, and a clamorous hollow wind bellowing down the chimneys and rumbling around the battlements and towers—just the right weather for the occasion, 44 said, nothing could improve it but an eclipse. That gave him an idea, and he said he would do an eclipse; not a real one, but an artificial one that nobody but Simon Newcomb could tell from the original Jacobs—so he started it at once, and it certainly did make those yawning old stone tunnels pretty dim and sepulchral, and also of course it furnished an additional uncanniness and muffledness to way-off footfalls, taking the harshness out of them and the edge off their echoes, because when you walk on that kind of eclipsy gloominess on a stone floor it squshes under the foot and makes that dull effect which is so shuddery and uncomfortable in these crumbly old castles where there has been such ages of cruelty and captivity and murder and mystery. And to-night would be Ghost-Night besides, and 44 did not forget to remember that, and said he wished eclipses weren't so much trouble after sundown, hanged if he wouldn't run this one all night, because it could be a great help, and a lot of ghastly effects could be gotten out of it, because all the castle ghosts turn out then, on account of its coming only every ten years, which makes it kind of select and distinguished, and still more so every Hundredth Year—which this one was—because the best ghosts from many other castles come by invitation, then, and take a hand at the great ball and banquet at midnight, a good spectacle and full of interest, insomuch that 44 had come more than once on the Hundredth Night to see it, he said, and it was very pathetic and interesting to meet up with shadowy friends that way that you haven't seen for one or two centuries and hear them tell the same mouldy things over again that they've told you several times before; because they don't have anything fresh, the way they are situated, poor things. And besides, he was going to make this the swellest Hundredth Night that had been celebrated in this castle in twelve centuries, and said he was inviting A 1 ghosts from everywhere in the world and from all the ages, past and future, and each could bring a friend if he liked—any friend, character no object, just so he is dead—and if I wanted to invite some I could, he hoped to accumulate a thousand or two, and make this *the* Hundredth Night of Hundredth Nights, and discourage competition for a thousand years.

We didn't see a soul, all the murky way from my door to the central grand staircase and half way down it—then we began to see plenty of people, our own and men from the village—and they were armed, and stood in two ranks, waiting, a double fence across the spacious hall—for the magician to pass between, if it might please him to try it; and Katrina was there, between the fences, grim and towering and soldierly, and she was watching and waiting, with her knife. I glanced back, by chance, and there was also a living fence *behind!* dim forms, men who had been keeping watch in ambush, and had silently closed in upon the magician's tracks as he passed along. Mary G. had apparently had enough of this grisly journey—she was gone.

When the people below saw that their plans had succeeded, and that their quarry was in the trap they had set, they set up a loud cheer of exultation, but it didn't seem to me to ring true; there was a doubtful note in it, and I thought likely those folks were not as glad they had caught their bird as they were letting on to be; and they kept crossing themselves industriously; I took that for a sign, too.

Forty-Four moved steadily down. When he was on the last step there was turmoil down the hall, and a volley of shoutings, with cries of "make way—Father Adolf is come!" then he burst panting through one of the ranks and threw himself in the way, just as Katrina was plunging for the disguised 44, and stormed out—

"Stop her, everybody! Donkeys, would you let her butcher him, and cheat the Church's fires!"

They jumped for Katrina, and in a moment she was struggling in the jumble of swaying forms, with nothing visible above it but her head and her long arm with the knife in it; and her strong voice was pouring out her feelings with energy, and easily making itself heard above the general din and the priest's commands:

"Let me at him—he burnt my child, my darling!" . . . . "*Keep her off, men, keep her off!*" . . . . "He is *not* the Church's, his blood is *mine* by rights—out of my way! I *will* have it!" . . . . "*Back! woman, back, I tell you—force her back, men, have you no strength? are you nothing but boys?*" . . . . "A hundred of you shan't stay me, woman though I be!"

And sure enough, with one massy surge she wrenched herself free, and flourished her knife, and bent her head and body forward like a foot-racer and came charging down the living lane through the gathering darkness—

Then suddenly there was a great light! she lifted her head and caught it full in her swarthy face, which it transfigured with its white glory, as it did also all that place, and its marble pillars, and the frightened people, and Katrina dropped her knife and fell to her knees, with her hands clasped, everybody doing the same; and so there they were, all kneeling, like that, with hands thrust forward or clasped, and they and the stately columns all awash in that unearthly splendor; and there where the magician had stood, stood 44 now, in his supernal beauty and his gracious youth; and it was from him that that flooding light came, for all his form was clothed in that immortal fire, and flashing like the sun; and Katrina crept on her knees to him, and bent down her old head and kissed his feet, and he bent down and patted her softly on the shoulder and touched his lips to the gray hair—*and was gone!*—and for two or three minutes you were so blinded you couldn't see your next neighbor in that submerging black darkness. Then after that it was better, and you could make out the murky forms, some still kneeling, some lying prone in a swoon, some staggering about, here and there, with their hands pressed over their eyes, as if that light had hurt them and they were in pain. Katrina was wandering off, on unsteady feet, and her knife was lying there in the midst.

It was good he thought of the eclipse, it helped out ever so much; the effects would have been fine and great in any case, but the eclipse made them grand and stunning—just letter-perfect, as it seemed to me; and he said himself it beat Barnum and Bailey hands down, and was by as much as several shades too good for the provinces—which was all Sanscrit to me, and hadn't any meaning even in Sanscrit I reckon, but was invented for the occasion, because it had a learned sound, and he liked sound better than sense as a rule. There's been others like that, but he was the worst.

I judged it would take those people several hours to get over that, and accumulate their wits again and get their bearings, for it had knocked the whole bunch dizzy; meantime there wouldn't be anything doing. I must put in the time some way until they should be in a condition to resume business at the old stand. I went to my room and put on my flesh and stretched myself out on a lounge before the fire with a book, first setting the door ajar, so that the cat could fetch news if she got hold of any, which I wished she might; but in a little while I was asleep. I did not stir again until ten at night. I woke then, and found the cat finishing her supper, and my own ready on the table and hot; and very welcome, for I hadn't eaten anything since breakfast. Mary came and occupied a chair at my board, and washed herself and delivered her news while I ate. She had witnessed the great transformation scene, and had been so astonished by it and so interested in it that she did not wait to see the end, but went up a chimney and stayed there half an hour freezing, until somebody started a fire under her, and then she was thankful and very comfortable. But it got too comfortable, and she climbed out and came down a skylight stairway and went visiting around, and a little while ago she caught a rat, and did it as easy as nothing, and would teach me how, sometime, if I cared for such things; but she didn't eat it, it wasn't a fresh rat, or was out of season or something, but it reminded her that she was hungry, so she came home. Then she said—

"If you like to be astonished, I can astonish you. The magician isn't dead!"

I threw my hands up and did the astonishment-act like an old expert, crying out—

"Mary Florence Fortescue, what *can* you mean!"

She was delighted, and exclaimed—

"There, it's just as I said! I *told* him you wouldn't ever believe it; but I can lay my paw on my heart, just so, and I wish I may never stir if I haven't *seen* him!—*seen* him, you hear?—and he's just as alive as ever he was since the day he was born!"

"Oh, go 'long, you're deceiving me!"

She was almost beside herself with joy over the success of her astonisher, and said—

"Oh, it's lovely, it's too lovely, and just as I *said* it would be—I *told* him you wouldn't, and it's come out just so!"

In her triumph and delight she tried to clap her hands, but it was a failure, they wouldn't clap any more than mushrooms. Then she said—

"Duplicate, would you believe he is alive if I should prove it?"

"Sho," I said, "come off!—what are you giving me?—as he used to say. You're talking nonsense, Mary. When a person is dead, *known* to be dead, permanently dead, demonstrably dead, you *can't* prove him alive, there isn't any *way*. Come, don't you know that?"

Well, she was just beaming, by now, and she could hardly hold her system together, she was that near to bursting with the victory she was going to spring on me. She skipped to the floor and flirted something to my foot with her paw; I picked it up, and she jumped into her chair again and said—

"There, now, he said you would know what that is; what is it?"

"It's a thing he calls a paper—Boston paper."

"That's right, that's what he said. And he said it is future English and you know present English and can read it. Did he say right?"

"The *fact* is right, but he didn't say it, because he's dead."

"You wait—that's all. He said look at the date."

"Very well. He didn't say it, because he's dead, and of course wouldn't think of it; but here it is, all the same—June 28, 1905."

"That's right, it's what he said. Then he said ask you what was the Founder's message to her disciples, that was in the other Boston paper. What was it?"

"Well, he told me there was an immense war going on, and she got tired having her people pray for peace and never take a trick for seventeen months, so she ordered them to quit, and put their battery out of commission. And he said nobody could understand the rest of the message, and like enough that very ignorance would bring on an immense disaster."

"Aha! well, it *did!* He says the very minute she was stopping the praying, the two fleets were meeting, and the uncivilized one utterly annihilated the civilized one, and it wouldn't have happened if she had let the praying go on. Now then, you didn't know *that,* did you!"

"No, and I don't know it yet."

"Well, you soon will. The message was June 27, wasn't it?"

"Yes."

"Well, the disaster was *that very day*—right after the praying was stopped—and you'll find the news of it in the very next day's paper, which you've got in your hand—date, *June 28.*"

I took a glance at the big headings, and said—

"M-y word! why it's absolutely *so!* Baker G., don't you know this is the most astounding thing that ever happened? It proves he *is* alive—nobody else could bring this paper. He certainly is alive, and back with us, after that tremendous abolishment and extinction which we witnessed; yes, he's alive, Mary, alive, and glad am I, oh, grateful beyond words!"

"Oh!" she cried, in a rapture, "it's just splendid, oh, just too lovely! I knew I could prove it; I knew it just as well! I thought he was gone, when he blazed up and went out, that way, and I *was* so scared and grieved—and isn't he a wonder! Duplicate, there isn't another necromancer in the business that can begin with him, now *is* there?"

"You can stake your tale and your ears on it, Mary, and don't you forget it—as he used to say. In my opinion he can give the whole trade ninety-nine in the hundred and go out every time, cross-eyed and left-handed."

"But he isn't, Duplicate."

"Isn't what?"

"Cross-eyed and left-handed."

"Who said he was, you little fool?"

"Why, you did."

"I never said anything of the kind; I said he could if he *was*. That isn't *saying* he was; it was a supposititious case, and literary; it was a figure, a metaphor, and its function was to augment the force of the—"

"Well, he *isn't*, anyway; because I've noticed, and—"

"Oh, shut up! don't I tell you it was only a *figure*, and I never meant—"

"I don't care, you'll never make *me* believe he's cross-eyed and left-handed, because the time he—"

"Baker G., if you open your mouth again I'll jam the boot-jack down it! you're as random and irrelevant and incoherent and mentally impenetrable as the afflicted Founder herself."

But she was under the bed by that time; and reflecting, probably, if she had the machinery for it.

Chapter 32

Forty-Four, still playing Balthasar Hoffman the magician, entered briskly now, and threw himself in a chair. The cat emerged with confidence, spread herself, purring, in his lap, and said—

"This Duplicate wouldn't believe me when I told him, and when

I proved it he tried to cram a boot-jack down my throat, thinking to scare me, which he didn't, *didn't* you, Duplicate?"

"Didn't I *what?*"

"Why, what I just *said.*"

"I don't know what you just said; it was Christian Silence and untranslatable; but I'll say yes to the whole of it if that will quiet you. Now then, keep still, and let the master tell what is on his mind."

"Well, this is on my mind, August. Some of the most distinguished people can't come. Flora McFlimsey—nothing to wear; Eve, ditto; Adam, previous engagement, and so on and so on; Nero and ever so many others find the notice too short, and are urgent to have more time. Very well, we've got to accommodate them."

"But how can we do it? The show is due to begin in an hour. Listen!"

Boom-m-m—boom-m-m—boom-m-m!—

It was the great bell of the castle tolling the hour. Our American clock on the wall struck in, and simultaneously the clock of the village—faint and far, and half of the notes overtaken in their flight and strangled by the gusty wind. We sat silent and counted, to the end.

"You see?" said I.

"Yes, I see. Eleven. Now there are two ways to manage. One is, to have time stand still—which has been done before, a lot of times; and the other one is, to turn time backward for a day or two, which is comparatively new, and offers the best effects, besides.

"'Backward, turn backward, O Time, in thy flight—
Make me a child again, just for to-night!'—

"—'Beautiful Snow,' you see; it hasn't been written yet. *I* vote to reverse—and that is what we will do, presently. We will make the hands of the clocks travel around in the other direction."

"But will they?"

"Sure. It will attract attention—make yourself easy, as to that. But the stunning effect is going to be the sun."

"How?"

"Well, when they see him come rising up out of the west, about half a dozen hours from now, it will secure the interest of the entire world."

"I should think as much."

"Oh, yes, depend upon it. There is going to be more early rising than the human race has seen before. In my opinion it'll be a record."

"I believe you are right about it. I mean to get up and see it myself. Or stay up."

"I think it will be a good idea to have it rise in the south-west, instead of the west. More striking, you see; and hasn't been done before."

"Master, it will be wonderful! It will be the very greatest marvel the world has ever seen. It will be talked about and written about as long as the human race endures. And there'll not be any disputing over it, because every human being that's alive will get up to look at it, and there won't be one single person to say it's a lie."

"It's so. It will be the only perfectly authenticated event in all human history. All the other happenings, big and little, have got to depend on minority-testimony, and very little of that—but not so, this time, dontcherknow. And this one's patented. There aren't going to be any encores."

"How long shall we go backwards, Balthasar?"

"Two or three days or a week; long enough to accommodate Robert Bruce, and Henry I and such, who have hearts and things scattered around here and there and yonder, and have to get a basket and go around and collect; so we will let the sun and the clocks go backwards a while, then start them ahead in time to fetch up all right at midnight to-night—then the shades will begin to arrive according to schedule."

"It grows on me! It's going to be the most prodigious thing that ever happened, and—"

"Yes," he burst out, in a rapture of eloquence, "and will round out and perfect the reputation I've been building for Balthasar Hoffman, and make him the most glorious magician that ever lived, and get him burnt, to a dead moral certainty. You know I've taken a lot of pains with that reputation; I've taken more interest in it than anything I've planned out in centuries; I've spared neither labor nor thought, and I feel a pride in it and a sense of satisfaction such as I have hardly ever felt in a mere labor of love before; and when I get it completed, now, in this magnificent way, and get him burnt, or pulverized, or something showy and picturesque, like that, I shan't mind the trouble I've had, in the least; not in the least, I give you my word."

Boom-m-m—boom-m-m—boom-m-m—

"There she goes! striking eleven again."

"Is it really?"

"Count—you'll see."

It woke the cat, and she stretched herself out about a yard and a half, and asked if time was starting back—which showed that she had heard the first part of the talk. And understood it of course, because it was in German. She was informed that time was about to start back; so she arranged herself for another nap, and said that when we got back to ten she would turn out and catch that rat again.

I was counting the clock-strokes—counting aloud—

"Eight . . . . nine . . . . ten . . . . eleven—"

Forty-Four shouted—

"Backward! turn backward! O Time in thy flight! Look at the clock-hands! Listen!"

Instantly I found myself counting the strokes again, aloud—

"Eleven . . . ten . . . . nine . . . eight . . . . seven . . . six . . . . five . . . . four . . . two . . . one!"

At once the cat woke and repeated her remark about re-catching the rat—saying it backwards!

Then Forty-Four said—

"see you'll—Count."

Whereupon I said—

"really? it Is"

And he remarked—the booming of the great castle clock mixing with his words—

"again. eleven striking goes! she There word (here his voice began to become impressive, then to nobly rise, and swell, and grow in eloquent feeling and majestic expression), my you give I least, the in not least; the in had, I've trouble the mind shan't I that, like picturesque, and showy something or pulverized, or burnt, him get and way, magnificent this in now, completed, it get I when and before; love of labor mere a in felt ever hardly have I as such satisfaction of sense a and it in pride (here his voice was near to breaking, so deeply were his feelings stirred) a feel I and thought, nor labor neither spared I've centuries; in out planned I've anything than it in interest more taken I've reputation; that with pains of lot a taken I've know You (here his winged eloquence reached its loftiest flight, and in his deep organ-tones he thundered forth his sublime words) certainty. moral dead a to burnt, him get and lived, ever that magician glorious most the him make and Hoffman, Balthasar for building been I've reputation the perfect and out round will and Yes,"—

My brain was spinning, it was audibly whizzing, I rose reeling, and was falling lifeless to the floor, when 44 caught me. His touch restored me, and he said—

"I see it is too much for you, you cannot endure it, you would go mad. Therefore I relieve you of your share in this grand event. You shall look on and enjoy, taking no personal part in the backward flight of time, nor in its return, until it reaches the present hour again and resumes its normal march forward. Go and come as you please, amuse yourself as you choose."

Those were blessed words! I could not tell him how thankful I was.

A considerable blank followed—a silent one, for it represented the unrepeated conversation which he and I had had about the turning back of time and the sun.

Then another silent blank followed; it represented the interval occupied by my dispute with the cat as to whether the magician was come alive again or not.

I filled in these intervals not wearily nor drearily—oh, no indeed, just the reverse; for my gaze was glued to that American clock—

watching its hands creeping backward around its face, an uncanny spectacle!

Then I fell asleep, and when I woke again the clock had gone back seven hours, and it was mid-afternoon. Being privileged to go and come as I pleased, I threw off my flesh and went down to see the grand transformation-spectacle repeated backwards.

It was as impressive and as magnificent as ever. In the darkness some of the people lay prone, some were kneeling, some were wandering and tottering about with their hands over their eyes, Katrina was walking backwards on unsteady feet; she backed further and further, then knelt and bowed her head—then that white glory burst upon the darkness and 44 stood clothed as with the sun; and he bent and kissed the old head—and so on and so on, the scene repeated itself backwards, detail by detail, clear to the beginning; then the magician, the cat and I walked backward up the stairs and through the gathering eclipse to my room.

After that, as time drifted rearward, I skipped some things and took in others, according to my humor. I watched my Duplicate turn from nothing into a lovely soap-bubble statue with delicate rainbow-hues playing over it; watched its skeleton gather form and solidity; watched it put on flesh and clothes, and all that; but I skipped the interviews with the cat; I also skipped the interview with the master; and when the clock had gone back twenty-three hours and I was due to appear drunk in Marget's chamber, I took the pledge and stayed away.

Then, for amusement and to note effects, 44 and I—invisible—appeared in China, where it was noonday. The sun was just ready to turn downward on his new north-eastern track, and millions of yellow people were gazing at him, dazed and stupid, while other millions lay stretched upon the ground everywhere, exhausted with the terrors and confusions they had been through, and now blessedly unconscious. We loafed along behind the sun around the globe, tarrying in all the great cities on the route, and observing and admiring the effects. Everywhere weary people were re-chattering previous conversations backwards and not understanding each other, and oh, they did look so tuckered out and tired of it all! and always there were groups gazing miserably at the town-clocks; in every city funerals were being held again that had already been held once, and the hearses and the processions were marching solemnly backwards; where there was war, yesterday's battles were being refought, wrong-end-first; the previously killed were getting killed again, the previously wounded were getting hit again in the same place and complaining about it; there were blood-stirring and tremendous charges of masses of steel-clad knights across the field —backwards; and on the oceans the ships, with full-bellied sails were speeding backwards over the same water they had traversed the day before, and some of each crew were scared and praying, some were gazing in mute anguish at the crazy sun, and the rest were doing profanity beyond imagination.

At Rouen we saw Henry I gathering together his split skull and his other things.

Chapter 33

SURELY Forty-Four was the flightiest creature that ever was! Nothing interested him long at a time. He would contrive the most elaborate projects, and put his whole mind and heart into them, then he would suddenly drop them, in the midst of their fulfilment, and start something fresh. It was just so with his Assembly of the Dead. He summoned those forlorn wrecks from all the world and from all the epochs and ages, and then, when everything was ready for the exhibition, he wanted to flit back to Moses's time and see the Egyptians floundering around in the Dead Sea, and take me along with him. He said he had seen it twice, and it was one of the handsomest and most exciting incidents a body ever saw. It was all I could do to persuade him to wait a while.

To me the Procession was very good indeed, and most impressive. First, there was an awful darkness. All visible things gloomed down gradually, losing their outlines little by little, then disappeared utterly. The thickest and solidest and blackest darkness followed, and a silence which was so still it was as if the world was holding its breath. That deep stillness continued, and continued, minute after minute, and got to be so oppressive that presently I was holding *my* breath—that is, only half-breathing. Then a wave of cold air came drifting along, damp, searching, and smelling of the grave, and was shivery and dreadful. After about ten minutes I heard a faint clicking sound coming as from a great distance. It came slowly nearer and nearer, and a little louder and a little louder, and increasing steadily in mass and volume, till all the place was filled with a dry sharp clacking and was right abreast of us and passing by! Then a vague twilight suffused the place and through it and drowned in it we made out the spidery dim forms of thousands of skeletons marching! It made me catch my breath. It was that grewsome and grisly and horrible, you can't think.

Soon the light paled to a half dawn, and we could distinguish details fairly well. Forty-Four had enlarged the great hall of the castle, so as to get effects. It was a vast and lofty corridor, now, and stretched away for miles and miles, and the Procession drifted solemnly down it sorrowfully clacking, losing definiteness gradually, and finally fading out in the far distances, and melting from sight.

Forty-Four named no end of those poor skeletons, as they passed by, and he said the most of them had been distinguished, in their day and had cut a figure in the world. Some of the names were familiar to me, but the most of them were not. Which was natural, for they belonged to nations that perished from the earth ten, and twenty, and fifty, and a hundred, and three hundred, and six hundred thousand years ago, and so of course I had never heard of them.

By force of 44's magic each skeleton had a tab on him giving his name and date, and telling all about him, in brief. It was a good idea, and saved asking questions. Pharaoh was there, and David and Goliath and several other of the sacred characters; and Adam and Eve, and some of the Caesars, and Cleopatra, and Charlemagne, and Dagobert, and kings, and kings and kings till you couldn't count them—the most of them from away back thousands and thousands of centuries before Adam's time. Some of them fetched their crowns along, and had a rotten velvet rag or two dangling about their bones, a kind of pathetic spectacle.

And there were skeletons whom I had known, myself, and been at their funerals, only three or four years before—men and women, boys and girls; and they put out their poor bony hands and shook with me, and looked so sad. Some of the skeletons dragged the rotting ruins of their coffins after them by a string, and seemed pitifully anxious that that poor property shouldn't come to harm.

But to think how long the pathos of a thing can last, and still carry its touching effect, the same as if it was new and happened yesterday! There was a slim skeleton of a young woman, and it went by with its head bowed and its bony hands to its eyes, crying, apparently. Well, it was a young mother whose little child disappeared one day and was never heard of again, and so her heart was broken, and she cried her life away. It brought the tears to my eyes and made my heart ache to see that poor thing's sorrow. When I looked at her tab I saw it had happened five hundred thousand years ago! It seemed strange that it should still affect me, but I suppose such things never grow old, but remain always new.

King Arthur came along, by and by, with all his knights. That interested me, because we had just been printing his history, copying it from Caxton. They rode upon bony crates that had once been horses, and they looked very stately in their ancient armor, though it was rusty and lacked a piece here and there, and through those gaps you could see the bones inside. They talked together, skeletons as they were, and you could see their jawbones go up and down through the slits in their helmets. By grace of Forty-Four's magic I could understand them. They talked about Arthur's last battle, and seemed to think it happened yesterday, which shows that a thousand years in the grave is merely a night's sleep, to the dead, and counts for nothing.

It was the same with Noah and his sons and their wives. Evidently they had forgotten that they had ever left the Ark, and could not understand how they came to be wandering around on land.

They talked about the weather; they did not seem to be interested in anything else.

The skeletons of Adam's predecessors outnumbered the later representatives of our race by myriads, and they rode upon undreamt-of monsters of the most extraordinary bulk and aspect. They marched ten thousand abreast, our walls receding and melting away and disappearing, to give them room, and the earth was packed with them as far as the eye could reach. Among them was the Missing Link. That is what 44 called him. He was an undersized skeleton, and he was perched on the back of a long-tailed and long-necked creature ninety feet long and thirty-three feet high; a creature that had been dead eight million years, 44 said.

For hours and hours the dead passed by in continental masses, and the bone-clacking was so deafening you could hardly hear yourself think. Then, all of a sudden 44 waved his hand and we stood in an empty and soundless world.

Chapter 34

"AND YOU are going away, and will not come back any more."

"Yes," he said. "We have comraded long together, and it has been pleasant—pleasant for both; but I must go now, and we shall not see each other any more."

"In this life, 44, but in another? We shall meet in another, surely, 44?"

Then all tranquilly and soberly he made the strange answer—

"*There is no other.*"

A subtle influence blew upon my spirit from his, bringing with it a vague, dim, but blessed and hopeful feeling that the incredible words might be true—even *must* be true.

"Have you never suspected this, August?"

"No—how could I? But if it can only be true—"

"It is true."

A gush of thankfulness rose in my breast, but a doubt checked it before it could issue in words, and I said—

"But—but—we have *seen* that future life—seen it in its actuality, and so—"

"It was a vision—it had no existence."

I could hardly breathe for the great hope that was struggling in me—

"A vision?—a vi—"

"Life itself is only a vision, a dream."

It was electrical. By God I had had that very thought a thousand times in my musings!

"Nothing exists; all is a dream. God—man—the world,—the sun, the moon, the wilderness of stars: a dream, all a dream, they have no existence. *Nothing exists save empty space—and you!"*

"I!"

"And you are not you—you have no body, no blood, no bones, you are but a *thought.* I myself have no existence, I am but a dream —your dream, creature of your imagination. In a moment you will have realized this, then you will banish me from your visions and I shall dissolve into the nothingness out of which you made me . . . . .

"I am perishing already—I am failing, I am passing away. In a little while you will be alone in shoreless space, to wander its limitless solitudes without friend or comrade forever—for you will remain a *Thought,* the only existent Thought, and by your nature inextinguishable, indestructible. But I your poor servant have revealed you to yourself and set you free. Dream other dreams, and better! . . . .

"Strange! that you should not have suspected, years ago, centuries, ages, æons ago! for you have existed, companionless, through all the eternities. Strange, indeed, that you should not have suspected that your universe and its contents were only dreams, visions, fictions! Strange, because they are so frankly and hysterically insane—like all dreams: a God who could make good children as easily as bad, yet preferred to make bad ones; who could have made every one of them happy, yet never made a single happy one; who made them prize their bitter life, yet stingily cut it short; who gave his angels eternal happiness unearned, yet required his other children to earn it; who gave his angels painless lives, yet cursed his other children with biting miseries and maladies of mind and body; who mouths justice, and invented hell—mouths mercy, and invented hell—mouths Golden Rules, and foregiveness multiplied by seventy times seven, and invented hell; who mouths morals to other people, and has none himself; who frowns upon crimes, yet commits them all; who created man without invitation, then tries to shuffle the responsibility for man's acts upon man, instead of honorably placing it where it belongs, upon himself; and finally, with altogether divine obtuseness, invites this poor abused slave to worship him! . . . .

"You perceive, *now*, that these things are all impossible, except in a dream. You perceive that they are pure and puerile insanities, the silly creations of an imagination that is not conscious of its freaks—in a word, that they are a dream, and you the maker of it. The dream-marks are all present—you should have recognized them earlier . . . . .

"It is true, that which I have revealed to you: there is no God, no universe, no human race, no earthly life, no heaven, no hell. It is all a Dream, a grotesque and foolish dream. Nothing exists but You. And You are but a *Thought*—a vagrant Thought, a useless Thought, a homeless Thought, wandering forlorn among the empty eternities!"

He vanished, and left me appalled; for I knew, and realized, that all he had said was true.

THE END

APPENDIXES

APPENDIX A

Marginal Notes

THIS LIST of marginalia includes those of Albert Bigelow Paine and F. A. Duneka as well as Mark Twain, but nothing added later than that has been included. The notes have been printed as written; the color of ink is specified only when it indicates that the note was written later than the manuscript page. Superscript letters and numbers have been lowered to the line. The notes have been keyed into the text approximately where they appear, and the location of the note on the manuscript page has been indicated.

The Chronicle of Young Satan
MANUSCRIPT

35.1	*'used' Probably Paine's or Clemens's note.*
36.23	'Mysterious Stranger' 'Harpers have the 3 opening pages' *Paine's notes.*
41.18	'fireside ghosts' *written and canceled in ink in top right corner.*
43.7	'at the end of the quarter' *in faint black ink at bottom.*
43.8	'1st form of Mys. Stranger abandoned for another form.' *Paine's note.*

70.21   'cat burnt, but the div.[idend] continues' *in ink in top
               left corner*. 'more com.[ment] on cat' *written and can-
               celed in ink in top right corner*.

71.7   'talks with animals' *in ink in top right corner*.

71.27   'Memory.' *in ink in top left corner*. 'Traum—dream' *in
               ink in top right corner*.

74.12   'He plans rocket.' *in ink in top right corner*.

81.12   'Satan often draws upon *future* history.' *in ink in top left
               corner*. 'Visit an asteroid, and a vast world outside our
               system.' *in ink in top right corner*.

89.12   'The com.[mission] will elect to tackle the cat and ignore
               the priest for a while.' *in ink in top right corner*.

162.11   'She snubs S[atan]?' *written and canceled in faint black
               ink in top left corner*. 'Tell Peter the news' *written and
               canceled in faint black ink in top right corner*.

TYPESCRIPT

43.8   'Duplicate of ms in safe' *Paine's note*.

51.25–   'Boys privately rescue them—2 or 3—and keep track of
52.11   them for years,—their lifetime is a 12th of ours—they
               raise families, have funerals, etc, they are invisible to all
               but the boys—they have tragedies and conflagrations and
               love passages and murders' *written and canceled in pencil
               in right margin*.

51.36   'Scene of terror—mother and child imploring—they and
               others come and look pleadingly up at the vast giants,
               and beg.' *written and canceled in pencil following* 'if we
               needed them.'

51.37–   'Now—50 years later?—they are a very numerous, and
52.11   are two nations, divided by a ridge, and have wars of suc-
               cession, and famous heroes, and crazy religions, and two
               languages.' *written and canceled in pencil in left margin*.

52.14   'Except a group found later' *written in pencil following*
               'five hundred poor creatures escaping.'

53.4   'He will let them see the little people, and understand them—tells them so—and maybe understand the speech of animals.' *written and canceled in pencil following* 'such as people have—Philip Traum.'

Schoolhouse Hill
MANUSCRIPT

175.title   'Schoolhouse Hill' [See "Textual Notes"]

175.title   ' "Mysterious Stranger" in Hannibal' 'Probably 1899—' *Paine's note.*

189.16   'Annie Fleming, niece' *written and canceled in pencil at top.*

189.27   'Disap' *written and canceled in pencil.*

191.4   'English—lovely, but native tongue is Cant—look at its reviews and papers.' *in pencil at top.*

193.2   'baggage' *written in ink at top and canceled in pencil. A reminder to mention Forty-four's lack of baggage.*

196.28   'Interlineations.' *in ink at top.*

200.3   'Prohibition Millerite All new ideas were wonderful but the same size—ill balanced.' *in pencil.* 'O had mental perception but no mental proportion' *in top right corner in pencil. O is surely Orion Clemens, who had died on 11 December 1897.*

207.17   'H. abolitionist not taken seriously or been lynched.' *in ink at top.*

214.7   'not *reared* in hell.' *in ink at top.*

218.16   'blankets fire name' *in ink at top.*

219.1   'Mys Stranger in Hannibal About 1899' *Paine's note.*

220.35   'Short-handing the boy's tale Crazy's history and misfortunes and his family and lost boy—Ratcliff.' *This note in pencil follows the broken-off end of MT's MS.*

No. 44, The Mysterious Stranger
MANUSCRIPT

221.1   '2nd form of Mysterious Stranger not to be used in any way *A. B. P.' Paine's note, written on a separate MS page.*

221.9   '1490.' *written and canceled in ink in top right corner.* 'The Mysterious Stranger. Put in (Description of the region from the "Young Satan.")' *written and canceled in ink at the top of the MS page.*

233.34   'called Polecat' *in ink at top center.*

234.6   'Insert others' *in ink in lower left corner.*

234.7   'knights' *in ink at top.*

254.27   'dirk, chevron' *in ink at top.*

255.5   '? 17 from bot of 14' *written and canceled in ink in lower left corner.*

259.25   'bottle-a'd ratting' *in ink at top.*

266.6   'I change my "intention" and pray for Doangiv to come.' *in pencil at top left.* 'wineglass.' *in ink at top right corner.*

271.1   'found 3 grosn' *written and canceled in dark blue ink in top left corner.*

312.9   'I think I tore up all the MS from page 174 (type) to this 259. SLC' *in blue-black ink at top left. In Paine's hand,* 'Mys stranger' *and* 'Probably 1901–3'.

313.12   'Xifixion' *written and canceled in blue-black ink at top left.*

330.4   'pone, coffee—pipe' *written and canceled in ink at top right.*

350.33   'chess.' *in ink in top left corner.*

353.19   'June 20/05 Burned the rest (30,000 words) of this book this morning. Too diffusive.' *in blue-black ink in lower left corner.*

400.17   'Mysterious Stranger' *in ink in top left corner.* 'His Dream-self to appear, a century later.' *in ink in top right corner.*

403.16   'those poor girls' *in ink in bottom right corner.*

403.17   '(Conclusion of the book.)' *in ink at top left.*

TYPESCRIPT

221.1   'One form of Mysterious Stranger. First pages missing *Should be destroyed*' *Paine's note.*

APPENDIX B

Working Notes and Related Matter

BECAUSE Mark Twain's notes bear directly on the texts and branch out in so many imaginative paths indirectly, the notes are translated into type as faithfully as possible.

They have been grouped on the basis of physical characteristics, comparisons with the manuscript, the matter treated within each set, internal cohesion, and topical references. When Mark Twain numbered his pages, his numbers have been printed. In addition, I have given a number to each manuscript leaf within a sequence.

No emendations have been made in Mark Twain's holograph notes. His ampersand has been retained, except in the case of the notebook entry. Single underlinings are presented as italics, double underlinings are rendered in small capital letters. Cancellations are included and marked by angle brackets, thus ⟨ ⟩; substitutions by vertical arrows, thus ↑↓, though context usually makes substitutions clear without the arrows; added words or phrases, by carets, thus ∧ ∧; additions at some later date in pencil or ink different from the original by boldface, thus **Marie;** and editorial explanation by square brackets, thus [ ]. Mark Twain's alternate readings are separated by slashes, thus Fischer/Stein. Doubtful readings are in square brackets, preceded by question marks.

St. Petersburg Fragment

Group A

These notes, on two sheets of Hotel Metropole stationery in black ink, were probably written just after Mark Twain's arrival in Vienna in 1897.[1] The notes on p. A-2 eventually found expression in "Three Thousand Years Among the Microbes" (*WWD*, pp. 433–553).

A-1

1

Human Race,
———

Destroy Moral Sense; or
" the Race?

———

Consultation with Crazy Fields & Oliver & D^r· Terry the great surgeon who hung his daughter in the cave. They make an ⟨⟨with Injun Joe,⟩ ∧ average intellectual forms ∧ of human insanity
Harem, 800 women
S. I^s [Sandwich Islands] copulation common
X^n one wife

∧ Brings Terry & Fields in out of the storm

———

But *before* that, explains who he is.
Takes 1000 books out of pocket; microscope to examine microbes which he gets out of his pocket.
Makes instant trips to China, heaven &c ∧

———

C. F. Always comparing himself with God.
People discussed: An Atheist now Catholic Why? Catholic now Atheist. Why?

———
[1] *MTSatan*, pp. 34–36.

Crazy Fields lost wife, then child; because wife nursed sm. pox patient who had no friend;

Tom Nash's ∧ mother ∧ took in a deserted child; it gave scarlet-fever death to 3 of her children & deaf[ness] to 2.

But don't look at merely the unhappy—consider the *happy*. Answer: Happiness is merely a preparation (a trap); their turn is coming; absolutely *none* escape.

The King? The young queen with her P Albert? Her turn will come. None escape.

A-2

CRAZY

VANITY

No support like it. Flattery—to think you are doing or suffering under the immediate notice of God & as a compliment to him & a glory—well, it will enable a man to be comfortable with the pains & rottennesses of 50 vile diseases upon him.

———

The first thing to do is to feed this vanity—show, by microbes he is God's especial pet

———

He is to find the diseases & tortures & microbes, & old Ferg will explain their function in rushing the glory of God

The Chronicle of Young Satan

Group A

This first group is probably the earliest set of working notes for "The Chronicle of Young Satan." It was written in pencil on a sheet of heavy buff paper identical to the original pp. 1–96 of the manuscript, probably in November 1897 before the composition of the first chapter. Later notes were added in ink after the first chapter was written, but before the second was begun.[1] These ink additions have been rendered in boldface type. A-2, on the verso, includes notes and a canceled paragraph from Mary Baker Eddy's *Science and Health*.

A-1

1

∧ Plenty Jews ∧

Marie

⟨Father⟩ Lueger, a drinking, spiteful, prying, over-godly, malicious priest. supplanter of Kitchelt [last 3 words circled in pencil]

Father Kitchelt ⟨Black⟩.

Margarethe (niece)

Nikolaus ∧ (Nick) ∧ Baumann	⟨Master Miller's⟩
⟨(Hank)⟩ **Tom Sawyer**	son of judge.
Seppi Wohlmeyer (Pole) **good**	the innkeeper's
but simple	
Thereodor Fischer ⟨Tom⟩ **Huck**	—sexton, organist, leader of
(I. **Son of Hans**	the village band, commune
Wilhelm Meidling ⟨Tom An-	tax collector & some other
drews⟩	things

---

[1] *MTSatan,* pp. 16–24.

The Bishop   **Philip Traum**

Procession to quiet Satan (table-
    rapping)
Bridge—(Satan built it)
    B. Langenau's tale of the Vir-
        gin—
Wayside shrines—crown &
    nails & paint
Old women & dogs harnessed
—& carrying bricks & mortar

The great noble ∧ Prince ∧—owner of the estate.
    His hunting—stags destroy crops.
    The forester (game-keeper)

Village ⟨Hasenfeld.⟩ Eseldorf.

Castle park wide

Other sid[e] river in a rich plain,
monkery in a grove.

Castle on heights—precipice
—long winding road to it—
it over looks river—boats &
rafts. Inn with garden in front
on bank.

New Jerusalem		Ghetto
Stephan	Lehrer	Jew
Edmund	Herold	J. Goldschmid⟨t⟩
	Bochner	I. Nussbaum
		Blumenduft

A-2

Ch. V.

We'll sing the wine-cup & the lass

⟨Finite belief can never do justice to ⟨t⟩Truth in any direction.
It limits all things & would compress Mind, which is infinite, beneath a skull-bone. Such belief can neither apprehend nor worship

human

the Infinite, & seeks to divide the one Spirit into many, to accommodate its finite sense of the divisibility of soul & substance.)

O witching are her pansy eyes   lashes
& silken are her   members
And chaste/coy/pure as is the mountain goat
And cold as   [last 4 lines written with page reversed]

Group B

This group of notes is composed of five half-sheets of lightweight, cream-colored stock identical to MS pp. 86–376 and 387–392. B-1, written in ink, is a plan for continuing the story, and was apparently written before Mark Twain reserved ten pages from his first section of the story and began the second section of manuscript in May 1899.[1] The other four pages are written in pencil. The note "Tell me my fortune for one day ahead—& Sep's for life. Did it." and the notes about Satan's glimpses into the past and future anticipate the episodes in the manuscript written after June 1900. Thus, the notes were probably written after Mark Twain laid the manuscript aside in October 1899, but before he resumed work in June 1900.

B-1

NOTES.

∧ Public inquire, Who *is* he?
Police want his details in their
book. Refuses. Arrested. ∧

S. will come "every day."
Jealousy of Wil[h]
S. after 3 days furnishes details of the 4 games, with notes to Wil, whose envy & jeal are further inflamed.

S. gets generally acquainted—also with Peter.

[1] *MTSatan*, p. 44.

W. tattles about the extraordinary music, to array pub. opinion against S. Talks this to draw fury away from Marget & settle it upon S.

S. associates freely with the worst & the best—they are all trivialities to him.

Says animals are far below the angels, but far above men.

_____

The days go on. People want to deed the village to the Virgin— but Prince Königsberg objects, being owner.

_____

Young princess Adelheid falls in l[ove] with S. He is indifferent, of course.

_____

Trial of Peter—he not present. Is begged by the boys to go & confer an immense happiness upon him to pay for his captivity & make him forget it. "I will—what shall it be?" "You choose it." He confers a happy insanity—imaginary kingship. Will not restore him—*knows* a happy insanity is best for all men. (Uses the figure of temporary kingship in a play as difference bet. man & angel, whose glory is permanent.

B-2

God has never kept the Sabbath. Doesn't even bank his fires Sat night, like the furnaces. [Written on separate MS page used by ABP to identify the working notes, and with the notation in his hand "Notes Mys. Stranger."]

B-3

1

On a trip to the Garden of Eden the eating of the apple is reproduced, & they notice that it is bitter, for Adam makes a wry face. He eats but half & throws it away. F. picks it up, furtively, & long afterward gets Satan drunk & he eats it—the idea being to give him the Moral Sense & Christianise him.

When sober he recognizes what has happened, & bitterly reproaches them. His great powers are gone, disease invades him, he has no way to earn his living; he begs it; will not accept help from them; becomes swiftly old & feeble; people no longer afraid of him; he is persecuted, but remains a heretic; so they torture him, convict him, damn him & burn him.

B-4

2

∧ *Adam's Fall.* ∧

Did the higher animals eat of the apple? No. But Adam's eating it brought suffering & death to them? Yes. Where is the justice in that?

———

Tell me my fortune for one day ahead—& Sep's for life. Did it.

———

Stoning the Jews. (passing remark)

———

Disease-germs. (Plague)

———

The *make* is a large part, & cannot be changed—from rabbit to tiger.

———

Seawonhake & Stella. Dana & chambermaid. The one's manliness was theory unsolidified by experience—& barren.

B-5

1

∧ *Nobility.* ∧

Let us make a trip into the future & see what they've got.

———

Civ. has advanced in many ways & you must grant that the nobility have assisted by notice & encouragement? *No.* They have never helped in *any* progress. Nor the priest. (religion). The church the aristocracy & the King stand for obstruction—they chock the wheels whenever they can. Progress moves in spite of them—then you lickspittle slaves get down on your knees & give *them* the praise—just as you do God for mercies never received.

Aristocracies are bred from villainies & whores.

Group C

These notes, in pencil, are on five consecutively numbered half-sheets of lightweight ochre stock, $7^{15}/_{16}$" by $4^{15}/_{16}$", with vertical chain-lines $1\frac{1}{8}$" apart. Mark Twain was reviewing pp. 1–85 of the manuscript; the numbers in the notes refer to manuscript pages. He may have written these notes just before his resumption of work in the summer of 1900.[1] Additions in ink have been rendered in boldface type.

C-1

1
Date, 1702.

———

 $\wedge$ The Host passes—Satan does not uncover. Is tried & imprisoned —in vain $\wedge$ [half-circled in pencil]

Eseldorf, the village.

Gretel Marx, the dairyman's widow.

Prince Königsberg.

 Young princess Adelheid his daugh, ⟨22⟩ **18.**
 "   **prince Adelbert, 17 ignorant & insolent.**

The Hussite Woman Adler

Father Adolf, the villain; belonged to the village Council & lorded it there, he is called "Town Bull" & "Hell's Delight" privately. Drunken & witty blackguard. Sings in a thundering bass "We'll sing the wine-cup & the lass." Swears "by God" & generally. profane words.

 $\wedge$ *No fear of the Devil—celebrated for it* $\wedge$

---
[1] *MTSatan*, p. 47.

Church of Our Lady of the Dumb Creatures

They try to burn the Hussite Adler as a witch; Satan enters into her & the fires do him no harm. [circled in pencil]

Boy—Gottfried Narr [added diagonally across the beginning of the entry above]

The village is solemnly deeded to the Virgin & she collects the taxes to a farthing. [circled in pencil]

Make an incident of Host & Suicide (11) Satan enters into the suicide & walks away

C-2

2

with the stake through him. [circled in pencil]

Make incident of plague-procession [half-circled in pencil] (12.)

The Interdict [circled in pencil]

The Dev. is always assuaged Dec. 9 (12)

14. One pilgrim to Rome got 14,000 years' for climbing steps of St. John Lateran on his knees, & came back & sold out in detail, 500 years at a time, & got rich.

Father Peter, village priest.

Marget, his niece—18.

Bishop Aloysius. (old fool)

21. Peter out 2 yrs—Adolf has his flock

Wilhelm Meidling, lawyer & M's sweetheart

22. *Solomon Isaacs* the creditor

THE 3 BOYS:

Hansel, tinker		**Fuchs, brewer**
	Rupert	**Marie** [1]

23. Nikolaus Baumann, **logy,** son of judge

Seppi Wohlmeyer **bright** son of "Golden Stag"

& I, Theordor Fischer, son of organist

&c &c &c.

---

[1] It is not clear whether Mark Twain meant "Rupert" and "Marie" which are interlined above "Baumann" and "son of judge" to be separate entries or alternative readings.

C-3

3

24. *Felix Brandt,* oldest serving man in ⟨*Castle Konradsburg.*⟩
== Castle Allerheiligenburg.
          29 Satan appears. [circled in pencil]
     44. In hell.
The boys go there with him, & find lost friends, who beg for
help. [circled in pencil]
          45 [circled in pencil]
          Satan on Human Race
          _____

          46. Make him build a city & drown it with
a bucket of water.

And railways	Creating the future [circled in
steamships	pencil]
bikes	
Modern cannon & guns	
smokeless powder	
bombs	

C-4

4

The village toughs pick a row with Satan, & make him fight. [half-
circled in pencil]
     S. as horse, dog, cat, &c.
          EMPEROR (or Gd. Duke?)
sends for him—has heard of him—is curious to see him. S. contemptuous—won't go. "Let him come here if he wants to see me."
"Arrest him, guard!" They fail. Garrison sent for. *It* fails. Report to
Vienna. Emperor comes—not in good humor—long journey. Satan
talks plainly to him—laughs at his office & his Church & priests.
          _____

          49. S's music.
          _____

C-5

5

50. PHILIP TRAUM (Satan's public name.

Satan shall proclaim & fully set forth the doctrine of SELFISHNESS whether it be printable or not.

And the *rest of it*. Moral Sense &c

64

1100 ducats odd. ∧ (1107) ∧ He will use 200 & put the rest at interest.

---

72. Father Peter wears spec⟨k⟩s.
73. Marie Lueger, Marget's ∧influential∧ pupil
    Marget falls in love with S. He plays spinet & speaks of the "Music of the spheres"
  76. Adolf's "ancient priory up the valley."
  80. Papas & the rest think the boys are lying about the 1107 ducats.
  83. Old Ursula, Peter's cook &c

Group D

These notes, on two half-sheets of Joynson Superfine paper, numbered consecutively, contain a reworking of Father Peter's trial and what seems to be an anticipation of the love-rivalry episode. They were probably written some time after Mark Twain's resumption of work in May 1899 but before June 1900. On the verso are canceled pp. 42–43 of an unidentified manuscript about publishing.

D-1

1

∧Tell how he displaced Father Peter∧

Plan.

Father Adolf (Lueger) summons the Devil to explain about that money. _∧*Grand time.* (night)_∧

Devil, frightened, says he stole it from 5 sacks one within the other (sacks produced⟨⟩) in court) which he kept in a secret hole in his sleeping room (secret hole produced)—900 of it was given him 2 years before when he went on pil to Rome by a traveler whom he protected from robbers & raised from the dead temporarily with St. John's tooth (his own) Adolf was only waiting till he could ⟨[? by]⟩ increase the sum to 1⟨3⟩500, when he was going to start a home for foundlings ("He's had a *factory*, this long time." "Right —charity begins at home" "He'll supply the foundlings, too") _∧Two strong parties—one for, the other agst Adolf._∧

Satan whispers "examine the date"—for the money was siezed the ⟨first⟩ 2^d day & brought into Court. Tableau—none of it is 2 yrs old. _∧Crowd goes over to Peter._∧ Judge is afraid of the Church, & yields when Adolf wants to inquire further of the Devil.

Does so. Devil confesses he changed date. Wonderful! Crowd goes back to Adolf.

D-2

2

Satan maddens Adolf—makes fun of him always. Adolf privately warms up Meidling's jealousy agst Satan

Meidling is the wonder of the region—the Admirable Crichton. Does all the old sleight of hand tricks & plays spinet—at exhibition Satan defeats him. Is a boxer & swordsman—Satan defeats him. Is the strong man—defeated again—finally, seeing Marg is in love with Satan, in a fury stabs him. S ⟨says, "It seems to me⟩ [1] laughs at him.

Adolf has Satan arrested & condemned to be burnt. They jail him; he comes out; they burn him, he doesn't mind it; they excommunicate him, they banish him he comes back. He is the terror of the place. Marg confesses her love—he despises it—says all human impulses are selfish & despicable. He comprehends them intellectually—no one can *realize* them but by eating the apple.

---

[1] " 'It seems to me" begins a new paragraph in the manuscript.

Schoolhouse Hill

Notebook Entry, November 1898

This sketch for the adventures of "little Satan, jr" with Huck and Tom, in St. Petersburg and in hell, immediately precedes in time the composition of "Schoolhouse Hill," but bears a relationship to the "Schoolhouse Hill" fragment in only a few particulars. It was written shortly after 8 November 1898 in Notebook 32.

Story of little Satan, jr, who came to ⟨Petersburg (Hannibal)⟩ went to school, was popular and greatly liked by ⟨Huck and Tom⟩ who knew his secret. The others were jealous, and the girls didn't like him because he smelt of brimstone. ∧*This* is the Admirable Crichton∧ He was always doing miracles—his pals knew they were miracles, the⟨y⟩ others thought them mysteries. He is a good little devil; ∧but swears, and breaks the Sabbath.∧ By and by he is converted, and becomes a Methodist. and quits miracling. In class meeting he confesses who he is—is not believed; his new co-religionists turn against him as a ribald humbug. He believes it is his duty as a Christian to forgive the people who despitefully use him; thinks it also his Xⁿ duty to hope for his father's pardon by God, and to pray for his papa—tries it; the church can't stand it. As he does no more miracles, even his pals⟨s⟩ fall away and disbelieve in him. When his fortunes and his miseries are at the worst, his papa arrives in state in a glory of hellfire and attended by a multitude of old-fashioned and showy fiends—and *then* everybody is at the boy-devil's feet at once and want to curry favor. He is grateful to hug his child to his breast once more, chides him gently for leaving hell without leave—but it was well enough to go out and try his hand at business and be competent for his future sovereignty—finds he has been rejected by Mary Lacy, who took him for crazy and who is now horribly sorry she didn't jump at the chance, since she finds that the Holy Family of Hell are not disturbed by the fire, but only their guests. Satan is glad his boy didn't marry beneath him—he is arranging with the shade of Pope Alexander VI to marry him to a descendant—and pending this he has allowed Aleck out on bail; and he is in his present traveling-suit with a vast position Lord Great Master of the Luggage—and he has another pope along who carries a ∧cold∧ stove-lid for Satan to sit on to keep from scorching the furniture. Satan gets drunk at a ⟨wedding⟩ banquet and promises to forever keep Cold Storage for any that come from that hellish and hospitable town—Jews included—he is no respecter of sects, if X^{ns} are—(no applause) fact is he wouldn't give a damn for the average $X^{n's}$ magnanimities (no applause)

When little Satan first came he was dreadfully profane, but good-natured, and would goodnaturedly thrash raftsmen, bullies, etc without letting it be seen that it was by miracle—and at jugglery shows he would go on the stage and not only make an omelet in a hat, but go on and make ice cream in it out of pounded glass, and mince-pies out of sand and sawdust, and so on. But after conversion he bore brutal mistreatment without resentment, he tried to win the raftsmen to Christ, he talked goody-goody sappy Sunday school talk to them and was in all ways an unattractive person and suitable to a heaven of the ⟨Petersburg⟩ average breed of X^{ns}.

In the early days he takes Tom and Huck down to stay over Sunday in hell—gatekeeper doesn't recognise him in disguise and asks for tickets—then is going to turn them out (it is raining) when LS privately tells who he is and is obsequiously received.

They see papa Satan on his throne under the vast crimson dome flaming with reflections from the ∧pleasure∧ Lake and they see the limitless red halls, palatial, full of sufferers swimming ashore but can't climb out—marble border too slippery. They help one or two out but the police interfere. They wipe the tears of the unbaptised babies roasting on the red hot floors—one is Tom's little niece that he so grieved to lose—still, as she deserves this punishment he is able to bear it (like Baxter looking over the balusters of heaven.)

Group A

These notes, in pencil, on a single sheet of mourning stationery, were probably written after Mark Twain laid aside the "Chronicle" manuscript in October 1898, but before he began composition of "Schoolhouse Hill" in November.

A-1

Loafer slips hand in his pocket to steal money—is grabbed by a harmless snake.

————

Animals are always infesting him.
He enters wounded tiger's cage & heals & pacifies it.
Being urged (it is a trick) he takes bare-back rider's place, & beats him & the jugglers out of sight

A-2

	∧ Proposes to join Pres. ch. Can't. Starts cch of Society for Eradication of the Moral Sense.
Faith Cure	————————————
Utterback	He preaches.
Incantations (witch)	————————————
Holy relics	But takes up no collection.
Virgin of this & that (cure)	————————————
Laying on of hands	This fills his pews.∧
Electric hands (Livy)	

Allopathy ⎫
Homeo ⎬ Enemies call frauds
Water-Cure ⎭

Pocket-potato for rheumatism

10,000 religions—& you *not mad*
You—intellectual!
If you had the sanity of the rats & other animals you would need no king
It is only madmen who need masters & looking after.

Group B

These notes, on an uncut sheet of Joynson Superfine paper, in black ink, probably preceded the composition of "Schoolhouse Hill."

B-1

1

∧Jim Colby (telegraph)∧

Becky Thatcher (Laura Hawkins)

Lucy Wright (L) Capt. Wright (Bowen)

Nancy Pratt (Mary Lacy)   ∧Mrs. Pratt

Cathy Pratt (Mary Miller   Squire Pratt, postmaster∧

Sally Fitch—(Bowen Sally)

⎰Margaret Stover (Ousley) ∧Merchant∧

⎱Olive Stover—(hunchback)

Fanny Brewster (*Helen Kercheval*) ∧tailor∧ [above 'Helen']

Cassy Gray (Artemissa Briggs).

Louisa Robbins (Mary Nash, *bad*.

Jenny Mason (Brady)

∧Sadie Hotchkiss (Hellfire) 15∧

⎰Hank Fitch (Will Bowen

⎱Sam   "   (Sam   "

Frank Robbins (Tom Nash, deaf & d.

Crazy Fields

George Pratt (Bill Pitts)   ⎱ Sid Sawyer

Flip Coonrod ∧fool—½ idiot∧ (Ben Coontz)⎰

⎰(Buck Johnson) ∧Charley Flanders∧ (Charley

⎪   Buchanan)

⎪Little Bob Turner—   "

⎱Bib   "   "   "

(Harry Slater (John Garth))

B-2

2

Jack Stillson (John Garth)
Henry Bascom (Beebe) ∧the bully∧ new rich man & slave trader
∧Jake his nigger∧
Ed. Sanders (Stevens) watch-maker
Kaspar Helder (poor little German cigar ∧(Garth's d—dest.∧
David Gray (John Briggs).
Gill Ferguson (Dawson, pop-eyed)
⟨H⟩ Sammy Wheeler (the timid)

Aunt Polly
Miss Pomeroy (Newcomb)
  ⟨Torrey⟩ Foster (Torrey)
Widow Dawson (Aunt Betsy Smith)
  "   Guthrie (Mrs. Holliday)
      ∧Mrs. Wheelright (Dutchka)∧
Dʳ· Wheelright (Dʳ· Peake)
Judge Taylor ⟨(pa)⟩ (Draper) magistrate
Deacon Hotchkiss & wife (Orion & Pamela)
                              interested in quack ways of curing
                              change religions

Group C

As were most of the working notes for "Schoolhouse Hill," this sheet
was written on the same paper and in the same ink as the manuscript. It
was interleaved between MS pp. 18 and 19 at 181.9–10 in the text, and
evidently was written as those pages were composed.

C-1

In school he must do all those books—⟨200⟩ 30—in average of ⟨3⟩ 5 minutes each—300 p. each—1 p. per second. Does the 30 books in 2½ hours.

Group D

This group consists of sixteen half-sheets of Joynson Superfine paper, in faint black ink, with later additions and corrections in pencil which have been rendered in boldface type. There is a break in the notes between D-5 and D-6. Forty-four appears in the notes as "404" or "94" through D-5, which is on the verso of a draft-letter to Henry Rogers dated 17 November 1898. D-1 through D-5 were probably written before the composition of "Schoolhouse Hill" and D-6 through D-16 after the first chapters were composed.

D-1

1

He is courteous to whores & niggers.
⟨Has been a week ↑a month↓ ↑2 days↓ in Paris & knows French,
∧ Spanish Italian German Latin & Greek. &c ∧⟩
Learns English in 2 days.
He is 15. Pretty mature, though.
Smiles "our property" when he sees Injun Joe & Jimmy Finn.
Cheery & good-natured, with an immortal's contempt for evanescent mortals, & can no more be angry with such, or insulted by them than by the tumble-bug to which he compares them.
Wonders at their interest in life—not worth the trouble; & at their childish ambitions to be circus clowns or kings or constables or Congressmen.

And they have to work so hard with clumsy hands & minds & their almost non-existent memories, to acquire & keep knowledge or an accomplishment of any kind—whereas

D-2

2

                                    The cat & dog & mice **X**
he masters the principles of an art or a science in a few hours, then in a few more he is perfect in it—piano, flute, skating, shooting, ∧ swimming, diving, ∧ astronomy, mathematics, drawing, painting, boxing, the bow (gauging the wind & distance by feet & inches).

Reads a book once & can never forget a detail of it, nor on what page & ⟨p⟩ line any detail is.

Recites in school. Takes all prizes.

X Always doing miracles—sometimes unconsciously. Does Indian jugglery—makes flowers & fruits spring up; makes clay birds & animals & gives them life.

X Gives life to a child's dough chickens & cats.

People who try to strike him (schoolmarm) & roughs—can't. Bricks, sticks & bullets don't ⟨har⟩ get to him.

D-3

3

                                    He is made of air **X**
X Walks through fire. Saves child—building falls in, he walks out. Spins top.

Smells of brimstone at first.

X food.

Appears & vanishes ∧ through bolted doors, ∧ like nothing.

On Lovers' Leap has a witches Sabbath & Tom & Huck see myriad devils &c

When he comes he knows nothing about men—has seen them in hell only. Never been from home before. Has run away this time.

By & by falls in love with Annie Fleming the Pres. pastor's ⟨girl⟩ child.

Can't understand prayer; "if you want a thing, *have* it."

He doesn't feel fire or pain, & can't comprehend how papa's prisoners or any one else can. Thinks it is all imagination.

Says men are moved by one impulse—selfishness—tries to prove it. This talk is with Rev. Fleming.

X Finds papa in books & Bible

D-4

4

He is Admirable Crichton—by & by all but Tom & Huck jealous & hostile. Conspire against him—he doesn't care.

Finally gets religion & stops doing miracles—allows himself to be struck, abused & insulted—turns the other cheek.

Prays for papa. All has gone well till then. He is turned out of the church for this.

X Is always transporting Tom & H to the ends of the earth in a jiffy—to fetch things needed to get them out of difficulties.

Animals are ⟨afraid⟩ **fond** of him ⟨& slink away when he comes.⟩ **They all follow him. He can talk with them.** **X**

No one knows where he eats & sleeps but H & T—it is in Paris. Papa has his chief agency there. **X**

D-5

5

∧ Slaughterhouse Point ∧

⟨Arrives at school. Calls himself 404—gives no other name. ∧ Dresses well. ∧⟩ ⟨Pocket full of money⟩

X Always has a half dollar & $5 & no more—but it never fails; pays his way; wants no change. Says his people are rich.

X Turns himself into birds, animals, fleas, &c. ⟨∧ Sometimes electric blue flames play about him ∧⟩

Takes to T & H at once, & they to him. Want to cross river, go fishing; no boat; wants them to fly over; can't understand why they can't; very well, he will fetch a boat,—disappears suddenly & comes rowing back from over river.

Has no fear of crosses & holy names—says papa hasnt. Says his papa has *not* been cheated by monks &c—a lot of Middle-Age lies. ∧ *T & H go to hell on a visit.* ∧ **He doesn't know** [in margin]

Papa *doesn't* buy souls—can get plenty for nothing.

He is No. ⟨404⟩ 94 Prince of the vintage of a certain century— doesn't know which one—no curiosity—hasn't inquired.   **X**

Soon picks up all languages.

D-6

6

∧ Old Ship of Zion ∧	∧ *Cross's schoolhouse on* ⟨P. S.⟩ *S. H. Hill*
	A coasting hill. ∧

Cadets of Temperance
Sunday school procesh & picnic
Campbellit[e] revival
Campmeeting
I O O F
Masons (procesh)
Fire Company Big 6 Joe Buckner ⟨Raymond
Mesmerism
Nigger Minstrels
⎧ Spirit rappings   ⎫
⎨ Materializing   ⎬
⎩ Knot-tying (Davenport) ⎭

44 joins the Cadets
Often wishes he was in hell.
Tells his secret in confidence to everybody in town—with an awful threat—so each thinks he alone possesses it—& each tries to get an advantage out of it.
Bessie Strong tries to convert him.

A ⟨Barnum⟩ wants to exhibit him

He must perform for a ch charity. Would it be right to use such money.

D-7

7

Why has he come to the world?

———

635 years ago he saw for the third time a human being ∧ thinks, a man ∧; ages before he had [seen] two at wide intervals of time, but they were ∧ too ∧ far away to be clear: one a man, he thinks, the other he thinks a child, but only head & shoulders showing, & they tossing so, in their torment (he sees *now* it was torment, but that was only a *name* to him then, *he* has had no personal experience of pain or unhappiness, papa's crime has not descended) couldn't make much out; they soon disappeared behind the billows.

But he *talked* with the third, & determined to go to the world next day & examine this curious race—& he has done it. "But *this* isn't next day."

"Yes, by our count it is."

D-8

8

He has come out of mere curiosity to see what perishable men are like; but now that he has read all about them, he hopes to find a way to rid them of the Moral Sense; they can [not] get to heaven without that, still, it is worth while, because without it *this* life wᵈ be innocent & happy, &, brief as it is it would be better to be happy than unhappy. He must think out a way. [half-circled]

His associates have always been his devil-⟨relatives⟩ ∧ brothers & sisters. ∧—a vast multitude, not named, but numbered. *They* have no wives nor children—there is no third generation.

They probably do not know their papa's history, as they have

438   *Appendixes*

never mentioned it in his hearing. They are happy & busy. So is papa.
Has seen papa 2 or 3 times per million years but has not talked with
him.

D-9

9

Has never seen a human girl or woman until now. **Except in
heaven**
X Hellfire Hotchkiss./**Annie Fleming.** He feels a strange & charming interest in her. By the books he gathers that this is "love"—the
kind that sex arouses. There is no such thing among his brothers &
sisters. He studies it in the books. It seems very beautiful in the books.
Presently the passion for Hl grows—becomes absorbing—is mutual.
Papa uneasy—he is the only person who knows 44's secret. 44 sees
that the happiness of hell ∧—which is purely intellectual— ∧ IS TAME
COMPARED TO THIS LOVE. [emphasis added in pencil] He has found
more in this random visit to earth than he bargained for.   **X**
In time he is obliged to tell his secret to Hl—horror! ⟨S⟩ Heart-
breaking scene. He has done *wrong?* Denies it. The word has no
real meaning to him, but only a

D-10

10

pallid dictionary meaning. The THING does not *exist* to his feeling &
comprehension. How?
Thought is merely a ∧ clumsy & inadequate ∧ translation of feeling
into speech. If we are so made that we can't *feel* right & wrong then
the words are mere air to us—the same as they would be to a grass-
hopper.
"It is like pain (physical). You may talk about it all you like, I
get only the dictionary/intellectual meaning, not the shadow of a
real comprehension, for I have never felt a pain. You *must* feel a

thought or the word that represents it has no value—talk to a stone of pain? No use. ⟨I⟩ You have coarse combinations of sounds which you blandly call music. Then you speak of the

D-11

11

music of the spheres. Is it actual music to your ear? No. Then the term is empty to you. To me it is ravishing—forever changing, never silent. How do you know, when a comet has swum into your system? Merely by your eye or your telescope—but I, I hear a ⟨strange sweet minor tone⟩ brilliant far stream of sound come ⟨singing⟩ winding across/through the firmament of majestic sounds & I know the splendid stranger is there without looking. Don't you see that to you people the phrase music of the spheres is wholly meaningless, wholly unfeelable,—like right & wrong to me?

⟨He suffers when they play piano, guitar, violin, banjo, flute—& sing. But he makes divine music himself. It is because he is listening to the music of the spheres & reproducing it. It makes the audience drunk

D-12

12

with delight—this is because his translation of it is ∧ coarsened & ∧ brought down to the low grade of their *feeling*; just as you can dilute champagne with milk until a cat will like it, & prefer it to straight milk, & get drunk on it. What is ch[ampagne]? I don't know; but by reading I perceive that it is the finest & most delicate of wines.

⟨D⟩ Vast dimensions of hell—which is a pigmy to heaven. Only *our* Adam fell—hl is for his chn alone; in the other worlds the Adams & the rest live millions of years till burnt out like the moon, then are ferried over to heaven *with their animals*. ALL ⟨*our*⟩ our animals go to heaven for they have no Moral Sense; also the Presbyterians; the rest go to hell.

Thinks if he can remove man's *vanity,* his Moral Sense may follow; his vanity in attributing merits to himself; & his fool idea that Selfishness is shameful; *he* didn't make it, & ⟨can't be⟩ the wisest thing

D-13

13

he can do is to raise its ideals & make it help toward making this life pleasant for all.

He has examined Selfishness by the books & found out that men have a misconception of the *thing,* consequently they have clothed the word with ∧ the rags of ∧ that misconception ⟨& made it a⟩ whereas they should clothe it in its proper garb the white of innocence. For it *is* innocent & remains so—it can do no wrong.

He has been in heaven; so vast; meet plenty of people from other worlds; & at long, long intervals a Presbyterian. They are not popular—avoided. Considered "queer" & of a low grade because they have been defiled with the Moral Sense.

Heaven is not according to a history which he has been reading "Pilgrim's Progress;" it is not so small; & Presbyterians are not so plenty as that.

D-14

14

He has read up, now, & knows all about papa & about Christ's great sacrifice for the Presbyterians. Admires Christ deeply. Likes to go to Church & SS & listen—at first. But quits, because they say such things about papa & his place.

He didn't know, before, that people suffered in Hl, & he does[n]'t feel it or appreciate it *now.* Is it the way the spectacle of a misdone Euclid problem makes one feel? "Oh, the feelings are not at all the *same.*" "Well, to me the pains of hell must remain a mere phrase—no meaning."

Has read the ⟨300⟩ 600 books, now, 300,000 pages in 160 hours of actual reading—he doesn't sleep, but loses time talking & at meals. This education has occupied him 10 days.

He can ∧'t∧ feel ⟨sudden⟩ anger, ⟨like an animal, but can't hold it;⟩ can't conceive of the spirit of revenge; nor of avarice, nor of

D-15

15

hoarding, nor of envy, nor of "ambitions" of any kind; nor of *jealousies;* nor of adulations; nor of obsequiousnesses; ⟨to monarchs or any⟩ nor of slaveries; nor of humilities; ⟨admir⟩ thinks well of the cat because she is the only independent; says there is no such thing as an independent human being—all are slaves; no such thing as freedom of thought freedom of opinion, freedom in politics & religion

Man is a poor thing; but if he can get back his original innocence he will be fine & worthy. [sidelined]

44 can love, like dog & others; & trust, like dog & others.

Praises of *him* he *cannot* understand—they are due to his Maker solely, ⟨he⟩—*bring this forward at* ONCE.

D-16

16

The sense of humor—what is that—in the books? Is rejoiced to find ⟨he⟩ it is in him, though in a sort of atrophied condition; but knows that even the smallest seed can be developed.

When they laughed in school he didn't understand it—had never heard a laugh before. Thinks it wᵈ improve heaven & his part of hell to import it.

And he couldn't understand the teacher's praise of his modesty; why should he [be] vain of his gifts & take credit for them?—they came from his Maker.

Group E

These notes consist of four consecutively numbered half-sheets of Joynson Superfine paper in black ink. E-2 is on the verso of a canceled p. 67 of the "Schoolhouse Hill" manuscript. The notes must have been written after that page was discarded.

E-1

1
⟨Nephew⟩ Son of Satan.
————

This world was 2 M yrs ago.

Man has been in it 7,000 yrs.

Remember seeing it made.

Satan ate the apple (& acquired not the knowledge of good & evil for he had that before, but the *disposition* to *do* evil (—as the sparks to fly upward or the water to run down hill.

⟨He⟩ Adam acquired the Moral Sense from the apple in a diseased form—*insanity* of mind & body; it decayed his body, filled it with disease-germs, & death resulted.

The angels have the Moral Sense, but not in diseased form—just the other way, the *healthy* way, disposition to avoid evil & dislike it. They are sane,

I was born in heaven; my ⟨father is an⟩ uncles are archangel ∧ s ∧, but it is

E-2

2

is no particular distinction; we have no rank-ambitions—care nothing for them.

Heaven is merely for God & the angels—these exist in billions—& for the people from this world. It is so recent that you see few; the Christians are so *very* recent that I ran across none.

Hell is solely for this world—the other Adams did not eat the apple, & the people & the animals never die. The animals in Heaven came from here—there are none in hell.

Satan has been in hell but 7 days, now; I have not seen him for 6 months (150,000 years). ⟨∧ I am so sorry for him—it is dreary there. ∧⟩

Our hour is about 41⅔ of your years.

I have ⟨myriads of⟩ several thousand brothers & sisters in hell— born since the Fall; I & ⟨another⟩ a myriad were born before the Fall. We often go & play with those others, but they

E-3

3

can't come to see us. They can come to me here, & they like to; will serve me gladly. It gives them a holiday & they cool off. They have horns, ∧ spiked ∧ tail & hoof, like papa. They are a part of the disease. They like to do wrong, I suppose—in fact they *must*, since they, like papa & you are morally & mentally insane. ∧ Satan's original host have large families ∧

If you could only get rid of the Moral Sense—& he!—& be like the animals; they haven't it, & Adam hadn't it. If you & he could be like the animals. The apple diseased his moral body & he feels the fire—he & Adam could not feel pain before, but only pleasure. I cannot feel pain either of body or mind, but only pleasure.

I have an intellectual ⟨knowledge⟩ notion of what pain is, ⟨but⟩ & an intellectual compassion for a sufferer, but as I don't *know* what pain is I can't *feel* the compassion. I am intellectually sorry for comets that are lost. but I cannot cry about it. No doubt you can.

E-4

4

The redeemed in heaven—I will go & hunt one up & see what he is like. Ah—he is ⟨disappointed.⟩ happy. Has lost the moral sense & is like the animals—& like the angels, who know evil but dislike it.

I find they are just like the immortals in the other planets.

I am No. 45 in in ∧ New ∧ series ∧ 9 ∧ 86,000,000. I have seen all my brothers & sisters at one time or another, & know them by Number & features. There are some billions of them—all in heaven except the few ⟨millions⟩ thousands born in hell in the past 7 days.

Group F

These notes are on two sheets of Joynson Superfine paper in black ink. They were written during the composition of "Schoolhouse Hill," but cannot be dated more precisely.

F-1

1

∧ Dʳ· Terry, great surgeon
contempt for human race
rough, but at bottom kind ∧

∧ Use the whole "Conscience" list
of religions for Major—"when I
was a x x x" ∧

⟨David Home's "Control"⟩

Mrs. Hooker & John ∧ 's ∧ ⟨Mr. & Mrs Horr⟩ "Control" told them what to eat, drink, think, believe ⟨& so they had ⟨become⟩ quit Presby—*before*,⟩ ⟨they⟩ & what to wear & how to vote. Mrs. H's self-sufficiency & talent, John's docility, & absence of any *special* talent except utter belief in his wife & God.

The Unbeliever ∧ Bob Ingersoll (Ira Jepson)∧ ⟨vain of it—just as the ex-Cath priest ⟨very few Irish⟩ was vain of his desertion &

courage, & was around telling the secrets of the priestly charnel-house to crowded (gratis) houses

Better get up a Catechism. Yes, 44 will do it. And it is printed: "Conscience" &c

Bring in corpses & examine microbes

Pass all the animals through, devils riding.

F-2

2

∧ Swedenborgian ∧

Report that Ferg., Meadows, & Major were drunk—hence the amazing reports. ∧ These men are not believed & they lose character ∧ 44 disappears, after catechism is printed & distributed—leaves the leaven to work & be discussed. It is attacked in conversation (pulpit?); some think successfully, some not. 44 as its author presently ignored —*he* does not exist, except in those drunken imaginations—Major must be the author. His denials are doubted.

"Go to bed & rest—begin next night; he will bring the others every night & take them back, per little devils. Meantime he will inspect the world daytimes & devour libraries for ten days.

Group G

This group of miscellaneous notes consists of five half-sheets of Joynson Superfine paper, written in pencil with additions in black ink. The additions in ink are rendered in boldface type.

G-1, G-2 (on the verso of G-1), and G-4 were grouped with the "Chronicle" working notes by DeVoto but both physical and internal evidence seem to place them with the notes for "Schoolhouse Hill."

G-1

ʌ *His Sermon—* ʌ   ʌ he is starting an Anti-Moral
                                                     Sense church. ʌ

Everything is insane—upside down.
The idle sit on thrones, the workers in the gutter
Seduced girl is punished, not the seducer
You say truth is mighty—the very words are a lie—
Murder will out   ʌ Might ɪs right ʌ

Your Napoleons want a fame which shall remain in this potatoe
after they have ascended into

I was present when some of the vast suns were swung out to light
this potatoe

You say killing is wrong & persuasion right—& you spend all your
money on wars & none on arbitration.

You punish attempted suicides—whereas if a man owns anything
at all (according to your own scheme of life) it is his life—a foolish
possession

G-2

2

you call life a gift to be grateful for—a boon—you mean the opposite

you generally decide that a suicide—the only tolerably sane person
among you—is temp. insane.

Your silly race is the despair of the few wise—& otherwise; but you
all try to hide it—⟨& y⟩ you call Pessimist names. You *are* all insane.

You speak admiring of the innocence of the lamb, yet wᵈ not be
innocent on the same terms

———

Papa ate apple & has moral sense

———

But none of us ch'n—⟨for we⟩

Like Adam he disobeyed like a dog & with a dog's merely intellectual conception of the guilt (& that is worthless—you have to feel
a thing to comprehend it—there is no *thought*

G-3

3

_∧ Fortunatus purse—get *anything*
out of pocket _∧
[sketch of thermometer]
In what do you differ from a thermo—a hand on you[r] ball will
raise you, but *you* can't put the hand there, & it would not be possible
for you to originate the idea of wishing you would put it there—
it *must* come from outside.

Devil's Sunday-School
The ?s & answers of "Conscience."

D^r· Wheelwright—⟨This⟩ It is my opinion that there is [something]
supernatural about this
His wife nods her h[e]ad as much as to say there—now you've
got the explanation

Sign of X—⟨crow⟩ not afraid of it.

Approves the Savior ⟨as God⟩_∧ —praises him. _∧

G-4

4

Adam's birth was 8500 million years ago.
⟨Why am I a boy at 5,000,000?⟩
The race has not changed a single shade in that time.
Ad would disobey—so w^d you; Cain was jealous; so are you; a

⟨murderer⟩ homicide—one in a family, for he had [s]isters—the mu[rder] average is the same to-day—3 in 10 of the men before me are murderers—100 present—the adultery committed by the eye is adultery—⟨murder⟩ homicide committed by *wish* is homicide

———

∧ *Ranks.* ∧ Your redeemed w⟨ore⟩ear crowns, aureoles, halos, for you are a childish lot & delight in vanities for the eye as glass beads delight savages. Your new Jerusalem & your pearly gates & so on— rather loud taste. *And* the music there!

You haven't changed one shade, in tastes or otherwise in 8500 million yrs.

G-5

⟨A⟩B 1

∧ No luggage, no wash.   ∧ *Blizzard.* ∧ **Hannah**
Plenty clothes—ain't
dressed as he was. ∧

Annie plays music—he suffers—finds her at home when he gets there. Then *he* plays?

Savage dog. *Animals were Adam's* loving *servants.* And so are *his* ∧
Talks with them. ∧ [half-circled]

He is made of air. ∧ Loaded the cat. ∧ [circled]

Furnishes food.   ∧ Takes from his pocket *any*thing;
50 cents & $5.   but it is previously empty. "Allow
Finds papa in books & Bible   me"—& he pulls a hairpin or
Turns himself into birds,   anything—candle. ∧
fleas, &c

Vanishes

Nigger Jake is sent to

When sense of humor is complete, he does the materializing at seances.

For the moment, Hotch is spiritualist, but not his Presbyterian wife.

Describe H's, Annie, Aunt Rachel & Uncle Jeff.

∧ His church prospers—for they don't take up a collection. Also, he gives away money freely. ∧ [in left margin]

Chess, cards, checkers,—stocking the cards. Drawing, painting. He quickly learns to talk with Tom Nash, then improves on the system.

Electricity ∧ Pipes—cigars. ∧ [half-circled]

G-6

1

Bring slathers of little red, ∧ *behind* ∧ cooling devils to print ms Bible &
feed the whole town ∧ (cold plate from cubboard to sit on ∧ pants—money—
—touch of love—
blizzard—

Bible—sermons—dialogues—in *Appendix*

No. 44, The Mysterious Stranger

Group A

These notes, on a single sheet of glossy pearl-gray Par Value tablet paper, are in the same dark blue ink as the first 171 pages of the manuscript and were probably written during their composition.

A-1

∧ lightning rod not permitted to search ∧	∧ Arthur tales— Go it, Galahad Launcelot ∧	∧ Japan rocket ∧

Notes.

Whenever a thing is large ∧ & bragable ∧, "Sho, you ought to see it in Sirius."

Whenever it is "advanced" Lord, you ought to see it in (get that name from Lady Duff Gordon.)

These snubs make me tired,—& Doan too.

I visit those places with 44.

44 hunts maj [magician] constantly with miracles—Satan comes—he takes the credit at first; then too late tries to get out of it.

He is burned at the stake (it is 44 in disguise).

Appears again—is destroyed in various ways, keeps coming to life.

∧ 150, gay & cheery ∧	∧ That *ass.* severe & mild, cold & warm, straight & crooked, so that no one could *bear* his gaze. ∧

∧ Beelze ∧   ∧ 2-year cholera ∧

Group B

This group of notes consists of six glossy buff-colored tablet sheets approximately 9″ by 5¾″, numbered consecutively, in the hand of Isabel V. Lyon. The notes were dictated some time after mid-November 1902 when she became Mark Twain's secretary and probably before the composition of the third chapter of "No. 44." [1] Spelling errors have been silently emended. The first two items, in Mark Twain's hand, in dark blue ink, have been rendered in boldface type.

B-1

1

Jesus! said Father Adolf. [in top left corner]
A drunken, armored knight.
A dethroned King in the cellar.
Pi.
Hell box.
Towel.
Strap oil.
Barty contributes money and is repaid.
I am told on and my trouble begins.
I explain to him what to do without speaking.
I shirked going to his room that night.
Some one propagates the suspicion that I am his friend.

B-2

2

Fischer and others begin to lean toward him, and I venture to say a good word to them for him.
There should have been a carouse in 44's honor that night.

---

[1] *MTSatan*, p. 57.

A conspiracy is brewing during several days against the master.
I pick up the facts from Fischer & Co.
The idea is to ruin him, oust him and put some one in his place.
44 is persecuted in all ways the first day.
At last Blume strikes him.

B-3

3

That is more than Fischer can stand.
He resents it.
That classes him with 44's friend, and the count begins to divide.
I privately work upon Fischer through Mar.
Some time Mar. and Maria will begin to be attracted toward 44.
Father Peter and his niece must come in here somewhere.
And perhaps the conspirators will purposely or by accident betray
the printing shop to Father Adolf.

B-4

4

Getting used to being in the opposition.
And finding a sort of support in Fischer.
I lose the bulk of my fears, and consort with 44 by night but not by
day.
I am astonished to find that he is quite willing to kill a good man.
Thinks it would be doing him a favor.
But spares Ernest—and all vicious men.
Because they did not make themselves.
And are not to blame for what they are and do.
They are entitled to large compassion.

B-5

5

I always find it impossible to budge him from that position.
Or get him to feel an insult or an injury.
The master's influence wanes little by little.
Perhaps by and by the magician will take the head of the table.
He is heavy hearted.
And finds solace in teaching 44.
44 explains what one's Dream-Self is.

Maria and her mother are feeling strong enough now.
To try again to oust Mar. and

B-6

6

her mother.
44 will take a hand.

Group C

This group of notes, in the hand of Jean Clemens, is on four Par Value tablet sheets, with writing on both the verso and the recto. The notes follow the second chapter of "No. 44," with a few omissions and changes in wording. Presumably Mark Twain dictated this passage to Jean for reference and omitted material not of immediate use. The changes are proposed shifts of plot direction. Jean's spelling, punctuation, and capitalization have been regularized. Later penciled corrections and additions by Mark Twain have been rendered in boldface type.

C-1

1.

Heinrich Stein, the master, was portly, of a grave and dignified carriage, with a large & benevolent face & calm deep eyes—a patient man whose temper could stand much before it broke. His head was bald, with a valance of silky white hair hanging around it, his face was clean shaven, his raiment was good & fine, but not rich. He was a scholar, & a dreamer & thinker, & loved learning & study, & would have submerged his mind all the days & nights in his books & been pleasantly & peacefully unconscious of his surroundings, if God had been willing. His complexion was younger than his hair; he was four or five years short of sixty.

C-2

2.

A large part of his surroundings consisted of his wife. She was well along in life, and was long & lean & flat-breasted, & had an active & vicious tongue & a diligent & devilish spirit, & more religion than was good for her, considering the quality of it. She hungered for money, & believed there was a treasure hid in the black deeps of the castle somewhere; & between fretting & sweating about that & trying to bring sinners nearer to God where any fell in her way she was able to fill up her time and save her life from getting uninteresting & her soul from getting mouldy. There was old tradition for the treasure, and the word of

C-3

3.

Balthasar Hoffman thereto. He had come from a ⟨great⟩ ∧ long ∧ way off, & had brought a great reputation with him, which he concealed ⟨fro⟩ in our family the best he could, for he had no more ambition to be burnt by the Church than another. He lived with us

on light salary & board, & worked the constellations for the treasure.
He had an easy berth & was not likely to lose his job if the constellations held out, for it was Frau Stein that hired him; & her faith
in him, as in all things she had at heart, was of the staying kind.
Inside the walls, where was safety, he clothed himself as Egyptians
and magicians should, & moved stately, robed in black velvet starred
& mooned ⟨& velveted⟩ & cometed & sun'd with the symbols of his
trade done in silver, & on his head a conical tower with ∧ like ∧ symbols glinting from it. When he at intervals went outside he left his
business suit behind, with good discretion, & went dressed like anybody else & looking the Christian etc. Very naturally we were all
afraid of him—abjectly so, I suppose I may say—though

C-4

4.

Ernest Wasserman professed that he wasn't, etc. etc.

To return to Frau Stein. This masterly devil was the master's
second wife, & before that she had been the widow Vogel. She had
brought into the family a young thing by her first marriage, & this
girl was now seventeen and a blister, so to speak; for she was a
second edition of her mother—just plain galley-proof, neither revised nor corrected, full of turned letters, wrong fonts, outs &
doubles, as we say in the printing-shop—in a word *pi,* etc. Moses
Haas said that whenever she took up an en-quad fact, just watch
her and you would see her try and cram it in where there wasn't
room for a 4-m space; & she'd do it, too, if she had to take the
sheep('s)-foot to it. That daughter kept the name she was born to—
Marie Vogel; it was her mother's preference & her own. Both were

C-5

5.

**Frau Stein—Maria ⟨Stein⟩ Vogel ["Stein" reinstated]—Marget
Regen**

proud of it, without any reason, etc. *Maria* [MT's italics] had plenty
of energy & vivacity & tongue, & was shapely enough but not pretty,
barring her eyes, which had all kinds of fire in them, according to

the mood of the moment—opal-fire, fox-fire, hell-f., & the rest. She hadn't any fear, broadly speaking. Perhaps she had none at all, except for Satan, & ghosts, & witches & the priest & the magician, & a sort of fear of God in the dark, & the lightning when she had been blaspheming & hadn't time to get in aves enough to square-up & cash-in. She ⟨ha⟩ despised Marget Regen & her mother the master['s] niece & dependent & bedridden ⟨moth⟩ sister. She loved Gustav Fischer who did reciprocate & hated all the rest.

Marget Regen was Maria's age—17. She was lithe & graceful & trim-built as a fish, & she was a blue-eyed blonde, & soft & sweet & innocent & shrinking & winning

C-6

6.

& gentle & beautiful; just a vision for the eyes, ⟨worshipful,⟩ [MT's cancellation] adorable, enchanting; but that wasn't the hive for her. She was a kitten in a menagerie.

She was a second edition of what her mother had been at her age. That poor meek mother! Yonder she ⟨lay⟩ had lain, partially paralysed, ever since her brother my master had brought her eagerly there a dear & lovely young widow 15 YEARS BEFORE, etc. [MT's emphasis]

Next was old *Katrina.* She was cook & housekeeper; her forebears had served the master's people & none else for 3 or 4 generations; she was 60 & served the master all his life, from the time she was a little girl & he a swaddled baby. She was erect, straight, 6 feet high, with the port & stride of a grenadier; she was independent & masterful, & her fears were limited to the supernatural. She believed that she could whip anybody on the place, & would have considered an invitation a favor. As far as her

C-7

7.

allegiance ⟨went⟩ stretched, she paid it with affection & reverence, but it did not extend beyond "her family"—the master, his sister &

Marget. She regarded Frau ⟨Vogel⟩ **Stein** & Maria as aliens & intruders, & was frank about saying so.

She had under her 2 strapping young wenches—Sara & Duffles (a nickname), and a manservant, Jacob, & a porter, Fritz. **& others**

Next, we have the printing force!

Adam Binks, 60 years old, learned bachelor, proof-reader, poor, disappointed, surly.

Hans Katzenyammer, 36, printer, huge, strong, freckled, redheaded, rough. When drunk, quarrelsome. Drunk when opportunity offered.

Moses Haas, 28, printer; a looker-out for himself; likely to say acid things about people & to people; take him all around, not a pleasant character.

Barty Langbein, 15; cripple; general-utility lad; sunny spirit; affectionate; could play the fiddle.

Ernest Wasserman, 17, apprentice; braggart, malicious, hateful, coward, liar, cruel, underhanded, treacherous.

C-8

8.

He and Moses had a sort of half-fondness for each other, which was natural, they having one or more traits in common, down among the lower grades of traits.

Gustav Fischer, 27, printer; large, well built, shapely & muscular; quiet, brave, kindly, a good disposition, just & fair; a slow temper to ignite, but a reliable burner when well going. He was about as much out of place as was Marget. He was the best man of them all, & deserved to be in better company.

Last of all comes *August Feldner*, 16, 'prentice. This is myself.

The stranger: No. 44, New series 864,962.
Martin v. Giesbach
Elisabeth v. Arnim
Emil Schwarz.

Group D

This group of notes consists of eleven note-size pages, 3″ by 4$\frac{11}{16}$″, in the blue-black ink of MS pp. 432–587, and must have been written in the course of composing that portion of the manuscript.

Group D

D-1

DISAPPEARANCE of the maid discovered.

———

Hurry the public betrothal before she publishes the scandal.

———

DISAPPEARANCE of $_\wedge$ me ⟨or⟩ and $_\wedge$ my Duplicate discovered.

———

Great excitement in castle.

———

Betrothal stops.

———

Distress is killing Marget's mother.

———

Rumor of 3 murders

———

The bodies found. Close all exits. Search. They find the murderer (44) with trinkets on him. Arrest him. *Torture* confession out of him. Behead him—he picks up head, puts

D-2

2

it in basket & walks off. While they stare, claps it on & becomes magician & disappears in thunder & lightning.

Big reputation.

44 invisible says it was I. The *real* magician will appear now.

FUNERALS

—the cat is around.

No consecrated ground—they lacked absolution. Buried with 44—
same ceremonies at night. Katrina & others grieve for cat & others.
(How long since K has seen this boy?)

D-3

3

The 3 murdered found again. Funerals.

The 3 found again. Funerals.

Stein declares he will pay no more funerals. They stop.

Upon reflection I find my way is *not* clear, for certainly Martin is
another & not I. It is he that is Lisbet's husband.

I must renounce that marriage & win her in my own person.
By & *by*.

Visit other centuries to ease my heart. Marry there, by compulsion

44 shows me dream-wonders & music of spheres, but I can't
describe them, there being nothing to compare them with.

D-4

P.O. DEPT. doesn't use [MT wrote 'used'] dreams so much now,
they use the late French King's post.

Katrina has dream?

Shall her implorations restore 44? I think so

---

44 must turn to animals.

———

Have him be a mountebank with trained animals—they talk together.

———

Adolf arrest the lot

D-5

INDULGENCE—murder produces one signed by Adolf, but he points out it only saves his soul, not his life. Court doubts, but yields. GHOST-NIGHT—castle full of spectres & wandering lights. Distant groans & cries—flight & pursuit, noiseless.

The murderer is I *or* my Duplicate, they can't tell which; I confess I did it but I won't *tell* which. The indulgence names the Duplicate & 44 claims to be he & that a duplicate is not human & not amenable to law. Court is uncertain.

D-6

The emperor said:

"They blame an emperor for his appetite for notice & praise: Look at God!"

His Majesty old Henry MMMMMDCXXII ⟨of savage⟩ The Blasphemous/Uncultured said—"Yes, I *am* fond of ⟨what the books call⟩ praises, processions, notice, attentions, reverence, fuss & feathers. Vanities? Are they? There was never ∧ a living creature nor even ∧ a god that didn't like them." [this paragraph canceled with a single line]

D-7

1

Kings and all. [circled] *All* ∧ men ∧ are so very very little, so microscopically little, not alone to the eye of God but when they searchin[g]ly & honestly examine them-[selves] it seems foolish to go thro the pretence of detecting differences & distinctions.

D-8

2

Let your condition be what it may, you will provide yourself with the same amount of unhappiness required by your born disposition —king & tramp alike.

D-9

3B

Pity—don't scoff at & despise & hate the race. It is ⟨sw⟩ victim of a *swindle,* & the arbitrary character of its nature makes it blameless. It has no responsibility.

(*Both* talk gently & earnestly.)

D-10

You wouldn't like *every*body to ⟨admire⟩ ⟨∧ applaud ∧⟩ ["admire" reinstated] you?

    ∧ Well . . . . no. ∧

You wouldn't like *any*body to admire all sides of your character?

    Why?

    Nemmine. ⟨Tell you⟩

Wouldn't you be satisfied if the "best people" admired as much of your character & conduct as *you* do?

    NO—(& that is honest.)

D-11

⟨B⟩ DREAM-LIFE

———

A funeral;
   accident;
   loss of wealth;
   "   " wife & child
Crossed in love—

It bites, it cuts, it tears,—but keep heart, it is not real.

———

There is but *one* person in the Universe—you are he, & you are
merely a wandering Thought.

Group E

These notes, in the blue-black ink of MS pp. 432–587, on four sheets of
Par Value tablet stock, were written during 1905.

E-1

1

1ˢᵗ· Cat passes through—she will bring news.

   ∧ 44 says ∧ Those boys are out of date in the matter of conveying
messages—go by Fr.[ench] K[ing]'s post, now. I remember the fat &
the lean kine.

   The *dreams* are all right enough, but the art of interpreting is
lost. 1500 yr ago they were getting to do it ∧ so ∧ badly it was
considered better to depend on ⟨augurs—do you know about those?
   Yes,⟩
chicken-guts & other naturally intelligent sources of prophecy,

recognising that when guts can't prophecy it is no use for Ezekiel to go into the business.

Prophecy went out with the chicken guts.

E-2

2

Everything at standstill because of the missing 3.

_∧ Search for them, must be missing 3 days _∧

By indulgence from Adolf:
Conspiracy to massacre the Duplicates. _∧ by the strikers. _∧
Cat overhears
Have to have signs passwords grips so as to tell who *are* Duplicates.
Cat reports them to August, & he, invisible, betrays them to Duplicates.
CAT [sidelined in margin]

Now is my chance, if I can only win her in my own name—
    Take father Peter's advice—he says Martin is quite another person —"green goods"

Then courts Marget—she is drawn to him, & he *may* be Emil, she doesn't know which he is but ⟨she⟩ her feelings tell her he is not *the* one. Yes, she concedes, he would answer all practical purposes; yet, lacking the essential one—love—no good. Sorry, but N. G. One parting kiss to meet no more. Take a hatful. I will not take advantage of your generosity—2 will do.
    The murdering is to happen *that night*—which is Ghost-Night— Adolf & other exorcisors there, to be pestered by 44

E-3

3

⟨DI⟩ BRONTOSAUR, all bones—"will be more effective that way" —prances around, reaches into 2^d story windows—

"Here comes Carnegie!"—it is the ⟨P⟩ Carnegio-Pittsburghio-Brontosoriass"—

They have an old love-grudge of tertiary times—they race all over town & region & fight, scaring everybody to death—

Summons St George from the past, Don Quixotte from the future & *try* to interest a tournament, but the boys ruther not—("it's Sunday").

44 thrashes the creatures (as the magic[ian]) leads them meekly, they kneel to a cardinal the minute they see him, & the cardinal's littl[e] boy⟨s⟩ takes a ride

E-4

4

Remember, *Katrina* cannot like the magician, he burnt her boy—she crosses herself & *attacks* him whenever they mee[t]—& she is the only one who dares defy him.

She's been waiting around ever since that tragedy, with a long carving-knife.

She thinks *he* has instigated the murders—she is so bitter against him that she attributes to him every evil that happens.

Group F

These miscellaneous notes, on the front and back covers of a Par Value tablet, although clearly not for "The Mysterious Stranger," were apparently written in Florence at the same time as the final chapter of "No. 44." The language of the last chapter parallels the first note on F-2.

F-1

1. Adam? He is part of the dream. [page torn] him by agreeing with his fad.

2. Father o' de Brotherhood? 'Sho! Cant ever get him to say anything but that.
3. Ad? Enthusiastic. He is the head-criminal—perpetuate his name.
4. Agree with his fad.
5. Full of his trouble; cares nothing for Ad.   Peters the inventor.

Adm's fad for life's failures came from wife.

Jemmy a wholesome spirit—practical, like x x poetic like x x x & both, like x x x x & literary by inheri[tance] from that uncle?

    Martha is doctor, like Mrs. G.   She is in deep sympathy with the Broken Reeds.

    Poem "The Derelict."

George Flinders [written in left margin]

    The squawkestrelle & penola

    Jemmy apparently no fad to work upon. Shall it turn out that he has one himself?—his love for her—& it operates by making him give up the monument scheme.

F-2

1. The intellectual & placid & sane-looking man whose foible is that life ∧ & God & the universe ∧ is a dream & he the only person in it—*not* a *person*, but a homeless & silly *thought* wandering forever in space.
2. The negro whitewasher (of the Brotherhood of Man) whose daughter (nurse) was lynched for poisoning the white child—it turns out she was innocent.
3. The N. E. farmer whose young daughter was beguiled away by . . . . he found her after 7 months' search, dying of starvation —had lived on 2 cans of condensed milk per week—afraid to go to her father who had never taken her mother's interest in the children, he being absorbed in the heathen. He rails at God, who could have saved her & didn't.
4. George Francis Train-looking man who lost wife & his 4 children in a week when was was 30. At 74 is glad they were taken— they escaped life. "God's only valuable gift to man—death." Has almost completed extermination-scheme—oxygen.

5 Young policeman refused $10,000 bribe & reported it. Is admired (with words) but is privately believed to be "a little off." Is little by little neglected, then dismissed. He laments his foolish act; the other policeman took the $10,000 & is now Chief of Police.

Page of Discarded Manuscript

This single discarded page of manuscript on cross-barred paper may be an early effort to explore the material used in these manuscripts. It may equally have come from some closely related manuscript: only once in the Mysterious Stranger stories is Traum or Satan or 44 characterized as "The Prince of Darkness."

1

The rain continued to beat softly upon the panes, & the wind to sigh & wail about the eaves. In the room there was no sound; both of us remained buried in thought. After a long time I roused myself & took up the thread where it had been broken off:

⟨"It was depressing—that which you said.⟩

"My perhaps over-warm eulogy ∧ of the character ∧ of my race, & my praise of its noble struggle against heavy odds toward higher & ever higher moral & spiritual summits, have not won from you even the slender kindness of a comment."

⟨He⟩ ∧ The Prince of Darkness ∧ answered gravely—

"Is not silence a comment?"

I had invited that thrust, & was ⟨sorry⟩ ashamed.

EXPLANATORY NOTES

The Chronicle of Young Satan

39.25   the Assuaging of the Devil.] This seems to be the kind of legend that Mark Twain invented freely in *A Tramp Abroad;* I have found no source for it. In "Sold to Satan" (1904) Satan says: "I used to buy Christian souls at fancy rates, building bridges and cathedrals in a single night in return, and getting swindled out of my Christian nearly every time that I dealt with a priest" (*Europe,* pp. 328–329).

65.13   Not a sparrow] See Matthew 10:29.

71.3   another fish] See Matthew 14:15–21, the miracle of the loaves and fishes.

79.3–4   all written down by the Pope] The rules for dealing with witchcraft as Mark Twain refers to them are probably based on a passage in W. E. H. Lecky's *History of the Rise and Influence of the Spirit of Rationalism in Europe* (London and Bombay, 1904), I, 6: "In 1484, Pope Innocent VIII. issued a bull, which gave a fearful impetus to the persecution, and it was he who commissioned the Inquisitor Sprenger, whose book was long the recognised manual on the subject, and who is said to have condemned hundreds to death every year."

79.17   It was charged] The charge that Gottfried Narr's grandmother "cured bad headaches by kneading the person's head and neck" refers to the Swedish Movement Cure of Jonas Henrik Kellgren, of Sanna, Sweden. In July 1899, the Clemenses took Jean there for treatment of the epileptic attacks she had suffered since 1896. The Kellgren treatment involved osteopathic exercises and manipulations (see SLC to Professor Heinrich Obersteiner, Vienna, 5 October 1897, TS in MTP; SLC to John Brisben Walker, Sanna, 30 July 1899, MTP; *MTHL*, pp. 706, 708). The inference is that Mark Twain wrote this passage in or after July 1899.

113.33   Man is to me as the red spider is to the elephant.] Compare Jonathan Edwards's "The God that holds you over the pit of hell, much in the same way as one holds a spider . . . abhors you, and is dreadfully provoked"; in "Sinners in the Hands of an Angry God," *A Series of Tracts on the Doctrines, Order and Polity of the Presbyterian Church in the United States* (Philadelphia, 1835), III, 13. Edwards's figure of the interdependence of links in a chain, moreover—in "Inquiry into the Freedom of the Will," *The Works of President Edwards* (New York, 1830), II, 45—resembles the image of a row of toppling bricks that Satan employs at 115.15–20 in a similar context.

154.33–34 a single daring man] The reference is presumably to Samuel Sewall's change of mind and heart after he had participated as a judge in the witchcraft trials of 1692 in Salem, Massachusetts.

156.36   pulled down the corner of his eye] This Italian gesture conveys polite but profound skepticism.

162.22   The shock unseated the old man's reason.] Madmen and claimants fascinated Clemens, from the Emperor Norton of San Francisco to Jesse Leathers. The madness of Father Peter is, however, a dramatic extension of Mark Twain's assertion "When we remember that we are all mad, the mysteries disappear and life stands explained" (*MTN,* July 1898, p. 345).

169.20   he struck Satan with his cane] In January 1896, Clemens made a note about the German hotelkeeper in India who cuffed one of the three native bearers bringing his luggage to his room (Notebook 28b, TS p. 22). Explaining the episode in *Following the Equator* (1897), he shows the "burly German" giving the bearer a brisk cuff on the jaw before telling him what he had done wrong. The arrogant—and harshly punished—white man of "Chronicle" probably derives from this memory.

Schoolhouse Hill

184.33   Quarante-quatre, sir.] Young Satan's name, Quarante-quatre or Forty-four (or Number 44, New Series 864,962, in "No. 44, The Mysterious Stranger") is challenging; it ought to mean something. Perhaps the name derives, as Henry Nash Smith has suggested, from Clemens's childhood acquaintance with the Levin boys of Hannibal. The first Jews he had ever seen, they were "clothed invisibly in the damp and cobwebby mould of antiquity" and the Old Testament. The youths of Dawson's school nicknamed them "Twenty-two"—"twice Levin" being twenty-two—in a much-repeated joke. But Smith makes his suggestion tentatively, recognizing that the extension to twice twenty-two is not much more than a possibility ("Mark Twain's Images of Hannibal," *University of Texas Studies in English*, XXXVII [1958], 20). Mark Twain writes in his working-notes for "Schoolhouse Hill," "I am No. 45 in New series 986,-000,000. I have seen all my brothers & sisters at one time or another, & know them by Number & features." And again, "He is No. ⟨404⟩ 94 Prince of the vintage of a certain century—doesn't know which one—no curiosity

—hasn't inquired." Finally, in his notebook for June and July 1897, Mark Twain wrote down some notes for a "New Huck Finn" in which the "Lev'n" boys were to be suspiciously regarded by the town, though Tom was to stand by them and have fights; then he has, "Instead of 11, call them 9 (Nein) and 18" (Notebook 32a, TS p. 60).

A further possibility is suggested in a newspaper letter entitled "A Mystery," probably written in 1868 to "EDS. HERALD" (clipping in MTP). Complaining of a deadbeat "Double" who had been writing squibs and borrowing money in his name, Mark Twain concludes: "I am fading, still fading. Shortly, if my distress of mind continues, there may be only four of us left. (That is a joke, and it naturally takes the melancholy tint of my own feelings. I will explain it: I am Twain, which is two; my Double is Double-Twain, which is four more; four and two are six; two from six leaves four. It is very sad.)" Thus, in a punning non-mathematical sense, 44 might be Twain twice doubled.

None of these explanations, however, seems wholly adequate. On the basis of present evidence I conclude that the number and name "44" indicate simply that "Satan's original host have large families," as the author says in his working notes for "Schoolhouse Hill."

186.30   held the age] "In poker the right possessed, under certain conditions, by the player to the left of the dealer of continuing in the game or dropping out" (*A Dictionary of Americanisms*, ed., Mitford M. Matthews [Chicago, 1951], I, 11). Mark Twain's familiarity with the term is demonstrated by its use in his Autobiographical Dictation of 12 February 1907: "He 'held the age,' as the poker-clergy say, and two can't talk at the same time with good effect."

191.10–11   the Fox-girl Rochester rappings] The reference is to Margaret Fox and her sister, of Rochester, New York, who were at the height of their fame throughout the country as spiritualists in 1849 and the early 1850's (*Appleton's Cyclopaedia of American Biography*).

214.3   "A day with us, is as a thousand years with you."] Compare Psalms 90:4, "For a thousand years in thy sight are but as yesterday when it is past, and as a watch in the night," and the words of the hymn, "O, God, our help in ages past."

216.8–9   *man is prone to evil as the sparks to fly upward*] MT alters the reading of Job 5:7, "Yet man is born unto trouble, as the sparks fly upward."

No. 44, The Mysterious Stranger

RATHER THAN define each printing term as it occurs in the text, I have assembled them here in a glossary. The definitions, often condensed, derive mostly from Herbert Simon and Harry Carter, *Printing Explained* (Leicester, 1931). As early as 1886, Clemens used many of these same terms in his speech, "The Compositor," delivered to a group of printers on Franklin's birthday; Hartford *Courant*, 20 January 1886. As late as 1909, in the essay "Is Shakespeare Dead?" Clemens would write: "If a man should write a book and in it make one of his characters say, 'Here, devil, empty the quoins into the standing galley and the imposing-stone into the hell-box; assemble the comps around the frisket and let them jeff for takes and be quick about it,' I should recognize a mistake or two in the phrasing, and would know that the writer was only a printer theoretically"; *What Is Man?*, pp. 336–337.

B.-A.   The nickname abbreviated on his slug which August Feldner finds so odious and humiliating even in retrospect stands for "bottle-assed"—from the printer's term meaning "type thickened, at the feet through . . . continual impression and improper planing down" according to Charles T. Jacobi in *The Printer's Vocabulary*

475

(London, 1888). MT's image of the "taper of a leather bottle" is more graphic in this context.

bearers | Strips of the same height as the type put in the form to make the ink-rollers run smoothly.

bed | The surface in the press against which the feet of the type rest.

box-partitions | The divisions forming compartments in the case.

case | A shallow wooden tray divided into compartments of different sizes in which printers keep type.

chase | A rectangular frame of iron in which pages of type are locked up before the whole is put on the bed of the press.

composition | Selecting types from the case, placing them in the composing-stick, and justifying each line of type.

compositor | One who sets up type, often shortened to "comp."

counter-sunk rails | Rails on which the type bed may be moved and adjusted under the platen.

devil | A printer's devil is the youngest or newest apprentice printer who performs much of the dirty work of a print-shop, such as washing type or inking forms, and who is often black with ink. The name may be associated with the belief that Faust was in league with the devil.

distribution | Dispersing washed type back into the case after printing has been completed.

double-leaded | See "leaded."

doubles | The compositor's common mistake of setting a word or phrase twice over; also used by pressmen to mean a sheet which is pulled twice.

em | The square of a body of type. The common method of measuring in America is by ems. The number of ems in a

	line is multiplied by the number of lines, and the result gives the quantity set.
en	Half the width of an em.
form	The collection of type pages and of wooden and metal furniture (or filler blocks) when they are locked up in the chase by means of quoins.
frisket	A thin metal frame covered with paper and linen hinged to the tympan of the press which serves to protect margins from ink-smears during the impression, to keep the sheets from moving, and to pull the paper away from the type when the tympan is raised.
galley	A metal tray with one open end on which type is placed as it is composed in lines in the stick.
galley-proof	A proof taken from type in the galley before the type has been made up into pages.
guide	A piece of reglet or lead which some compositors used to keep their place in the copy hanging in front of them on the upper case. MT plainly considered the use of a guide the mark of an inferior compositor.
hell-box	A box into which battered or broken type-metal is thrown.
imposing-stone	A stone-topped table or a flat, firm surface to which type is transferred from the galley and upon which it is locked up in the chase.
ink-ball	A covered ball on a handle used for inking galleys. The ink-roller was reserved for inking the form prior to printing.
jeff for takes	To play a game of chance with em-quads to determine which compositor has first choice of takes.
justify	To space elements within a line of type so that the length will come out exactly as it should be. Only a skilled compositor justifies well.
leaded	Set with leads or strips of type-metal less than type-high to create interlinear space between lines of type.

lock up   To fit quoins in a form and tighten them so as to hold the type and the furniture firmly within the chase.

lye-hopper   A device used in the process of producing a wood-ash lye solution used to clean type after printing.

out   An omitted word or words in the galley of type, usually corrected by resetting a good many lines to accommodate the omission.

over-run   "Over-running a page" means to carry words backwards or forwards in correcting.

pi   A hodge-podge of mixed up type, often the result of "pi-ing the form"—dropping the form and spilling out the lines of type.

platen-springs   Springs designed to lift the platen off the impression.

proof-slip   A trial print made from a galley for the printer's reader or the author to scrutinize and mark mistakes or alterations on.

prove a galley   To make a proof-slip from a galley.

quads   Quadrats, or blocks of type metal less than type high and of varying thicknesses used as spacing material within the line of type.

quoins   Wedges of wood or metal often used in pairs to tighten or lock up forms.

reglets   Strips of wood less than type high and of various thicknesses. Springy and resilient, they keep type matter efficiently under pressure in the form.

rule   Composing-rule, a strip of metal placed over a line of type in the stick to make it easier to drop letters into the next line.

sheep-foot   An iron claw hammer used to tighten quoins in the chase.

signature   A sheet of paper making four or more pages when folded and often having an identifying letter or figure at the bottom of the first page.

solid
: Set without leads; that is, having no horizontal space between the lines of type.

space
: A hair-space is less than one-half em.

standing form
: A form stored for re-use.

standing galley
: A galley upon which matter is emptied; here, a galley where units of type are kept for re-use, firmly tied up.

stick
: The composing stick is a narrow, flanged metal tray, closed at one end and with an adjustable stop at the other. The compositor holds the stick in his left hand and assembles several lines of type in it with his right.

strap-oil
: Concerns an initiation trick in the print-shop: presumably dispatching a new apprentice to the saddler's shop for "strap-oil" and then paddling him for failing to find it.

strike galley-proof
: See "prove a galley" above.

take
: A take is a section of copy given to one compositor when there are several compositors working at a single job. A "fat" take is an assignment which requires little exertion, such as poetry or leaded matter as opposed to a "lean" take of closely written pages of prose. See "jeff for takes" above.

tie up
: To tie up dead matter is to wind printer's cord several times around a page or unit of type matter that has already been printed. Dead matter may be stowed away to be washed and distributed at some future time, or it may be held for use again.

token
: Half a ream, once 240 and now 250 sheets of paper.

towel
: In his speech to the Typothetae of 1886 MT noted that one of the apprentice's duties was to replace the towel,

"which was not considered soiled until it could stand alone."

turned
letters

Letters set upside down.

tympan

In a hand-press, the thin wooden frame across which is stretched cloth or parchment and upon which the sheet about to be printed is laid.

type

A single letter or mark of punctuation cast on the top surface of a block of type metal. One of the apprentice's duties was to gather up type dropped to the floor by the compositors, and to put the good type in the pi-pile and the broken type in the hell-box.

work off

To print off.

wrong fonts

The mistake in composition of using a letter of the wrong size or of different design from the rest.

238.25

"Number 44, New Series 864,962."] For the name 44, see the "Schoolhouse Hill" explanatory note at 184.33.

251.33

the honorable rank of apprentice] In "Tom Sawyer's Conspiracy," one finds similar praise of the printer's art, along with definitions of Hell, Printer's Devil, Pi, and composing stick and rule, in an essay by Tom that ends: "let all the nations bless the name of Guttingburg and Fowst which done it amen / TOM SAWYER / printer" (*HH&T*, p. 190).

302.13

"I should be the only one."] Compare this to the Pudd'nhead Wilson maxims: "If Christ were here now, there is one thing he would *not* be—a Christian," and "There has been only one Christian. They caught Him and crucified Him early" (*MTN*, pp. 328, 344).

309.7

"The Lord gave, the Lord hath taken away] See Job 1:21.

311.19–20

when he runs up against himself in a mirror] Mark Twain used this metaphor of the doppelgänger created by a reflection in a mirror in a passage of the holograph manuscript, later canceled, of *A Connecticut Yankee in King Arthur's Court.*

339.4–5   "I've never heard it before!"] Many names of Dream-Selves were first suggested in "My Platonic Sweetheart," which Mark Twain wrote in July 1898 (*MTHL,* p. 676).

340.6   "Elisabeth von Arnim!"] Presumably Mark Twain borrowed this name for Marget Regen's Dream-Self from Elisabeth (Bettina) von Arnim, a vivacious young woman who idolized Goethe, quarreled with his wife, and was forbidden his house. After Goethe's death she wrote a highly romantic and fantastic account of their friendship, elaborating upon Goethe's letters to her.

343.20–21   Box and Cox lodgers in the one chamber] The comparison is especially apt since Box was a journeyman printer in John Maddison Morton's farce of 1847, *Box and Cox.*

354.23   a tall man] The tall man in the clownish costume introduced by 44 is playing the character of both Mr. Bones and Banjo, the end men in the Negro minstrel show. Mark Twain recalled how the first such show he ever saw burst upon Hannibal in the early 1840's as a "glad and stunning surprise." Thereafter he preferred the Christy minstrel troupe and the others to any opera (Bernard DeVoto, ed., *Mark Twain in Eruption* [New York, 1940], pp. 110–118). "Buffalo Gals" dates from the earliest minstrel shows; Stephen Foster wrote "Old Folks at Home" for Christy in 1851.

362.20   in catapult, or cataplasm] Mark Twain had long before amused his children with cat-languages and an elaborate "Cat Tale"; see Frederick Anderson, ed., *Concerning Cats* (San Francisco, 1959), reprinted in Bernard DeVoto, ed., *Letters from the Earth* (New York, 1962), pp. 125–134.

362.23   "It's a poem] The poem not yet written is Felicia Heman's "Casabianca." It was an absolute standby in "exhibitions" when Mark Twain was a boy in the Hannibal schools (Hannibal *Morning Journal,* 4 June 1902).

364.14–15   talk into the thing which he brought in] Mark Twain
             was one of the very first writers to use an early form of the
             dictaphone (*MTHL*, pp. 451–452, 592, 637–638).

369.29–30   Oh, this human life] Schwarz's lament voices a frequent
             mood of Mark Twain in the years of his composing the
             Mysterious Stranger manuscripts. He understands the
             meaning of Wilbrandt's play, *The Master of Palmyra*, to
             be that human life in its varying aspirations is childish,
             ridiculous, trivial, cheap, capricious, and momentary
             (*Hadleyburg*, p. 219). He also argues that men are "sorry
             shows and shadows . . . poor things . . . only candles"
             in "The Memorable Assassination" (*What Is Man?*,
             p. 170).

383.29   a prodigious war] The Russo-Japanese War, drawing to
             a conclusion as Mark Twain wrote, after the heavy losses
             suffered by the Russian army at Mukden in February-
             March 1905, and following the destruction of the Rus-
             sian fleet in the battle of Tsushima on 27 May. At the
             time Mrs. Eddy sent her telegram, the Czar had initiated
             pour parlers through President Theodore Roosevelt. "The
             Czar's Soliloquy" in the *North American Review* for
             March makes Mark Twain's views clear: he was pro-
             foundly disappointed by the signing of the peace treaty
             in August, at Portsmouth, N.H., because he hoped for
             the overthrow of the Czar in Russian defeat.

384.31   He is speaking of Atia] Mark Twain wrote passages about
             Atia's dream and divination by chicken-entrails both at
             this point in "No. 44" and in the piece "As Concerns In-
             terpreting the Deity." Both were written in this same
             summer of 1905 (*What Is Man?*, pp. 268–269; see also
             Appendix B).

388.18   that nobody but Simon Newcomb could tell] Simon
             Newcomb (1835–1909) was a distinguished American
             astronomer whose more than 500 publications include
             "The Recurrence of Solar Eclipses." I have not identified
             "the original Jacobs."

393.17–18   the very minute she was stopping the praying, the two fleets were meeting] Since the battle of Tsushima took place on 27–28 May 1905 rather than on 27 June, Mark Twain appears to be shuffling dates in order to make a joke at the expense of Mary Baker Eddy.

395.10   Flora McFlimsey—nothing to wear] William Allen Butler's poem about Miss Flora M'Flimsey who had "Nothing to Wear," first published in *Harper's Weekly* of 7 February 1857, was enormously popular and inspired many imitations and replies.

395.27   " 'Backward, turn backward] In "Is Shakespeare Dead?" Mark Twain quotes these first two lines of Elizabeth Akers Allen's poem "Rock Me to Sleep" to illustrate how a popular poem may be claimed by a dozen people (*What Is Man?*, p. 351). The poem was first published in the *Saturday Evening Post* of 9 January 1860.

         Mark Twain had written in his notebook on 6 January 1897 an idea for a farce or sketch involving a backward shift in time, a dream backward in time, in which Chaucer was to appear (Notebook 31, TS pp. 41–43).